The Glannon Guide to Secured Transactions

The Glannon Guide to Secured Transactions

Learning Secured Transactions Through Multiple-Choice Questions and Analysis

Third Edition

Scott J. Burnham
Frederick N. and Barbara T. Curley Professor of Law
Gonzaga University School of Law (retired)

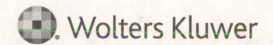 Wolters Kluwer

ISBN 978-1-4548-5008-3

Library of Congress Cataloging-in-Publication Data
Names: Burnham, Scott J., author.
Title: The Glannon guide to secured transactions : learning secured
  transactions through multiple-choice questions and analysis / Scott J.
  Burnham, Frederick N. and Barbara T. Curley Professor, Gonzaga University
  School of Law (ret.).
Description: Third edition. | New York : Wolters Kluwer Law & Business,
  [2017] | Includes index.
Identifiers: LCCN 2017047312| ISBN 9781454850083 | ISBN 1454850086
Subjects: LCSH: Security (Law) — United States. | Security (Law) — United
  States — Problems, exercises, etc. | LCGFT: Study guides.
Classification: LCC KF1050.Z9 B87 2017 | DDC 346.7307/4 — dc23 LC record available at https://
lccn.loc.gov/2017047312

SUSTAINABLE FORESTRY INITIATIVE   Certified Sourcing
www.sfiprogram.org
SFI-00756

About Wolters Kluwer Legal & Regulatory U.S.

Wolters Kluwer Legal & Regulatory U.S. delivers expert content and solutions in the areas of law, corporate compliance, health compliance, reimbursement, and legal education. Its practical solutions help customers successfully navigate the demands of a changing environment to drive their daily activities, enhance decision quality, and inspire confident outcomes.

Serving customers worldwide, its legal and regulatory portfolio includes products under the Aspen Publishers, CCH Incorporated, Kluwer Law International, ftwilliam.com, and MediRegs names. They are regarded as exceptional and trusted resources for general legal and practice-specific knowledge, compliance and risk management, dynamic workflow solutions, and expert commentary.

For my students. *Gloria discipuli gloria magistri est.*

Contents

Acknowledgments

I am indebted to The University of Montana School of Law and the Gonzaga University School of Law for their support of this project.

I also wish to thank Nick Jones, Amy Lord, David Lord, and Maggie Sampsel, former students at The University of Montana School of Law, and Erik Kukuk, former student at the Gonzaga University School of Law, for their research assistance.

I gratefully acknowledge the permission granted by the American Law Institute (ALI) and the Uniform Law Commission (ULC) to reprint portions of the Uniform Commercial Code. Copyright 2002.

Finally, I am grateful to all those involved in the editorial process at Aspen Publishers, including the anonymous reviewers, who made this a better book.

1

A Very Short Introduction

CHAPTER OVERVIEW
A. Introduction to Secured Transactions
B. Answering Multiple-Choice Questions
C. How to Use This Book

A.   Introduction to Secured Transactions

This book has three goals: (1) to provide you with a concise overview of Secured Transactions that will be helpful whether you are taking the course or preparing for the bar; (2) to help you use multiple-choice questions to assess your understanding of the material and to improve your skills at taking multiple-choice exams; and (3) to develop your skills in statutory analysis and interpretation.

Secured Transactions is a cumulative subject. You must begin by learning some basic concepts and vocabulary and then use those concepts and vocabulary to build your understanding of the subject. If you are working with this book as you take the course, you might find that the order of topics here differs from that used in your class. Don't be concerned about that. As long as you see how all the pieces fit together, the order doesn't really matter. I believe, however, that I have designed a sequence that flows logically, allowing you to learn in a coherent fashion. In addition, if you are reading the book for a final course review or for bar review, I think you will find it helpful to see the topics from a different organizational perspective. Although this book is not a detailed treatise, it emphasizes the main contours of the subject; if you are using it to prepare for the bar exam, I think you will find it addresses the main points on which you are most likely to be examined.

You won't know whether you understand a concept until you are asked to apply it to a particular fact situation. You will find at least one multiple-choice question at the end of each section that will ask you to apply your knowledge of the material to solve problems. In the analysis that follows each question, you will find not only the best response but also the reasoning process that led to that conclusion. The analysis will discuss the rules, usually found in the statutes, in the context of particular facts. Because you are learning skills of legal analysis, the questions and analysis will help you when you are assessed, whether the assessment uses multiple-choice questions or some other format.

Secured Transactions is a statutory course, requiring you to become familiar with Article 9 of the Uniform Commercial Code (hereafter, UCC or Code). Unless you are a very unusual person, reading statutes is probably not one of your favorite things to do. However, since the answers to most questions regarding secured transactions are found in the Code, you must develop the habit of reading the relevant Code sections, particularly when answering the multiple-choice questions. Although many individual sections are laid out in the reading, it will be helpful if you have a copy of the complete Code handy in order to see the big picture and to consult other sections that are referenced.

B.   Answering Multiple-Choice Questions

The answer to a legal question is a function of both the facts and the rules. In order to properly analyze the question, you must appreciate the facts, knowing which ones are important, and you need to be able to apply the correct rule in the particular factual situation. Multiple-choice tests can help you develop and improve your legal analysis skills.

The following section is designed to assist you in answering multiple-choice questions. A multiple-choice question consists of a fact pattern that ends with a *question*. Following the question is a series of *options* or *responses*, one of which is correct, and the rest of which (sometimes called the *distractors*) are incorrect. Sometimes two responses may appear to be correct, but one is the *best* response.

As with any exam, follow instructions. If your score is simply the sum of the right answers and there is no penalty for wrong guesses, don't leave any blanks. If only one answer is required, don't choose two responses. As with any exam, pay attention to the "call of the question": that is, answer the question that is asked. For example, suppose the question asks:

Which of the following is *not* a category of collateral under Article 9?

Here, the question asks you to do the opposite of what you normally do: it asks that you choose the *wrong* response rather than the right response. If you miss a little word like *not* when you read the call of the question, you are likely to go astray.

Some multiple-choice questions simply ask you to recall information. Consider the following example:

> A bank takes a security interest in the equipment of a corporation. In which state should the bank file the financing statement?
>
> **A.** The state where the equipment is located.
> **B.** The state where the corporation has its principal place of business.
> **C.** The state where the corporation is incorporated.
> **D.** The state whose law governs the security interest.

These questions require that you know the rule, and little analytical reasoning is involved. Such questions reward those who have learned the rules. Alternatively, your instructor may give an open-book exam, perhaps limiting the allowed materials to the Code. In that case, you can verify the answer by finding the relevant statute. The question then rewards those who are familiar with the Code, who know where to find things and so do not need to research them for the first time.

Other questions may draw on the materials used in class, asking you to recall what you read or discussed. Here is an example:

> Which of the following best states the holding of *In re Bollinger Corp.?*
>
> **A.** An evidentiary function is served by requiring a signed security agreement.
> **B.** A financing statement cannot operate as a security agreement.
> **C.** A security agreement can be oral if the parties clearly intended to create it.
> **D.** A security agreement can be found in context from a number of documents.

These questions reward students who have read the material and paid attention in class. The answer cannot be deduced through logic, and even in an open-book exam, there may not be time enough to find the answer.

Most multiple-choice questions, however, require analysis. You should approach these questions using the traditional essay examination technique known by the acronym IRAC: Issue, Rule, Analysis or Application, Conclusion. An essay examination provides a set of facts. In responding, you deduce the *issue* raised by these facts; recall the appropriate *rule* that applies to the issue; and *analyze* or *apply* the rule to the facts to come to a *conclusion*.

A multiple-choice question similarly begins with facts from which you must determine the issue. Determining the issue for a multiple-choice question will often be easier than for an essay exam question, because the facts for an essay can be complex, raising many issues, while a multiple-choice question is usually narrow, raising only a single issue. To spot the issue, it is helpful to know your course's syllabus or the table of contents of the course material, which can serve as a checklist for the topic areas within which issues arise. Except for Chapter 20, which contains review questions, this book places the questions in the section that covers the relevant topic, so it may be less helpful in developing your broad issue-spotting skills. The following tips can nevertheless serve as guidelines.

The facts in the question will suggest the relevant issue. Ask yourself why the author included certain facts: they were probably intended to raise a certain issue. Consider the following facts:

> The President of ABC Corporation made a telephone call to a Loan Officer of the Bank. During the call, the Bank agreed to loan ABC $100,000, and ABC granted the Bank a security interest in its accounts.

While you can't be sure it is relevant until you have read the entire problem, a light should go on when you read that the President of ABC "made a telephone call" to the Bank. Why did the drafter of the question include that particular fact, rather than just stating that the parties made an agreement? A good working hypothesis is that, because the drafter bothered to mention it, the fact that this transaction was *oral* will be significant in answering the question; it suggests that the issue might involve the enforceability of an oral agreement. Look for words or phrases in fact statements that trigger particular issues.

Once you have determined the issue, you will need to employ the relevant rule. In Secured Transactions, the relevant rule will often be found in a statute from UCC Article 9. Familiarity with the organization of Article 9 will help you find the relevant rule. After determining the relevant rule, apply the facts to the rule and come to a conclusion. On an essay exam, you would write out all of your thinking as you followed the steps, but on a multiple-choice exam, the next step is to select the best response from those offered in the question.

Sometimes the responses offered contain only conclusions; at other times they contain both conclusions and analysis, such as the reason behind the conclusion. Consider this question:

A security agreement between Bank and Company is silent on the recovery of expenses and attorney's fees incurred in connection with the enforcement of the agreement. On Company's default, Bank incurs reasonable expenses of $1,000 and reasonable attorney's fees of $2,000. What may Bank recover?

A. Neither the expenses nor the attorney's fees, because neither is permitted by the statute.

B. The expenses only, because the statute permits expenses, but permits attorney's fees only if provided for by agreement.

> **C.** The attorney's fees only, because the statute permits attorney's fees, but permits expenses only if provided for by agreement.
> **D.** Both the expenses and the attorney's fees, because both are permitted by the statute.

Another set of possible responses to the same question might look like this:

   A. 0.
   B. $1,000.
   C. $2,000.
   D. $3,000.

These two sets of responses are functionally equivalent. The first set of responses contains a conclusion and the underlying analysis, that is, the reason for the conclusion. The second set of responses contains only the conclusions the test-taker would reach by following the analysis provided in each of the responses in the first set. In responding to answers of the second type, you will need to reason from what you know from the facts given and analyze each answer in terms of the appropriate rule. In this example, you know that the expenses are $1,000 and the attorney's fees are $2,000; therefore you will quickly see that the response "$1,000" represents "expenses and not attorney's fees." From the facts, then, you must reason through whether one, both, or neither of the costs are allowed.

You will often be able to eliminate immediately two responses as erroneous or irrelevant, thus narrowing the field to two responses that seem equally correct. In distinguishing among the responses, the following techniques may help you find the best response:

- Review the facts to determine whether you are being tested on a factual distinction. One response might be correct when the debtor is *commercial*, another when the debtor is a *consumer*. Or one response might be correct when the collateral is *inventory*, another when the collateral is *equipment*.
- Make sure you are applying the right rule. Rule A might lead you to one response, while Rule B might lead you to another.
- Check whether you are being tested on the exception to a rule. Applying the rule might lead you to one response, while the exception might lead you to another.

In this book, a question will sometimes be labeled a *Statute reader* when it focuses on your ability to read the text of a statute, and the analysis following a question will sometimes include a section labeled *Note on test-taking* when it points out some of these techniques.

C.   How to Use This Book

This book can be used in two ways. One approach is to read the material in each section and then take the multiple-choice assessment. This approach will help you to master the material and to determine whether you have understood it. The second approach is to take the assessment first. If the analysis seems familiar to you, you probably understand the material and can move on to the next section; if the analysis seems unfamiliar, you should read the explanatory material preceding the question. This approach works well when you are looking for multiple-choice questions on which to practice.

If you have any comments about the book, positive or negative, do not hesitate to send an e-mail to me at burnham@gonzaga.edu.

2

Working with the Uniform Commercial Code

CHAPTER OVERVIEW
A. **Introduction**
   1. **It Is Not Uniform**
   2. **It Is Not Commercial**
   3. **It Is Not a Code**
B. **Working with the Code**
C. **Closer**
✦ **Burnham's Picks**

A. Introduction

What is secured transactions all about? Let's begin with a review of contract remedies. Assume that two parties have entered into a contract, such as a contract for the sale of goods. Who has to perform first?

If it is a *cash* or *barter* transaction, the exchange is simultaneous. If, for example, I agree to sell my car to you for $5,000, I have to tender you the car at the same time you tender the $5,000. Under the rule of constructive conditions of exchange, each performance is a condition of the other. If you don't tender me the $5,000, I don't have to tender you the car. This rule protects me in the event you refuse to pay me.

But if the transaction is a *credit* transaction, the creditor must perform first and then hope that the debtor pays the debt. For example, if I agree to sell my car to you for $5,000, payable in 30 days, I have to tender the car immediately and wait 30 days for payment of the debt. If, after the 30 days, you refuse to pay me, what is my remedy? If you said "take back the car," you need a review of Contracts. The remedy for breach of contract gives the

7

nonbreaching party the expectancy, that is, what that party would have had if the contract had been performed. Here, my expectancy is $5,000. To recover it, I must obtain a judgment and execute on your property. I have taken a risk by extending credit.

Having learned my lesson, the next time I extend credit I might try to reduce my risk by obtaining the right to take property from the debtor in the event of default. In that event, the credit is said to be *secured* by that property. The right to take or keep possession of the property may arise by operation of law. That is, the jurisdiction may have enacted a statute that gives certain creditors the right to take the property of certain debtors to satisfy a debt. These statutes include "mechanic's liens" that allow those who have improved certain personal property to obtain a lien on that property to secure payment for their labors. Alternatively, the creditor's right to take possession of the debtor's property may arise *consensually,* by contract. In the contract, the debtor (or a third person) may agree that the creditor can take this interest in certain *personal property* if the debtor defaults on payment of the debt.

The body of law that we call *secured transactions* is concerned only with a transaction that involves *credit secured consensually by personal property.* This is the subject matter of the law of secured transactions.

Article 9 of the UCC tells the creditor how to enter into a security agreement and successfully structure this transaction by taking a security interest in property that will be effective against the debtor, against other creditors, and against other parties, including the trustee in bankruptcy in the event of the debtor's bankruptcy. On the other hand, it tells debtors, other creditors, and other parties, including the trustee in bankruptcy, how to defeat the security interest so they can assert their claim to the property free of the claim of the secured creditor.

Before we get into the details of Article 9, let's look at the more general backdrop of the UCC. Where does the UCC come from? It is a project of the Uniform Law Commission (ULC), formerly known as the National Conference of Commissioners on Uniform State Laws, with the assistance of the American Law Institute (ALI), the folks who bring us the *Restatements of Law.* The ULC is a private group that attempts to draft model codes that (1) get the law right, and (2) are enactable by state legislatures. The UCC is the most successful of all the uniform laws promulgated by the ULC; most of it, including Article 9, has been enacted in all 50 states and the District of Columbia. In addition, the ULC has promulgated a Model Tribal Secured Transactions Act for adoption by Indian tribes.

In working with the UCC, however, remember:

- It is not uniform.
- It is not commercial.
- It is not a code.

1. *It Is Not Uniform*

A Uniform Law is, of course, just a model. It has no mandatory authority until it has been enacted through a state's legislative process. Each enacting state is free to create local variations and in fact often does. Furthermore, after the initial enactment, revisions of a Uniform Law are frequently proposed by the ULC. You will therefore find that, like other Uniform Laws, variations in Article 9 occur from jurisdiction to jurisdiction, depending on how many local changes the legislature has made and whether the legislature has kept current with proposed revisions.

A major revision of Article 9 was promulgated in 2000 and was enacted by all the states and by some tribes. In most jurisdictions, Revised Article 9 became effective on July 1, 2001. In this book, I will sometimes refer to the pre-2001 version, as case law developed under it will often continue to be relevant as precedent. When necessary to make a distinction, I will call the pre-2001 version "former Article 9," and the post-2001 version "Revised Article 9." To make things more complicated, Article 9 underwent an overhaul in 2010; this latest version, which the uniform version says is effective on July 1, 2013, is referred to as "Amended Article 9." I will be indicating some of the significant changes made in Amended Article 9. There are some complicated rules found in Part 8 of Amended Article 9, known as the "Transition Provisions," that must be applied when a transaction entered prior to the effective date of Amended Article 9 is affected by those amendments. Those provisions will not be discussed in this book because they come up infrequently. Finally, unless otherwise indicated, when I refer to "Article 9," I am referring to the uniform version of Amended Article 9 and all citations will reflect where provisions are found in that uniform version of Article 9. To recap, in this book:

- "former Article 9" refers specifically to the version in effect prior to July 1, 2001.
- "Revised Article 9" refers specifically to the version effective July 1, 2001.
- "Amended Article 9" refers specifically to the version effective July 1, 2013.
- "Article 9" refers generally to the uniform version of Revised Article 9 that includes the changes made by Amended Article 9.

After it has become law, the Code is then codified in the statutes of the enacting jurisdiction. Many jurisdictions use different numbering systems for the Code, but that is a superficial distinction. The uniform version of § 9-204(b)(1), for example, was codified in Montana as § 30-9A-204(2)(a) and in Oregon as § 79.0204(2)(a), but the text is the same. More importantly, when you cite a Uniform Code section as authority, or when you cite a case from another jurisdiction construing a Code section, you must find the comparable section in your jurisdiction and check to be sure the text is the same as the text of the section as enacted in your jurisdiction. Furthermore, when you cite a case decided under former Article 9 that discusses a Code section, you must be sure that the former Code section is substantively similar to the Amended Code section. To help you navigate between former Article 9, Revised Article 9, and Amended Article 9, it may be helpful to use the table of corresponding Code sections that can be found in many Code publications.

The concepts and definitions in UCC Article 1 apply throughout the Code, including Article 9. A Revised Article 1 was promulgated in 2001 and has been enacted in every state, although many states did not enact the uniform version. Because Revised Article 1 has become the norm, it is referred to as Article 1 in this book. Here is a table indicating where the corresponding sections that we will be working with can be found in Revised Article 1 and pre-Revision Article 1:

Revised Article 1	Pre-Revision Article 1
1-103(b)	1-103
1-201(b)(20)	1-201(19)
1-203	1-201(37)
1-204	1-201(44)
1-301	1-105
1-302(a)	1-102(3)
1-309	1-208

Question 1. Is the same version of the UCC found in every state?

A. Yes, because as federal law, it is uniform throughout the states.
B. Yes, because each state has enacted the uniform version.
C. No, because the numbering system is different in each state.
D. No, because state legislatures often make changes to the uniform version.

Analysis. The uniform version of the UCC is promulgated by the ULC, but to become law, it must be enacted in each state. Therefore, **A** is an incorrect response, because the UCC is state law, not federal law. Even though ULC doesn't like it, each state usually makes some changes to the uniform version. Therefore, **B** is not a correct response. The changes to the numbering system are superficial; you need to look past that to the substance of each section. Therefore, **C** is not a correct response. Because many states make changes to the substance of the official text, **D** is the correct response.

2. *It Is Not Commercial*

The word *commercial* is often used to distinguish a transaction between two businesses from a *consumer* transaction. For purposes of the Code, however, the word *commercial* is used in the broad sense of involving commerce, making a consumer transaction just one kind of commercial transaction. The Code governs both kinds of transactions and, most of the time, does not distinguish between them. Recall, for example, that Article 2 applies to *all* sales of goods, whether the transaction is the sale of 50,000 pens from the Bic Company to IBM, the sale of a pen from The Office Supply Company to you, or the sale of my pen to you.

Similarly, Article 9 applies to secured transactions involving a giant corporation putting up its inventory to secure a $5 million loan and to an individual putting up household goods, such as a washer or dryer, to secure a $500 loan. Article 9, however, has some rules that apply only to consumers, some that apply only to businesses, and some that are purposely left to the courts to resolve when they apply.

Why didn't the drafters take advantage of the revision process to resolve ambiguous provisions that have been interpreted differently by different state courts? Here is a bit of history. It will soon become apparent to you that Article 9 is not exactly debtor-friendly. It was written largely by creditors for creditors. Believing that they were unable to influence the revision process, supporters of consumer interests threatened to protest the enactment of Revised Article 9 in each state legislature. The drafters then agreed to a compromise: the revision would leave consumers no worse off than they had been under former Article 9, and consumer interests would not oppose enactment. So where former Article 9 had been ambiguous, with some court decisions resolving the ambiguity in ways favorable to consumers, the drafters of Revised Article 9 often clarified the ambiguity in a new rule, but stated that the clarification expressly did not apply to consumers. Keep an eye out for such rules; they often contain language such as "except in consumer transactions."

Question 2. Both former § 9-504(3) and Revised § 9-611 provide that, after repossession of the goods, the secured party must give the debtor "reasonable notification" of when the sale of the goods will take place. Under former Article 9, there were a lot of claims by debtors that the amount of notice was not reasonable. The revisers wanted to put an end to that issue by establishing a "safe harbor," an amount of time that would be considered reasonable. Revised § 9-612 provides:

§ 9-612 Timeliness of Notification Before Disposition of Collateral.

(a) Except as otherwise provided in subsection (b), whether a notification is sent within a reasonable time is a question of fact.

(b) In a transaction other than a consumer transaction, a notification of disposition sent after default and 10 days or more before the earliest time of disposition set forth in the notification is sent within a reasonable time before the disposition.

Assume that in your jurisdiction, two cases interpreted former § 9-504(3). The *Smith Co.* case held that 15 days' notice was not reasonable for the sale of a business's equipment, and the *Jones* case held that 15 days' notice was not reasonable for the sale of a consumer's automobile. Which of the cases are still good law under Revised § 9-612?

A. Both *Smith Co.* and *Jones*.
B. *Smith Co.* only.
C. *Jones* only.
D. Neither *Smith Co.* nor *Jones*.

Analysis.   Revised § 9-612 provides that 10 days' notice is considered reasonable. So *Smith Co.*, which dealt with a business transaction, has been overruled by statute. Therefore **A** and **B** cannot be correct. But *Jones* involves a consumer transaction. In order to avoid opposition to Revised Article 9, the ULC decided that consumers would be no worse off under Revised Article 9 than they had been under former Article 9. As a result, you will frequently see exceptions for consumer transactions in Revised Article 9. For example, the rule in Revised § 9-612(b) applies only to "a transaction other than a consumer transaction." Therefore, the rule in *Jones* is still good law in the state. **D** cannot be the correct response, and **C** is correct.

3. *It Is Not a Code*

We generally use the word *code* in contrast to the common law as a source of law. Codes generally represent the exclusive law in the area. The UCC, however, has been called a "common law" code because of the extent to which it is supplemented by the common law. Section 1-103(b), one of the most important provisions in the Code, expressly provides for this supplementation:

> Unless displaced by the particular provisions of [the Uniform Commercial Code], the principles of law and equity, including the law merchant and the law relative to capacity to contract, principal and agent, estoppel, fraud, misrepresentation, duress, coercion, mistake, bankruptcy, or other validating or invalidating cause shall supplement its provisions.

Recall also that the Code generally provides default rules for a transaction while enabling the parties to vary the provisions, thus preserving freedom of contract. Section § 1-302 provides in part:

§ 1-302. Variation by Agreement.

(a) Except as otherwise provided in subsection (b) or elsewhere in [the Uniform Commercial Code], the effect of provisions of [the Uniform Commercial Code] may be varied by agreement.

(b) The obligations of good faith, diligence, reasonableness, and care prescribed by [the Uniform Commercial Code] may not be disclaimed by agreement. The parties, by agreement, may determine the standards by which the performance of those obligations is to be measured if those standards are not manifestly unreasonable.

This principle of freedom of contract is less applicable to Article 9, however, for Article 9 tends to be regulatory. If a creditor does not comply with it, the creditor does not get the benefit of a security interest. Section 9-602 enumerates specific rules that the debtor or obligor may not agree to waive or vary.

Furthermore, Article 9 is supplemented by many other statutes. Frequently, merely finding your way around the Code is necessary but not sufficient to resolve all the issues raised in a secured transaction. As state law, Article 9 is subject to (1) other state law regulating the transaction, and (2) preemption by federal law. Even if you have determined the result under Article 9, you may not have found all relevant law. See §§ 9-201(b) & (c). That other relevant law, some of which will be discussed in this book, includes law in the following areas:

- Property exempted from execution
- Consumer protection acts
- Penalties for defrauding creditors
- Criteria for UCC searches
- Perfection of titled goods
- Judicial lien creditors
- Creditors with a lien arising by operation of law
- Agricultural liens
- Federal tax liens
- Bankruptcy

Question 3. In a transaction governed by Colorado law, a farmer in Fort Morgan, Colorado, granted a security interest in his farm products to First Bank. General Mills then bought grain (a farm product) from the farmer. Here are the applicable statutes:

Colorado Revised Statutes Annotated § 4-9-320. Buyer of goods

(a) . . . a buyer in ordinary course of business, other than a person buying farm products from a person engaged in farming operations, takes free of a security interest created by the buyer's seller, even if the security interest is perfected and the buyer knows of its existence.

7 United States Code § 1631(d). Purchases free of security interest
[A] buyer who in the ordinary course of business buys a farm product from a seller engaged in farming operations shall take free of a security

interest created by the seller, even though the security interest is perfected; and the buyer knows of the existence of such interest.

Based only on what you read in these statutes, does General Mills take the grain free of First Bank's security interest?

A. No, because the Colorado Code provides that a person buying farm products from a farmer does not take free of a security interest.

B. No, because the U.S. Code provides that a person buying farm products from a farmer does not take free of a security interest.

C. Yes, because the Colorado Code provides that a person buying farm products from a farmer takes free of a security interest.

D. Yes, because the U.S. Code provides that a person buying farm products from a farmer takes free of a security interest.

Analysis.   Response **C** cannot be right because it does not correctly state the rule found in the Colorado statute. The statute provides that "a buyer in ordinary course of business, other than a person buying farm products from a person engaged in farming operations, takes free of a security interest created by the buyer's seller." The general rule is that a buyer takes free of a security interest. But there is an exception for a person buying farm products. So, under the Colorado rule, a person buying farm products does *not* take free of a security interest. Similarly, **B** cannot be right because it does not correctly state the U.S. Code rule.

The U.S. Code provision states that "a buyer who in the ordinary course of business buys a farm product from a seller engaged in farming operations shall take free of a security interest created by the seller." So, under the U.S. Code rule, a person buying farm products takes free of a security interest. Since both **A** and **D** state the rule correctly for the respective jurisdiction, which one governs? Even though Colorado law governs the transaction, and **A** correctly states the Colorado rule, where there is both a federal rule and a state rule on a point, the federal rule generally preempts the state rule. So **D**, the federal rule, is the correct response. As we will see in Chapter 15.C, the federal Food Security Act, from which this statute is taken, was enacted by Congress with the intention of overriding the relevant state law of secured transactions.

B.   Working with the Code

What sources assist you in trying to comprehend a Code section? Remember the first rule of statutory interpretation: read the statute. You will find that in most statutory compilations, the Code section is followed by Official Comments. Because these comments are not enacted by the legislature, they do not have the force of law. They are merely persuasive. However, the Comments to Article 9 are very helpful and often contain illustrations that will assist you in applying a Code section. Do not neglect to consult them. Speaking of persuasive authority, you might also want to become familiar with the treatise by White and Summers, *Uniform Commercial Code.* There are other sources on the Code, some of them very good, but White and Summers seems to be the source most frequently cited by courts.

Question 4. The sections of UCC Article 9 are followed by Official Comments. What is the legal significance of the Official Comments to the sections?

A. They are part of the statute that is enacted into law in every state.
B. They are mandatory authority in states that have enacted the Code.
C. They are highly persuasive authority in states that have enacted the Code.
D. They have no more persuasive authority than any other secondary source on the Code.

Analysis. When the ULC promulgates a Uniform Law, it often promulgates Official Comments as well. But because the state legislatures do not enact the Official Comments, **A** is not correct. Similarly, the only authority that is "mandatory" is authority enacted by the legislature, so **B** cannot be correct. The Official Comments are only "persuasive" authority. However, because the Official Comments express the views of the drafters of the Code, they are close to the source and are considered highly persuasive, so **C** is a better response than **D**. **C** is the correct response.

C. Closer

Question 5. Which of the following statements about secured transactions is true?

A. Some provisions in Article 9 may be varied by the parties' agreement and may be supplemented by the common law.
B. The law of secured transactions is primarily found in federal law.
C. Like Article 2, Article 9 applies only to commercial transactions and not to consumer transactions.
D. All the law governing a secured transaction can be found in UCC Article 9.

Analysis.   The law of secured transactions is primarily found in UCC Article 9, which is state law, so **B** is not true. However, not all the law governing a secured transaction can be found in Article 9; since other law must be consulted, **D** is not correct. Both Article 2 and Article 9 apply to consumer transactions as well as to commercial transactions, so **C** is not correct. According to § 1-302, parties have some freedom of contract to vary Code provisions, and § 1-103(b) provides that the Code is supplemented by principles of law and equity, so **A** is correct.

 # Burnham's Picks

Question 1	**D**
Question 2	**C**
Question 3	**D**
Question 4	**C**
Question 5	**A**

3

What Is a Security Interest?

CHAPTER OVERVIEW

A. What Is a Secured Transaction?

B. Is It Better to Be a Secured Creditor Than an Unsecured Creditor?

C. Does a Transaction Create a Security Interest?

D. Closers

✧ Burnham's Picks

A.   What Is a Secured Transaction?

I n order to understand what a secured transaction is, we will first examine credit transactions that are *not* secured transactions. Consider these typical credit transactions:

- Brenda Buyer wants to buy a new dishwasher from Sears. The dishwasher costs $300 but Brenda has only $100 in cash available. Sears agrees to sell the dishwasher to Brenda, and she agrees to make installment payments over time that include interest.
- Vann's TV and Appliance wants to buy 100 big-screen TVs from Mitsubishi for $100,000. First Bank agrees to finance Vann's purchase of the TVs, and Vann's agrees to make payments over time that include interest.

Assume that each of these debtors defaults by not making payments. At the time of the default, Brenda owes Sears $300, and Vann's owes First Bank $100,000. What remedies do Sears and First Bank have against the debtors? (If you get this wrong, your Contracts grade may be in jeopardy.) The creditor is entitled to the expectancy: what the nonbreaching party would have had if the contract had been performed. In these cases, that is the amount of the remaining debt. The creditor can obtain a judgment for that amount and seek to enforce the judgment by executing on it, for example, having the sheriff seize property of the debtor. Note that under the facts you were given, without a judgment, Sears has no right to recover the dishwasher, and First Bank has no right to recover the TVs. This analysis suggests that creditors such as Sears and First Bank would like to obtain such a right.

Now assume, as is usually the case, that these debtors have other creditors. What determines whether Sears and First Bank come out ahead of the other creditors? It is simply a race: the first creditor to successfully execute on property is entitled to that property. This analysis suggests that creditors would like to have priority over other creditors. Suppose Brenda has $100,000 in debts, and a rich uncle gives her $50,000. Can she use the money to pay other creditors but give nothing to Sears? Sure. The debtor has no obligation to pay the creditors in any particular order of priority. This analysis suggests that creditors will seek to obtain some leverage that will give the debtor an incentive to pay them first.

How hard will it be for the creditors to recover from the debtors? We won't go into the details of what a creditor needs to do to get a judgment and convert that judgment to money, but the long and short of it is, it isn't easy. One impediment to the collection of a judgment from an individual debtor such as Brenda is exemption statutes, which enumerate property that may not be seized to satisfy a judgment. For example, if a statute exempts an automobile worth up to $20,000 from execution, then the sheriff can't take a car of Brenda's that is worth less than that to satisfy the judgment. These statutes vary widely from state to state. The Kansas statute, which is typical of state exemption statutes, looks like this:

> **§ 60-2304. Personal property; articles exempt**. Every person residing in this state shall have exempt from seizure and sale upon any attachment, execution or other process issued from any court in this state, the following articles of personal property:
>
> (a) The furnishings, equipment and supplies, including food, fuel and clothing, for the person which is in the person's present possession and is reasonably necessary at the principal residence of the person for a period of one year.
>
> (b) Ornaments of the debtor's person, including jewelry, having a value of not to exceed $1,000.
>
> (c) Such person's interest, not to exceed $20,000 in value, in one means of conveyance regularly used for the transportation of the person or for transportation to and from the person's regular place of work, except that the value limitation specified in this subsection shall not apply when the means of conveyance is a vehicle designed or equipped, or both, for handicapped persons, as defined in K.S.A. 8-1,124 and amendments thereto.
>
> (d) A burial plot or crypt or any cemetery lot exempt from process pursuant to K.S.A. 17-1302 and amendments thereto.
>
> (e) The books, documents, furniture, instruments, tools, implements and equipment, the breeding stock, seed grain or growing plants

stock, or the other tangible means of production regularly and reasonably necessary in carrying on the person's profession, trade, business or occupation in an aggregate value not to exceed $7,500.

Finally, what effect will it have on the creditors if the debtors file for bankruptcy before the debt is repaid? In a Chapter 7 liquidation (so called because it is addressed in Chapter 7 of the Federal Bankruptcy Code), the unencumbered assets of the debtor are sold and the proceeds are divided pro rata among the creditors. To compute the amount that each creditor will recover, create a fraction using the total assets as the numerator and the total debts as the denominator. Then multiply each debt by that fraction to obtain the amount of the debt the creditor will recover. For example, if total assets are $10,000 and total debts are $100,000, then each creditor will recover 10,000/100,000 or 1/10 of its debt.

Question 1. Assume that Brenda has $100,000 in debts, including the $300 debt to Sears, and $10,000 in nonexempt assets, including the dishwasher. Vann's has $20 million in debts, including the $100,000 debt to First Bank, and $1 million in assets, including the Mitsubishi big-screen TVs. Assuming all creditors are unsecured, if Brenda and Vann's file for bankruptcy under Chapter 7, what will Sears and First Bank recover?

A. Sears $300; First Bank $100,000.
B. Sears $30; First Bank $5,000.
C. Sears $300; First Bank $200,000.
D. Sears $0; First Bank $0.

Analysis. Brenda's assets of $10,000 must be allocated among creditors seeking to recover $100,000 in debts. The assets over the debts gives us a fraction of 10,000/100,000, which is .10 or 10 percent. Each creditor will receive 10 percent of its debt, or "10 cents on the dollar." So Sears will recover 10 percent of its $300 debt, which is $30. Similarly, each creditor of Vann's will recover 1/20 or .05 or 5 percent of its debt, or "5 cents on the dollar." So First Bank will recover $5,000 of its $100,000 debt. The option that matches those amounts is **B**.

Now let's change the hypothetical. Sears and First Bank learned their lesson about how hard it is to obtain a remedy when structuring credit transactions this way. So they wrote their contracts with their debtors so that, in addition to promising to pay the debt, the debtors granted them the right to repossess certain property in the event of default. Under one of these "security agreements," Brenda agreed that, in the event of default, Sears has certain rights to the dishwasher, and Vann's agreed that, in the event of default, First

Bank has certain rights in the TVs, including, in both cases, the right to take possession of the property. The interest that Brenda and Vann's granted in their property is a *security interest.* The interest arose *consensually*, that is, by contract between the parties.

The transactions are now Article 9 secured transactions because the creditor followed the requirements of § 9-203: a *debtor authenticated* a *security agreement*; that is, a *record* in which the *debtor* granted the *secured party* a *security interest* in certain *collateral.* This vocabulary is defined in the following Code sections:

debtor	§ 9-102(a)(28)
authenticated	§ 9-102(a)(7)
record	§ 9-102(a)(70)
security agreement	§ 9-102(a)(74)
secured party	§ 9-102(a)(73)
security interest	§ 1-201(b)(35)
collateral	§ 9-102(a)(12)

Question 2. In the transaction between Brenda and Sears, what is the security interest?

A. The contract that Brenda entered into with Sears.
B. Brenda's ownership of the dishwasher.
C. Sears's rights with respect to the dishwasher.
D. Brenda's debt to Sears.

Analysis. According to § 9-102(a)(74), Brenda's agreement with Sears is a security agreement, so **A** is not a correct response. According to § 1-201(b) (35) and § 9-102(a)(12), *security interest* means "an interest in personal property . . . which secures payment or performance of an obligation." Brenda granted Sears a security interest when she granted Sears an interest in the dishwasher, including the right to take possession if she did not pay her obligation. Therefore, the security interest is the interest of Sears, not the interest of Brenda, so **C** is the correct response.

Now assume under our new hypothetical that each of these debtors defaults in its payments. The creditors have the remedy provided in § 9-609(a)(1): "After default, a secured party . . . may take possession of the collateral." This sounds as if Sears can grab the dishwasher and First Bank can grab the TVs without going to court and without going through execution. That is exactly what it means! "Wait a minute," you say. "Isn't it unconstitutional for one person to take the property of another without due process of law?" No. It is unconstitutional for the *state* to take property without due process of law. Repossession pursuant to a security interest is a *private* action with no state involvement.

If the debtors have other creditors, do Sears or First Bank come out ahead of them? Yes! Section 9-201(a) provides that "[e]xcept as otherwise provided in [the Uniform Commercial Code], a security agreement is effective according to its terms between the parties, against purchasers of the collateral, and *against creditors*." What do you think the rule is if some of those other creditors are also secured creditors? According to § 9-322(a), the creditor who is "perfected" has priority over those who are unperfected. We will spend a good deal of time on *perfection* in Chapters 12 through 14, but essentially it is a system for giving notice of the security interest. In general, the first secured party to give notice has priority over the others. If Brenda's rich uncle gives her $50,000, she is still free to use the money to pay creditors other than Sears, but as a rational debtor she is likely to want to pay the creditors who have the most leverage. Sears has leverage because it can repossess the dishwasher if she does not pay. Unsecured creditors might not be in as good a bargaining position to obtain payment.

Those pesky state exemption statutes are less of an impediment for secured creditors than for unsecured creditors. The Kansas statute states that the property is "exempt from seizure and sale upon any attachment, execution or other process issued from any court in this state." With a secured transaction, we are talking about a private remedy that does not involve process issued from a court. So the creditor is free to take a security interest in property that is listed in the exemption statute and repossess it on the debtor's default.

Finally, what effect will it have on the secured creditors if the debtors file for bankruptcy before the debt is repaid? In bankruptcy, some of the property of the debtor (called *exempt property* and often the same property listed in the exemption statute) cannot be claimed by creditors. But the nonexempt property of the debtor (called the debtor's *estate*) is available for creditors to satisfy their debts. However, if a secured party has an interest in property, whether it is exempt or not, the security interest of the creditor will remain and will have to be satisfied. So when a debtor is in bankruptcy, it is a considerable advantage for a creditor to be a secured creditor.

Question 3. ABC Motors sells a car to John for $25,000, taking a $5,000 down payment from John and John's promissory note (formal promise to pay) for $20,000. John defaults in payments on the note. On these facts, what is the remedy of ABC Motors?

A. Repossess the car.
B. Sue John for $20,000, get a judgment, and execute on the car.
C. Sue John for $20,000, get a judgment, and execute on John's nonexempt property.
D. Either A or C.

Analysis. *Note on test-taking.* In reading this question, it is important to notice a fact that is *not* given. The facts do not state that ABC Motors took a security interest in John's property, so do not read that fact in. Unless the instructor or the question tells you otherwise, answer a question based on the facts that are given and do not supply additional facts.

Without a security interest, ABC Motors cannot repossess the car. Therefore, response **A** is incorrect, and **D** must also be incorrect if **A** is incorrect. The creditor must proceed by getting a judgment and executing on it. **C** is a better answer than **B** because it is more complete; ABC Motors's remedy is not limited to executing on the car. In fact, in most jurisdictions a car is exempt property, so ABC might have limited or no rights to execute on it.

Question 4. Creditor 1 loans $50,000 to Dewey Cheatam, a Kansas lawyer. When Cheatam defaults, Creditor 1 gets a judgment and asks the sheriff to execute on Cheatam's property. The sheriff executes on Cheatam's car, which is worth $25,000, and his law office equipment, which is worth $25,000. After an appropriate proceeding, how much of the value of this property is Creditor 1 entitled to?

A. $0 on the car and $0 on the office equipment.
B. $5,000 on the car and $17,500 on the office equipment.
C. $20,000 on the car and $7,500 on the office equipment.
D. $25,000 on the car and $25,000 on the office equipment.

Analysis. As in the previous question, this is an unsecured loan. An additional important fact is that this question involves execution on a judgment in Kansas. The relevant rule is therefore the Kansas exemption statute. Without any property protected by an exemption statute, the correct answer would be **D,** but that is not correct under the statute. A careful reading of Kansas Statutes Annotated § 60-2304 indicates that there are special rules for cars in subsection (c) and for tools of the trade in subsection (e). The statute only provides some protection, up to $20,000 on the car and up to $7,500 on the office equipment. Since the creditor may recover $5,000 on the car and $17,500 on the office equipment, **B** is the correct response.

Question 5. Creditor 2 loans $50,000 to Dewey Cheatam, a Kansas lawyer, and takes a security interest in Cheatam's car and law office equipment. When Cheatam defaults, Creditor 2 repossesses Cheatam's car, which is worth $25,000, and his law office equipment, which is worth $25,000. After an appropriate proceeding, how much of the value of this property is Creditor 2 entitled to?

A. $0 on the car and $0 on the office equipment.
B. $5,000 on the car and $17,500 on the office equipment.
C. $20,000 on the car and $7,500 on the office equipment.
D. $25,000 on the car and $25,000 on the office equipment.

Analysis. *Note on test-taking.* These facts are very similar to the facts of the previous question. An assessor who asks both is probably trying to determine whether you can spot the distinction and determine whether it makes a difference in the outcome.

In this question, the creditor obtained a security interest and is repossessing pursuant to a security interest rather than executing on a judgment. Because the creditor is not executing on a judgment, the exemption statute does not apply. The relevant rule is found in Article 9, which permits the parties to negotiate what property will be collateral. Since none of the limitations of the exemption statute apply, the correct response must be **D.** We see in these two questions the power of the security interest.

B. Is It Better to Be a Secured Creditor Than an Unsecured Creditor?

As we have seen, a secured transaction is a *consensual* lien, agreed to by both parties. It can be created only by contract. In such a contract, could Vann's agree to use its accounts receivable as collateral instead of the TVs? Both? All its personal property? All its property, both personal and real? In general, yes, because of the principle of freedom of contract. Could Brenda agree to use her TV as collateral in the transaction with Sears instead of the dishwasher? Both? All her personal property? All her property, both personal and real? It won't surprise you that we will see that there are more restrictions on freedom of contract in a consumer transaction, that is, one entered into for personal, family, or household purposes. But the important thing to realize is that the collateral is not just limited to the property financed by the transaction. On default, how much of that property can the secured party repossess? In theory, the secured party can repossess all the property in which it has a security interest. But as we will see, the secured party must then dispose of the property in a reasonable manner. The creditor can't recover more than the amount of the obligation (plus certain expenses allowed by law), and must return the balance to the debtor.

Given this freedom to bargain, why would creditors want a credit transaction to be secured? Why would debtors? The policy argument is that the availability of secured credit reduces the cost of credit and makes credit more widely available. After all, one element in setting an interest rate is the amount of risk; if the risk that the creditor will not be repaid is lowered, the cost of credit should be lowered as well.

You should be convinced by now that it is better to be a secured creditor than an unsecured creditor. The remainder of this book will look at these issues:

- How does a creditor get to be a secured creditor?
- What is the scope of a security interest?
- What are the priorities among secured creditors?
- What are the priorities between secured creditors and other parties?
- What happens to security interests in bankruptcy?

First, let's look at the transactions that create a security interest.

C.   Does a Transaction Create a Security Interest?

As you can imagine, security interests began as a kind of "hostage taking" by creditors. If I agree to loan you $500, but I am concerned that you might not repay me, I might say, "I'll hold on to your gold ring until you pay me back." This crude transaction, called a *pledge*, satisfies the requirements of an Article 9 security interest. Section 9-109(a) provides in part:

§ 9-109. Scope.

(a) **General scope of article.** Except as otherwise provided in subsections (c) and (d), this article applies to:

(1) a transaction, regardless of its form, that creates a security interest in personal property or fixtures by contract.

Recall that § 1-201(b)(35) provides that "'[s]ecurity interest' means an interest in personal property or fixtures which secures payment or performance of an obligation." In our example, I have an interest in your gold ring that secures your payment of $500 to me. We never thought of this as a secured transaction, but what matters is the substance of the transaction, not what the parties intend or what they label it.

For example, John agrees to sell Mary his automobile for $12,000. Mary doesn't have the cash available, so John agrees to accept payments of $1,050 a month for 12 months. Then a light goes on in John's head. It dawns on him that Mary might stop making payments, and he would have no easy remedy. He gets a bright idea and says to her, "Not that I don't trust you, but why don't I keep the title to the car in my name until you finish paying? When you have paid, I'll give you the title." That seems fair to Mary, so she agrees, and they sign a contract to that effect.

Did John and Mary create a security interest? Yes. In the language of § 1-201(b)(35), there is "an interest in personal property . . . which secures payment . . . of an obligation." The interest in personal property is John's interest in the car. The obligation is Mary's promise to make the payments. The property secures the payments because John is saying he will take back the car if she does not pay. The fact that he does this by retaining title is not relevant to the creation of the security interest. Section 9-202 provides as follows:

> **§ 9-202. Title to Collateral Immaterial.**
> . . . . the provisions of this article with regard to rights and obligations apply whether title to collateral is in the secured party or the debtor.

D.   Closers

> **Question 6.** *Statute reader.* Homer wants to buy a new couch from Fast Freddie's, but his credit is not good. Fast Freddie's agrees that it will sell Homer the couch for $600 on credit if Homer promises to pay the debt and Flanders agrees to grant Fast Freddie's a security interest in his lawn mower to secure the debt. All the parties agree. Under Article 9, who is a *debtor*? Hint: read § 9-102(a)(28).
>
> **A.** Homer.
> **B.** Flanders.
> **C.** Both Homer and Flanders.
> **D.** Fast Freddie's.

Analysis.   This is a good lesson in statute reading, because it shows that the words used in statutes do not always have their ordinary meaning. We think of Homer as a debtor because he incurred a financial obligation, but according to § 9-102(a)(28), "debtor" means "a person having an interest, other than a security interest or other lien, in the collateral, whether or not the person is an obligor." And according to the relevant part of § 9-102(a)(59), "obligor" means "a person that, with respect to an obligation secured by a security interest . . . owes payment or other performance of the obligation." Therefore, Homer, who owes payment of the obligation, is an obligor, but he is not a debtor for purposes of Article 9 because he does not have an interest in the collateral. Since Flanders has an interest in the collateral, he is the debtor, so **B** is the correct answer. The reason for this rule is that Article 9 is only concerned with secured debts and governs the security interest, not the financial obligation.

By the way, you may be wondering how Flanders could be bound by a contract where he did not appear to get anything. Recall that the consideration for a promise does not have to go to the promisor; in return for his promise to grant a security interest, Flanders bargained for something from Fast Freddie's — the sale on credit to Homer. That is the consideration for his promise.

> **Question 7.** Pursuant to a state statute permitting it to do so, an auto repair shop retains possession of a car when the owner fails to pay for the repairs. Why is this not an Article 9 secured transaction?
>
> A. The repair shop is not extending credit.
> B. The credit is not secured.
> C. The right to retain the car is not given consensually.
> D. The transaction does not involve personal property.

Analysis. This is an easy one if you applied the rule from § 9-109 and you noted the word *not* in the question. The repair shop is extending credit, so **A** is not correct, and the credit is secured by the car, which is personal property, so **B** and **D** are not correct. According to § 9-109, "this article [Article 9] applies to: (1) a transaction, regardless of its form, that creates a security interest in personal property or fixtures *by contract*." The facts state that the lien of the auto repair shop was created by statute. Because the lien arises by operation of law, and not consensually by contract, **C** is the correct response.

> **Question 8.** Homer contracts to buy a couch for $600 on credit from Fast Freddie's. The contract states that Fast Freddie's will keep the title to the couch until Homer pays all amounts due. Homer defaults on his payments, and Fast Freddie's attempts to repossess. Can Fast Freddie's repossess the couch?
>
> A. Yes, because the retention of title by a seller creates a security interest.
> B. Yes, because general principles of contract law permit a seller the remedy of repossession when a buyer does not pay.
> C. No, because Homer did not grant a security interest in the couch.
> D. No, because a creditor may not take a security interest in household goods.

Analysis. We know that **B** is a wrong answer; in contract law, the principle of the expectancy permits the seller to recover what it would have had if the contract had been performed; here this means the money owed. According to § 1-201(b)(35), a security interest arises when there is "an interest in personal property which secures payment of an obligation." When Fast Freddie's reserved title until it was paid, it created a security interest. Section 9-202, Title to Collateral Immaterial, provides that "the provisions of this article with regard to rights and obligations apply whether title to collateral is in the secured party or the debtor." It therefore appears that **C** is wrong and **A** is correct. The general rule is that the parties have freedom of contract to enumerate the collateral, so **D** does not correctly state an exception, and we can stick with **A** as the correct response.

✹ Burnham's Picks

Question 1	**B**
Question 2	**C**
Question 3	**C**
Question 4	**B**
Question 5	**D**
Question 6	**B**
Question 7	**C**
Question 8	**A**

4

Overview of Secured Transactions

CHAPTER OVERVIEW

A. A Secured Transactions Roadmap
B. Classification of Collateral
  1. Introduction
  2. Goods
  3. Intangible Property
  4. Quasi-Tangible Property
  5. Fixtures
C. Consumer Transactions
D. Purchase Money Security Interests
E. Closers
✦ Burnham's Picks

A. A Secured Transactions Roadmap

Before we look at the details of secured transactions, let's look at the big picture.

In Chapter 5, we will first determine which transactions are within the scope of Article 9 before examining *attachment*. *Attachment* is the word used in the Code for what occurs when a security interest becomes effective; an invisible tag can be said to "attach" to the collateral, signifying that a creditor has an interest in it. In Chapter 6 we will look at how a security interest is created, and in Chapter 7 we will see what the scope of that interest is.

Assuming the security interest attaches to the collateral, we will explore in Chapters 8 through 10 what happens when the debtor defaults on the security agreement. In these chapters, you will meet our friend the Repo Man, a figure often involved in default because one of the distinctive features of a security interest is the general availability of self-help repossession. Sometimes third parties, known as *secondary obligors,* become involved in the transaction on behalf of the debtor; we will explore the interests of those parties in Chapter 11.

Chapters 12 through 14 explore what the Code calls *perfection*. *Perfection* in Code terminology means a security interest that has attained the status whereby third parties are deemed to have knowledge of the security interest. The best-known form of perfection is the filing of a document called a *financing statement*, and we will explore a typical filing system. Notice that in this book, perfection is not examined until after default by the debtor has been considered. We use this organization to emphasize that—although you may forget this important principle from time to time—perfection is irrelevant as between the creditor and the debtor, for obvious reasons: the debtor does not need notice of the security interest. So for the secured party to make a claim against the debtor, the security agreement must have *attached* to the collateral, but the security interest does not need to be *perfected*.

Often, however, another party may be involved in the picture, one who is competing with the secured creditor for the debtor's property. We will therefore spend a great deal of time on issues of *priority*. The question is who has first claim to the collateral as between various parties: the secured party versus a buyer (Chapter 15), the secured party versus another secured party (Chapter 16), and the secured party versus various other creditors (Chapter 17). In resolving these disputes, perfection becomes a key factor, for a secured creditor generally obtains priority by being first to file or otherwise to perfect the security interest. In Chapter 18, the priority dispute is between a party who has an Article 9 security interest in a *fixture*, an item that occupies the gray area between personal property and real property, and a party who has a real property security interest in the property to which the fixture is attached.

We conclude in Chapter 19 with an exploration of how bankruptcy affects security interests. When a debtor declares bankruptcy, the result is that the claims of many creditors are adversely affected, even to the point of being discharged. Secured creditors make out a lot better than unsecured creditors when the debtor declares bankruptcy, for if a security interest has been effectively granted, then the secured party has an interest in the property that remains despite the debtor's bankruptcy. There is one important catch, however: to remain effective when the debtor declares bankruptcy, the security interest has to be perfected.

Question 1. A debtor has effectively granted a creditor a security interest in a piece of equipment. The creditor, however, has neglected to file a financing statement. The debtor defaults, and the creditor seeks your opinion as to whether the creditor may have the Repo Man repossess the equipment. Would you advise the creditor that it is legal to repossess the equipment?

A. Yes, because the security interest has attached.

B. No, because the security interest has not attached.

C. No, because the security interest was not perfected.

D. No, because the creditor must obtain a court judgment before taking the debtor's property.

Analysis.   You are told that the debtor granted an effective security interest in the equipment, so there has been attachment. Therefore, **B** is not correct. For the secured party to take action against the debtor, perfection is not required, so **C** is not correct. Article 9 allows self-help repossession, so **D** is not correct. All that is required for a creditor to have the right to repossess the debtor's property on default is attachment, so **A** is correct.

Question 2. A debtor has effectively granted a creditor a security interest in a piece of equipment. The creditor, however, has neglected to file a financing statement. The debtor declares bankruptcy, and the creditor seeks your opinion as to whether the security interest is effective. Is it?

A. Yes, because the security interest has attached.
B. No, because the security interest has not attached.
C. No, because the security interest was not perfected.
D. No, because secured creditors lose their security interests in bankruptcy.

Analysis.   *Note on test-taking.* This question shows a change in the facts from the previous question. In Question 1, the debtor is in default, but in Question 2 the debtor has declared bankruptcy. If faced with both questions, ask yourself in your analysis whether that fact makes a difference.

You are told that the debtor granted an effective security interest in the equipment, so there has been attachment. Therefore, **B** is not correct. The creditor is not proceeding against the debtor here, but against a third party, the trustee in bankruptcy. As against that party, perfection is required, so attachment is not sufficient. Therefore, **A** is not correct. **D** is not correct because security interests are generally effective in bankruptcy, but they are not effective in bankruptcy unless perfected, so **C** is correct.

The lesson here is that the secured party should perfect to preserve its interest in the event the debtor declares bankruptcy.

B.   Classification of Collateral

1. Introduction

The classification of collateral is an important aspect of Article 9. One reason classification is important is because when drafting the security agreement and financing statement, the creditor often describes the collateral using the Code classifications. See § 9-108(b)(3). It is helpful to think of the creditor as asking the debtor what personal property the debtor will use to secure the debt. That property is the *collateral,* defined in § 9-102(a)(12) as "the property subject to a security interest." Note that the classifications require us to look at the property from the debtor's point of view; when the debtor answers the creditor's question, the debtor will be describing the property in its hands. For example, a security agreement might provide the following:

1. Grant of Security Interest
   Debtor grants a security interest in the Collateral to Secured Party to secure the payment or performance of the Obligations.
2. *"Collateral."* The Collateral consists of all of the following personal property of Debtor, wherever located, and now owned or hereafter acquired, including:
   2.1. Accounts;
   2.2. Chattel paper, including equipment leases and conditional sales agreements;
   2.3. Inventory, including property held for sale or lease and raw materials;
   2.4. Equipment, including property used in the Debtor's business, machinery, and production machines;
   2.5. Instruments, notes, negotiable instruments, and negotiable certificates of deposit;
   2.6. Investment property;
   2.7. Documents, including documents of title, warehouse receipts, and bills of lading;
   2.8. Deposit accounts;
   2.9. Debtor's claim for interference with contract against Big Soda Pop Company;
   2.10. Letter-of-credit rights; and
   2.11. General intangibles, including payment intangibles, licenses, intellectual property, and tax returns.

The classifications are also important because Article 9 frequently has different substantive rules for different classifications. Although Article 9 generally addresses security interests in personal property, in fact it contains a bundle of rules that depend on which kind of personal property is involved. Once you determine the classification, you will know which rules to follow to structure a transaction involving that kind of collateral. Some of these rules are outlined in the Official Comments to § 9-101, which provide a helpful overview of Article 9. For example, the rules on how to perfect the security interest differ depending on the classification of the collateral. If you need to know how to establish priority in Deposit Accounts, see Official Comment 4.e. Alternatively, if you represent a seller of machinery that businesses purchase on credit to use as equipment, you will want to become familiar with all Code sections that relate to equipment. You can find an index to Article 9 organized by collateral in a number of secondary sources.

The following table organizes the various classifications of collateral. I have divided the collateral into two groups defined in the Code, Goods and Fixtures, and two groups not defined in the Code, Quasi-Tangible Property and Intangible Property. Here is the list of classifications within these four categories, along with citations to the definitions in the Code:

Goods (§ 9-102(a)(44)):

> Consumer goods (§ 9-102(a)(23))
> Equipment (§ 9-102(a)(33))
> Farm products (§ 9-102(a)(34))
> Inventory (§ 9-102(a)(48))

Intangible property (not a Code classification, but a name used here for property having no significant physical form):

> Accounts (§ 9-102(a)(2)) (health-care-insurance receivables, defined in § 9-102(a)(46), are a subcategory of accounts)
> Deposit accounts (§ 9-102(a)(29))
> General intangibles (§ 9-102(a)(42)) (payment intangibles, defined in § 9-102(a)(61), and software, defined in § 9-102(a)(76), are subcategories of general intangibles)
> Commercial tort claims (§ 9-102(a)(13))
> Letter of credit rights (§ 9-102(a)(51))

Quasi-tangible property (not a Code classification, but a name used here for property that historically consisted of a piece of paper but that today might take electronic form):

> Instruments (§§ 9-102(a)(47) and 3-104) (promissory notes, defined in § 9-102(a)(65), are a subcategory of instruments)
> Investment property (§ 9-102(a)(49))
> Documents (for example, warehouse receipts and bills of lading) (§§ 9-102(a)(30), 1-201(b)(15), 7-202)
> Chattel paper (§ 9-102(a)(11))

Fixtures (§ 9-102(a)(41))

Let's further explore the Code classifications.

2. Goods

"Goods" are defined in § 9-102(a)(44) as "all things that are movable," which is similar to the Article 2 definition in § 2-105. Identifying the subcategory of "consumer goods" can be very important, not only for identifying the applicable Article 9 rules but because a great deal of non–Article 9 law may apply to a consumer transaction. Chapter 4.C discusses consumer transactions in detail. In order for goods to be "farm products," as defined in § 9-102(a)(34), the debtor must be engaged in a "farming operation," as defined in § 9-102(a)

(35), with respect to the goods. The farm products are the crops, livestock, and supplies used in the operation, but if the farm products are subjected to a manufacturing process, they usually become inventory. For example, if a farmer grows tomatoes and at a farm stand sells both harvested tomatoes and canned tomatoes, the tomatoes from the crops grown likely remain farm products while the canned tomatoes have become inventory.

"Inventory" is defined in § 9-102(a)(48) as follows:

> (48) "Inventory" means goods, other than farm products, which:
>   (A) are leased by a person as lessor;
>   (B) are held by a person for sale or lease or to be furnished under a contract of service;
>   (C) are furnished by a person under a contract of service; or
>   (D) consist of raw materials, work in process, or materials used or consumed in a business.

Note that the categories of goods are mutually exclusive, so if goods are farm products, like the harvested tomatoes in the previous paragraph, they can't be inventory. Inventory can be held for either sale or lease, so the automobiles owned by a car rental business are inventory. The materials used or consumed in a business are also inventory, so the oil used to cook french fries at a fast-food restaurant is inventory even though it is not sold as such. Similarly, the napkins and plastic forks used by customers are inventory because they are used up in a short period of time. At a fancier restaurant, however, the linen napkins and metal silverware are not inventory because they have a long period of use.

"Equipment" is defined in § 9-102(a)(33) by what it is not—goods that are not inventory, farm products, or consumer goods. So in our previous example, the linen napkins and silverware are equipment. Similarly, a tractor used in a farming operation or a law book used by a lawyer is equipment.

Question 3. Bitterroot Motors sells automobiles. Its customers include both corporations that will use the vehicles for business purposes and individuals who will use the vehicles for personal use. First Bank intends to make a loan to Bitterroot Motors, taking a security interest in the automobiles. How should the security agreement describe the collateral using Code classifications?

A. Inventory.
B. Inventory and equipment.
C. Inventory and consumer goods.
D. Inventory, equipment, and consumer goods.

Analysis.   While the automobiles may be equipment in the hands of business customers and consumer goods in the hands of individual customers, the Code classifies collateral from the point of view of the debtor. In the hands of

Bitterroot Motors, the debtor in the loan transaction, the automobiles are held for sale. Imagine that First Bank asks Bitterroot Motors, "What do you have for collateral?" The answer will be "inventory," which is defined at § 9-102(a) (48) in part as "goods, other than farm products, which . . . are held by a person for sale or lease." The automobiles are held by Bitterroot Motors for sale. Therefore, **A** is correct, and **B, C,** and **D** are not.

Question 4. Bitterroot Motors buys a van from Ford on credit and grants Ford a security interest in the van. Bitterroot Motors plans to use the van as a "courtesy car" to shuttle customers from their homes or offices to the repair shop while their cars are being repaired. After a couple of years of this use, Bitterroot Motors plans to sell the courtesy car. What Article 9 classification best describes the collateral?

A. Inventory.
B. Equipment.
C. Consumer goods.
D. "Courtesy car."

Analysis.   Admittedly, the Code definition of "equipment" in § 9-102(a)(33) is not helpful, for it merely says that equipment consists of goods that are not anything else. But Official Comment 4.a. to § 9-102 explains:

> In general, goods used in a business are equipment if they are fixed assets or have, as identifiable units, a relatively long period of use, but are inventory, even though not held for sale or lease, if they are used up or consumed in a short period of time in producing a product or providing a service.

Here, the van is held not primarily for sale but for use in the operation of the business. Response **B** is therefore correct. Because the van is equipment, it is not inventory or consumer goods, so **A** and **C** are not correct. While "courtesy car" does accurately describe the collateral, and would be a sufficient description in a security agreement, the call of the question asked for the Code classification. So while **D** is not incorrect as a description of the collateral, **B** is a better response to the question.

3. Intangible Property

Let's now look at intangible property. Remember that Article 9 governs security interests in personal property, and that term governs a wide spectrum of property, some of which may not have tangible form. Usually, the intangible property represents a *right* of the debtor. For example, suppose The Oxford Cafe lets me run up a tab, and I owe it $100. The Oxford has some property of value—a right to claim $100 from me, but that right does not take any particular tangible form. I can write the Oxford an IOU or send them a letter stating that I owe the money, but that writing does not have any legal significance. While the Oxford can assign that debt to another person, transferring that writing is not meaningful. We call that right of the Oxford an *account*. "Account" is defined in pertinent part in § 9-102(a)(2):

> (2) "Account" . . . means a right to payment of a monetary obligation, whether or not earned by performance, (i) for property that has been or is to be sold, leased, licensed, assigned, or otherwise disposed of, (ii) for services rendered or to be rendered.

You are probably familiar with the concept of accounts as money owed to a business. For example, if my dentist provides me with services and sends me a bill for $150 payable in 30 days, his right to payment is an *account*, also called an *account receivable*. If some of the obligation was to be paid by my medical insurance, then he has a "health-care insurance receivable," defined in § 9-102(a)(46), which is a form of account. Accounts financing is very significant in the commercial world, because many businesses want to obtain cash now instead of when the account is paid. They therefore grant a security interest in their accounts, or sell their accounts, in order to get cash.

Don't confuse accounts with deposit accounts. A "deposit account" is an account the debtor maintains with a bank. Although we don't usually think of it this way, when we have a bank account, we are a creditor of the bank. Therefore, the bank owes us money, and we have a property interest in that right to receive money from the bank. As we will see, there can be practical problems in foreclosing on this property, a problem that is compounded because the bank in which the funds are held may also be a creditor of the debtor. A "letter of credit right" is a right created under a letter of credit, which is an Article 5 transaction. This transaction is frequently used in international transactions, but because it involves a complex interaction with Article 5, it is beyond the scope of this work.

If certain collateral is not within the scope of Article 9, it does not mean that a creditor can't take a security interest in that property. For example, under § 9-109(c)(12), Article 9 does not apply to tort claims. If someone ran me over and broke my leg, I would have a tort claim against that person. A creditor might loan me money and expect to be paid out of the proceeds I recovered from the tortfeasor. The creditor's claim would be governed by law other than Article 9, such as the common law. One exception to this rule is that a creditor can take an Article 9 security interest in a "commercial tort claim," as defined in § 9-102(a)(13). These are the tort claims that you probably didn't study in your class in Torts, such as tortious interference with contract. One special rule with respect to this classification of collateral is that the security agreement can't define it by type of collateral but must spell it out with particularity. See § 9-108(e)(1). That is why the example at the beginning of this section, which used the Code categories of collateral, made an exception in 2.9, where it stated with particularity "Debtor's claim for interference with contract against Big Soda Pop Company" instead of the more general "Commercial tort claims."

Like equipment, the category of "general intangible" is also a residual classification; it is defined by the exclusion of a number of other categories enumerated in § 9-102(a)(42). Because of this definition, the drafter has to be careful. A grant of a security interest in "general intangibles" does not grant the creditor a security interest in categories that are enumerated in the exclusions from that definition. Property that doesn't fit within the excluded categories, and so would fall into general intangibles, includes software, licenses such as liquor licenses, and intellectual property such as copyrights, trademarks, and patents.

Question 5. A company owns a warehouse. Part of the warehouse burned down, allegedly because of the negligence of the neighboring business, and the company has made a claim against the business for the loss. The company is attempting to obtain credit from a lender, and the lender would like to take a security interest in this claim. How should the parties characterize this collateral under the Code?

A. Accounts.
B. General Intangible.
C. Commercial tort claim.
D. Trick question—this is not a Code transaction.

Analysis. While the company is claiming that the business owes it money, the claim is not a "right to payment of a monetary obligation," as defined in § 9-102(a)(2), so it can't be an account. A is therefore incorrect. While security interests in tort claims in general are not Code transactions, there is an exception for commercial tort claims. This is a commercial tort claim as defined in § 9-102(a)(13), so the correct response is **C**. *Extra credit*—note that when the parties come to draft their security agreement, they should not use the Code characterization but should describe the collateral as "commercial tort claim against neighboring business." See § 9-108(e)(1).

---

4. *Quasi-Tangible Property*

Let's now look at quasi-tangible property. This property was historically pieces of paper, but today might be what the Code calls *records*—information found either on a tangible medium such as paper or in electronic form. Quasi-tangible property evidences a right and also embodies a right, so that a person may transfer the right to a third party by transferring the piece of paper or, in the modern age, by making an effective electronic transfer. For example, if I owe the Oxford Café $100, and I write them a check for $100, or I give them a promissory note for $100, then they can transfer to a third party the right to obtain that money from me by transferring that piece of paper. Recall that we can contrast this with intangible property, such as an account, which represents a right not embodied in any particular piece of paper.

An "instrument," defined in § 9-102(a)(47), is "a negotiable instrument or any other writing that evidences a right to the payment of a monetary obligation." The most common instruments are promissory notes and checks, though checks seem to be rapidly disappearing as electronic funds transfers replace them. Negotiable instruments are the subject of Article 3. A "document," defined in § 9-102(a)(30) is a document of title, which is the subject of Article 7. One of the most common documents is the *warehouse receipt*. A farmer may store his crop in a silo and obtain a warehouse receipt for it. If it is negotiable, then the person who possesses that document has the right to obtain the crop.

The last few decades have seen an explosion in the kind of products available in the securities and financial markets beyond old-fashioned stocks and bonds, and "investment property," defined in § 9-102(a)(49), is Article 9's attempt to keep up by allowing creditors to obtain security interests in this kind of personal property.

"Chattel paper" is defined in pertinent part in § 9-102(a)(11):

> (11) "Chattel paper" means a record or records that evidence both a monetary obligation and a security interest in specific goods.

What does this mean? Assume I purchase a new $25,000 Sienna from Bitterroot Motors, and I arrange with the company's financing arm that I will pay $5,000 down and the $20,000 balance in monthly payments over the next four years. If that was all there was to it, then Bitterroot Motors would merely have an account, my promise to pay the obligation. But Bitterroot Motors, having lawyers who took this course when they were in law school, knows how to get better security than my mere promise to pay. They have prepared the transaction so that I sign a promissory note for $20,000 and I also grant Bitterroot Motors a security interest in the car, allowing Bitterroot Motors to repossess the car if I fail to make monthly payments. Note that the Code calls this documentation a *record* (defined in § 9-102(a)(70)) because even though historically it is called *paper*, it may today take electronic rather than tangible form. Bitterroot Motors now has two things: (1) an instrument, the promissory note that evidences a monetary obligation, and (2) a security interest in the car that evidences a security interest in specific goods. Since these records "evidence both a monetary obligation and a security interest in specific goods," in the words of § 9-102(a)(11), it has *chattel paper*.

Question 6. Tina Smith purchased a car to use for pleasure from Bitterroot Motors on credit, giving Bitterroot Motors a promissory note and granting it a security interest in the car. How would you classify the collateral in the Bitterroot Motors–Smith transaction?

A. Consumer goods.
B. Inventory.
C. Accounts.
D. Chattel paper.

Analysis.   Always remember: *Classify the collateral from the point of view of the debtor*. In this transaction, Smith is the debtor. Section 9-102(a)(23) defines "consumer goods" as "goods that are used or bought for use primarily for personal, family, or household purposes." Since Smith is using the car for pleasure, it is consumer goods, so **A** is correct and **B, C,** and **D** are incorrect. As a footnote, recall that many special rules, both in Article 9 and in other law, apply to consumer transactions.

Question 7. Tina Smith purchased a car to use for pleasure from Bitterroot Motors on credit, giving Bitterroot Motors a promissory note and granting it a security interest in the car. Bitterroot Motors now goes to First Bank to borrow money. First Bank asks Bitterroot Motors what it has for collateral, and Bitterroot Motors offers First Bank the documentation of transactions with Smith and with similar customers. How would you classify the collateral in the Bitterroot Motors–First Bank transaction?

A. Consumer goods.
B. Inventory.
C. An account.
D. Chattel paper.

Analysis.   Always remember: *Classify the collateral from the point of view of the debtor*. In this transaction, Bitterroot Motors is the debtor. Section 9-102(a)(11) defines "chattel paper" as "a record or records that evidence both a monetary obligation and a security interest in specific goods." The promissory note evidences a monetary obligation, and the security interest in the car evidences a security interest in specific goods. Therefore, since both elements of the definition are satisfied, the collateral is chattel paper. **D** is correct, and **A, B,** and **C** are incorrect.

5. *Fixtures*

Finally, "fixtures" are also goods. They are defined in § 9-102(a)(41) as "goods that have become so related to particular real property that an interest in them arises under real property law." Since fixtures appear to be part of real property, this classification is important when there is a contest between a party secured by personal property and a party secured by real property. For example, if Bank A has a mortgage (an interest secured by real property) on a building housing a law firm, and Bank B has a security interest in the law firm's equipment, the banks might get into an argument about who has claim to built-in bookcases that are firmly attached to the wall. I know you can't stand the suspense, but Chapter 18 discusses this and other problems that arise with fixtures.

C.   Consumer Transactions

We saw in Chapter 2.A.2 that Article 9 will often have special rules for consumer transactions.

What is a consumer transaction? Consistent with the definition in most consumer protection statutes, § 1-201(b)(11) provides that "'[c]onsumer' means an individual who enters into a transaction primarily for personal, family, or household purposes." Article 9 adds a definition of "consumer goods" in § 9-102(a)(23) that provides that "'[c]onsumer goods' means goods that are used or bought for use primarily for personal, family, or household purposes." So if I buy a baseball card for my personal collection on credit and grant the seller a security interest in the baseball card, then I am a *consumer* who has granted an interest in *consumer goods*. Section § 9-102(a)(24) calls this a *consumer goods transaction*:

> (24) "Consumer-goods transaction" means a consumer transaction in which:
> (A) an individual incurs an obligation primarily for personal, family, or household purposes; and
> (B) a security interest in consumer goods secures the obligation.

Our example is an easy case, because both the obligation secured and the collateral have a personal, family, or household purpose. But things are not always so clear-cut, and Article 9, in its usual thorough fashion, provides for other possibilities. For example, suppose I take out a loan to paint my house and grant the lender a security interest in my stock in Cisco Systems Inc. Here, the obligation secured has a household purpose, but the collateral is not consumer goods but investment property. This is not the narrower *consumer-goods transaction* but the broader *consumer transaction*, as defined in § 9-102(a)(26):

> (26) "Consumer transaction" means a transaction in which (i) an individual incurs an obligation primarily for personal, family, or household

purposes, (ii) a security interest secures the obligation, and (iii) the collateral is held or acquired primarily for personal, family, or household purposes. The term includes consumer-goods transactions.

In other words, all consumer-goods transactions are consumer transactions, but not all consumer transactions are consumer-goods transactions. When you read Code rules that apply to consumers, keep an eye out for whether they apply to just a "consumer-goods transaction" or to the more general "consumer transaction."

When you see that a transaction involves a consumer, a warning light should go on. In addition to special treatment under Article 9, consumer transactions are subject to a great deal of regulation, both state and federal. In such a transaction, not only may Article 9 have a special rule, but compliance with Article 9 alone may not be sufficient.

Question 8. In order to obtain a loan to renovate her law office, attorney Mary Moe grants the lender a security interest in her personal baseball-card collection. Which of the following describes this transaction?

A. Consumer goods.
B. Consumer-goods transaction.
C. Consumer transaction.
D. None of the above.

Analysis.   It is true that the baseball-card collection is consumer goods, for in the words of § 9-102(a)(23) it is used "primarily for personal, family, or household purposes," but *consumer goods* does not describe the transaction, so response **A** is incorrect. The transaction is neither a consumer-goods transaction nor a consumer transaction, for one element of those transactions as defined in § 9-102(a)(24) and (26) is that the individual "incurs an obligation primarily for personal, family, or household purposes." Here, while the collateral is consumer goods, the obligation was incurred for a business purpose (renovating the law office) rather than for a personal, family, or household purpose. Since this element is not satisfied, **B** and **C** are incorrect, and the correct response is **D.** Therefore, the general rules of Article 9—not the special rules applicable to consumers—apply to this transaction.

D.   Purchase Money Security Interests

While we are introducing concepts that will be useful in our later discussions, let's explore the concept of the *purchase money security interest* (PMSI), which is often vocalized as "PIM-zee." This concept is important in many aspects of secured transactions, especially regarding the priorities among creditors that we will discuss in Chapter 16. The definition of PMSI in § 9-103 is quite convoluted, but the heart of it is in § 9-103(a)(2):

> "purchase-money obligation" means an obligation of an obligor incurred as all or part of the price of the collateral or for value given to enable the debtor to acquire rights in or the use of the collateral if the value is in fact so used.

In other words, a security interest in collateral is a PMSI if either (1) a seller sold the debtor the collateral in which it took a security interest, or (2) a lender loaned the money to the debtor that the debtor used to buy the collateral. Not so hard, is it?

One issue that occasionally comes up is whether a lender has a PMSI when the debtor commingles the money with other funds before using it to purchase the collateral. For example, assume a lender loaned the debtor $5,000 and took a security interest in a piece of equipment that the debtor planned to buy with the money. The debtor put the loan proceeds in its bank account and then wrote a check on that account to purchase the equipment. Whether the lender has a PMSI depends on whether, in the words of the statute, "the value is in fact so used," that is, whether the $5,000 that the lender loaned the debtor was the same $5,000 that the debtor used to acquire the collateral. This question poses a "tracing" problem: can the money paid be "traced" to the money lent? One way lenders avoid this problem is to give the debtor a two-party check. For example, the lender might make its check payable to both the debtor and the seller. Because negotiating the check requires the indorsement of the seller, it would have to be used to purchase the collateral.

Question 9. Vann's TV and Appliance wants to buy 100 big-screen TVs from Mitsubishi for $100,000. First Bank agrees to finance Vann's purchase of the TVs, and Vann's agrees to make payments over time that include interest. Vann's grants First Bank a security interest in its entire inventory. First Bank gives Vann's a check for $100,000 payable to Vann's and Mitsubishi, and Vann's uses that check to purchase the TVs. Does First Bank have a PMSI in the inventory of Vann's?

A. Yes, in the entire inventory.
B. Yes, but only in the 100 big-screen TVs.
C. No, because First Bank did not sell the TVs to Vann's.
D. No, because the loan from First Bank was not used to acquire the TVs.

Analysis.   A lender obtains a PMSI if the money loaned is used to acquire the collateral. Here, First Bank structured the transaction to make it clear that the money was so used. Therefore, **C** and **D** are incorrect. However, even though First Bank has a security interest in Vann's entire inventory, it has a PMSI only in the collateral that the debtor acquired with the money it loaned to the debtor. Because that collateral is the 100 big-screen TVs, **B** is correct, and **A** is incorrect.

Note on test-taking. You had to read carefully for the call of the question. If the question had asked, "Does First Bank have a *security interest* in the inventory of Vann's," then the correct response would be **A**. But the correct response turns on the fact that the question asked whether the bank had a *PMSI* in the inventory.

Question 10. A consumer purchased a clothes washer from Sears for $469 and used his Sears credit card to pay for the transaction. The sales receipt, which the consumer signed, conspicuously stated: "Purchased under my Sears account and security agreement, incorporated by reference. I grant Sears a security interest in this merchandise."

Did the transaction create a PMSI?

A. Yes, because Sears sold the debtor the collateral in which it took a security interest.
B. Yes, because Sears loaned the money to the consumer that the consumer used to buy the collateral.
C. No, because the statute provides that there is no PMSI in consumer goods.
D. No, because the transaction is for less than $500.

Analysis.   Section 9-103(a)(2) provides that "'purchase-money obligation' means an obligation of an obligor incurred as all or part of the price or the collateral." Under the facts, the obligation of the consumer was incurred as all of the price of the washer. Since a security interest was created that is a purchase-money obligation, the correct response is **A**. In Chapter 6.B you can see what this PMSI looks like. A PMSI can also be created as described in **B**, but under these facts, Sears sold the consumer the collateral and did not loan the consumer the money used to purchase the collateral, so **B** is incorrect. **C** is incorrect because there is no distinction in the creation of a PMSI between a consumer transaction and a transaction that is not a consumer transaction. In Chapter 14.E, we will see that there is a distinction when it comes to perfection of the PMSI. **D** is incorrect because there is no particular monetary amount required to create a PMSI.

E.   Closers

Question 11. Homer bought a sofa for his living room on credit from Friendly Sofa Co., signing a contract in which Homer promised to pay Friendly $100 a month for 12 months and granted Friendly a security interest in the sofa. If Friendly granted First Bank a security interest in this collateral, how would you describe the collateral in the Friendly–First Bank transaction?

A. An account.
B. Chattel paper.
C. A document.
D. Consumer goods.

Analysis. *Always characterize the goods in the hands of the debtor.* In the Friendly–First Bank transaction, the debtor is Friendly. It has Homer's promise to pay, which evidences a monetary obligation, and it has a security interest in the goods, the sofa. This record constitutes "chattel paper" under § 9-102(a)(11), so **B** is the correct response.

Question 12. Farmer Wicks stored 50,000 bushels of wheat in the Farmer's Co-op grain elevator and received a receipt for the wheat. First Bank then loaned Wicks $10,000 and took a security interest in the receipt. How would you characterize the collateral?

A. Goods.
B. Farm Products.
C. Document.
D. General Intangible.

Analysis. Although wheat is a good and, more specifically, a farm product, First Bank did not take a security interest directly in the wheat. It took a security interest in the receipt, which represents the right to receive the wheat. This collateral is quasi-tangible property because the person who has this particular receipt is entitled to obtain the wheat from the warehouse. It is a *document* as defined in § 9-102(a)(30) (the particular document is a *warehouse receipt*, as described in § 1-201(b)(42)), so **C** is the correct response.

 ## Burnham's Picks

Question 1	A
Question 2	C
Question 3	A
Question 4	B

Question 5	**C**
Question 6	**A**
Question 7	**D**
Question 8	**D**
Question 9	**B**
Question 10	**A**
Question 11	**B**
Question 12	**C**

5

The Scope of Article 9

CHAPTER OVERVIEW
A. **Introduction**
B. **§ 9-109(a) "Except as otherwise provided in subsections (c) and (d)"**
C. **§ 9-109(a)(1) "a transaction, regardless of its form, that creates a security interest in personal property or fixtures by contract"**
D. **§ 9-109(a)(2) "an agricultural lien"**
E. **§ 9-109(a)(3) "a sale of accounts, chattel paper, payment intangibles, or promissory notes"**
F. **§ 9-109(a)(4) "a consignment"**
G. **Closers**
✦ **Burnham's Picks**

A. Introduction

To what transactions does Article 9 apply? Section 9-109 provides the following:

> § 9-109. Scope.
>
> (a) Except as otherwise provided in subsections (c) and (d), this article applies to:
>
> (1) a transaction, regardless of its form, that creates a security interest in personal property or fixtures by contract;
>
> (2) an agricultural lien;
>
> (3) a sale of accounts, chattel paper, payment intangibles, or promissory notes;
>
> (4) a consignment.

Let's look at each of the items listed in this provision.

B.   § 9-109(a) "Except as otherwise provided in subsections (c) and (d)"

Note that subsection (a) of § 9-109 begins by telling us what transactions Article 9 does *not* apply to. Those exclusions are contained in subsections (c) and (d). Here are a few highlights from that list of exclusions:

Federal Preemption.   A federal law that governs security interests preempts the state law. We saw an example of that in Chapter 2.A: the federal Food Security Act preempts state law with respect to purchasers of farm products. We will see in Chapter 14.D that there are a number of federal filing schemes that preempt state filing schemes.

Real Property.   Each state's scheme for creating, transferring, and filing liens on real property is similar to that in Article 9, but each has its own rules. You may study this topic in a course in real estate transactions; it sometimes also comes up in courses that combine the study of liens on real and personal property. Watch out for transfers that combine both a real property interest and a personal property interest. Each interest must be given its own treatment under the appropriate statutes. Also watch out for *fixtures*, which occupy the gray area between real property and personal property. Fixtures are essentially items of personal property that are firmly attached to the real property, such as elevators and built-in bookcases. We will examine security interests in fixtures in Chapter 18.

Liens Arising by Operation of Law.   Broadly speaking, a security interest is a lien because it is an interest in property that secures payment of a debt. For Article 9 purposes, we are interested only in the security interests that arise consensually, by contract. Some liens can arise not by agreement but by operation of law. For example, if I have my car repaired and do not pay the repair shop, a statute in my jurisdiction may grant the repair shop a lien on my car, permitting the repair shop to retain the car to secure payment, even if I never agreed to grant the lien. That lien arises by operation of law rather than consensually. Because of that, the lien is not an Article 9 security interest.

> **Question 1.** Seller sold a farm, including portable irrigation equipment, to Buyer on contract for deed. A contract for deed is a financing agreement in which real property is sold on the installment plan, with the seller holding title to the property until the buyer has made all the payments. Buyer then obtained a loan from Bank, giving Bank a security interest in equipment. Buyer then defaulted as to Seller and Bank. What law determines who has priority in the irrigation equipment?

> **A.** Federal law, because the property is a farm.
> **B.** State real property law, because the transaction is primarily a real estate transaction.
> **C.** State real property law, because the irrigation equipment is a fixture.
> **D.** Article 9, because the irrigation equipment is personal property.

Analysis. As we have seen, the federal Food Security Act may govern the sale of farm products but not the sale of the farm itself, so **A** is incorrect. We are told that the irrigation equipment is "portable," so it cannot be a fixture, so **C** is incorrect. Note that the seller held title until all payments are made. As we saw in the previous chapter, a personal property transaction structured that way creates a security interest. This transaction will probably be bifurcated, with real property law governing the lien on the real property and Article 9 governing the lien on the personal property, which includes the irrigation equipment. So **B** is not the correct response with respect to the irrigation equipment, and **D** is the correct response.

Let's now look at the transactions enumerated in § 9-109(a) to which Article 9 *does* apply.

C. § 9-109(a)(1) "a transaction, regardless of its form, that creates a security interest in personal property or fixtures by contract"

This subsection reiterates the principle that substance governs over form: it doesn't matter what the parties call the transaction; what matters is its legal effect. We saw applications of this principle in the last chapter, where parties created security interests in personal property by contract without realizing it. For example, a seller might have retained title to property in order to secure payment. The effect of that action is to make a sale with retention of a security interest, for even though the form of the transaction is the retention of title, the substance is that the seller is retaining an interest in the property to secure payment.

The issue of whether a security interest has been created frequently arises with transactions that the parties characterize as a "lease." It is the fundamental characteristic of a lease that the goods revert to the lessor at the end of the lease term. Therefore, if the lessee materially defaults under a lease of personal property, the lessor, who remained the rightful owner, may take it back. See § 2A-525. Also, a lessor does not have to file to give third parties notice of its interest in order to have priority over them. In the event of bankruptcy, as we discussed in the previous chapter, the trustee in bankruptcy takes control of the debtor's property for the benefit of the creditors. But if the debtor leased the property, the property itself does not fall into the debtor's estate but remains the property of the lessor, with the trustee having control only of the lessee's leasehold interest.

If, however, the transaction the parties called a lease is deemed not to be a true lease but a sale with retention of a security interest, the alleged lessor will lose to a secured party who is entitled to priority or to the bankruptcy trustee who prevails over unperfected security interests. It is thus often important for Article 9 purposes to determine whether the transaction is a sale or a lease. There are other occasions when it is necessary to make the same determination. For one thing, the law governing a sale is Article 2, while the law governing a lease is Article 2A. For another, the transaction may have different tax consequences. For our present purposes, it is often necessary to determine whether a transaction is a lease or a sale with reservation of a security interest in order to determine whether the creditor should have complied with Article 9 to obtain priority over other creditors or the bankruptcy trustee. To help resolve whether a transaction is a lease or a security interest, the drafters of the Code included in Article 1 a provision directly addressing the point:

§ 1-203. Lease Distinguished from Security Interest.

(a) Whether a transaction in the form of a lease creates a lease or security interest is determined by the facts of each case.

(b) A transaction in the form of a lease creates a security interest if the consideration that the lessee is to pay the lessor for the right to possession and use of the goods is an obligation for the term of the lease and is not subject to termination by the lessee, and:

(1) the original term of the lease is equal to or greater than the remaining economic life of the goods;

(2) the lessee is bound to renew the lease for the remaining economic life of the goods or is bound to become the owner of the goods;

(3) the lessee has an option to renew the lease for the remaining economic life of the goods for no additional consideration or for nominal additional consideration upon compliance with the lease agreement; or

(4) the lessee has an option to become the owner of the goods for no additional consideration or for nominal additional consideration upon compliance with the lease agreement.

(c) A transaction in the form of a lease does not create a security interest merely because:

(1) the present value of the consideration the lessee is obligated to pay the lessor for the right to possession and use of the goods is substantially equal to or is greater than the fair market value of the goods at the time the lease is entered into;

(2) the lessee assumes risk of loss of the goods;

(3) the lessee agrees to pay, with respect to the goods, taxes, insurance, filing, recording, or registration fees, or service or maintenance costs;

(4) the lessee has an option to renew the lease or to become the owner of the goods;

(5) the lessee has an option to renew the lease for a fixed rent that is equal to or greater than the reasonably predictable fair market rent for the use of the goods for the term of the renewal at the time the option is to be performed; or

(6) the lessee has an option to become the owner of the goods for a fixed price that is equal to or greater than the reasonably predictable fair market value of the goods at the time the option is to be performed.

(d) Additional consideration is nominal if it is less than the lessee's reasonably predictable cost of performing under the lease agreement if the option is not exercised. Additional consideration is not nominal if:

(1) when the option to renew the lease is granted to the lessee, the rent is stated to be the fair market rent for the use of the goods for the term of the renewal determined at the time the option is to be performed; or

(2) when the option to become the owner of the goods is granted to the lessee, the price is stated to be the fair market value of the goods determined at the time the option is to be performed.

(e) The "remaining economic life of the goods" and "reasonably predictable" fair market rent, fair market value, or cost of performing under the lease agreement must be determined with reference to the facts and circumstances at the time the transaction is entered into.

In determining whether a transaction is a lease or a sale with reservation of a security interest, one of the most significant factors is whether anything of value reverts to the original owner of the goods at the end of the term of the agreement. Assume, for example, that a widget has a retail market value of $4,000 and an economic life of two years (that is, it will decline in value until it has no value at the end of two years). Business sees the widget for sale at Sears for $4,000. Not having that much cash, Business agrees to buy it on the installment plan. Business agrees to pay $400 per month for 12 months and to grant Sears a security interest in the widget. This is obviously a sale with retention of a security interest. Nothing reverts back to Sears at the end of the agreement. Sears has the right under Article 9 to repossess the collateral (the widget) in the event of Business's default. Whether Sears will prevail over other creditors or over the bankruptcy trustee, however, depends on whether Sears's security interest is perfected and has priority. On the other hand, if Sears said, "We will lease the widget to you for a year for $300 per month. At the end of 12 months, you must return it to us," then it is a true lease, because there is something of value that reverts to the lessor at the end of the lease term.

> **Question 2.** Buyer sees a widget for sale at Sears. The widget has a retail market value of $4,000 and an economic life of two years. Sears says, "Instead of selling this widget to you, we will lease it to you for a year. You must make lease payments of $400 per month. At the end of 12 months, it is yours." Using the guidance of § 1-203, do you think a court would find that Sears has a true lease or a security interest?
>
> **A.** True lease, because the parties cast the transaction in the form of a lease.
> **B.** True lease, because the lessee is to pay the lessor for the right to use the goods for the term of the lease and is not subject to termination by the lessee.
> **C.** Security interest, because the lessee has an option to become the owner of the goods for no additional consideration.
> **D.** Security interest, because the original term of the lease is equal to or greater than the remaining economic life of the goods.

Analysis.   Section 1-203(a) makes clear that the issue is to be "determined by the facts of each case." Therefore, the intentions of the parties as expressed in their agreement are of no effect, so **A** is not correct. We are told that the economic life of the widget is two years, so **D** is not correct factually. **B** is factually correct, but the conclusion is not. According to § 1-203(b)(4), even if the agreement has those characteristics of a lease, it can still be a sale with reservation of a security interest if "the lessee has an option to become the owner of the goods for no additional consideration." Since the lessee has that option, **C** is correct. The reason is that there is nothing to revert to the lessor at the end of the lease term, as there would be in a true lease.

Many cases fall between the two extremes of everything reverting back to the lessor and nothing reverting back to the lessor. For example, assume Sears said, "At the end of 12 months you have an option. Either return the widget to us or pay us an additional $10, and it is yours." See § 1-203(b)(3). It seems fair to assume that if the widget had an economic life of two years, then it still had a value of more than $10 at the end of one year. Therefore, the $10 is a "nominal" amount; that is, it does not reflect the value of the widget and is a mere formality. To put it another way, under the "economic realities" test, a reasonable person in the shoes of Business would always exercise this option. Therefore, this is not a lease but a sale with a reservation of a security interest. On the other hand, assume Sears said, "We will lease the widget to you for a year for $300 per month. At the end of 12 months, you have an option. Either return it to us or pay us an additional $1,200, and it is yours." The amount of $1,200 is probably not nominal but a reflection of the value of the widget at the end of one year. Therefore, a reasonable person would not necessarily exercise the option. This is a true lease. The mere fact that there is an option to buy at the end of the term is not the determining factor; the real question is whether the option is for a nominal amount.

The owner of goods who enters into an agreement that is not clearly a true lease faces a problem. If a court holds that the transaction is a sale with retention of a security interest, the original owner may lose priority and will lose to the trustee in the event of Business's bankruptcy if it does not perfect. Therefore, the owner should file in case this transaction is held to be a sale with retention of a security interest. Such a filing, where the party claims not to have a security interest but files in case it does not prevail on that issue, is described as a "precautionary filing" in Official Comment 2 to § 9-505. That section provides as follows:

§ 9-505. **Filing and Compliance With Other Statutes and Treaties for Consignments, Leases, Other Bailments, and Other Transactions.**

(a) **Use of terms other than "debtor" and "secured party."** A consignor, lessor, or other bailor of goods or a buyer of a payment intangible or promissory note may file a financing statement, or may comply with a statute or treaty described in Section 9-311(a), using the terms "consignor", "consignee", "lessor", "lessee", "bailor", "bailee", "owner", "registered owner", "buyer", "seller", or words of similar import, instead of the terms "secured party" and "debtor".

(b) **Effect of financing statement under subsection (a).** This part applies to the filing of a financing statement under subsection (a) and, as appropriate, to compliance that is equivalent to filing a financing statement under Section 9-311(b), but the filing or compliance is not of itself a factor in determining whether the collateral secures an obligation. If it is determined for another reason that the collateral secures an obligation, a security interest held by the consignor, lessor, bailor, owner, or buyer which attaches to the collateral is perfected by the filing or compliance.

Question 3. A widget has a retail market value of $4,000 and an economic life of two years (that is, it will decline in value until it has no value at the end of two years). Bob and Ray agreed that Bob would lease the widget to Ray for $400 per month for one year. At the end of the year, Ray has the option either to return the widget to Bob or to pay Bob $10 and keep it. On advice of counsel, Bob filed a financing statement listing Ray as debtor and the widget as collateral. In determining whether this transaction is a lease or a sale with retention of a security interest, what weight should be given to the fact that Bob filed a financing statement?

A. It creates an irrebuttable presumption that the transaction is a security interest.

B. It creates a presumption that the transaction is a security interest, but the party claiming to be a lessor can present evidence to rebut the presumption.

C. It depends on whether Bob described the parties as "lessor" and "lessee" instead of "secured party" and "debtor" in the financing statement.

D. It is not a factor in determining whether the transaction is a security interest.

Analysis. As we have seen, under the § 1-203 analysis, the facts indicate that this is a sale with a reservation of a security interest because, under § 1-203(b)(4), the lessee has the option to become the owner of the goods for nominal additional consideration. However, § 9-505(b) provides that when a party makes a precautionary filing, "the filing or compliance is not of itself a factor in determining whether the collateral secures an obligation." Therefore, **D** is correct, and all the other responses are incorrect.

D. § 9-109(a)(2) "an agricultural lien"

Although we may think of the term *agricultural lien* as describing any lien on agricultural products, it is actually a term of art having a particular meaning in Article 9. The definition in § 9-102(a)(5) provides:

"Agricultural lien" means an interest in farm products:

(A) which secures payment or performance of an obligation for:

(i) goods or services furnished in connection with a debtor's farming operation; or

(ii) rent on real property leased by a debtor in connection with its farming operation;

(B) which is created by statute in favor of a person that:

(i) in the ordinary course of its business furnished goods or services to a debtor in connection with a debtor's farming operation; or

(ii) leased real property to a debtor in connection with the debtor's farming operation; and

(C) whose effectiveness does not depend on the person's possession of the personal property.

While former Article 9 did not apply to statutory liens, Revised Article 9 expressly provided that Article 9 applies to agricultural liens. Section 9-109(a)(2) provides that "this article applies to . . . an agricultural lien." The change is more limited than that section suggests, however, for not *all* of Article 9 applies to agricultural liens, and the applicable provisions apply only to agricultural liens as defined in the statute. Note that under the statutory definition, an agricultural lien is "created by statute." Under § 9-109(a)(1), Article 9 applies only to a security interest that is created consensually, by contract. Therefore, although Article 9 applies to agricultural liens, only those parts of Article 9 that expressly refer to agricultural liens, rather than those that refer to security interests, are applicable to agricultural liens. There are, in fact, few sections that expressly apply to agricultural liens.

Don't confuse an agricultural lien with a security interest in farm products. For Article 9 purposes, a security interest is a consensual lien, arising only by contract between the creditor and the debtor, while an agricultural lien is a creature of statute, arising when the creditor satisfies the statutory requirements, irrespective of the consent of the debtor. Furthermore, the definition limits agricultural liens to the statutes that do not make the lien dependent on possession. The statute determines the scope of the lien and may determine its priority. If the statute does not provide a priority, the Article 9 default rule found in § 9-322 governs priority. As we will see in Chapter 17.D, frequently the holder of an agricultural lien is in conflict with a secured creditor who holds a security interest in the same crop.

Here is an example of an agricultural lien from the Revised Statutes of Nebraska:

> **§ 52-1201. Lien on crops; authorized.**
> Any person, including any public power district, cooperative, firm, or corporation, who contracts or agrees to furnish (1) seed to be sown or planted or (2) electrical power or energy, or both, used in the production of crops shall have a lien upon all crops produced from the seed furnished or produced with the electrical power or energy furnished to secure the payment of the purchase price of the seed or the cost of the electrical power or energy used.

Question 4. Ingmar Johnson is a rancher in Valentine, Nebraska. When taking out a loan with First Bank, he granted the bank a security interest in his wheat crop. He then bought seed on credit from Seedco in order to plant his crop and promised to pay Seedco when the crop was harvested. At harvest time, he defaulted on his payments to First Bank and Seedco. Is the transaction between Johnson and Seedco within the scope of Article 9?

A. Yes, because it is an Article 9 security interest.
B. Yes, because it is an agricultural lien.
C. No, because transactions arising under statutes outside of Article 9 cannot be within the scope of Article 9.
D. No, because it is an unsecured loan.

Analysis. Note that under the facts, Johnson did not consensually grant Seedco a security interest in his crops. Therefore, response **A** is incorrect, as no security interest was created by contract. But Revised Statutes of Nebraska § 52-1201 grants Seedco a lien under these facts. Therefore, **D** is incorrect, as Seedco does have a lien that secures the loan. The choice is between **B** and **C**. This lien arose under a statute outside of Article 9. However, it satisfies the Article 9 definition of an *agricultural lien* in § 9-102(a)(5), and § 9-109(a)(2) provides that an agricultural lien is within the scope of Article 9. Therefore, although that lien was created by another statute, it is within the scope of Article 9, so **C** is incorrect, and **B** is correct. What this means in practice is that the priority between the Bank and Seedco will be determined under Article 9.

E.   § 9-109(a)(3) "a sale of accounts, chattel paper, payment intangibles, or promissory notes"

We saw in the previous chapter that Article 9 applies to security interests in accounts and chattel paper. Recall the example in which Bitterroot Motors granted First Bank a security interest in those classifications of collateral. What is significant for our present purpose in exploring the scope of Article 9 is that subsection 3 of § 9-109(a) states that Article 9 applies to a *sale* of certain classifications of collateral, most importantly, accounts and chattel paper, and not just to a security interest in this collateral. Contrast this rule with the rule for the sale of goods. If Bitterroot Motors sells a car to me for cash, it is not an Article 9 transaction. So we are looking at an exception to Article 9 that applies only when accounts and chattel paper are sold.

We saw that when Bitterroot Motors needs cash, it could go to the bank and ask for a loan secured by its accounts and chattel paper. "Wait a minute," you say. "Does that mean that the bank can take possession of the accounts and chattel paper if Bitterroot Motors is in default?" Yes, that is exactly what it means. "How does it do that?" you ask. I could say that will be covered in a later chapter. I could also tell you to look at § 9-607(a)(1). The long and short of it is that the secured party (the bank) will take by assignment whatever rights the debtor (Bitterroot Motors) has against the obligor of the account or chattel paper. If I owed money to Bitterroot Motors, on default by Bitterroot Motors, I would be instructed to make my payments to the bank, and the bank would have whatever rights Bitterroot Motors would have against me. The main point is that the transaction between the bank and Bitterroot Motors is a secured transaction governed by Article 9.

Bitterroot Motors has another alternative to get the money it needs. It goes to Midtown Factors and asks for some money. Midtown says, "What do you have to sell?" Bitterroot Motors says, "accounts and chattel paper." Midtown says, "We will buy your accounts and chattel paper for 10 percent less than the face value." Bitterroot Motors agrees. After the transfer is complete, I am instructed to make my payments to Midtown. This is a sale rather than a secured transaction. Midtown Factors is the owner of the accounts and chattel paper rather than a secured party with a security interest in them. Nevertheless, this transaction is also governed by Article 9. Why? Because the passage we started with, § 9-109(a)(3), says so. Why does it say so? Official Comment 4 to § 9-109 tells us:

> This approach generally has been successful in avoiding difficult problems of distinguishing between transactions in which a receivable secures an obligation and those in which the receivable has been sold outright. In many commercial financing transactions the distinction is blurred.

In other words, since it may be hard to distinguish between a transaction in which accounts and chattel paper have been sold and a transaction in which security interests in accounts and chattel paper have been granted, the transactions are treated the same for Article 9 purposes.

This distinction makes little difference to me, the person whose obligation is either used as collateral or sold, but it makes a difference to creditors of Bitterroot Motors. When a second creditor comes along to see what collateral Bitterroot Motors has, it does its due diligence by checking the filings to see if anyone has either taken a security interest in accounts and chattel paper or bought accounts and chattel paper. If the second creditor does not find a filing by Midtown, it can file and get priority in those accounts over Midtown. Do you recall that we said in the last chapter that it is important to classify the collateral because different classifications of collateral may receive different treatment? This is a good example. In most cases, a sale is not an Article 9 transaction. The sale for $250 of a floor waxing machine belonging to Bitterroot Motors, for example, has nothing to do with Article 9.

Note, by the way, that for purposes other than Article 9, the distinction between the sale of accounts and granting a security interest in accounts remains important. For example, assume Bitterroot Motors borrowed $20,000 from the bank secured by $25,000 worth of accounts and chattel paper. Bitterroot Motors defaulted, and the bank recovered only $15,000 from the account debtors to apply to the debt. How much does Bitterroot Motors owe the bank? The answer is $5,000, because Bitterroot Motors has an obligation to pay a total of $20,000 to the bank regardless of how much the collateral proves to be worth. Alternatively, assume Bitterroot Motors sold $25,000 worth of accounts and chattel paper to Midtown Factors for $22,500. Midtown Factors recovered only $15,000 from the account debtors. How much does Bitterroot Motors owe Midtown Factors? The answer is nothing. For this purpose, the sale price of the accounts was $22,500, and it is irrelevant how much they are worth to the buyer.

> **Question 5.** Bitterroot Motors goes to Midtown Factors to obtain financing. Midtown says, "What do you have to sell?" Bitterroot Motors says, "Accounts and chattel paper." Midtown says, "We will buy your accounts and chattel paper for 10 percent less than the face value." Bitterroot Motors agrees and sells Midtown $100,000 worth of accounts and chattel paper for $90,000. Is this transaction governed by Article 9?
>
> **A.** Yes, because in reality Midtown has secured a loan to Bitterroot Motors with the accounts and chattel paper.
> **B.** Yes, because Article 9 governs the sale of accounts and chattel paper.
> **C.** No, because this is an outright sale with no reservation of a security interest.
> **D.** No, because the sale of accounts and chattel paper is specifically excluded from the transactions to which Article 9 applies.

Analysis.   § 9-109(a)(3) provides that "this article applies to: . . . (3) a sale of accounts, chattel paper, payment intangibles, or promissory notes." Therefore, **B** is correct, and the other responses are incorrect.

F.   § 9-109(a)(4) "a consignment"

In the transaction described as a consignment, the owner of goods (the "consignor") delivers them to a seller (the "consignee") for sale. If the consignee sells the goods, she pays the consignor a share of the proceeds. If the consignee does not sell the goods, she returns them to the consignor. A problem arises when the consignee has given a creditor a security interest in inventory and the consigned goods look like inventory. For example, if Bank has a security interest in the inventory of Joe's Store, and Mary consigns her goods to Joe's Store, on default by Joe's Store, Bank can repossess Mary's goods.

This doesn't seem fair to poor Mary. On the other hand, when Bank looked over the inventory that Joe's Store offered as collateral, it reasonably assumed that Mary's goods were part of that inventory. The challenge for the drafters of Article 9 was to be fair to Mary while also being fair to Bank. Initially, based on this subsection and § 9-103(d), it looks like the solution was to make a consignment an Article 9 transaction. This would mean that people like Mary would have to take a security interest in the consigned goods, file notice of that interest, and obtain priority in order to come in ahead of creditors like Bank. While that may be a theoretically fair solution, many consignors are not sophisticated enough to follow that procedure.

That is not the approach the drafters took. While they did make a consignment an Article 9 transaction, they manipulated the Code definition of "consignment" in order to bring fewer transactions within its scope. Section 9-102(a)(20) provides:

> (20) "Consignment" means a transaction, regardless of its form, in which a person delivers goods to a merchant for the purpose of sale and:
>> (A) the merchant:
>>> (i) deals in goods of that kind under a name other than the name of the person making delivery;
>>> (ii) is not an auctioneer; and
>>> (iii) is not generally known by its creditors to be substantially engaged in selling the goods of others;
>> (B) with respect to each delivery, the aggregate value of the goods is $1,000 or more at the time of delivery;
>> (C) the goods are not consumer goods immediately before delivery; and
>> (D) the transaction does not create a security interest that secures an obligation.

Notice that a transaction is a consignment under subsection (A) only if the merchant who receives the goods "deals in goods of that kind; . . . is not an auctioneer; and . . . is not generally known by its creditors to be substantially engaged in selling the goods of others." In the three situations outlined, creditors should know from the circumstances that the goods are not part of the regular inventory of the merchant. So in that event, the transaction is not a consignment for purposes of Article 9.

Question 6. Mary delivered $2,000 worth of quilts to Joe's Consignment Shop with the understanding that Joe would try to sell the quilts for Mary and would return to her any unsold quilts. A creditor who had a security interest in Joe's inventory repossessed Mary's quilts on Joe's default. Was the transaction a consignment for purposes of Article 9?

A. Yes, because Mary delivered the goods to Joe's for sale but did not sell them to Joe's.

B. Yes, because Joe's creditors would not know that he was substantially engaged in selling the goods of others.

C. No, because Joe's dealt in goods of that kind.

D. No, because Joe's creditors would know that he was substantially engaged in selling the goods of others.

Analysis. For many purposes, this transaction would be a consignment, but many such transactions are not consignments for purposes of Article 9, so we will assume A is not a complete response and look further. Under § 9-102(a)(20) (A)(i), the transaction is a consignment if the merchant "deals in goods of that kind." The theory of that provision is that a creditor should know that goods are not part of inventory if they differ considerably from the goods regularly sold by the merchant. For example, if a tire retailer had a stock of quilts to sell, a reasonable creditor would assume they were not part of inventory. Here, that factor does not appear to be present, so **C** is not a good answer. Would creditors generally know that Joe's Consignment Shop is substantially engaged in selling the goods of others? I think it is evident from the name. Therefore, **D** is correct, and Article 9 does not apply to this transaction. Because most stores receiving consignments don't have such obvious names, many consignment issues turn on whether the merchant is "generally known by its creditors to be substantially engaged in selling the goods of others" under § 9-102(a)(20)(A)(iii).

The statute removes two other transactions from the scope of a consignment. Unless "the aggregate value of the goods is $1,000 or more at the time of delivery," then it is not a consignment under Article 9. This part of the statute protects "rack stuffers" who place goods of small value in stores for the stores to sell for them. Also, the transaction is a consignment if "the goods are not consumer goods immediately before delivery." So if a person delivers to a merchant goods that are used for personal, family, or household purposes (the definition of consumer goods in § 9-102(a)(23)) for the merchant to sell for them, then the transaction is not a consignment under Article 9. This provision protects the consumer who makes a consignment agreement with a merchant.

Question 7. Dave Patterson wanted to sell his car, which has a "Blue Book" value of $5,000. His friend Joe Quarter runs Quarter's Used Car Lot. Quarter does not usually take cars on consignment, but as a favor to Dave, Quarter agreed to do so. Quarter then defaulted on its obligation to First Bank, which had a security interest in Quarter's inventory. Pursuant to the security agreement, First Bank took possession of all the cars on the lot, including Patterson's. Was the transaction between Patterson and Quarter a consignment for purposes of Article 9?

A. Yes, because Quarter deals in goods of the same kind as the goods that were consigned.
B. Yes, because Quarter is not generally known by its creditors to sell the goods of others.
C. No, because the car is worth only $5,000.
D. No, because the car is consumer goods.

Analysis. Section 9-109(a)(4) brings a consignment within the scope of Article 9. Since he did not protect himself by obtaining a security interest, it appears that Patterson might lose his car. But it is only a consignment if the transaction fits the definition. Response **A** reflects the rule found in § 9-102(a)(20)(A)(i). Since Quarter deals in goods of the same kind, it appears that Patterson might lose his car. Response **B** reflects the exception found in § 9-102(a)(20)(A)(iii). The exception does not apply to our fact situation, however, because the facts state that "Quarter does not usually take cars on consignment." Therefore, it can't be "generally known by its creditors to be substantially engaged in selling the goods of others." Response **C** would be a good response if the car were worth less than $1,000, for according to § 9-102(a)(20)(B), a transaction is a consignment only if the value of the goods is more than $1,000. However, § 9-102(a)(20)(C) states that the transaction is a consignment if the consigned goods "are not consumer goods immediately before delivery." Here, the car *was* consumer goods in the hands of Patterson immediately before delivery to Quarter Cars. Therefore, that element is not satisfied, so the transaction is not a consignment and not within the scope of Article 9. The correct response is **D**.

G. Closers

Question 8. Quarter Cars entered into an agreement described as an "automobile lease" with Smith. Under the agreement, Smith was obligated to make payments of $180 per month for three years and had an option to buy the car at the end of that period for $10. The agreement also provided that, on default, Quarter had the right to terminate the lease and take back the car. Quarter Cars made no filing. Smith defaulted on his payments. Which advice would you give Quarter Cars?

A. The car belongs to Quarter, so it can take back the car because Smith broke a lease.

B. The car belongs to Quarter, but it must sue for a money judgment.

C. The car belongs to Smith, but Quarter can repossess because it has a security interest.

D. The car belongs to Smith, but Quarter cannot repossess because it did not perfect its security interest.

Analysis.   Under § 1-203(b)(4), this transaction probably does not create a true lease because "the lessee has an option to become the owner of the goods for no additional consideration or for nominal additional consideration upon compliance with the lease agreement." Therefore, there is a sale with reservation of a security agreement. Since Quarter has reserved the right to take back the car, it has a security agreement. The correct response is **C**. **D** is not correct because perfection is not relevant as between the creditor and the debtor.

Question 9. According to § 9-109, Article 9 applies to "a transaction, regardless of its form, that creates a security interest in personal property or fixtures by contract." Which of the following transactions does Article 9 *not* apply to?

A. Real estate mortgages.
B. Consignments of automobiles to a seller of automobiles.
C. Sales of chattel paper.
D. Agricultural liens.

Analysis.   § 9-109 provides in pertinent part:

SCOPE.

(a) **General scope of article.** Except as otherwise provided in subsections (c) and (d), this article applies to:

(1) a transaction, regardless of its form, that creates a security interest in personal property or fixtures by contract;

(2) an agricultural lien;

(3) a sale of accounts, chattel paper, payment intangibles, or promissory notes;

(4) a consignment.

The transactions listed in § 9-109 include all of the responses except real estate mortgages. A real estate mortgage is a secured transaction, but it is not an *Article 9* secured transaction because the obligation is secured with real property rather than personal property. Therefore, the correct response is **A,** and all the other responses are incorrect.

 # Burnham's Picks

Question 1	**D**
Question 2	**C**
Question 3	**D**
Question 4	**B**
Question 5	**B**
Question 6	**D**
Question 7	**D**
Question 8	**C**
Question 9	**A**

6

Creation of a Security Interest

CHAPTER OVERVIEW

A. Introduction
B. Sample Agreements
C. Is There a Security Agreement Authenticated by the Debtor?
D. Does the Security Agreement Contain a Description of the Collateral?
E. Closers
✦ Burnham's Picks

A. Introduction

The requirements for the creation of a security interest are found in § 9-203, which provides in part as follows:

(b) **Enforceability.** Except as otherwise provided in subsections (c) through (i), a security interest is enforceable against the debtor and third parties with respect to the collateral only if:

(1) value has been given;

(2) the debtor has rights in the collateral or the power to transfer rights in the collateral to a secured party; and

(3) one of the following conditions is met:

(A) the debtor has authenticated a security agreement that provides a description of the collateral and, if the security interest covers timber to be cut, a description of the land concerned;

(B) the collateral is not a certificated security and is in the possession of the secured party under Section 9-313 pursuant to the debtor's security agreement.

Let's review these requirements:

1. *Value has been given.* See § 1-204 for the definition of *value.* Essentially, the debtor has to get something in return for granting the security interest. Usually this will be goods that are sold to it or money that is loaned to it. In that context, *value* is the same as *consideration* in contract law. But value can exist even when consideration does not. For example, creditor and debtor enter into a security agreement in which debtor grants creditor a security interest in a computer in return for a loan. The loan is the value as well as consideration. Later, the computer declines in value, and the creditor demands additional collateral. The debtor agrees that a printer will also be collateral for the loan. Under the common law of contracts, there is no consideration for the debtor's promise of the printer as collateral. The creditor has already given the debtor the loan and gives the debtor nothing new in return for the promise of rights in the printer. But § 1-204(2) provides that there is value if a person acquires rights "as security for . . . a preexisting claim."

   AND

2. *The debtor has rights in the collateral.* This makes sense. You can't grant an interest in property that you don't have. On the other hand, you can grant only what you do have. Always ask what rights the debtor has in the property in which it is granting a security interest to the creditor. That will be the extent to which the secured party has rights. For example, a rich uncle promises John, who is 19, a new $50,000 Mercedes when he turns 21 on the condition that he does not smoke or drink before then. At the time the promise is made, Mary loans John $10,000 and takes a security interest in the Mercedes. At that moment, John has only a contract right to the car, and that right is contingent on his not smoking or drinking before he is 21. So Mary has only a contingent security interest that will not attach unless and until John gets the car.

   AND

3. Either:

   A. *A security agreement authenticated by the debtor provides a description of the collateral.* Note that the Code now uses the term *authenticated* rather than *written* in order to accommodate electronic commerce. The agreement must be authenticated only by the debtor, not by both parties. The agreement must contain a description of the collateral. Because most transactions involve an authenticated security agreement, we will focus our attention on this type of transaction. We will first look to whether the two requirements for a security agreement are satisfied: (1) authenticated by the debtor and (2) provides a description of the collateral

      OR

   B. *The collateral is in the possession of the secured party pursuant to a security agreement.* See § 9-313. Sometimes the term *pledge* is used to describe the transaction in which the creditor is in possession of the collateral. According to this provision, the pledge agreement can be oral.

OR

C and D. A couple of things that are too esoteric for us to study in a survey book.

When the last of these events has occurred, the security interest is said to have "attached." See § 9-203(a), which provides as follows:

(a) **Attachment.** A security interest attaches to collateral when it becomes enforceable against the debtor with respect to the collateral, unless an agreement expressly postpones the time of attachment.

Think of *attachment* as Article 9 placing a tag on the collateral that says, "This personal property secures a debt to a creditor."

Is it a big deal to have a security agreement? You bet. Section 9-201(a) provides the following general rule:

§ 9-201. General Effectiveness of Security Agreement

Except as otherwise provided in [the Uniform Commercial Code], a security agreement is effective according to its terms between the parties, against purchasers of the collateral, and against creditors.

Hmmm, I wonder who could have drafted Article 9? As we will see, Article 9 is very creditor-friendly. Nevertheless, we will see a number of exceptions to this sweeping general rule. But always remember that if no exception applies, this is the general rule.

> **Question 1.** John and Mary Smith are the joint owners of 1,000 shares of stock in Cisco Systems. John went to the bank and borrowed $10,000 and signed a security agreement granting the bank a security interest in the Cisco Systems stock. What interest does the bank have in the collateral?

> **A.** No interest, because the stock was owned jointly by John and Mary.
> **B.** An interest in 500 shares, representing John's share of the stock.
> **C.** An interest in John and Mary's joint tenancy in 1,000 shares.
> **D.** A tenancy in common with Mary in 1,000 shares.

Analysis.   It is clear that John authenticated a security agreement and that he received value. The only other requirement for attachment is that he have rights in the collateral. It is easy to determine what the bank's interest is if we focus on John's interest: what did he have to give to the bank? The answer is he had a joint tenancy with Mary in the stock. Therefore, that is what the bank has an interest in. So the correct response is **C**. Note that if John died before Mary, the bank would have no collateral. In a joint tenancy, the survivor gets the entire interest; since John would no longer have an interest in the stock, the bank would have no interest. If John survived and defaulted, the bank could sever the joint tenancy, and it would then have a tenancy in common with Mary in 1,000 shares.

> **Question 2.** On Monday, Pat and Mike were having a few drinks at the local tavern when Pat asked Mike if he could borrow $500. Mike responded, "It's not that I don't trust you, but I'd feel a lot better about it if I could hold on to your Ted Williams rookie baseball card until you pay it back." "It's a deal," Pat said, and they shook hands on it. On Tuesday, Pat gave the baseball card to Mike and on Wednesday, Mike gave $500 to Pat. When, if ever, did a security interest attach to the baseball card?
>
> **A.** Never, because the requirements for attachment were not satisfied.
> **B.** On Monday, when they made the agreement.
> **C.** On Tuesday, when Pat gave Mike the baseball card.
> **D.** On Wednesday, when Mike gave Pat the $500.

Analysis.   Response **A** is incorrect, for all the requirements for attachment were satisfied. Mike gave value, and Pat had an interest in the collateral. Although there was no authenticated security agreement, that is not necessary under § 9-203(b)(3)(B) when the collateral "is in the possession of the secured party." The security interest attaches when the last of these events occurs. Under these facts, value was given, according to the definition of "value" in § 1-204(1), when Mike made a "binding commitment" to loan Pat $500, not when Pat got the money. The last act necessary for attachment was Mike's possession of the baseball card on Tuesday, so **C** is the correct response. Note that this transaction is subject to misunderstanding, for other than the oral exchange, it appears to be a sale of the baseball card for $500.

Question 3. John and Mary are having lunch and discussing the sale of John's car to Mary. John wants $1,000 for it, but Mary doesn't have that much cash. John says, "I'll let you pay $100 each month if I can take the car back if you don't pay." Mary agrees. John writes these notes on a napkin:

> John's Toyota Corolla
> $1,000
> $100 per month
> take back if no pay

At John's request, Mary initials the napkin, they shake hands, and he gives her the keys. Six months later, Mary misses a monthly payment. Can John take the car back?

A. Yes, because there is an authenticated security agreement.
B. Yes, because the oral agreement is enforceable.
C. No, because John did not sign the writing.
D. It depends on whether parol evidence of the security agreement is admissible to supplement the writing.

Analysis. We can eliminate response **C** because § 9-203(b)(3)(A) requires authentication only by the debtor, not by the secured party. We can also eliminate **B,** because an oral security agreement is enforceable only if the collateral is in the possession of the secured party, and that is not the case here. In addition to authentication by the debtor, are the other elements of § 9-203 satisfied? Value has been given because John has promised the car. Mary has rights in the collateral, since she has purchased the car. The document contains a description of the collateral. Is the document that has been authenticated—the napkin—a security agreement? Recall that under § 9-102(a)(74), *security agreement* means "an agreement that creates or provides for a security interest." And a *security interest,* according to § 1-201(b)(35) means "an interest in personal property or fixtures which secures payment or performance of an obligation." The language "take back if no pay" evidences that a security agreement was created by this transaction. So the correct response is **A.** The question of whether the writing contains the entire agreement of the parties is a question to be resolved by the parol evidence rule. But we do not need to introduce evidence outside the writing in this case, so **D** is not a correct response.

B. Sample Agreements

As long as they comply with the § 9-203 requirements, security agreements may vary greatly in their sophistication. In the last question, for example, because John had written "take back if no pay" on the napkin that Mary initialed, a security interest was created. Between sophisticated parties, a complex agreement is often drafted. You can find examples in many online sources or form books. Below are three simpler agreements. Example 1 is a security agreement buried in the middle of a seven-page software sales and licensing agreement. Example 2 is entered into by a customer of Sears when he bought a washer and charged it on his Sears card; this transaction is unusual because most credit card purchases do not include a security agreement. Example 3 is typical of those used in consumer transactions. With respect to each of these agreements, note the presence of all the elements of a security agreement under § 9-203(b):

1. Value has been given.
2. The debtor has rights in the collateral.
3. It is authenticated by the debtor and provides a description of the collateral.

This provision is buried in the middle of a seven-page software license:

6.0 PAYMENT.

Upon and subject to credit approval by Company, payment terms shall be net thirty (30) days from shipping date. All payments shall be made in U.S. currency unless otherwise agreed. If at any time Customer is delinquent in the payment of any invoice or is otherwise in breach of this Agreement, Company may, in its discretion, and without prejudice to its other rights, withhold shipment (including partial shipments) of any order or may, at its option, require Customer to prepay for further shipments. Any sum not paid by Customer when due shall bear interest until paid at a rate of 1.5% per month (18% per annum), or the maximum rate permitted by law, whichever is less. Customer grants Company a security interest in Products purchased under this Agreement to secure payment for those Products purchased. If requested by Company, Customer agrees to execute financing statements to perfect this security interest.

Example 1: Security Agreement

SEARS
MISSOULA, MT 02259

RETAIN FOR COMPARISON WITH MONTHLY
STATEMENT OR FOR RETURN OR EXCHANGE

SALESCHECK #
022590266731

DELIVER TO: CUSTOMER
CUSTOMER: SCOTT J. BURNHAM
DELIV. DATE: 01/04/19 NORMAL
DELIV INSTR: ON ORDER

TRAN#   PG/STORE   REG#   ASSOC#
6731   20 02259   026   1883

MERCHANDISE ORDERED
LOCAL DELIVERY

26 28902   A/WASHER W SAL   469.88t
                        ORDERED
SETUP OR DELUXE
        DELIVERY FEE   30.00
        SUBTOTAL   499.88
        TAX 00.000%   .00

CARD TYPE: SEARS ACCOUNT
ACCT #: S0055113601136/001/000
STATE: MT
12/29/18 SEARS ACCOUNT TOTAL 499.88

PURCHASED UNDER MY SEARS ACCOUNT AND
SECURITY AGREEMENT, INCORPORATED BY
REFERENCE, I GRANT SEARS A SECURITY
INTEREST IN THIS MERCHANDISE UNTIL
PAID, UNLESS PROHIBITED BY LAW.
$499.88

PURCHASED BY

Example 2: Security Agreement on Credit Card Receipt

FIRST BANK

Security Agreement (Consumer)

In this Security Agreement, the words **I**, **me**, **my** and **mine** mean anyone who signs below. **You** and **your** mean First Bank.

I agree to give you a security interest in my property that's described below. If I don't repay any amounts I may owe you, or break a promise I've made in any loan or credit agreement I may

have with you, you can take this property and sell or use it as described below.

By granting you a security interest in this collateral, I intend to provide you with security for payment and performance of all my obligations to you which now exist or may exist in the future.

The collateral. Any of my property covered by your security interest is called "collateral." Any additions and replacements to the property, or any proceeds from the sale of the property are also part of the collateral. The collateral in this agreement is: (give full description using year, make, model and serial numbers)

_____
_____
_____
_____
_____
_____

Where I will keep the collateral. I'll keep the collateral in
_____ County, Missouri. I won't remove the collateral from Missouri without your written permission.
□ I live in the same county where I'll keep the collateral.
□ I live in _____ County, Missouri.
The collateral □ will □ won't be attached to real estate.
If it will, the owner of the real estate is

_____
and this is the real estate it will be attached to: (give legal description)_____
_____
_____
_____
_____
_____

Ownership and use of the collateral. I promise that I own the collateral and that there are no other claims, liens or security interests against it. I won't sell, lease or give the collateral to anyone else. I will use it carefully and keep it in good repair. I will not use or permit anyone to use the collateral in violation of any law.

The collateral is used primarily for:
□ personal purposes   □ business   □ farming

I agree to help you do all that's necessary to protect your security interest in the collateral.

I □ am □ am not using money you are lending me to buy the collateral. If I am, you will have what is called a "purchase money security interest" in the collateral. This will give you more protection against others who might claim the collateral is theirs.

Property Insurance and Taxes. I'll keep the collateral insured for its full value against loss and damage with an insurance company that you accept. The policies must say that you are to be paid if there's a loss. I'll deliver the policies to you, if you request.

If the collateral is lost or damaged, you can use the insurance proceeds to replace or repair it, or to repay any amounts I owe you.

I'll also pay all taxes and fees on the collateral. You can insure the collateral, or pay any tax or fee if I don't (although you don't have to). If you do pay taxes or fees, I'll repay you with interest at the highest rate allowed by law.

Default and repossession. I will be in default:

1. If I don't make a payment when due or I don't fully repay any loan I may have with you.
2. If I break any promise I have made to you in this agreement, under any loan note or in connection with any loan transaction between us.
3. If I become insolvent or file bankruptcy.
4. If a lien is put on the collateral, or if it's confiscated.
5. If the collateral is misused, or in danger of depreciating too much.
6. If I do anything that reduces my ability or willingness to repay.
7. If I die or become incompetent.
8. If my insurance is cancelled.

If I am in default, I will deliver the collateral to you upon request, or you can enter wherever the collateral is located and take it yourself without notice or other legal action. You can sell the collateral after giving me ten days notice. You can use the proceeds of the sale toward what I owe you. You can add to what I owe you the costs of repossession, sale, court costs and reasonable attorney's fees, if any. I'll pay any difference between the sale proceeds and what I owe you. If you owe me any money, you can use it to pay off this difference.

Law that applies. This agreement will be governed by Missouri law. Because you excuse one default by me does not mean later occurrences of default will be excused. I've read this agreement and received a copy. I understand it contains all my rights and responsibilities. No oral statements will be binding. All changes must be approved by you in writing. My heirs and legal representatives will also be responsible under this agreement.

_____Date _____

_____Date _____

Example 3: Typical Security Agreement Used in Consumer Transactions

C.   Is There a Security Agreement Authenticated by the Debtor?

You, of course, will always properly draft a security agreement. But your client may put you in the position of trying to argue that a security interest has attached even though there is no possession of the collateral and no authenticated security agreement. In a number of litigated cases, the creditor is able to produce a number of documents that seem to evidence a security agreement. Frequently, one of those documents is a financing statement. Recall from Chapter 4.A that a financing statement is the document filed by the creditor to perfect the security interest in order to give third parties notice of the transaction. You can see what a financing statement looks like in § 9-521. See Chapter 12.A.

You might think that a financing statement is good evidence of a security agreement, but virtually all the cases say that a financing statement alone is not sufficient. For one thing, the financing statement may be filed at any time, even before a security agreement is entered into. For example, a creditor might begin negotiations by asking the debtor to authorize the filing of a financing statement so the creditor can obtain priority. If those negotiations subsequently fail, however, there might be a filed financing statement but no security agreement. Furthermore, as we shall see, the description of the collateral in the financing statement can be broader than the description in the security agreement. For example, the security agreement might grant a security interest in an "RX7 Copy Machine," but the financing statement might indicate "equipment." In that case, the financing statement would not be good evidence of what the parties agreed to in their contract. The financing statement also does not show that value has been given. Finally, the financing statement does not have to be signed by either party, so the financing statement cannot constitute a security agreement authenticated by the debtor. Don't be confused when a judge states in a case that "the security agreement can be the financing statement." That simply means that as an alternative to filing the standard form financing statement, the creditor can satisfy the filing requirement by filing the security agreement.

In many cases, however, the creditor is able to produce not only a financing statement but a promissory note evidencing a promise to pay the value that was given and correspondence between the parties evidencing that particular items of property were to be collateral for the loan. Under the "composite document" rule, many jurisdictions have found that these documents are enough, in the absence of a unitary agreement, to constitute a security agreement.

Question 4. Donald sent an e-mail to Steven, asking Steven if he could borrow $10,000 for one year at 10 percent interest, with the obligation secured by Donald's baseball-card collection. Steven responded that he would have to see the collection. The parties then got together at

Donald's house. After looking at the collection, Steven said, "It's a deal. You can hold on to the collection subject to my security interest." They shook hands, and Steven gave Donald a check for $10,000. The next day, Steven filed a financing statement indicating that the baseball-card collection was the collateral. Donald did not repay the loan, and Steven sought to exercise his Article 9 rights to the baseball-card collection. Did a security interest attach to the baseball-card collection?

A. No, because the debtor never authenticated a security agreement.
B. Yes, because the filing of the financing statement satisfies the requirement of an authenticated security agreement.
C. Yes, because the e-mail from Donald satisfies the requirement of an authenticated security agreement.
D. Yes, because in most jurisdictions the documents and circumstances would satisfy the "composite document rule."

Analysis.   Section 9-203(b)(3)(A) provides that a security interest attaches when "the debtor has authenticated a security agreement that provides a description of the collateral." Here, there is no document that constitutes an agreement, because although Donald's e-mail proposes an agreement, it does not constitute one. Therefore, response **C** is not correct. The financing statement is not enough to indicate that there is an agreement, since it can be filed at any time by the creditor alone. Therefore, response **B** is not correct. It would appear that response **A** is correct. However, in most jurisdictions, a "composite document" can substitute for the formal grant of a security interest. As stated in *In re Bollinger Corp.*, 614 F.2d 924 (3d Cir. 1980):

> When the parties have neglected to sign a separate security agreement, it would appear that the better and more practical view is to look at the transaction as a whole in order to determine if there is a writing, or writings, signed by the debtor describing the collateral which demonstrates an intent to create a security interest in the collateral.

Here it would appear that the exchange of e-mails, the check, and the financing statement considered together would constitute a composite document that would satisfy § 9-203(b)(3)(A). Therefore, response **D** is the best choice.

Question 5. Donald sent an e-mail to Steven asking Steven if he could borrow $10,000 for one year at 10 percent interest, with the obligation secured by Donald's baseball-card collection. Steven responded that he would have to see the collection. The parties then got together at Donald's house. After looking at the collection, Steven said, "It's a deal. But I am going to hold on to the collection until you pay." They shook hands; Steven then gave Donald a check for $10,000, and Steven took the collection. Steven never filed a financing statement. Donald did not repay the loan, and Steven sought to exercise his Article 9 rights to the baseball-card collection. Did a security interest attach to the baseball-card collection?

A. No, because the debtor, Donald, never authenticated a security agreement.

B. No, because Steven never filed a financing statement.

C. Yes, because the collateral is in the possession of the creditor, Steven, pursuant to a security agreement.

D. Yes, because in most jurisdictions the documents and circumstances would satisfy the "composite document rule."

Analysis. *Note on test-taking.* Sometimes instructors include two questions that initially seem very similar. In order to answer the second one correctly, it is helpful to spot the difference and understand its significance. Here, there is a difference in the facts between Question 4 and Question 5. In Question 4, Steven said, "You can hold on to the collection subject to my security interest." But in Question 5, Steven said, "But I am going to hold on to the collection until you pay." To answer Question 5 correctly, you needed to spot this difference and understand its significance.

We can immediately eliminate response **B,** because filing is not necessary for attachment. Response **A** is correct in stating that the debtor never authenticated a security agreement. But there are alternate ways to have a security agreement attach. Section 9-203(b)(3)(B) provides that a security interest attaches when the collateral "is in the possession of the secured party under Section 9-313 pursuant to the debtor's security agreement." In other words, possession is a substitute for an authenticated agreement. Here, the parties did enter into an oral security agreement under which the debtor gave possession to the creditor, so **C** is the correct response. It could be argued that **D** may also be true, in that the e-mails and the check could satisfy the "composite document rule," but there is no reason to get into that factual inquiry. **C** is a better response because it relies on the language of the statute that is enacted in all jurisdictions and it is clearly satisfied by the facts.

D. Does the Security Agreement Contain a Description of the Collateral?

Recall that § 9-203(b)(3)(A) requires that the authenticated security agreement contain "a description of the collateral." This is key because the security agreement is a type of contract, and the subject matter of the contract is obviously a material term. In a number of litigated cases, a party contends that the creditor did not properly comply with this requirement. Sometimes a debtor challenges the description, but more often the challenge is brought by a competing creditor or by the trustee in bankruptcy acting on behalf of the creditors. In those disputes among creditors, the issue is often which party is entitled to priority in the collateral. However, the issue of priority is never reached if one creditor can knock off a competing creditor by proving that the competitor's security interest never attached.

Section 9-108 tells us what is a sufficient description of collateral for purposes of § 9-203(b)(3)(A):

§ 9-108. Sufficiency of Description.

(a) **Sufficiency of description.** Except as otherwise provided in subsections (c), (d), and (e), a description of personal or real property is sufficient, whether or not it is specific, if it reasonably identifies what is described.

(b) **Examples of reasonable identification.** Except as otherwise provided in subsection (d), a description of collateral reasonably identifies the collateral if it identifies the collateral by:

(1) specific listing;

(2) category;

(3) except as otherwise provided in subsection (e), a type of collateral defined in [the Uniform Commercial Code];

(4) quantity;

(5) computational or allocational formula or procedure; or

(6) except as otherwise provided in subsection (c), any other method, if the identity of the collateral is objectively determinable.

(c) **Supergeneric description not sufficient.** A description of collateral as "all the debtor's assets" or "all the debtor's personal property" or using words of similar import does not reasonably identify the collateral.

(d) **Investment property.** Except as otherwise provided in subsection (e), a description of a security entitlement, securities account, or commodity account is sufficient if it describes:

(1) the collateral by those terms or as investment property; or

(2) the underlying financial asset or commodity contract.

(e) **When description by type insufficient.** A description only by type of collateral defined in [the Uniform Commercial Code] is an insufficient description of:

(1) a commercial tort claim; or

(2) in a consumer transaction, consumer goods, a security entitlement, a securities account, or a commodity account.

Note that this section provides in subsection (a) that the description is sufficient if it "reasonably identifies what is described" and that subsection (b) goes on to explain what constitutes a reasonable description. Most creditors will identify the collateral by either a specific listing under subsection (b)(1) or by a type of collateral defined in the Code under subsection (b)(3). For the latter purpose, see the list of Code Classifications in Chapter 4.B. For example, if the debtor is a car rental agency who grants a security agreement in the cars, the creditor could describe the collateral as either "cars available for rental," as a specific listing under subsection (b)(1), or "inventory," as a type of collateral defined in the Code under subsection (b)(3).

There are two exceptions in subsection (e) to the general rule that a description of collateral by type is sufficient. It provides as follows:

> (e) **When description by type insufficient.** A description only by type of collateral defined in [the Uniform Commercial Code] is an insufficient description of:
>> (1) a commercial tort claim; or
>> (2) in a consumer transaction, consumer goods, a security entitlement, a securities account, or a commodity account.

One exception is "a commercial tort claim." You probably didn't spend a lot of time in Torts class discussing commercial torts. Commercial tort claims are defined in § 9-102(a)(13) as tort claims that arise in the course of a business and do not include claims for personal injury. Examples of commercial tort claims include tortious interference with contract, defamation, and injury to business property. A law firm pursuing a tort claim against Green Environment, Inc., on behalf of Smokestack Industries, Inc., for example, might take a security interest in the claim in order to secure its legal fees. It would have to specifically describe the collateral as something like "defamation claim against Green Environment, Inc."

The other exception is "in a consumer transaction, consumer goods, a security entitlement, a securities account, or a commodity account." So if an individual entered into a security agreement for personal, family, or household purposes, using as collateral certain consumer goods and stocks that were acquired for personal, family, or household purposes, the transaction would be a "consumer transaction" as defined in § 9-102(a)(26). The security agreement could not describe the collateral as "consumer goods and investment property." It would have to more specifically describe the items as, for example, "baseball-card collection and 1,000 shares Cisco Systems."

A policy question arose under former Article 9 as to whether a creditor could use a supergeneric description like "all of debtor's personal property." Debtors argued that taking a security interest in all property was overreaching, while creditors claimed that the description accurately described the collateral because the security agreement did, in fact, grant the creditor a security interest in all of the property. That question is now resolved in § 9-108(c), which provides that "[a] description of collateral as 'all the debtor's assets' or 'all the debtor's personal property' or using words of similar import does not reasonably identify the collateral." Note, however, that this provision is not saying that the creditor can't *take* a security interest in all of the debtor's property; the creditor just can't *describe* it that way. For example, as we saw in Chapter 4.B, a security agreement drafted pursuant to this section could provide as follows:

2. *"Collateral."* The Collateral shall consist of all of the following personal property of Debtor, wherever located, and now owned or hereafter acquired, including:

    2.1 Accounts;

    2.2 Chattel paper, including equipment leases and conditional sales agreements;

    2.3 Inventory, including property held for sale or lease and raw materials;

    2.4 Equipment, including property used in the Debtor's business, machinery, and production machines;

    2.5 Instruments, notes, negotiable instruments, and negotiable certificates of deposit;

    2.6 Investment property;

    2.7 Documents, including documents of title, warehouse receipts, and bills of lading;

    2.8 Deposit accounts;

    2.9 Debtor's claim for interference with contract against Texaco;

    2.10 Letter-of-credit rights;

    2.11 General intangibles, including payment intangibles, licenses, intellectual property, and tax returns.

I don't want to confuse you by talking too much about financing statements at this point. The content of the financing statement is discussed in Chapter 12.C. But it may be helpful to point out that the rules in § 9-108 we have discussed apply only to the description of the collateral in the security agreement and *not* to the description of the collateral in the financing statement. The rule applicable to financing statements is found in § 9-504, which provides as follows:

> **§ 9-504. Indication of Collateral.** A financing statement sufficiently indicates the collateral that it covers if the financing statement provides:
>
>   (1) a description of the collateral pursuant to Section 9-108; or
>
>   (2) an indication that the financing statement covers all assets or all personal property.

The reason these rules are different should become clear when you consider the function of each document. The security agreement is the contract that describes which collateral secures the transaction; the financing statement merely puts third parties on notice of the transaction. For example, it makes a big difference whether the security agreement describes the collateral as "one RX7 copy machine" or "all of debtor's equipment." If the description "one RX7 copy machine" is used, the security interest would attach only to the copy machine; but if the phrase "all of debtor's equipment" is used, the security interest would attach to all equipment. But whether the collateral was "one RX7 copy machine" or "all of debtor's equipment," the description "equipment" in the financing statement would put third parties on notice to make further inquiry into what the collateral is. As a practical matter, creditors often put in the financing statement the description from the security agreement.

Question 6. A creditor wishes to take a security interest in all the assets of a business debtor. The security agreement between the creditor and the debtor describes the collateral as "all the debtor's personal property, including accounts, chattel paper, inventory, equipment, instruments including promissory notes, investment property, documents, deposit accounts, letter of credit rights, general intangibles, and supporting obligations." Is this description of the collateral sufficient under Article 9?

A. Yes, because it is a description by type of collateral defined in the Code.
B. Yes, because it puts third parties on inquiry notice.
C. No, because it is supergeneric.
D. No, because public policy does not allow a creditor to take a security interest in all the debtor's personal property.

Analysis. According to 9-108(c), a supergeneric description is not sufficient. However, here the drafter has expanded upon the supergeneric language "all the debtor's personal property" by adding particular types of collateral. Section 9-108(b)(3) provides that "a description of collateral reasonably identifies the collateral if it identifies the collateral by: . . . a type of collateral defined in [the Uniform Commercial Code]." That is what the creditor has done here, so **A** is the correct response. Note, however, that the creditor's security interest attaches only to those types and not to any that are not enumerated.

Question 7. Brown & Williamson Tobacco Co. has a claim against CBS Inc. for tortious interference with a contract between Brown & Williamson and one of its employees, Jeffrey Wigand. To finance the lawsuit, Brown & Williamson borrows money from First Bank and grants First Bank a security interest in the claim. In the security agreement, First Bank should describe the collateral as:

A. Intangible property.
B. General intangibles.
C. Commercial tort claims.
D. A claim against CBS Inc. for tortious interference with a contract between Brown & Williamson and one of its employees, Jeffrey Wigand.

Analysis.   Responses **A**, **B**, and **C** are types of collateral under the Code. Under the general rule of § 9-108(b)(3), such a description reasonably identifies this collateral. But this question is testing you for the exception to the general rule. Under the exception in § 9-108(e), a description by type is *not* sufficient when the collateral is a commercial tort claim or collateral in a consumer transaction. Here, the collateral is a commercial tort claim, so **D** is the correct response. This claim, by the way, fueled the plot of the movie *The Insider*.

Question 8. Bank loans debtor money and takes a security interest in certain property of a debtor, describing the collateral in the security agreement as "all of the debtor's equipment." Bank's financing statement describes the collateral as "all of the debtor's equipment and inventory." Has a security interest attached to debtor's inventory?

A. Yes, because that collateral is described in the security agreement.
B. Yes, because that collateral is described in the financing statement.
C. No, because that collateral is not described in the security agreement.
D. No because that collateral is not described in the financing statement.

Analysis.   According to § 9-203(b)(3)(A), for attachment to take place, there must be a security agreement that "provides a description of the collateral." It is irrelevant that inventory is described in the financing statement, because that is not sufficient for attachment. Here, inventory is not described in the security agreement, so the correct response must be **C**.

E.   Closers

Question 9. Austin Furniture Company Inc. sells home furniture at retail outlets. On February 1, Austin asked First Bank to loan it $100,000, payable on February 1 two years later, and First Bank agreed. First Bank prepared the loan documents, and both parties signed them. At this point, what do the parties have?

A. An agreement that is not a security agreement.
B. A security agreement that is unperfected.
C. A security agreement that is perfected.
D. No agreement.

Analysis. Since both parties signed the documents, they have an agreement. However, there is no mention in the facts of a security agreement. Therefore, the correct answer is **A.**

Question 10. Austin Furniture Company Inc. sells home furniture at retail outlets. On February 1, Austin asked First Bank to loan it $100,000, to be distributed on March 1 and payable on February 1 two years later, and First Bank agreed. First Bank prepared the loan documents, which provided that Austin granted First Bank a security interest in its "inventory of furniture now owned or hereafter acquired," and both parties signed them. At this point, do the parties have a security agreement?

A. Yes, because all the elements are satisfied.
B. No, because value has not yet been given.
C. No, because Austin does not yet have rights in the collateral that will be "hereafter acquired."
D. No, because there is not a sufficient description of the collateral.

Analysis. Under § 1-204(1), *value* includes "a binding commitment to extend credit." Therefore, Austin obtained value even though it has not yet received the money. The description of the collateral as "inventory" is sufficient, for a description by category satisfies § 9-108. It is true that the security interest does not attach to the future inventory until Austin has rights to it, but since the interest does attach to the existing inventory, there is a security agreement with respect to that collateral. As explained in the next chapter, as soon as Austin acquires new inventory, the security interest will attach to it. Since all the elements of § 9-203 are satisfied, the correct answer is **A.**

Burnham's Picks

Question 1	C
Question 2	C
Question 3	A
Question 4	D
Question 5	C
Question 6	A
Question 7	D
Question 8	C
Question 9	A
Question 10	A

7

The Security Interest as a "Floating Lien"

CHAPTER OVERVIEW

A. The "Floating Lien"
  1. Sale or Exchange
  2. Proceeds
  3. After-Acquired Property
  4. Future Advances
B. Sale or Exchange
  1. The General Rule
  2. First Exception: "When the Secured Party Authorized the Disposition"
  3. Second Exception: "Except as Otherwise Provided in This Article"
C. Proceeds
D. After-Acquired Property
E. Prohibitions Against Security Interests in Certain Property
F. Future Advances
G. Closers
✦ Burnham's Picks

A.   The "Floating Lien"

Once a security interest is created, what collateral does it cover and what debts does it secure?

Obviously, it covers the collateral enumerated at the time of the agreement and secures the debt stated in the agreement. But the scope of the security interest is greater than that. It has been called a "floating lien" because it floats over collateral not enumerated in the agreement and debts not stated in the agreement. The following concepts demonstrate this breadth.

1. Sale or Exchange

The *general rule* of § 9-315(a)(1) is that the security interest continues in collateral "notwithstanding sale, lease, license, exchange, or other disposition thereof." Recall the hypotheticals in Chapter 3.A in which Brenda granted Sears a security interest in her dishwasher and Vann's granted First Bank a security interest in its inventory of Mitsubishi TVs. If Brenda sells her dishwasher, or Vann's sells a Mitsubishi TV, under the general rule the security interest floats to the property in the hands of the new owner. After the security interest has attached to collateral, it *automatically* remains attached to the collateral after disposition. Don't be alarmed if it dawns on you that this rule may give a bank the right to repossess the TV you just bought. This is the general rule, and there will be exceptions.

2. Proceeds

The *general rule* of § 9-315(a)(2) is that the security interest "attaches to any identifiable proceeds of collateral." Proceeds is defined in § 9-102(a)(64)(A) as "whatever is acquired upon the sale, lease, license, exchange, or other disposition of collateral." If Brenda sells her dishwasher or Vann's sells a Mitsubishi TV, under the general rule the security interest floats to the proceeds of the sale in the hands of the debtor. After the security interest has attached to collateral, it *automatically* attaches to the proceeds of collateral.

3. After-Acquired Property

The *general rule* of § 9-204(a) is that the security agreement "may create or provide for a security interest in after-acquired collateral." Note that the security agreement *may create or provide for* this interest; it is not automatic, but must be drafted into the agreement to be effective. Under such a clause, the creditor may take as collateral not just property in which the debtor presently has rights, but property in which the debtor may have rights in the future.

Such a provision is essential to protect the creditor who takes a security interest in collateral that turns over, such as inventory or accounts. If the creditor took a security interest in "inventory" and that meant only the inventory the debtor had at the time the agreement was signed, such as the cars for sale in a new car lot, that collateral would soon be depleted and the debt would be unsecured. The careful drafter will provide for a security interest in "all inventory now owned or hereafter acquired," so that the security interest will attach to after-acquired property.

Review question: *When* does the security interest attach to the after-acquired collateral? You recall from Chapter 6 that § 9-203 provides that in order for attachment to occur, "the debtor has rights in the collateral," so the security interest attaches to after-acquired collateral when the debtor acquires rights to that collateral, usually by buying it.

4. *Future Advances*

The *general rule* of § 9-204(c) is that "a security agreement may provide that collateral secures . . . future advances or other value, whether or not the advances or value are given pursuant to commitment." In other words, under the concept of future advances, the security interest does not float over additional collateral, but the same collateral floats over a new extension of credit. Again, the coverage *may include* this provision: like the interest in after-acquired property, it is not automatic, but must be drafted into the agreement to be effective. The careful drafter will provide that the security interest "secures all future advances as well as all obligations now existing."

Let us explore these concepts in greater detail.

B.   Sale or Exchange

1. *The General Rule*

The general rule, § 9-201(a), provides (emphasis added):

> Except as otherwise provided in [the Uniform Commercial Code], a security agreement is effective according to its terms between the parties, *against purchasers of the collateral,* and against creditors.

And § 9-315(a)(1) provides in part:

> Except as otherwise provided in this article and in Section 2-403(2):
>   (1) a security interest or agricultural lien continues in collateral notwithstanding sale, lease, license, exchange, or other disposition thereof unless the secured party authorized the disposition free of the security interest or agricultural lien.

So, the general rule is: when both the secured party and a transferee claim rights to the collateral, the secured party prevails unless an exception applies.

Question 1. Farmer Brown buys a "Model A irrigation system" and finances $100,000 of the purchase price with First Bank, giving the bank a security interest in the irrigation system. Two years later, Brown trades his Model A system to Farmer Smith for a cheaper Model B system plus $10,000 in cash. After the sale, Farmer Brown stops making his payments to First Bank. Under the general rule, can the bank repossess the Model A system, which is now owned by Farmer Smith?

A. Yes, because the security interest "continues in collateral notwithstanding sale."

> **B.** Yes, because Smith is held to have impliedly granted a security interest.
> **C.** No, because the security interest is cut off when there is a sale.
> **D.** No, because Smith had no knowledge of the security interest.

Analysis.   *Note on test-taking.* The "call of the question" here is to apply the "general rule." Even if you are aware of some applicable exception, you must ignore it when answering the question.

It may not seem intuitive, but the general rule says *yes*! First Bank can take the equipment out of the hands of Smith, because, according to § 9-315 (a)(1), the security interest "continues in collateral notwithstanding sale." Therefore, response **A** is correct, and the other responses are incorrect.

It may not seem fair to buyers that the security interest remains attached when they acquire the collateral. Let's look at the exceptions to see when buyers fall under them.

2. First Exception: "When the Secured Party Authorized the Disposition"

The first exception occurs in § 9-315(a)(1). The security interest continues in the collateral notwithstanding the sale of the collateral unless the secured party authorizes the sale. Remember the significance of determining whether the debtor's sale of the collateral is "authorized" for purposes of § 9-315(a)(1). The general rule is that the security interest remains attached even after the sale. If the debtor's sale of the collateral was authorized, the secured party loses its security interest in the collateral, that is, the tag is removed and the buyer "takes free" of the security interest.

For example, assume First Bank took a security interest in Brown's irrigation system, and Brown sold the equipment to Smith. If First Bank authorized the sale, Smith would take the irrigation equipment free of the security interest. In that event, First Bank could still recover the money it loaned by suing Brown on the debt, but it would lose the advantage of having a security interest. So it is unlikely that a creditor would be foolish enough to let go of its security interest in equipment by authorizing the sale. On the other hand, the situation is different when the collateral is inventory rather than equipment. A creditor generally wants the debtor to sell inventory because that's how the debtor earns the money to pay the debt. So it won't surprise you that a sale from inventory subject to a security interest is generally authorized unless the creditor or the circumstances indicate otherwise.

Parties are free to provide in the security agreement whether a sale is authorized. In interpreting such a provision, courts will use the principles of law and equity incorporated in the Code by § 1-103(b).

Question 2. First Bank has a security interest in all of the inventory of the Two Dot General Store. The store sells sugar to a customer. Is the sale "authorized" for purposes of § 9-315(a)(1)?

A. Yes, because it is a sale from inventory.
B. No, because it is a sale of equipment.
C. No, because sales must be affirmatively authorized by the secured party.
D. No, because this is not the kind of inventory sale that a secured party would authorize.

Analysis.   The correct response is **A.** Absent other circumstances, the secured creditor is presumed to authorize sales from inventory.

Question 3. First Bank has a security interest in all of the inventory of the Two Dot General Store. The owners sell the store—inventory, building, and equipment—to Megalo Mart. Is the sale of inventory "authorized" for purposes of § 9-315(a)(1)?

A. Yes, because it is a sale from inventory.
B. No, because it is a sale of equipment.
C. No, because sales must be affirmatively authorized by the secured party.
D. No, because this is not the kind of inventory sale that a secured party would authorize.

Analysis.   *Note on test-taking.* The responses here are the same as the responses to the previous question, but the facts have changed. In that situation, the assessor is probably testing whether you are alert to a fact that would produce a different response.

Here, the fact change is that the sale is not the ordinary sale of inventory to a customer but the bulk sale of the entire inventory to another business. It is unlikely that the secured party would authorize this kind of disposition of the collateral, so the best response is **D.**

Question 4. First Bank extends credit to Wally Congdon, a cattle rancher, and obtains a security interest in Congdon's cattle. The security agreement expressly provides in bold print that Congdon cannot sell cattle without the prior written consent of the bank. Despite this provision in its standard form security agreement, First Bank's usual practice is to permit ranchers who use cattle as collateral for loans to sell the cattle without first obtaining written consent. On four occasions, Congdon

> sells cattle with the knowledge of the bank but without first obtaining the bank's written consent, and the bank does not object. On the fifth occasion, the bank claims that Congdon is in breach of the security agreement. Is he?
>
> A. Yes, because the security agreement provides that he must obtain the bank's written consent.
> B. No, because the Code does not allow a secured party to require consent to sell the collateral.
> C. No, because the secured party affirmatively authorized the sale of the cattle.
> D. No, because the secured party would be held to have waived the condition of written consent.

Analysis. This is a tough one. We can eliminate response **B** because it is not a correct statement of the law, and we can eliminate response **C** because it is not a correct statement of the facts. We are left, as we often are in multiple-choice analysis, with two responses that might be correct: **A,** which seems to be a correct statement, and **D,** which would provide an exception to that statement. Is the waiver exception applicable? The facts may ring a dim bell from first-year Contracts. You learned there that a waiver is a knowing relinquishment of a legal right. It is imposed by a court in equity when a person is lulled into thinking that they do not have to perform as required by the contract. Note that principles of law and equity are read into the Code under § 1-103(b). Here, it is likely that a court would find that, despite the language in the contract, the bank gave up its right to require consent when it repeatedly led Congdon to believe that consent was not required. Therefore, **D** is the better response. Some drafters attempt to draft around this result by putting a "no-wavier" clause in the contract providing that the creditor's failure to act on one or more occasions does not bar them from taking action on another. Courts will usually not honor this provision, finding that the creditor waived it as well. The creditor's best course of action is to send the debtor notice that in spite of past waivers, the creditor may take action if there is a breach in the future. This retraction of a waiver is likely to be effective.

3. Second Exception: "Except as Otherwise Provided in This Article"

A second exception occurs under § 9-315(a). How can a lawyer or a law student reading § 9-315(a) discover *where* Article 9 otherwise provides that a disposition of collateral cuts off the security interest? The lawyer or law student remembers, of course, to look to the Official Comments, in this case, Comment 2 to § 9-315, the third paragraph of which begins as follows:

This Article contains several provisions under which a transferee takes free of a security interest or agricultural lien. For example, Section 9-317 states when transferees take free of unperfected security interests; Sections 9-320 and 9-321 on goods, 9-321 on general intangibles, 9-330 on chattel paper and instruments, and 9-331 on negotiable instruments, negotiable documents, and securities state when purchasers of such collateral take free of a security interest, even though perfected and even though the disposition was not authorized.

Note the importance in solving Code problems of making various classifications: of the parties, of the status of perfection, and of the collateral. We start with the party competing with the secured creditor, here, a *transferee*. To find the right section, we classify the security interest as *perfected or unperfected*, and we classify the *collateral*. Voila! We go to the right section!

I know you can't stand the suspense, but we're not going to look at those exceptions until Chapter 15. If you want to know the answer, take a peek at that chapter.

C.   Proceeds

The general rule of § 9-315(a)(2) is that "a security interest attaches to any identifiable proceeds of collateral." This happens automatically; it does not have to be stated in the security agreement. A secured party relying on § 9-315(a)(2) must establish that the property is proceeds. *Proceeds* is defined in § 9-102(a)(64), which provides:

"Proceeds" . . . means the following property:

(A) whatever is acquired upon the sale, lease, license, exchange, or other disposition of collateral;

(B) whatever is collected on, or distributed on account of, collateral;

(C) rights arising out of collateral;

(D) to the extent of the value of collateral, claims arising out of the loss, nonconformity, or interference with the use of, defects or infringement of rights in, or damage to, the collateral; or

(E) to the extent of the value of collateral and to the extent payable to the debtor or the secured party, insurance payable by reason of the loss or nonconformity of, defects or infringement of rights in, or damage to, the collateral.

Note that each of those subsections refers to the *collateral*, which is defined in § 9-102(a)(12) to include "proceeds to which a security interest attaches." If we plug that definition into § 9-102(a)(64)(A), then we see that proceeds are acquired upon the disposition of proceeds. In other words, the proceeds of proceeds are proceeds! No matter how many times the proceeds change form, they are still proceeds as long as they are "identifiable," that is, traceable back to the collateral.

Question 5. Farmer Brown buys a "Model A irrigation system" and finances $100,000 of the purchase price with First Bank, giving the bank a security interest in the irrigation system. Two years later, Brown trades his Model A system to Farmer Smith for a cheaper Model B system and $10,000 in cash. Brown buys a used Toyota with $5,000 of the cash and puts the rest into his bank account, which had no other money in it. Farmer Brown defaults on his payments to First Bank. Which of the following property secures the debt?

I.   The Model A system.
II. The Model B system.
III. The Toyota.
IV. The cash in the bank.

    A. I only.
    B. I and II only.
    C. I, II, and IV only.
    D. I, II, III, and IV.

Analysis.   *Note on test-taking.* As a general rule, there is only one correct response to a multiple-choice question. Assessors may use other techniques to indicate that more than one answer may be correct, such as the form used here. To approach a question such as this, it is probably best to check off which items in the list I through IV satisfy the question and then to match your choices to the responses in **A** through **D**.

We know from part B of this chapter that item I is correct, for the general rule is that the security interest continues in collateral notwithstanding disposition. The other items refer to property that is not the original collateral, so if the security interest attaches, it is because of the rule of proceeds. Is each item proceeds of the Model A system? The Model B system and the cash are proceeds because under § 9-102(a)(64)(A) they are "acquired upon the sale, lease, license, exchange, or other disposition of collateral." Therefore items II and IV are correct. The Toyota is more problematic, because it was not acquired upon the disposition of the collateral, if we think of the collateral as the Model A system. But if it was acquired with proceeds, it is proceeds. You are told that the cash was used to buy the Toyota and that there is no other money in the bank account, so the Toyota is identifiable as proceeds of the collateral. Item III is also proceeds. Since the property enumerated in items II, III, and IV are all proceeds, the security interest automatically attaches to them under § 9-315(a)(2). The "call of the question" did not ask which items are proceeds, but which items secure the debt. Our response must therefore include item I as well, so the correct response is **D**.

Recall that in Chapter 4.D we raised the issue of whether the lender can "trace" the funds used to purchase the collateral in order to establish that it has a purchase money security interest (PMSI). Similarly, the issue of whether the proceeds are *identifiable* frequently arises when cash from the sale of the collateral is "commingled" with other cash so that it loses its separate identity. We made it easy in the last question by noting that there was no other money in the bank account into which the cash was placed. To avoid the commingling problem, creditors frequently require debtors to deposit amounts received from the sale of collateral in a special escrow account reserved only for those funds. But what if Brown put the $10,000 into a bank account that already had $5,000 in it and then wrote a check on that account for $5,000 to buy the Toyota and spent the remaining $10,000 on an entry fee to the World Series of Poker? Was the money used to buy the Toyota or the entry fee identifiable proceeds? How can proceeds deposited in a bank account be identifiable?

The answer to that last question is codified in § 9-315(b). Subsection (b)(2) directs us to methods of "tracing" that are not found in the Code. One of those methods of tracing, used in trust accounting, is the "lowest intermediate balance rule." Under that rule, deposits of proceeds always go to the bottom of the account; deposits of nonproceeds go to the top, and withdrawals come off the top. That way the proceeds sit on the bottom and are the last to be drawn on. So the lowest balance between the time the proceeds were deposited and the time the accounting is made must be proceeds.

Question 6. On January 10, S lends D $10,000 and obtains a security interest in all of D's inventory. As of January 10, D's bank account has a $3,000 balance (not from proceeds). D then makes the following deposits and withdrawals.

- On January 13, D deposits $9,000 from the sale of a vacant lot.
- On January 16, D deposits $4,000 from the sale of the inventory.
- On January 18, D withdraws $6,000 from the bank account for rent, payroll, and other expenses.

What is the extent of S's security interest in D's bank account under § 9-315(b)?

A. $1,000.
B. $3,000.
C. $4,000.
D. $7,000.

Analysis.   It should be immediately apparent that the answer cannot be **D,** for only $4,000 was deposited from the sale of inventory. The key to solving a "lowest intermediate balance rule" problem is to take each step chronologically. We start on January 10 with $3,000 of nonproceeds in the account. On January 13, $9,000 is deposited. Because it is not proceeds, it goes to the top of the account. On January 16, $4,000 in proceeds is deposited. It sits on the bottom of the account, under the $12,000 in nonproceeds. On January 18, a withdrawal of $6,000 of nonproceeds is made. This comes off the top. So there is now $10,000 in the account, of which $4,000 is proceeds. **C** is the correct response.

Question 7. On January 10, S lends D $10,000 and obtains a security interest in all of D's inventory. As of January 10, D's bank account has a $3,000 balance (not from proceeds). D then makes the following deposits and withdrawals:

- On January 13, D deposits $4,000 received from the sale of inventory.
- On January 16, D withdraws $6,000 from the account for payroll, rent, and other expenses.
- On January 30, D deposits $9,000 from the sale of a vacant lot.

What is the extent of S's security interest in D's bank account under § 9-315(b)?

A. $1,000.
B. $3,000.
C. $4,000.
D. $7,000.

Analysis.   It should be immediately apparent that the answer cannot be **D**, for only $4,000 was deposited from the sale of inventory. To solve a "lowest intermediate balance rule" problem, take each step chronologically. We start on January 10 with $3,000 of nonproceeds in the account. On January 13, $4,000 in proceeds is deposited. It sits on the bottom of the account, under the $3,000 in nonproceeds. On January 16, a withdrawal of $6,000 of nonproceeds is made. This comes off the top, taking the $3,000 in nonproceeds and $3,000 in proceeds, leaving $1,000 in the account, all of which is proceeds. On January 30, $9,000 is deposited. Because it is not proceeds, it goes to the top of the account. So there is now $10,000 in the account, of which $1,000 is proceeds. **A** is the correct response.

D. After-Acquired Property

Section 9-204(a) contains the basic rule regarding after-acquired property clauses:

> (a) **After-acquired collateral.** Except as otherwise provided in subsection (b), a security agreement may create or provide for a security interest in after-acquired collateral.

In order to have the security interest attach to after-acquired property, the creditor must put an after-acquired property clause in the security agreement. In commercial (as opposed to consumer) transactions, after-acquired property clauses are universally found and operate in a straightforward manner.

For example, a security agreement dated March 1 between First Bank and Doctor Green states that the collateral is "all accounts now owned by debtor as well as any and all accounts that may hereafter arise or be acquired by Debtor." On March 1, Dr. Green has $10,000 worth of outstanding bills to patients. The security interest attaches to these bills, which are Dr. Green's accounts. On April 1, Dr. Green bills a patient $1,000. Because of the after-acquired clause in the security agreement, the security interest attaches to this account as well.

Collateral such as accounts and inventory frequently turns over as bills are paid and new bills issued or as goods are sold and the inventory replenished. For this reason, creditors sometimes neglect to include an after-acquired property clause, thinking it is only logical that the debtor was granting a security interest in future accounts and inventory and not just those in which the debtor has an interest at the time the security agreement was entered into. This language is at best ambiguous. For example, if the security agreement with Dr. Green had stated that the collateral was "all accounts," there might be an argument as to whether that language meant only existing accounts or future accounts as well. The prudent creditor wants to avoid litigation about the meaning of language and will include the "after-acquired" language to avoid this issue.

The rule differs with respect to consumer goods. Recall that consumer goods are goods that are used "primarily for personal, family, or household purposes," according to § 9-102(a)(23). When the collateral is consumer goods, § 9-204(b)(1) limits the right of the creditor to secure the debt with after-acquired property to property acquired within 10 days after the secured party gives value. It provides as follows:

> (b) **When after-acquired property clause not effective**. A security interest does not attach under a term constituting an after-acquired property clause to:
>
> > (1) consumer goods, other than an accession when given as additional security, unless the debtor acquires rights in them within 10 days after the secured party gives value.

This provision provides some consumer protection, preventing consumer debtors from granting a security interest in property that they later acquire.

Question 8. Doctor Green is a dentist who collects baseball cards as a hobby. On March 1, First Bank and Dr. Green enter into a security agreement that states that the collateral is "all accounts now owned as well as any and all accounts that may hereafter be acquired by Debtor." Dr. Green bills Derek Jeter $1,000 on March 8 and bills Alex Rodriguez $1,000 on April 1. Assuming First Bank gave Dr. Green the money on March 1, to which of the following collateral does the security interest attach?

A. The Derek Jeter bill only.
B. The Alex Rodriguez bill only.
C. Both the Derek Jeter bill and the Alex Rodriguez bill.
D. Neither the Derek Jeter bill nor the Alex Rodriguez bill.

Analysis. The bills can be characterized as accounts. The security agreement contains an after-acquired property clause that covers accounts. According to § 9-204(a), the after-acquired property clause is enforceable. Therefore, it attached to both accounts. The correct response is **C**.

Question 9. Doctor Green is a dentist who collects baseball cards as a hobby. On March 1, First Bank and Dr. Green enter into a security agreement that states that the collateral is "all baseball cards now owned as well as any and all baseball cards that may hereafter be acquired by Debtor." Dr. Green acquires a Dom DiMaggio card on March 8 and a Ted Williams card on April 1. Assuming First Bank gave Dr. Green the money on March 1, to which of the following collateral does the security interest attach?

A. The Dom DiMaggio card only.
B. The Ted Williams card only.
C. Both the Dom DiMaggio card and the Ted Williams card.
D. Neither the Dom DiMaggio card nor the Ted Williams card.

Analysis. The baseball cards can be characterized as consumer goods. The security agreement contains an after-acquired property clause that covers baseball cards. According to § 9-204(b)(1), the creditor may secure the debt only with consumer goods acquired within 10 days after the secured party gives value. Since First Bank gave value on March 1, the security interest attaches to the Dom DiMaggio card acquired on March 8, but not to the Ted Williams card acquired on April 1. Therefore, the correct response is **A**.

E.   Prohibitions Against Security Interests in Certain Property

Not all personal property is subject to Article 9. Section 9-109(d) contains a list of transactions to which Article 9 does not apply. Section 9-109(d)(4) for example, qualifies the rule that a sale of accounts is an Article 9 transaction by providing that "[t]his article does not apply to: . . . a sale of accounts . . . as part of a sale of the business out of which they arose." Furthermore, § 9-109 (c) provides that [t]his article does not apply to the extent that . . . a statute, regulation, or treaty of the United States preempts this article."

An example of federal preemption is the Credit Practices Rules in 16 C.F.R. 444. Do you remember from Contracts poor Ms. Williams, who was rescued from the predatory creditor when the court held that the credit practice might be unconscionable? See *Williams v. Walker-Thomas Furniture Company*, 350 F.2d 445 (D.C. Cir. 1965). The Federal Trade Commission has stepped in and enacted regulations that discourage lenders from taking security interests in certain kinds of consumer property. These rules provide in part:

§ 444.2 Unfair credit practices.

(a) In connection with the extension of credit to consumers in or affecting commerce, as commerce is defined in the Federal Trade Commission Act, it is an unfair act or practice within the meaning of Section 5 of that Act for a lender or retail installment seller directly or indirectly to take or receive from a consumer an obligation that: . . .

(4) Constitutes or contains a nonpossessory security interest in household goods other than a purchase money security interest.

"Household goods" is defined as follows in § 444.1(i):

Household goods. Clothing, furniture, appliances, one radio and one television, linens, china, crockery, kitchenware, and personal effects (including wedding rings) of the consumer and his or her dependents, provided that the following are not included within the scope of the term household goods:

(1) Works of art;

(2) Electronic entertainment equipment (except one television and one radio);

(3) Items acquired as antiques; and

(4) Jewelry (except wedding rings).

Question 10. *Statute reader.* A consumer wishes to buy a $1,000 washer-and-dryer set on credit from Strongarm Finance Co. for household purposes. Advise Strongarm whether it is permitted to take a security interest in each item of the consumer's personal property listed below:

A. The washer and dryer.

B. A 2004 Toyota Camry.

C. Clothing.

D. Color TVs in the den and bedroom.

E. "Good" china that Strongarm will hold on to.

F. Wedding ring.

G. Spouse's wedding ring.

H. Picasso painting.

Analysis.   Note that the FTC Credit Practices Rules only apply to consumers. Since the consumer is purchasing for household use, the Rules apply. Let's take the items one at a time:

A. The washer and dryer are the items being sold by Strongarm, so the security interest in them is a PMSI. See Chapter 4.D to review that concept. Section 444.2(a)(4) forbids a security interest in household goods "other than a purchase money security interest." Therefore, since the security interest in the washer and dryer is a PMSI, it is permissible.

B. A car is not within the definition of *household goods* in § 444.1(i); therefore, the security interest in the Toyota is permissible.

C. Clothing is within the definition of *household goods* in § 444.1(i); therefore, the security interest is not permissible.

D. "One television" falls within the definition of *household goods* in § 444.1(i); therefore, the security interest is permissible in one of the TVs but not in the other.

E. Section 444.2(a)(4) forbids a security interest in household goods that is *nonpossessory*. Although china is within the definition of household goods, since Strongarm will hold on to it, the security interest is possessory and is permissible.

F. While jewelry is excepted from the definition of *household goods*, wedding rings are excepted from the exception, so the security interest is not permissible.

G. The definition of household goods includes the property "of the consumer and his or her dependents." So if it is an item in which the creditor cannot take a security interest from the debtor (and as we have seen, a wedding ring is such an item), then it cannot take a security interest in that property from the consumer's dependents either. Therefore, assuming the spouse is a dependent, a security interest in the wedding ring of the spouse is not permissible.

H. "Works of art" are excepted from the definition of household goods, so the security interest is permissible.

So **A, B, D** (in one), **E,** and **H** are permitted; **C, F,** and **G** are not permitted.

Incidentally, note that a violation of this rule constitutes an "unfair act or practice." The Federal Trade Commission can bring a claim for a violation, but private claims are not permitted under the FTC Act. The debtor would have to bring a claim under the state Consumer Protection Act, which is likely to recognize violations of FTC rules as *per se* violations of the state act.

F.   Future Advances

A security interest can "float" not only as to the collateral encumbered but also as to the obligations that are secured by that collateral. A security interest can secure not only the payment of antecedent or present debts but also the payment of future debts. Section 9-204(c) provides:

> (c) **Future advances and other value.** A security agreement may provide that collateral secures, or that accounts, chattel paper, payment intangibles, or promissory notes are sold in connection with, future advances or other value, whether or not the advances or value are given pursuant to commitment.

Assume, for example, that D borrows $10,000 from Creditor 1 on January 11. D signs a security agreement that contains a future advances clause. On June 19, D borrows an additional $20,000 from Creditor 1 but does not sign a security agreement. According to § 9-204(c), because of the operation of the future advances clause, the June 19 loan is secured by the same collateral that secured the January 11 loan.

One issue that sometimes arises is whether there are any limitations on the scope of future advances clauses. Will any and all debts of a debtor to a creditor be secured because of the future advances clause in the security agreement, even if those obligations are different in kind? For example, on March 1, debtor borrows $20,000 from First Bank to purchase a new car and grants the bank a security interest in the car. The security agreement contains a future advances clause. On April 1, debtor overdraws her checking account at First Bank, creating a debt to the bank. Can the bank repossess the car, arguing that the overdraft is an obligation secured by the car?

One answer to this question is that it is a matter of careful drafting. Under that approach, if the parties clearly provide in their agreement that the obligations of the debtor do not have to be related or of the same type, then the future advances clause is effective. This is the approach taken by Official Comment 5 to § 9-204, which provides in part:

> [T]he parties are free to agree that a security interest secures any obligation whatsoever. Determining the obligations secured by collateral is solely a matter of construing the parties' agreement under applicable law. This Article rejects the holdings of cases decided under former Article 9 that applied other tests, such as whether a future advance or other subsequently incurred obligation was of the same or a similar type or class as earlier advances and obligations secured by the collateral.

This is a good opportunity to point out that the Official Comments do not have the force of law. This comment obviously stretches the point when it says that "[t]his Article rejects the holdings of cases decided under former Article 9," for the text of § 9-204(c) says no such thing. Therefore, as a matter of policy, courts are still free to police these so-called "dragnet clauses" that bring all transactions into the scope of the future advances clause. Under that approach, a court may rule that the later obligation is not secured if it is not similar to or related to the earlier obligation.

Question 11. Debtor borrowed $10,000 from Creditor 1 on January 11. Debtor signed a security agreement that contained a future advances clause. Creditor 1 immediately perfected by filing. On February 11, Debtor paid Creditor 1 in full. On June 19, Debtor borrowed $20,000 from Creditor 2. The security agreement with Creditor 2 listed the same collateral that Creditor 1 had listed. Creditor 2 perfected by filing. On July 7, Debtor borrowed an additional $10,000 from Creditor 1 with no grant of a security interest. On August 29, Debtor declared bankruptcy. Assuming (as we shall see later) that priority goes to the first secured creditor to file or perfect, who has priority in the collateral?

A. Creditor 1, because it was first to file or perfect.
B. Creditor 1, because the July 7 transaction created the only effective security interest.
C. Creditor 2, because the loan had been paid back to Creditor 1 when it made its transaction.
D. Creditor 2, because it was first to file or perfect.

Analysis. *Note on test-taking.* Since the topic for this section is future advances clauses, you should expect the correct response to turn on the future advances clause.

And indeed it does! The January 11 security agreement contained a future advances clause. Therefore, when Creditor 1 and Debtor entered into another transaction on July 7, that obligation was a future advance that is secured by the original collateral. When was notice of that transaction filed? On January 11. Since priority goes to the first to file or perfect, Creditor 1 has priority over Creditor 2. The fact that the loan was paid back is irrelevant. The correct response is **A.** When we study perfection, we will see that Creditor 2 would have found the filing and become aware of the relationship between Creditor 1 and Debtor.

Question 12. On January 11, Debtor borrowed $30,000 from S and signed a security agreement granting S a security interest in equipment. On March 3, Debtor borrowed an additional $20,000 from S. Under which of the following circumstances will this new loan also be secured by the equipment described in the January 11 agreement?

I. Debtor signs a security agreement on March 3, granting S a security interest in the equipment.
II. Debtor does not sign a second security agreement, and the January 11 security agreement provides that the equipment is to serve as collateral for "all debts now owed by Debtor to S and all debts of Debtor to S that are hereafter incurred."
III. Debtor does not sign a second security agreement, and the January 11 security agreement does not contain any "future advances" language.

A. I only.
B. I and II only.
C. III only.
D. I, II, and III.

Analysis.   *Note on test-taking.* This is another form that a question can take when there is more than one correct answer, but in this form you choose only one of the responses. The best approach is to determine whether each of the items listed as I through III is correct and then choose the response that contains those choices.

Here, I is a correct choice. The equipment would be collateral for this loan because the new security agreement says so. Item II is also a correct choice. Even if there is no new grant of a security interest, the future advances clause in the original security agreement would bring this loan within its scope. Item III is not a correct choice. If there is no new security agreement and no future advances clause in the original security agreement, the second loan is unsecured. Therefore, since I and II are correct choices, **B** is the correct response.

G.   Closers

Question 13. First Bank took a security interest in Farmer Brown's tractor. The tractor was destroyed in a lightning storm, and Brown recovered $5,000 from the insurance company for the loss. Brown put the $5,000 into a bank account that had $2,000 in it. He then took $3,000 out of the account to spend on a vacation, and, on his return from vacation, he used the remaining $4,000 in the account, together with a $16,000 gift from his brother, to purchase a car. Does First Bank have a security interest in the car?

A. No, because the car is not the identifiable proceeds of the collateral.
B. Yes, to the extent of $5,000.
C. Yes, to the extent of $4,000.
D. Yes, to the extent of $3,000.

Analysis.   The insurance money is proceeds from the tractor. When those proceeds were placed in the bank account, they went to the bottom under the "intermediate balance rule," and the $2,000 went to the top. The $3,000 withdrawal came off of the top of the account, leaving $4,000 in proceeds that was used to purchase the car. The correct answer is **C**.

> **Question 14.** AP took a security interest in a couch it sold to Homer
> Simpson on credit for $1,000 and properly perfected. Simpson
> complained to the Federal Trade Commission that AP committed an unfair
> or deceptive act or practice. Did AP violate the Credit Practices Rule?
>
> **A.** Yes, because the couch is household goods.
> **B.** No, because the couch is not household goods.
> **C.** No, because AP took a PMSI.
> **D.** No, because the security interest was possessory.

Analysis. A couch is household goods as defined in FTC Rule 444.1(i), for
the definition includes "furniture." However, Rule 444.2(a)(4) prohibits "a
nonpossessory security interest in household goods *other than a purchase
money security interest*." Here, since AP is taking a security interest in household goods that it sold, the security interest is a PMSI. Therefore, **C** is the correct response.

 # Burnham's Picks

Question 1	**A**
Question 2	**A**
Question 3	**D**
Question 4	**D**
Question 5	**D**
Question 6	**C**
Question 7	**A**
Question 8	**C**
Question 9	**A**
Question 10	**A, Yes; B, Yes; C, No; D, Yes (in one); E, Yes; F, No; G, No; H, Yes**
Question 11	**A**
Question 12	**B**
Question 13	**C**
Question 14	**C**

8

Secured Party v. Debtor

A. Introduction

> Q: What happened to the guy who didn't pay for his exorcism?
> A: He got repossessed.

A security agreement is a contract between a creditor and a debtor governed by Article 9 of the UCC that creates a lien on personal property to secure payment or performance of an obligation.

Of course, creditors don't want to have to enforce their lien by repossessing property—they want to get paid. Generally, so long as the debtor is making payments, the secured party is not concerned about its rights to the collateral, although a prudent creditor will monitor it. Even when the debtor misses payments, the secured party generally tries to "persuade" the debtor to make the payments before looking to the collateral.

Assume, for example, that First Bank made a loan to Local Manufacturer Inc. and obtained a security interest in Manufacturer's equipment. Manufacturer misses a payment. First Bank really does not want to repossess Manufacturer's equipment. Manufacturer can't make any money without its equipment, and First Bank does not want to have to sell Manufacturer's equipment. First Bank really wants Manufacturer's money. Accordingly, First Bank will "work with" Manufacturer in an effort to obtain payment. Furthermore, if its informal efforts to work out a payment scheme with Manufacturer are unsuccessful, First Bank can sue Manufacturer. The fact that First Bank has a security interest does not bar it from pursuing its other remedies. Section 9-601(a)(1) provides:

Rights after Default; Judicial Enforcement.

(a) **Rights of secured party after default.** After default, a secured party has the rights provided in this part and, except as otherwise provided in Section 9-602, those provided by agreement of the parties. A secured party:

(1) may reduce a claim to judgment, foreclose, or otherwise enforce the claim, security interest, or agricultural lien by any available judicial procedure.

By far the most significant right "provided in this part" is the § 9-609(a) remedy of self-help repossession:

Secured Party's Right to Take Possession after Default.

(a) **Possession; rendering equipment unusable; disposition on debtor's premises.** After default, a secured party:

(1) may take possession of the collateral; and

(2) without removal, may render equipment unusable and dispose of collateral on a debtor's premises under Section 9-610.

(b) **Judicial and nonjudicial process.** A secured party may proceed under subsection (a):

(1) pursuant to judicial process; or

(2) without judicial process, if it proceeds without breach of the peace.

Accordingly, "after default" by the debtor, the secured party (often aided by its attorneys) sometimes must look to its rights under the security agreement and under Article 9 as to the available collateral. Before the creditor acts, it must make sure the action it wishes to take is permitted by the agreement and by the law of the relevant jurisdictions. For example, while we have just seen that § 9-609 of the uniform version of Article 9 permits self-help repossession without involving a court, Model Tribal Secured Transactions Act § 9-609 provides (emphasis added):

Secured Party's Limited Right to Take Possession after Default.

(a) **Consent or judicial process.** Unless otherwise agreed, a secured party has at the time of or after default the powers described in subsection (b), but *such powers may be exercised only pursuant to judicial process or with the debtor's consent.* Such consent is effective only if expressed after default by means of a separate dated and signed personal statement in the debtor's handwriting, describing the powers to be exercised by the secured party and expressly acknowledging and waiving the debtor's right to require that such exercise be pursuant to judicial process.

(b) **Possession, rendering equipment unusable and assembly of collateral.** Under the circumstances of subsection (a) the secured party may:

(1) take possession of the collateral.

So in a particular jurisdiction that has enacted that provision, most likely an Indian Reservation, self-help repossession is not permitted.

In most jurisdictions, secured creditors who are unable or unwilling to exercise the self-help remedy may seek a remedy under *replevin* or *claim and delivery* statutes. These statutes permit a person who has an interest in particular property to bring an expedited action to recover that property.

Question 1. Under § 9-609, "After default, a secured party . . . may take possession of the collateral . . . without judicial process." Why isn't it unconstitutional to take another person's property without due process of law?

A. Because the debtor has agreed by contract to give up constitutional rights.
B. Because the creditor can only take possession if it gets a court order.
C. Because the Constitution contains an exception for security interests.
D. Because there is no state action.

Analysis. Responses **B** and **C** are inaccurate statements of the law. The Fourteenth Amendment to the U.S. Constitution provides in pertinent part, "nor shall *any State* deprive any person of life, liberty, or property, without due process of law." If the repossession occurs without state action, then it is not within the Constitution, so **A** is incorrect, and the correct response is **D**.

Question 2. First Bank has taken a security interest in an automobile belonging to a debtor who is a tribal member residing on an Indian reservation. The debtor has stopped making payments, and First Bank asks for your advice about repossession of the collateral. Your research reveals that the reservation has adopted a version of Article 9 that provides, "In taking possession, a secured party must either obtain the consent of the debtor when the default occurs or obtain a judicial order of repossession." Which of the following advice would you give the bank?

A. Repossess the car from the reservation as long as it can be done without breach of the peace.
B. Get an order from the Tribal Court on the reservation before repossessing the vehicle.
C. Get an order from a state court that has jurisdiction over Article 9 transactions before repossessing the vehicle.
D. Get an order from a Federal District Court before repossessing the vehicle.

Analysis. If the tribe had enacted the uniform Article 9, the correct response would be **A,** because of § 9-609(b)(2). When working across jurisdictional boundaries, however, it is always wise to check the local law of the jurisdiction. Here, the tribe has enacted its own rules to govern default and repossession, and those rules require a court order. Because of the sovereign status of tribes, the tribal court rather than the state or federal courts would have jurisdiction over property on the reservation. The correct response is **B.**

Question 3. Debtor contracted to buy a couch for $600 on credit from Freddie's. The contract granted Freddie's a security interest in the couch. Debtor defaulted on his payments, and Freddie's wants to know if it can repossess the couch. The state statute on exempt property provides that "[a] judgment debtor is entitled to exemption from execution on the following property: (1) the judgment debtor's interest, to the extent of a value not exceeding $600 in any item of property, in household furnishings and goods."

Would you advise Freddie's that it can repossess the couch?

A. Yes, because repossession by a secured party is not execution against a judgment debtor.
B. Yes, because the couch is not exempt property under the statute.
C. No, because the statute specifically prohibits execution on household furnishings of that value.
D. No, because Freddie's did not perfect its security interest.

Analysis. This should be a good review question on the exemption statutes we looked at in Chapter 3.A. The key to answering the question is that exemption statutes enumerate property that may not be used to satisfy a *judgment.* Note that the statute affects a "judgment debtor," not a debtor subject to a security interest. It does not prohibit secured creditors from taking a security interest in the enumerated property or from taking possession of that property. Since the statute is not relevant, **B** and **C** are incorrect. You also recall from Chapter 4.A that perfection is irrelevant as between the creditor and the debtor, so **D** is incorrect. Therefore, the correct response is **A.**

Before we look at repossession, let's back up a step, for before proceeding to take possession of the collateral, the secured party should make sure there has been a default.

B.   What Is *Default*?

Default is an extremely significant concept in secured transactions. According to § 9-601(a), all of Part 6 of Article 9 is applicable only "after default." Nevertheless, the word *default* is not defined in Article 9. Nonpayment is an obvious act of default. But beyond that, the drafters of the Code left the definition of *default* to the security agreement. See, for example, the provision labeled "Default and repossession" in the First Bank Security Agreement in Chapter 6.B, which enumerates a number of events of default. Assume that under that agreement, the debtor had borrowed $20,000 from the bank and granted the bank a security interest in his boat. The debtor, who lives in Missouri, takes the boat to a lake in Kansas for the weekend. The president of the bank spots the boat at the lake and declares a default. Is the debtor in default? Technically, yes. The events of default include "If I break any promise I have made to you in this agreement," and one of the promises under "Where I will keep the collateral" states, "I won't remove the collateral from Missouri without your written permission."

Creditors should be cautious before declaring a default, however, for they can pay dearly for repossessing property when there was no default. Taking property in which you have no right constitutes the intentional tort of conversion. In addition, the repossession may involve a trespass and other criminal acts. If the goods are consumer goods, Consumer Protection Acts in most jurisdictions allow the prevailing party to recover treble damages and attorney's fees. So the message is clear: make sure the debtor is in default before repossessing the collateral.

An interesting issue arises when the agreement provides that the secured party may accelerate payment or take other steps "if Secured Party deems payment of Debtor's obligations to Secured Party to be insecure," or words of similar effect. In other words, the debtor has not actually missed payments, but circumstances have led the secured party to believe that the debtor's collapse is imminent. The plot of the Denzel Washington movie *Mississippi Masala* turned on this issue. Washington's character ran a rug-cleaning business in a small town. Word began to spread of a romance between him and a young woman, and many people in the town, including some using his rug-cleaning services, disapproved of the relationship. The news that he was losing customers eventually reached the bank that had financed his business. Section 1-309 has a rule governing this "nervous banker's clause":

Option To Accelerate At Will.
A term providing that one party or that party's successor in interest may accelerate payment or performance or require collateral or additional collateral "at will" or when the party "deems itself insecure," or words of similar import, means that the party has power to do so only if that party in good faith believes that the prospect of payment or performance is impaired. The burden of establishing lack of good faith is on the party against which the power has been exercised.

This issue is further compounded by the problem of determining what constitutes lack of "good faith." Under Pre-Revision Article 1, the definition of "good faith" is the subjective standard of "honesty in fact." Under Revised Article 1, the definition of good faith in § 1-201(b)(20) also includes the objective standard of "reasonable commercial standards of fair dealing." In exercising good faith under the objective standard, a creditor would have to be reasonable, but under the subjective standard, it would merely have to be honest. Many jurisdictions that enacted Revised Article 1 nevertheless retained the old standard for good faith — subjective only. Many times the outcome of a case turns on which standard is applied.

Question 4. Debtor financed his purchase of a truck with Bank. Debtor signed a security agreement granting Bank a security interest in the truck. Debtor also signed an installment note providing for 48 monthly payments, with each payment due on the first of the month. The security agreement expressly says that failure to make a payment on time is an event of default. Debtor almost never made a payment on time. Bank sent Debtor letters complaining about the late payments, but it accepted them. Debtor is now late again in making a payment, and Bank has had enough. Can Bank treat Debtor as being in default and repossess Debtor's truck?

A. Yes, because Article 9 provides that failure to pay on time is an event of default.

B. Yes, because the agreement provides that failure to pay on time is an event of default.

C. No, because it is unconscionable to repossess property merely because of late payment.

D. No, because Bank has waived its right to insist on strict performance of the contract.

Analysis.   Responses **A** and **C** can be eliminated because they do not accurately state the law. As often happens with multiple-choice questions, this one reduces the choices to two plausible responses. Response **B** is a generally correct statement, and had Bank acted the first time payment was late, it would be correct. But as we saw in Chapter 7.B.2, under the doctrine of *waiver*, a creditor can be estopped from exercising a right if it has led the other party to believe that the right will not be strictly enforced. Here, the facts probably constitute a waiver, making **D** the correct response.

Note that sometimes an agreement contains an antiwaiver clause. For example, the First Bank agreement in Chapter 6.B states, "Because you excuse one default by me does not mean later occurrences of default will be excused." Most courts will find that actions speak louder than words and will give no weight to this provision. This does not mean the creditor has no remedy, however. The solution to the creditor's problem is to write a letter to the debtor making it clear that, although the creditor has not strictly enforced its rights in the past, it will do so in the future. With this notice, the debtor is no longer "lulled" into thinking that the creditor has waived its rights.

Question 5. Bank has loaned a widget seller money secured by seller's inventory of widgets. Bank has read credible reports of a serious downturn in the widget business, and it wants to demand additional security under the "nervous banker's clause" in the security agreement. The law of the relevant jurisdiction is the uniform version of Revised Article 1. If the issue goes to court, what standard would a court apply in determining whether Bank was entitled to demand additional security?

A. Whether the term in the security agreement was fairly negotiated.
B. Whether a reasonable bank would have made the demand.
C. Whether Bank honestly believed that the prospect of payment was impaired.
D. Whether Bank honestly believed that the prospect of payment was impaired and a reasonable bank would have made the demand.

Analysis. Under § 1-309, the "nervous banker's clause" is enforceable if the bank has a good faith belief that the prospect of payment is impaired. Therefore, **A** is an incorrect response. The applicable definition of good faith in § 1-201(b)(20) provides that "good faith . . . means honesty in fact and the observance of reasonable commercial standards of fair dealing." Therefore, the bank must be both honest and reasonable in its belief that it may exercise its rights under the agreement, so **D** is the correct choice.

Note that, as a practical matter, it is much harder for the bank to live up to this standard than to live up to the honesty standard. Assume the bank exercised its right, and the seller sued, claiming the bank did not act in good faith. If the jurisdiction has retained only the subjective standard, the seller would have to prove that the bank acted dishonestly, that its motives were other than to secure payment. This would be very hard to do. If the jurisdiction has adopted the uniform version of Article 1, which contains both the subjective and the objective standards, the seller could alternately prove that the bank acted unreasonably, which it could do by putting experts on the stand to testify that in this situation they would not have exercised that clause. This will be much easier to do.

C. Repossession of the Collateral

As we have seen under § 9-609(b), on default, the secured party has a right to repossess the collateral without obtaining a court order and without first notifying the debtor. A number of possible questions arise under this section. One that we have already addressed is whether the debtor was in default. Another is whether the seized property is collateral. For example, a bank has a security interest in a debtor's car. The debtor defaults and the bank employs the Repo Man to seize the debtor's car. The debtor now contends that some gold coins she bought for her husband were in the glove compartment. If the collateral was defined as the car, then the bank is not entitled to the gold coins, and it must inventory and return all property that it was not entitled to repossess.

A significant issue is whether the repossession was done without a "breach of the peace," in the words of § 9-609(b)(2). Article 9 does not define the phrase *breach of the peace,* and considerable case law exists interpreting and applying the phrase. The determination is highly fact-specific, but a superficial summary would indicate that the following constitute breaches of the peace:

- The use of force or threats of force.
- A potential for violence.
- Entering a closed structure on the debtor's property.

In the movie *Repo Man,* the repo men hired by the creditor (who is, by the way, responsible for the actions of the repo men) use various methods to repossess cars. Some, like throwing a rat into the car in order to induce the driver to abandon it, probably constitute a breach of the peace, while others, like hot-wiring the car and driving it away from the curb in the middle of the night, are probably not. Some creditors are now experimenting with devices that could disable a car by remote control. The creditor would claim that the device is an extension of § 9-609(a)(2), which provides that the secured party "without removal, may render equipment unusable."

There is such a strong policy against breaches of the peace that the Code does not permit a party to waive or vary this rule. Section 9-602(6) provides:

Waiver and Variance of Rights and Duties.
Except as otherwise provided in Section 9-624, to the extent that they give rights to a debtor or obligor and impose duties on a secured party, the debtor or obligor may not waive or vary the rules stated in the following listed sections: . . .
(6) Section 9-609 to the extent that it imposes upon a secured party that takes possession of collateral without judicial process the duty to do so without breach of the peace.

It is obvious from this summary that it is easy for the debtor to prevent the creditor from repossessing the collateral by putting it where it would require a breach of the peace to get to it, for example, by keeping it in a locked structure. So why are there so many peaceful repossessions? One answer may be that people are not aware that they may refuse to turn over the property. Another may be that they realize they are going to have to pay the debt and this is one way to do it. That explanation may have particular relevance, as we shall see in Chapter 11, when there are secondary obligors who are responsible for the debt. If, for example, the officers of a corporation are responsible for the corporation's debts, they will want the creditor to apply the corporation's assets to the debt before going after their personal assets. While they may be of questionable deterrent value, criminal statutes may also discourage noncooperation. For example, Alaska Statutes § 11.46.730 provides:

Defrauding creditors.

(a) A person commits the crime of defrauding creditors if

(1) knowing that property is subject to a security interest, the person

(A) with intent to defraud, fails to disclose that security interest to a buyer of that property; or

(B) destroys, removes, conceals, encumbers, transfers, or otherwise deals with that property with intent to hinder enforcement of that security interest. . . .

(c) Defrauding creditors is a class A misdemeanor unless that secured party, judgment creditor, or creditor incurs a pecuniary loss of $500 or more as a result to the defendant's conduct, in which case defrauding secured creditors is

(1) a class B felony if the loss is $25,000 or more;

(2) a class C felony if the loss is $500 or more but less than $25,000.

In the movie *Country*, Sam Shepard and Jessica Lange play the Ivys, family farmers trying to protect their assets from secured creditors. In one scene, their neighbors ask the Ivy family for permission to put their sheep temporarily in the Ivys' corral. The unspoken reason is to hide the sheep from the creditors. One wonders if the Ivys knew that this was a criminal act or if they would have refused permission if they had known.

Question 6. John loaned Mary $1,000 payable on October 1 and took a security interest in Mary's tickets to Red Sox games at Fenway Park. On October 2, Mary had not paid John, so he visited her office. She was not there, but she was expected back momentarily, so the receptionist, who knew John, allowed him to wait in Mary's office. On her desk, John spotted tickets to the World Series games at Fenway Park. He grabbed the tickets and left a note for Mary that said, "Ha Ha! I took the tickets. John." What is Mary's best claim against John?

A. Mary was not in default.
B. John did not give Mary notice before he took the tickets.
C. John's taking the tickets from Mary's office was a breach of the peace.
D. None of the above is a good defense.

Analysis. By the terms of the agreement, Mary was in default, and the Code does not require notice. So **A** and **B** are incorrect. Under § 9-609(b)(2), a secured party may take possession of the collateral "without judicial process, if it proceeds without breach of the peace." Here, the repossession took place without force, without the potential for violence, and without entering an enclosed structure, so there was probably no breach of the peace. The best response is **D**.

Question 7. Debtor was in default under a security agreement, and the agreement listed a small tractor as the collateral. At night, the tractor was kept on an open lot surrounded by a chain-link fence on debtor's property. The fence had a gate secured by a chain with a lock on it. The Repo Man went to the property in the middle of the night, when no one was present, cut the chain with bolt cutters, opened the gate, and removed the tractor without incident. Is a court likely to consider this repossession to involve a "breach of the peace"?

A. Yes, because Repo Man had to enter debtor's property.
B. Yes, because Repo Man had to open a closed gate.
C. Yes, because Repo Man had to cut through a chain to open the gate.
D. No, because there was no potential for violence since no one was present.

Analysis.   While this is a close question, the best response is **C**. It is generally permissible for secured parties to enter a debtor's property and to go through gates in order to repossess collateral but not to break into enclosed or locked structures.

Question 8. A creditor and debtor state in the security agreement, "On default, the secured party shall have the right to take possession of the collateral, even if such repossession involves a breach of the peace." Does this agreement violate Article 9?

A. No, § 1-302 provides that the Code rules are default rules that the parties are free to vary by agreement.
B. No, it does not expressly violate Article 9, but a jurisdiction would likely determine that the agreement was contrary to public policy.
C. Yes, the parties may not waive or vary the rule on breach of the peace.
D. Yes, and the creditor is subject to a $500 liability for including this language in the agreement.

Analysis.   We noted in Chapter 2.A.3 that § 1-302 provides that the Code rules are default rules that the parties are free to vary by agreement. However, that provision applies only "except as otherwise provided." It should not surprise you that this is one of the rules that the parties are specifically not permitted to vary. See § 9-602(6). Therefore, **C** is correct because this exception to freedom of contract is expressly provided in the Code. Curiously, there was no such express provision in former Article 9, but courts nevertheless would not enforce such a provision as a matter of policy, so under former Article 9, **B** would have been the correct response. The Code does not go so far as the remedy in response **D**, however.

D.   Closer

> **Question 9.** On February 1, AP and First Bank entered into a loan agreement and a security agreement. On March 1, after First Bank had loaned the money to AP, the president of First Bank read an accurate report in *The Wall Street Journal* about financial difficulties at AP. The president asks you whether First Bank can declare a default and demand immediate payment of the loan. Is First Bank permitted to do this?
>
> A. Yes, if there is a provision in the contract that says the bank can call the loan if it deems itself insecure.
> B. Yes, if there is a provision in the contract that says the bank can call the loan if it deems itself insecure and the action is taken in good faith.
> C. Yes, if the bank acts in good faith even if there is no such provision in the contract.
> D. No, because even if it is in the contract, such a provision is not enforceable.

Analysis.   Under § 1-309, such a provision in a loan agreement is enforceable if it is exercised in good faith. The definition of *good faith* in § 1-201(b)(20) includes both the subjective standard of honesty and the objective standard of reasonableness; therefore, if it declares a default, the bank must be prepared to justify it on those grounds. The correct answer is **B.**

 ## Burnham's Picks

Question 1	**D**
Question 2	**B**
Question 3	**A**
Question 4	**D**
Question 5	**D**
Question 6	**D**
Question 7	**C**
Question 8	**C**
Question 9	**B**

D. Closer

Question 9. On February 1, AE and First Bank entered into a loan agreement and a security agreement. On March 1, after First Bank had loaned the money to AE, the president of First Bank read an account report in The Wall Street Journal about financial difficulties at AE. The president asks you whether First Bank can declare a default, and demand immediate payment of the loan. Is First Bank permitted to do this?

A. Yes, if there is a provision in the contract that says the bank can call the loan in a deeply held insecurity.

B. Yes, if there is a provision in the contract that says the bank can call the loan if it deems itself insecure and the action is taken in good faith.

C. Yes, if the bank acts in good faith even if there is no such provision in the contract.

D. No, because even if it is a requirement, such a provision is not enforceable.

Analysis. Under § 1-309, such a provision in a loan agreement is enforceable if it is exercised in good faith. The definition of good faith in § 1-201(b)(20) includes both the subjective standard of honesty and the objective standard of reasonableness; therefore, if it declares a default, the bank must be prepared to justify it on those grounds. The correct answer is B.

Burnham's Picks

Question 1	D
Question 2	B
Question 3	A
Question 4	D
Question 5	D
Question 6	D
Question 7	C
Question 8	C
Question 9	B

9

Disposition of the Collateral After Repossession

CHAPTER OVERVIEW
A. Care of the Collateral
B. Redemption
C. Retention
D. Resale
E. Collection of Intangibles
F. Closers
✴ Burnham's Picks

A.   Care of the Collateral

We are now at the point where the secured party has repossessed the collateral. We will explore the different ways in which the collateral may be disposed of by the creditor. Think of them as the three Rs: redemption, retention, and resale. But before the collateral is disposed of, it may spend some time in the hands of the creditor.

The rules governing the creditor's rights and duties with respect to care of the collateral it has repossessed are found in § 9-207:

Rights and Duties of Secured Party Having Possession or Control or Collateral.

(a) Duty of care when secured party in possession.

Except as otherwise provided in subsection (d), a secured party shall use reasonable care in the custody and preservation of collateral in the secured party's possession. In the case of chattel paper or an instrument, reasonable care includes taking necessary steps to preserve rights against prior parties unless otherwise agreed.

(b) Expenses, risks, duties, and rights when secured party in possession.

Except as otherwise provided in subsection (d), if a secured party has possession of collateral:

(1) reasonable expenses, including the cost of insurance and payment of taxes or other charges, incurred in the custody, preservation, use, or operation of the collateral are chargeable to the debtor and are secured by the collateral;

(2) the risk of accidental loss or damage is on the debtor to the extent of a deficiency in any effective insurance coverage;

(3) the secured party shall keep the collateral identifiable, but fungible collateral may be commingled; and

(4) the secured party may use or operate the collateral:

(A) for the purpose of preserving the collateral or its value;

(B) as permitted by an order of a court having competent jurisdiction; or

(C) except in the case of consumer goods, in the manner and to the extent agreed by the debtor.

"Wait a minute," you say. "What is this provision doing in Part 2 (Attachment) rather than Part 6 (Default) of Article 9?" Hint: review § 9-203(b)(3)(B), discussed in Chapter 6.A. Right! You recall that a security interest may attach when the collateral is in the possession of the secured party. So, it makes sense that the same rules govern the rights and duties of the secured party having possession of the collateral, whether the secured party possesses the collateral originally or obtains it through repossession after default. Those rules are designed to keep the collateral productive rather than idle.

Question 1. A secured creditor properly repossessed a commercial fishing boat from the debtor. Because the boat had been poorly maintained, the creditor spent $10,000 on repairs. The creditor also paid $1,000 to keep insurance on the boat current. Because the market for boat sales was weak, the creditor decided to lease the boat to a commercial fisherman for $750 per week. What is the rule with respect to this income and expenses?

A. Because the boat remains the property of the debtor until it is sold, the secured creditor had no right to incur expenses or receive income.

B. The secured creditor may incur expenses to make the boat more attractive for a sale and may keep it insured, but the secured creditor may not use the boat without the permission of the debtor.

C. The secured creditor may incur reasonable expenses, such as the repairs and the insurance, and may rent out the boat; the expenses will be charged to the debtor and the income will be used to pay off the debt.

D. The secured creditor may incur reasonable expenses, such as the repairs and the insurance, and may rent out the boat; the secured creditor is liable for the expenses and may retain the income.

Analysis. The correct response is **C**. See § 207(b)(1) and (4). It is in the interest of the debtor to have the creditor spend money on maintenance, because that should help secure a higher price if the collateral is later sold. It is also in the interest of the debtor for the creditor to make commercial use of the collateral prior to sale because the income will be applied toward the debt.

B.   Redemption

In redemption, the debtor pays the obligation and recovers the collateral. Section 9-623 provides:

> **Right to Redeem Collateral.**
>   (a) **Persons that may redeem.** A debtor, any secondary obligor, or any other secured party or lienholder may redeem collateral.
>   (b) **Requirements for redemption.** To redeem collateral, a person shall tender:
>   (1) fulfillment of all obligations secured by the collateral; and
>   (2) the reasonable expenses and attorney's fees described in Section 9-615(a)(1).
>   (c) **When redemption may occur.** A redemption may occur at any time before a secured party:
>   (1) has collected collateral under Section 9-607;
>   (2) has disposed of collateral or entered into a contract for its disposition under Section 9-610; or
>   (3) has accepted collateral in full or partial satisfaction of the obligation it secures under Section 9-622.

According to § 9-602, the provision that restricts freedom of contract, the debtor may not waive or vary these rules. However, this is not a blanket restriction. Section 9-624(c) provides that except in a consumer transaction, a debtor may waive the right to redeem the collateral if it does so in an authenticated agreement after default.

But redemption is not as simple as just paying the obligation that led to the default. For one thing, under § 9-623(b)(1), the debtor must "tender . . . fulfillment of all obligations." Most loan agreements provide that if one installment is missed, the entire balance accelerates. In other words, after acceleration, the debtor's obligation is to pay not just the missed installments but the entire principal balance. For another, § 9-623(b)(2) provides that the creditor may also recover "the reasonable expenses and attorney's fees described in Section 9-615(a)(1)." Under that section, the secured party is always entitled to reasonable expenses incurred and is entitled to reasonable attorney's fees "to the extent provided for by agreement." Because these factors make the cost of redemption so high, it is rare that a debtor who defaulted on installment payments can pay the full obligation plus expenses and attorney's fees after default. Furthermore, the right to redemption is terminated when the collateral is disposed of, so the debtor has to raise the money quickly. In short, redemption rarely occurs.

Question 2. Debtor entered into an installment sales agreement with Creditor for the purchase of a car for $11,000. Under the agreement, Debtor made a down payment of $1,000 and promised monthly payments of $400 for three years. The contract contained an acceleration clause and gave the creditor a security interest in the car. When Debtor missed two monthly payments of $400, Creditor determined that Debtor was in default and repossessed the car. At the time Debtor defaulted, the principal balance due was $8,000. Creditor scheduled a sale of the car for July 1. On June 30, Debtor asked Creditor what Debtor would have to pay to redeem the car. What is the amount required for the "fulfillment of all obligations secured by the collateral"?

A. Because the car is scheduled to be sold the next day, it is too late to redeem the collateral.
B. $800.
C. $8,000.
D. $8,000 plus interest to June 30.

Analysis.   Under § 9-623(c)(2), redemption may occur anytime before the creditor has disposed of the collateral, so **A** is incorrect. Because of the acceleration clause, the amount due is the principal balance of $8,000 and not the missed payments of $800, so **B** is not correct. Because the amount of $8,000 was computed on the date Debtor defaulted, the amount of the obligation on a later date would include that amount plus interest. So the correct answer is **D**.

Question 3. In calculating the amount Debtor will have to pay to redeem the collateral, a creditor wants to include reasonable expenses incurred in repossessing and storing the collateral and reasonable attorney's fees that the creditor paid. What is the rule on the creditor's recovery of expenses and attorney's fees?

A. The creditor can recover neither reasonable expenses nor attorney's fees unless they are provided for in the contract.
B. The creditor can recover reasonable expenses but can recover attorney's fees only if they are provided for in the contract.
C. The creditor can recover reasonable attorney's fees but can recover expenses only if they are provided for in the contract.
D. The creditor can recover both reasonable expenses and attorney's fees even if they are not provided for in the contract.

Analysis. Section 9-623(b)(2) provides that the creditor may recover "the reasonable expenses and attorney's fees described in Section 9-615(a)(1)." That section provides:

> **Application of Proceeds of Disposition; Liability for Deficiency and Right to Surplus.**
>
> (a) **Application of proceeds.** A secured party shall apply or pay over for application the cash proceeds of disposition in the following order to:
>
> > (1) the reasonable expenses of retaking, holding, preparing for disposition, processing, and disposing, and, to the extent provided for by agreement and not prohibited by law, reasonable attorney's fees and legal expenses incurred by the secured party.

Under § 9-615(a)(1), expenses may be recovered automatically, but attorney's fees may be recovered only "to the extent provided for by agreement." Therefore, the creditor may recover expenses, but it may recover attorney's fees only if they were provided for in the contract. So **B** is the correct response.

C.   Retention

In retention, also known as "strict foreclosure," the creditor agrees to discharge the debt in return for the debtor agreeing to let the creditor keep the collateral. Section 9-620 provides the rules for retention. These rules are a bit complicated, but here they are:

> **§ 9-620. Acceptance of Collateral in Full or Partial Satisfaction of Obligation; Compulsory Disposition of Collateral.**
>
> (a) **Conditions to acceptance in satisfaction.** Except as otherwise provided in subsection (g), a secured party may accept collateral in full or partial satisfaction of the obligation it secures only if:
>
> > (1) the debtor consents to the acceptance under subsection (c);
> >
> > (2) the secured party does not receive, within the time set forth in subsection (d), a notification of objection to the proposal authenticated by:
> >
> > > (A) a person to which the secured party was required to send a proposal under Section 9-621; or
> > >
> > > (B) any other person, other than the debtor, holding an interest in the collateral subordinate to the security interest that is the subject of the proposal;
> >
> > (3) if the collateral is consumer goods, the collateral is not in the possession of the debtor when the debtor consents to the acceptance; and
> >
> > (4) subsection (e) does not require the secured party to dispose of the collateral or the debtor waives the requirement pursuant to Section 9-624.

(b) **Purported acceptance ineffective.** A purported or apparent acceptance of collateral under this section is ineffective unless:

    (1) the secured party consents to the acceptance in an authenticated record or sends a proposal to the debtor; and

    (2) the conditions of subsection (a) are met.

(c) **Debtor's consent.** For purposes of this section:

    (1) a debtor consents to an acceptance of collateral in partial satisfaction of the obligation it secures only if the debtor agrees to the terms of the acceptance in a record authenticated after default; and

    (2) a debtor consents to an acceptance of collateral in full satisfaction of the obligation it secures only if the debtor agrees to the terms of the acceptance in a record authenticated after default or the secured party:

        (A) sends to the debtor after default a proposal that is unconditional or subject only to a condition that collateral not in the possession of the secured party be preserved or maintained;

        (B) in the proposal, proposes to accept collateral in full satisfaction of the obligation it secures; and

        (C) does not receive a notification of objection authenticated by the debtor within 20 days after the proposal is sent.

(d) **Effectiveness of notification.** To be effective under subsection (a)(2), a notification of objection must be received by the secured party:

    (1) in the case of a person to which the proposal was sent pursuant to Section 9-621, within 20 days after notification was sent to that person; and

    (2) in other cases:

        (A) within 20 days after the last notification was sent pursuant to Section 9-621; or

        (B) if a notification was not sent, before the debtor consents to the acceptance under subsection (c).

(e) **Mandatory disposition of consumer goods.** A secured party that has taken possession of collateral shall dispose of the collateral pursuant to Section 9-610 within the time specified in subsection (f) if:

    (1) 60 percent of the cash price has been paid in the case of a purchase-money security interest in consumer goods; or

    (2) 60 percent of the principal amount of the obligation secured has been paid in the case of a non-purchase-money security interest in consumer goods.

(f) **Compliance with mandatory disposition requirement.** To comply with subsection (e), the secured party shall dispose of the collateral:

    (1) within 90 days after taking possession; or

    (2) within any longer period to which the debtor and all secondary obligors have agreed in an agreement to that effect entered into and authenticated after default.

(g) **No partial satisfaction in consumer transaction.** In a consumer transaction, a secured party may not accept collateral in partial satisfaction of the obligation it secures.

According to § 9-602, the provision that restricts freedom of contract, the debtor may not waive or vary these rules. The Code wants to encourage retention, which facilitates a resolution of the dispute between the creditor and the debtor at low cost. On the other hand, because of the possibility that a creditor could take advantage of a debtor when the value of the collateral is greater than the amount of the debt, there are a number of restrictions on retention. According to § 9-620(c), retention must be agreed to after default and not in the security agreement. Furthermore, if the debtor is a consumer, there can be no partial satisfaction. That is, the parties cannot agree that the debtor will still owe some of the debt after the creditor retains the collateral. There is also a restriction on retention of consumer goods when the debtor has paid 60 percent of the price if the security interest is a PMSI or 60 percent of the obligation if the security interest is not a PMSI.

To effectuate partial satisfaction in a commercial transaction, the debtor must consent in an authenticated record. See § 9-620(c)(1). To effectuate full satisfaction in either a commercial or consumer transaction, either (1) the debtor must consent in an authenticated record, or (2) the creditor must send the debtor a proposal and the creditor does not receive an authenticated objection to it within 20 days after it is sent. See § 9-620(c)(2).

Question 4. Creditor loans Debtor $20,000 secured by Debtor's inventory. Debtor defaults, and Creditor repossesses the inventory. Creditor believes that the inventory is worth $15,000 and wishes to keep the inventory and reduce the debt owed by Debtor to $5,000. Which of the following would accomplish this?

A. Creditor sends Debtor a letter stating that it has reduced the amount of the debt to $5,000 pursuant to a provision in the security agreement that states, "Debtor hereby renounces its right to consent to retention. Creditor may retain collateral after repossession after reducing the amount of the debt by the reasonable value of the collateral."

B. Creditor sends Debtor a letter proposing that Creditor keeps the inventory and reduces the debt owed by Debtor to $5,000. Debtor receives the letter but does not respond to it within 20 days.

C. Creditor meets with Debtor, and they orally agree that Creditor keeps the inventory and reduces the debt owed by Debtor to $5,000 and they shake hands on it.

D. Creditor sends Debtor a letter proposing that Creditor keeps the inventory and reduces the debt owed by Debtor to $5,000. Debtor receives the letter and responds in 30 days that the proposal is accepted.

Analysis.   According to § 9-620(c), retention must be agreed to after default and not in the security agreement. Therefore, response **A** is incorrect. To effectuate retention, § 9-620(a) requires either the debtor's agreement in an authenticated record under § 9-620(c) or the debtor's failure to respond within 20 days to an authenticated proposal. Either of these methods requires an authentication, which is defined in § 9-102(a)(7) as follows:

"Authenticate" means:

(A) to sign; or

(B) with present intent to adopt or accept a record, to attach to or logically associate with the record an electronic sound, symbol, or process.

Therefore, the agreement cannot be oral, so response **C** is incorrect. At first blush, it might appear that both responses **B** and **D** would satisfy the requirements for retention, but note that here Creditor proposes a *partial* retention: after the agreement is made, Debtor still has an obligation to Creditor. Under § 9-620(c)(1), "a debtor consents to an acceptance of collateral in partial satisfaction of the obligation it secures only if the debtor agrees to the terms of the acceptance in a record authenticated after default." So under these circumstances, Debtor's failure to respond to a proposal is not sufficient; Debtor's affirmative agreement is required. The only correct response is **D**.

Question 5. Creditor loans Debtor $20,000 to remodel her kitchen and takes a security interest in Debtor's personal baseball-card collection. Debtor defaults, and Creditor repossesses the baseball-card collection. Creditor believes that the collection is worth $15,000 and wishes to keep the collection and reduce the debt owed by Debtor to $5,000. Which of the following would accomplish this?

A. Creditor sends Debtor a letter proposing retention on these terms. Debtor receives the letter, but she does not respond to it within 20 days.

B. Creditor meets with Debtor, and they orally agree to retention on these terms and shake hands on it.

C. Creditor sends Debtor a letter proposing retention on these terms. Debtor receives the letter, and she responds in 30 days that the proposal is accepted.

D. None of the above.

Analysis.   *Note on test-taking*. This question is very similar to the previous question, except for a fact difference. The assessor is probably testing for your ability to spot the difference and to determine whether it would call for a different conclusion.

The difference is that the collateral is a personal baseball-card collection instead of inventory. Is this a consumer transaction? Section 9-102(a)(26) provides:

> "Consumer transaction" means a transaction in which (i) an individual incurs an obligation primarily for personal, family, or household purposes, (ii) a security interest secures the obligation, and (iii) the collateral is held or acquired primarily for personal, family, or household purposes. The term includes consumer-goods transactions.

Here, all three elements are satisfied, so this is a consumer transaction rather than a commercial transaction. Note that the elements would not be satisfied if the baseball-card collection was collateral for a business loan because the fact that the collateral is consumer goods is not sufficient to make a business transaction a consumer transaction. When the transaction is a consumer transaction, § 9-620(g) provides that there can be no partial satisfaction. Here, Creditor has proposed that the entire debt is not discharged, so this is partial satisfaction. Since there can be no such agreement in a consumer transaction, the correct response is **D.**

D. **Resale**

In resale, the secured party sells the goods and applies the proceeds to the debt. Usually the creditor's repossession of the collateral is followed by resale. This remedy is very similar to the Article 2 remedy for a seller whose buyer defaults, leaving seller with the goods. See § 2-706. Sections 9-610 and 9-611 govern the secured party's disposition of the collateral and the notice requirement. The rules balance the debtor's interest in having the creditor obtain the most money possible from the sale of the collateral against the creditor's interest in disposing of the collateral in an efficient and timely manner. They provide in part:

> **§ 9-610. Disposition of Collateral after Default.**
>
> (a) **Disposition after default.** After default, a secured party may sell, lease, license, or otherwise dispose of any or all of the collateral in its present condition or following any commercially reasonable preparation or processing.
>
> (b) **Commercially reasonable disposition.** Every aspect of a disposition of collateral, including the method, manner, time, place, and other terms, must be commercially reasonable. If commercially reasonable, a secured party may dispose of collateral by public or private proceedings, by one or more contracts, as a unit or in parcels, and at any time and place and on any terms.
>
> (c) **Purchase by secured party.** A secured party may purchase collateral:

(1) at a public disposition; or

(2) at a private disposition only if the collateral is of a kind that is customarily sold on a recognized market or the subject of widely distributed standard price quotations.

§ 9-611. Notification Before Disposition of Collateral.

(a) **"Notification date."** In this section, "notification date" means the earlier of the date on which:

(1) a secured party sends to the debtor and any secondary obligor an authenticated notification of disposition; or

(2) the debtor and any secondary obligor waive the right to notification.

(b) **Notification of disposition required.** Except as otherwise provided in subsection (d), a secured party that disposes of collateral under Section 9-610 shall send to the persons specified in subsection (c) a reasonable authenticated notification of disposition.

(c) **Persons to be notified.** To comply with subsection (b), the secured party shall send an authenticated notification of disposition to:

(1) the debtor;

(2) any secondary obligor. . . .

(d) [**Subsection (b) inapplicable: perishable collateral; recognized market.**] Subsection (b) does not apply if the collateral is perishable or threatens to decline speedily in value or is of a type customarily sold on a recognized market.

It will not surprise you that § 9-602(7) provides that "[s]ections 9-610(b), 9-611, 9-613, and 9-614, which deal with disposition of collateral" are among those rules that the debtor may not waive or vary. Some of the possible issues presented by the notice and resale rules include whether the disposition was preceded by "reasonable authenticated notification" to all parties entitled to notice under § 9-611(b) and whether "every aspect" of the disposition was "commercially reasonable" under § 9-610(b). Note that notice is not required under § 9-611(d) if the collateral is perishable or if it is sold on a recognized market. These exceptions seem reasonable, for the creditor should not wait if the collateral may perish, and if the purpose of notice is to allow the debtor to redeem the collateral or try to obtain a better price, those purposes are not relevant when the price is determined by a market.

Debtors have been very creative in finding something about either the notification or the disposition that was not reasonable. For example, they have claimed that the seller held the sale too quickly (or waited too long), that the time between the notice and the sale was too long (or too short), that the sale should have been public (or private), that the sale should have been at retail (or wholesale). If the collateral was sold for less than its market value, debtors have frequently claimed that the sale was presumptively unreasonable, even if they could point to no other factor that made the sale unreasonable. If a court found for the debtor in such a case, former Article 9 only provided that the debtor could recover for "any loss caused" by the noncompliance. Courts were all over the board in determining what the remedies were if the notice or the disposition was not reasonable.

Revised Article 9 responded to some of these issues by creating "safe harbor" provisions for the creditor to follow and by creating a presumptive measure of the loss if the notice or sale was not reasonable. For example, § 9-612 provides that notification sent 10 days or more before the disposition is sent within a reasonable time, and § 9-613 contains a form of notification that is sufficient for a commercial transaction. If the creditor follows the "safe harbor" rules, the debtor will not be able to claim that the disposition was not commercially reasonable.

Recall, however, that because of the compromise discussed in Chapter 2.A.2, these changes expressly do not apply to consumer transactions. Because § 9-612 does not apply to consumer transactions, consumers are free to claim that any amount of notice was not reasonable. Furthermore, § 9-614 contains a "safe harbor" form of notification in a consumer goods transaction. In § 9-627, the Code insists that the fact that a greater amount could have been obtained by a different method of sale does not itself preclude the secured party from establishing that the disposition was made in a commercially reasonable manner. While these provisions might reduce litigation, courts will probably continue to weigh in on issues involving the reasonableness of the notice and the sale.

The secured party is free to purchase the collateral if the sale is a public sale. Although *public sale* is not defined in the Code, Official Comment 7 to § 9-610 states that "a 'public disposition' is one at which the price is determined after the public has had a meaningful opportunity for competitive bidding." The secured party may also purchase at a private sale if the collateral is sold on a recognized market so that the price is readily determined. See § 9-610(c). One restriction, however, is found in § 9-615(f). Under this provision, if the secured party purchases for a price lower than would have been paid by a transferee who was not the secured party, the proceeds may be calculated as the amount that would have been realized in a disposition to such a party.

Question 6. Olivia borrows $5,000 from Bank and grants Bank a security interest in her car. Sabrina agrees to cosign Olivia's obligation. The debt is not paid, and Bank repossesses Olivia's car. To whom is Bank required to send notice of the sale of the collateral?

A. Olivia only.
B. Sabrina only.
C. Both Olivia and Sabrina.
D. Neither Olivia nor Sabrina.

Analysis. Even though only Olivia is a debtor with an interest in the collateral, Sabrina has an interest in the sale because she is liable for any deficiency that remains after the proceeds of the sale are applied to the debt. Therefore, both parties have an interest in the sale, so § 9-611(c) requires that both be given notice. The correct response is **C**. In Chapter 10, we will learn more about "secondary obligors" such as Sabrina.

Question 7. Seller is aware of the § 9-610(b) rule that permits a secured party to dispose of collateral after default and requires that every aspect of the disposition must be "commercially reasonable." Seller is also aware of § 1-302(a), which provides that "the effect of provisions of the code may be varied by agreement," and of § 9-602, which prohibits varying some rules. Seller wants to draft language in the security agreement that will make it harder for a debtor to claim that a resale was not commercially reasonable. Seller asks you which of the following statements is true:

A. Seller can waive its duty to dispose of collateral in a commercially reasonable manner by agreement with its customers, but only in a transaction other than a consumer transaction.

B. Seller can waive its duty to dispose of collateral in a commercially reasonable manner by agreement with its customers, but only if the waiver is unambiguous and conspicuous and the agreement is authenticated by the customer after default.

C. Seller and its customers can determine, by agreement, standards of commercially reasonable behavior, but those standards cannot be manifestly unreasonable.

D. Seller and its customers cannot determine, by agreement, standards of commercially reasonable behavior.

Analysis. Section 9-602 contains a list of provisions that cannot be waived or varied despite the freedom of contract permitted by § 1-302. According to § 9-602(7), the debtor may not waive or vary the rules of § 9-610(b). However, § 9-603(a) permits the parties to determine by agreement the standards measuring the fulfillment of the rights of a debtor if the standards are not "manifestly unreasonable." The same language is used in § 1-302(b). Therefore, the correct answer is **C**.

Question 8. First Bank made a car loan to Mary, retaining a security interest in the car. Mary defaulted, and the bank properly repossessed the car. According to the *Blue Book* publication of used-car values, the car had an average wholesale value of $4,000 and an average retail value of $6,000. After proper notice, the bank sold the car at a public auction for $3,900. Mary then saw the car being advertised for sale at a used-car lot for $6,000 and now claims that the bank's disposition of the car was commercially unreasonable. Was the sale commercially unreasonable?

A. No, because the price itself does not indicate that the sale was commercially unreasonable.
B. No, because the bank held a public sale.
C. Yes, because the bank could have held a private sale.
D. Yes, because the bank could have sold the car at retail itself.

Analysis.   The car was sold for a lot less than its retail value and somewhat less than its wholesale value. While the bank could theoretically have sold the car at retail, such a sale would have cost the bank a great deal in time, effort, advertising, insuring, storage, and so on. Even though it won't make Mary feel better, our economist friends will tell her that the difference between wholesale and retail price represents the investment required to get that higher price. Therefore, it was reasonable for the bank to forego those expenses and sell at an auction, where the buyers will be expected to pay wholesale prices. Section 9-627(a) provides:

> **Determination of Whether Conduct Was Commercially Reasonable.**
> (a) **Greater amount obtainable under other circumstances; no preclusion of commercial reasonableness.** The fact that a greater amount could have been obtained by a collection, enforcement, disposition, or acceptance at a different time or in a different method from that selected by the secured party is not of itself sufficient to preclude the secured party from establishing that the collection, enforcement, disposition, or acceptance was made in a commercially reasonable manner.

The mere fact that there could have been a private sale is not enough to make the public sale unreasonable. Section § 9-627(a) wants to eliminate this kind of second-guessing and intends to focus instead on the reasonableness of the disposition that was used. Therefore, **C** alone is not sufficient.

The sale therefore appears to have been commercially reasonable, and the best response is **A.**

E.   Collection of Intangibles

So far we have talked about the secured party's remedies when the debt is secured by goods. It is easy to visualize the process of repossessing and reselling goods. But recall that a debtor can use intangibles, such as the obligations owed to the debtor, as collateral for the obligations the debtor owes to others.

How does the secured party take possession of intangible collateral? For example, dentist Dr. Jim Lonborg bills his patients for the services he renders. In the hands of Lonborg, the obligations of Jim Rice, Carl Yastrzemski, Jerry Remy, and other patients are *accounts*. If Lonborg grants State Street Bank a security interest in his accounts as collateral for a $10,000 loan and then defaults, State Street Bank has rights to that collateral. Section § 9-607 provides in part:

Collection and Enforcement by Secured Party.

(a) **Collection and enforcement generally.** If so agreed, and in any event after default, a secured party:

(1) may notify an account debtor or other person obligated on collateral to make payment or otherwise render performance to or for the benefit of the secured party;

(2) may take any proceeds to which the secured party is entitled under Section 9-315;

(3) may enforce the obligations of an account debtor or other person obligated on collateral and exercise the rights of the debtor with respect to the obligation of the account debtor or other person obligated on collateral to make payment or otherwise render performance to the debtor, and with respect to any property that secures the obligations of the account debtor or other person obligated on the collateral;

(4) if it holds a security interest in a deposit account perfected by control under Section 9-104(a)(1), may apply the balance of the deposit account to the obligation secured by the deposit account; and

(5) if it holds a security interest in a deposit account perfected by control under Section 9-104(a)(2) or (3), may instruct the bank to pay the balance of the deposit account to or for the benefit of the secured party. . . .

(c) **Commercially reasonable collection and enforcement.** A secured party shall proceed in a commercially reasonable manner if the secured party:

(1) undertakes to collect from or enforce an obligation of an account debtor or other person obligated on collateral; and

(2) is entitled to charge back uncollected collateral or otherwise to full or limited recourse against the debtor or a secondary obligor.

It is probably easiest to think of this transaction in terms of the concept of *assignment* from Contracts. Essentially, the debtor has assigned its interest in the accounts to the secured party, who now "stands in the shoes" of the assignor in collecting the obligations from the "account debtors." For example, assume that at the time of Lonborg's default, Jim Rice owes Lonborg $2,000. State Street Bank can send a letter to Rice stating that his account has been assigned by Lonborg to State Street Bank as collateral for a loan, that Lonborg is now in default on that loan, and that Rice should now pay the $2,000 he owes Lonborg directly to State Street Bank.

Recall that under the law of assignment, the assignee "stands in the shoes" of the assignor and is subject to having the debt reduced by any claims or defenses that the account debtor had against the assignor. Section 9-404(b) provides:

> (b) **Account debtor's claim reduces amount owed to assignee.** Subject to subsection (c) and except as otherwise provided in subsection (d), the claim of an account debtor against an assignor may be asserted against an assignee under subsection (a) only to reduce the amount the account debtor owes.

For example, assume that Lonborg's records indicate that Rice owes $2,000, but Rice claims that he only owes $1,000. Rice asserts this defense against the bank, and the bank settles this dispute by accepting $1,500 as full payment of Rice's obligation to Lonborg. This settlement is binding on Lonborg. Note, however, that the claim may only be asserted "to reduce the amount the account debtor owes." For example, if Rice had a substantial malpractice claim against Lonborg, the bank has no liability to Rice on this claim.

An interesting issue arises if the contract between Rice and Lonborg states, "Rights under this contract may not be assigned." After receiving notice of the assignment, can Rice refuse to pay the bank because of this provision? You would think the answer would be yes, because generally parties have freedom of contract to put restrictions on the assignment of rights. But accounts financing is such an important part of our economy that the provision will not be enforced. Section 9-406(d) provides in part that "an agreement between an account debtor and an assignor or in a promissory note is ineffective to the extent that it . . . prohibits . . . the assignment or transfer of . . . the account, chattel paper, payment intangible, or promissory note." This rule recognizes the importance of accounts financing in the U.S. economy and does not permit contractors to interfere with the system. So in spite of that language, the assignment is effective, and Rice must pay the bank.

Question 9. Dr. Jim Lonborg bills his patients for the services he renders. Lonborg then grants State Street Bank a security interest in these accounts as collateral for a $10,000 loan from the bank. Lonborg defaults on his loan to the bank. What are State Street Bank's rights as to its collateral?

A. The bank may contact the patients and instruct them to make their payments to the bank.
B. The bank may wait until payments are made to Lonborg and then take them.
C. Both of the above.
D. Neither of the above.

Analysis.   The obligations of Lonborg's patients are *accounts* as defined in § 9-102(a)(2). Section 9-607 permits the secured party to notify "account debtors," as defined in § 9-102(a)(3), such as the dentist's patients, to make their payments directly to the bank. As a practical matter, however, the bank may wait until payments are made to the debtor before taking possession of the payments. This practice may be less disruptive of relations between the debtor and the account debtor. For example, it is not unusual for the creditor to have someone sit in the debtor's office to receive checks that arrive in the mail or to receive payments by operating the debtor's cash register. Therefore, the correct answer is **C**.

Question 10. Dr. Jim Lonborg bills his patients for the services he renders. Lonborg then grants State Street Bank a security interest in these accounts as collateral for a $10,000 loan from the bank. Lonborg defaults on his loan to the bank, and the bank notifies the account debtors, instructing them to pay the bank. After receiving notice, patient Jim Rice refuses to pay the bank because the contract between Rice and Lonborg says, "Rights under this contract may not be assigned." Can the bank recover payment from Rice?

A.   No, because a secured party may not recover directly from account debtors.

B.   No, because a contract right may not be assigned when the contract contains an express nonassignment clause.

C.   Yes, because the common law rule is that nonassignment clauses are not enforceable.

D.   Yes, because Article 9 expressly makes ineffective nonassignment clauses that restrict the assignment of obligations to pay money.

Analysis.   The credit economy depends on the free availability of accounts financing. Therefore, an agreement between the debtor and a third party that purports to prevent the assignment of the right to receive money is not enforceable, despite the common law rule to the contrary. Recall that the legislature is free to enact statutes that change the common law, as it did when enacting § 9-406(d). Therefore, the correct response is **D**.

F.   Closers

Question 11. A secured party properly repossesses the collateral of a debtor. Six months later, the debtor discovers that the creditor has stored the collateral and has no plans to sell it. What would you advise the debtor?

> **A.** The creditor has violated Article 9, because a sale must be held within 10 days.
>
> **B.** It is likely, but not conclusive, that the creditor has failed to act in a commercially reasonable manner.
>
> **C.** After a reasonable time has passed, the creditor is deemed to have retained the collateral and the debt is discharged.
>
> **D.** Under the common law, the creditor has converted the property.

Analysis. The best answer is **B.** A and C simply misstate the law. Retention under § 9-620 requires affirmative action by the creditor; it does not happen by operation of law. There is no time limit within which a sale must be held; the standard is what is commercially reasonable under § 9-610(b). While a six-month delay does not seem reasonable, it is possible that the delay is commercially reasonable if, for example, there is a slump in the market and the creditor is waiting for a recovery. Mere delay in sale would probably not constitute a conversion. After all, it is in the creditor's interest to dispose of the collateral to recover on the debt, so creditors have nothing to gain by delay.

> **Question 12.** A Co. regularly sells refrigerators to B Co. according to a sales agreement that says that B's payment is due 60 days after delivery. The contract also says that "neither party may assign rights or delegate duties under this agreement." A Co. borrowed money from C Credit Co. and granted C a security interest in A's accounts. When A defaulted on its debt to C, C sent B a letter that was also signed by A. The letter stated, "Pursuant to a security agreement between A and C, your obligation to A has been assigned to C. Please pay C." When B's payment to A becomes due, should B pay C?
>
> **A.** No, because under contract law, a nonassignment clause is not effective.
>
> **B.** No, because under Article 9, a clause restricting the assignment of a right to receive money is effective.
>
> **C.** Yes, because under Article 9, a clause restricting the assignment of a right to receive money is not effective.
>
> **D.** Yes, because under Article 9, the secured party always wins.

Analysis. Section 9-406(d) provides in part that "an agreement between an account debtor and an assignor or in a promissory note is ineffective to the extent that it . . . prohibits . . . the assignment or transfer of . . . the account, chattel paper, payment intangible, or promissory note." Therefore, the language in the contract between A Co. and B Co., while effective to prevent the delegation of other duties and the assignment of other rights, is not effective to restrict the assignment of a right to receive money. The correct answer is **C**.

Question 13. A bank properly repossesses an automobile from a consumer. The bank looks up the value of the automobile in the *Blue Book,* a publication that lists the value of used cars, purchases the car from itself for that amount, and properly credits the debtor with the proceeds. Did this disposition of the collateral violate Article 9?

A. No, because a secured party may purchase collateral at a private sale if the collateral is the subject of widely distributed standard price quotations.

B. No, because a creditor may dispose of the collateral by either public or private proceedings, as long as the sale is commercially reasonable.

C. Yes, because a secured party may not purchase consumer goods at a private sale.

D. Yes, because the *Blue Book* is not the kind of standard price quotation contemplated by the Article 9 rules on purchase at a private sale.

Analysis. Response **B** states the general rule of § 9-610(b). However, that general rule is subject to the exception stated in § 9-610(c), which governs the purchase by a secured party:

> (c) **Purchase by secured party.** A secured party may purchase collateral:
>
> > (1) at a public disposition; or
> >
> > (2) at a private disposition only if the collateral is of a kind that is customarily sold on a recognized market or the subject of widely distributed standard price quotations.

There is no special rule for consumer goods in this provision, so **C** is incorrect. Therefore, it comes down to whether the *Blue Book* is a "widely distributed price quotation." According to Official Comment 9 to § 9-610, it is not:

> 9. **"Recognized Market."** A "recognized market," as used in subsection (c) and Section 9-611(d), is one in which the items sold are fungible and prices are not subject to individual negotiation. For example, the Philadelphia Stock Exchange is a recognized market, whereas the markets for used automobiles are not.

It would appear that there is more room to negotiate an automobile price than an item such as a stock or a commodity. Therefore, while **A** states the rule correctly, it does not apply to this transaction, so **D** is the correct answer.

Burnham's Picks

Question 1	C
Question 2	D
Question 3	B
Question 4	D
Question 5	D
Question 6	C
Question 7	C
Question 8	A
Question 9	C
Question 10	D
Question 11	B
Question 12	C
Question 13	D

10

Sale and Deficiency

CHAPTER OVERVIEW
A. The Sale
B. Remedies of the Debtor
C. Closers
✦ Burnham's Picks

A. The Sale

We will now explore what happens after the sale is held. The secured party now has a pot of money, formally known as the "proceeds of disposition," to distribute. Section 9-615(a) contains a pretty straightforward enumeration of how those proceeds are to be applied:

Application of Proceeds of Disposition; Liability for Deficiency and Right to Surplus.

(a) **Application of proceeds.** A secured party shall apply or pay over for application the cash proceeds of disposition in the following order to:

(1) the reasonable expenses of retaking, holding, preparing for disposition, processing, and disposing, and, to the extent provided for by agreement and not prohibited by law, reasonable attorney's fees and legal expenses incurred by the secured party;

(2) the satisfaction of obligations secured by the security interest or agricultural lien under which the disposition is made;

(3) the satisfaction of obligations secured by any subordinate security interest in or other subordinate lien on the collateral if:

(A) the secured party receives from the holder of the subordinate security interest or other lien an authenticated demand for proceeds before distribution of the proceeds is completed; and

(B) in a case in which a consignor has an interest in the collateral, the subordinate security interest or other lien is senior to the interest of the consignor; and

(4) a secured party that is a consignor of the collateral if the secured party receives from the consignor an authenticated demand for proceeds before distribution of the proceeds is completed.

First, the proceeds are applied to reasonable expenses and, if provided for by agreement, to reasonable attorney's fees. Second, they are applied to the satisfaction of the debt. Third, they are applied to any subordinate security interests or other liens if the secured party has received an authenticated demand from the holder of that lien. The concept of a "subordinate lien" will be clearer after we have looked into priorities in Chapter 16. There can, of course, be a number of liens attached to the collateral. For purposes of this chapter, we are assuming that the secured party who has repossessed and is conducting a sale has first claim to the collateral.

Finally, according to § 9-615(d), any *surplus* that is left is paid to the debtor. If there is a balance due, then the debtor is liable for that *deficiency*. In a consumer goods transaction, § 9-616 provides that the creditor must send the debtor an explanation of how the surplus or deficiency was calculated. Unless there is additional collateral available, that deficiency is an unsecured debt, and the creditor must proceed to judgment to enforce it. Although a debtor may make an affirmative claim that a sale was not commercially reasonable, this claim is more often raised as a defense when the creditor sues for a deficiency.

Note that the Code does not say that in order to repossess and sell the collateral the secured party must have priority over other secured parties. However, as a practical matter, junior creditors are discouraged from exercising their rights in collateral when a senior creditor is involved. For one thing, while under § 9-617 the buyer at the sale takes free of subordinate security interests, a senior security interest remains attached and is not lost. For another, the senior secured party may have a claim against the junior party for conversion of its interest. As a practical matter, a junior party will not repossess, and if it does, under § 9-611(c) it must notify the senior party, who will often take over the sale. See also § 9-609.

According to § 9-617, the buyer at the sale takes the debtor's rights in the collateral free of the security interest under which the sale was made and free of any subordinate security interest or lien. If the buyer has acted in good faith, then the buyer has these rights even if it is later determined that the sale was not commercially reasonable.

According to §§ 9-610(d) and (e), a sale includes the same warranty of title that applies to a sale under Article 2. You will recall that Article 2 provides that a buyer of goods gets a warranty of good title under § 2-312(1). However, the seller may disclaim the warranty of good title under § 2-312(2) or under § 9-610(f), which provides:

(f) **Record sufficient to disclaim warranties.** A record is sufficient to disclaim warranties under subsection (e) if it indicates "There is no warranty relating to title, possession, quiet enjoyment, or the like in this disposition" or uses words of similar import.

Depending on the circumstances, a buyer might get an implied warranty of merchantability at a foreclosure sale. Under § 2-314, this warranty is given only if "the seller is a merchant with respect to goods of that kind," which the seller at the foreclosure sale might not be. Also, the implied warranty of merchantability can be disclaimed if the seller uses the proper language under §§ 2-316(2) and (3) (a). Finally, this warranty may be excluded by usage of trade under § 2-316(3)(c).

Question 1. After disposing of the collateral, a creditor wants to apply the proceeds of the disposition to reasonable expenses incurred in arranging the disposition and to reasonable attorney's fees that the creditor paid. What is the rule on the creditor's recovery of expenses of disposition and attorney's fees?

A. The creditor can recover neither reasonable expenses nor attorney's fees unless they are provided for in the contract.

B. The creditor can recover reasonable expenses but can recover attorney's fees only if they are provided for in the contract.

C. The creditor can recover reasonable attorney's fees but can recover expenses only if they are provided for in the contract.

D. The creditor can recover both reasonable expenses and attorney's fees even if they are not provided for in the contract.

Analysis.   Sound familiar? This is the same rule we applied in Chapter 9.B when we had a question about the recovery of expenses and attorney's fees when the debtor redeemed the collateral. The rule has not changed. § 9-615(a) (1) provides:

> **Application of Proceeds of Disposition; Liability for Deficiency and Right to Surplus.**
>   (a) **Application of proceeds.** A secured party shall apply or pay over for application the cash proceeds of disposition in the following order to:
>   (1) the reasonable expenses of retaking, holding, preparing for disposition, processing, and disposing, and, to the extent provided for by agreement and not prohibited by law, reasonable attorney's fees and legal expenses incurred by the secured party;

Under § 9-615(a)(1), expenses may be recovered automatically, but attorney's fees may be recovered only "to the extent provided for by agreement." Therefore, the creditor may recover expenses, but may recover attorney's fees only if they were provided for in the contract. So **B** is the correct response.

> **Question 2.** Second Bank conducts a proper sale of a vehicle owned by John Zilch. After expenses, there is a surplus due Zilch of $8,000. Before the proceeds have been distributed, Second Bank receives written notice from two other creditors of Zilch who demand payment from the sale proceeds. Auto Title Lenders is owed $4,000 by Zilch and has presented evidence that the vehicle is subject to a security interest it obtained after Second Bank got its security interest. Mary Smith has presented evidence that she obtained a judgment against Zilch in the amount of $4,000 before Auto Title Lenders got its security agreement. Which of these claims should Second Bank pay out of the surplus due Zilch?
>
> **A.** Auto Title Lenders only.
> **B.** Mary Smith only.
> **C.** Both Auto Title Lenders and Mary Smith.
> **D.** Neither Auto Title Lenders nor Mary Smith.

Analysis.   Section 9-615(a)(3)(A) provides:

> **Application of Proceeds of Disposition; Liability for Deficiency and Right to Surplus.**
>   (a) **Application of proceeds.** A secured party shall apply or pay over for application the cash proceeds of disposition in the following order to: . . .
>   (3) the satisfaction of obligations secured by any subordinate security interest in or other subordinate lien on the collateral if:
>   (A) the secured party receives from the holder of the subordinate security interest or other lien an authenticated demand for proceeds before distribution of the proceeds is completed.

Here, Auto Title Lenders has a subordinate security interest. Mary Smith has a judgment against Zilch, but it is not a lien on the collateral. A judgment does not attach to particular property until the sheriff levies on that property. Therefore, Second Bank should pay Auto Title Lenders but not Mary Smith, so the correct response is **A.**

> **Question 3.** Terry Johnson recently bought a truck at a repo auction for $5,000. The auction was conducted by a bank that rarely sells automobiles. After the purchase, however, two things happened. First, a lender named Auto Title Lenders told Terry that it had a security interest in the truck that was perfected after the interest of the lender that conducted the sale had been perfected. Auto Lenders demanded payment of $4,000, or it would repossess the truck. Second, the truck was giving Terry problems, and a mechanic told Terry it had a serious alignment problem that would cost $4,000 to fix. Terry wants to know if

> there is any recourse for this situation. Terry is quite sure that there was
> no written disclaimer of warranties in connection with the sale. What
> would you advise Terry?
>
> A. Auto Title Lenders' claim is good, and Terry has no warranty of
>   merchantability claim.
> B. Auto Title Lenders' claim is good, but Terry has a warranty of
>   merchantability claim.
> C. Auto Title Lenders' claim is not good, and Terry has no warranty of
>   merchantability claim.
> D. Auto Title Lenders' claim is not good, and Terry has a warranty of
>   merchantability claim.

Analysis. Under § 9-617(a)(3), the sale discharges subordinate liens. Since the security interest of Auto Title Lenders is subordinate, it is discharged, so the claim is not good.

Responses **A** and **B** cannot be correct. Under § 2-314, unless disclaimed, a warranty of merchantability is given by a seller who is a merchant with respect to goods of that kind. Here, because it rarely sells automobiles, the bank is probably not a merchant with respect to automobiles. Therefore, **D** cannot be correct, and the correct response is **C**.

B.   Remedies of the Debtor

Assume that the secured party is found not to have complied with one of the debtor protection provisions, such as the § 9-609 requirement that the repossession not involve a "breach of the peace" or the § 9-610 requirements that the resale be "commercially reasonable" and that the debtor receive "reasonable notification." What can the debtor do about it? Section 9-625(b) provides that "a person is liable for damages in the amount of any loss caused by a failure to comply with this article."

Because it can be difficult for a debtor to prove actual damages, statutory damages are also available in consumer goods transactions under § 9-625(c) and in all transactions under § 9-625(e). Most of the latter involve violations of filing requirements that we will discuss in Chapter 12. One relevant to this chapter, however, is a pattern of failure to send the explanation of calculation of deficiency in a consumer transaction. Note that the remedies for noncompliance under § 9-625 are only the remedies available under the statute. As we have mentioned, in an appropriate case, a remedy may be available under the common law or under consumer protection law.

Section 9-625(c)(2) contains a little-used remedy for the debtor when the collateral is consumer goods:

(2) if the collateral is consumer goods, a person that was a debtor or a secondary obligor at the time a secured party failed to comply with this part may recover for that failure in any event an amount not less than the credit service charge plus 10 percent of the principal amount of the obligation or the time-price differential plus 10 percent of the cash price.

In this statute, the cash price is the price the buyer would have paid if the buyer had paid cash instead of buying on credit. Similarly, the credit service charge or time price differential is the cost of credit, that is, the difference between the cash price and the credit price. So if a television set retails for $1,000, but the buyer can obtain it on credit by making 12 payments of $100, then the cash price is $1,000, and the credit service charge or time price differential is $200.

Because the proceeds from the sale may not be sufficient to satisfy the debt, the expenses, and attorney's fees, creditors may pursue a debtor for the "deficiency." Frequently, this claim motivates the debtor to assert that the creditor did not comply with Article 9. Section 9-626 explains what happens in that event. First, in the deficiency action, the creditor does not need to affirmatively prove compliance with Article 9, but if the debtor raises the issue, the creditor has the burden of proof. See § 9-626(a)(2). If the creditor fails to prove that the collection, enforcement, and disposition complied with Article 9, then an issue arises as to the relief the debtor is entitled to. Former Article 9 did not dictate an applicable rule, and courts developed three rules applicable to this situation. See Official Comment 4 to § 9-626. Under the "offset rule," the injured party got a remedy like expectation damages in contract: the amount the debtor would have had had the creditor complied with the statute.

Courts in many jurisdictions used a "rebuttable presumption" rule. Under this rule, the presumption was that a commercially reasonable sale would have realized the amount that would satisfy the debt, the expenses, and attorney's fees. Because a commercially reasonable sale with proper notice would have netted this amount, the creditor was entitled to nothing. The creditor, however, was allowed to rebut this presumption by proving how much the collateral would have sold for at a commercially reasonable sale. The deficiency or surplus would then be calculated based on that amount.

For example, assume the debt plus expenses and attorney's fees totaled $10,000 and the collateral was sold at a sale for $6,000. The creditor sought a deficiency of $4,000. The debtor raised the issue that the sale was not commercially reasonable, and the creditor did not satisfy the burden of proving that the sale was commercially reasonable. Under the "rebuttable presumption" rule, it would be presumed that at a commercially reasonable sale, the collateral would have been sold for $10,000, so the creditor is entitled to no deficiency. But if the creditor rebuts the presumption by proving that the collateral would have sold for $8,000, then the creditor is entitled to a deficiency of $2,000, the amount the creditor would have had if there had been a sale for that amount.

Other jurisdictions adopted the "absolute bar" rule. Under that rule, if the creditor failed to comply with Article 9, the creditor was "absolutely barred" from recovering any deficiency. In other words, it could not rebut the presumption.

Revised Article 9 codified the "rebuttable presumption" rule in § 9-626(a) (3), so all jurisdictions must follow that rule—with one exception. Remember the compromise between the consumers and the creditors described in Chapter 2.A.2. Because the rebuttable presumption rule would not be as favorable to consumers in jurisdictions that had adopted the absolute bar rule, the drafters could not deprive them of that benefit. Sure enough, if you look closely at § 9-626(a), the rule is prefaced by the language, "In an action arising from a transaction, *other than a consumer transaction*, in which the amount of a deficiency or surplus is in issue, the following rules apply." So in a consumer transaction, you would have to research the law in your state. Some states have enacted non-uniform versions of § 9-626(a) that eliminate the language "other than a consumer transaction," thus making the rule applicable to all transactions. In other states, you would have to study the case law to predict which rule the court would apply in the event the creditor could not prove the sale was commercially reasonable in a consumer transaction.

Question 4. A creditor makes a loan to a business debtor secured by equipment. The debtor defaults, and the creditor repossesses the collateral and sells it for $6,000. Because the debt and expenses came to $10,000, the creditor seeks a deficiency of $4,000. The court finds that the sale was not commercially reasonable. The creditor proves that in a commercially reasonable sale, the collateral would have sold for $8,000. How much is the creditor entitled to as a deficiency judgment against the debtor?

A. $0.
B. $2,000.
C. $4,000.
D. $8,000.

Analysis.   This is not a consumer transaction. Under the "rebuttable presumption rule" of § 9-626, if the sale is not commercially reasonable, it is presumed that the collateral would have sold for the amount of the debt and expenses, here $10,000. If that is the case, then the deficiency equals $0. However, the creditor can rebut that presumption by proving what the collateral would have sold for in a commercially reasonable sale, here $8,000. In that event, the deficiency is calculated as the amount the creditor would have had if there had been a reasonable sale of the collateral. Here, the deficiency would be $10,000 minus $8,000 for a total of $2,000. Therefore, the correct response is **B**.

> **Question 5.** A creditor makes a loan to an individual debtor to enable the debtor to take a vacation. The debt is secured by the debtor's baseball-card collection. The debtor defaults and the creditor repossesses the collateral and sells it for $6,000. Because the debt and expenses came to $10,000, the creditor seeks a deficiency of $4,000. The court finds that the sale was not commercially reasonable. The creditor proves that in a commercially reasonable sale, the collateral would have sold for $8,000. How much is the creditor entitled to as a deficiency judgment against the debtor?
>
> **A.** $0.
> **B.** $2,000.
> **C.** $4,000.
> **D.** It depends on the jurisdiction.

Analysis. *Note on test-taking.* The facts of this question are almost the same as the facts of the previous question. The assessor is probably testing you on whether you can determine whether that factual change is significant.

Under the "rebuttable presumption rule" of § 9-626, the deficiency would be $10,000 minus $8,000 for a total of $2,000. However, under the new facts, the debtor is incurring the debt for personal, family, or household purposes and is using collateral that is held for personal, family, or household purposes. This is a consumer transaction as defined in § 9-102(a)(26), so the "rebuttable presumption rule" is not applicable. Section 9-626(b) provides:

> (b) **Exception for non-consumer transactions; no inference.** The limitation of the rules in subsection (a) to transactions other than consumer transactions is intended to leave to the court the determination of the proper rules in consumer transactions. The court may not infer from that limitation the nature of the proper rule in consumer transactions and may continue to apply established approaches.

Therefore, the correct response is **D.**

> **Question 6.** *Statute reader.* Debtor buys a car from Seller for $12,000 that Debtor will use for personal purposes. Debtor promises to pay $300 per month for 60 months and grants Seller a security interest in the car. Debtor defaults. Seller repossesses the car and resells it, but in the process, Seller fails to comply completely with the requirements of Article 9. How much can Debtor recover from Seller under § 9-625(c)(2)?
>
> **A.** $6,000.
> **B.** $7,200.
> **C.** $12,000.
> **D.** $18,000.

Analysis. Section 9-625(c)(2) applies because the collateral is consumer goods. It provides:

> (2) if the collateral is consumer goods, a person that was a debtor or a secondary obligor at the time a secured party failed to comply with this part may recover for that failure in any event an amount not less than the credit service charge plus 10 percent of the principal amount of the obligation or the time-price differential plus 10 percent of the cash price.

What is the cash price? It is the price the buyer would have paid if the buyer had paid cash, which here is $12,000. What is the credit service charge or time price differential? It is the cost of credit, that is, the difference between the cash price and the credit price. Here, the goods had a cash price of $12,000. But Debtor is making 60 payments of $300 or $18,000, so the credit service charge is $6,000. Plugging these numbers into the formula, Debtor is entitled to $6,000 plus 10 percent of $12,000, which is $6,000 plus $1,200, or $7,200. Therefore, the correct response is **B**.

C. Closers

> **Question 7.** The security agreement between Debtor and Creditor provides that, in the event of default, the Debtor will pay the Creditor's attorney's fees incurred in collecting the debt. Creditor properly repossessed Debtor's inventory. Attorney for Creditor reasonably charged $3,000 for legal advice in connection with the foreclosure, sale, and distribution of the proceeds. Creditor reasonably spent $2,000 on expenses related to the sale. Out of the proceeds from the sale, which of the following payments is Creditor permitted to make?
>
> A. $3,000 to the attorney.
> B. $2,000 for expenses.
> C. Both the $3,000 and the $2,000.
> D. Neither the $3,000 nor the $2,000.

Analysis. Under § 9-615(a)(1), the creditor can recover reasonable expenses but can recover attorney's fees only if they are provided for in the contract. Here, attorney's fees were provided for in the contract, so the correct answer is **C**.

Here's a follow-up question. Assume the contract provided that Debtor will pay the Creditor's attorney's fees incurred in collecting the debt, but when Creditor sued, Debtor prevailed. Does Creditor have to pay Debtor's attorney's fees? The answer in many jurisdictions is yes. In California, for example, by statute a one-sided attorney's fees provision must be read as if it were reciprocal.

Question 8. First Bank repossessed inventory from AP Furniture and held a sale that was not commercially reasonable. The amount of the debt was $100,000, and the sale price was $80,000, leaving a deficiency of $20,000. What is the Article 9 rule in this situation?

A. The reasonable sale price is presumed to be $100,000, but First Bank can rebut the presumption.
B. The reasonable sale price is presumed to be $80,000, but AP can rebut the presumption.
C. First Bank cannot recover a deficiency.
D. Whether First Bank can recover a deficiency is up to the case law of each state.

Analysis.   This is not a consumer transaction, so under the "rebuttable presumption" test codified in § 9-626(a), **A** is the correct response. If, for example, First Bank can prove that the reasonable sale price was $80,000, then First Bank may recover a deficiency of $20,000.

 # Burnham's Picks

Question 1	**B**
Question 2	**A**
Question 3	**C**
Question 4	**B**
Question 5	**D**
Question 6	**B**
Question 7	**C**
Question 8	**A**

Secondary Obligors

A.   Introduction

Up to this point we have looked at transactions involving a single creditor and a single debtor. But the financial world is often more complicated than that. Assume for example, that Peter asks Creditor for a loan and Creditor wants more security than Peter has to offer. Paul agrees to help Peter get the loan. Here is one way the transaction could be structured:

- Peter promises to repay Creditor, and
- Paul promises Creditor that he will be liable for the obligation.

Article 9 is not concerned with this transaction, because it does not involve a security interest. Nevertheless, we'll spend a minute looking at it. If Peter and Paul are both liable on the same obligation, Paul is commonly called a *cosigner*. The Federal Trade Commission (FTC) Credit Practices Rules define *cosigner* as "a natural person who renders himself or herself liable for the obligation of another person without compensation." 16 C.F.R. § 444.1(k). Many people have misunderstandings about what it means to cosign. Some people think, for example, that the creditor has to go after the principal debtor before going after the cosigner or that the cosigner is only liable to the creditor for half of the obligation. Some creditors may encourage these misunderstandings to induce a person to cosign. To address these misunderstandings, the FTC created a rule that prohibits "unfair or deceptive cosigner practices" in a consumer transaction and requires the creditor to give the cosigner a statement that explains his or her responsibilities. That rule, found in 16 C.F.R. § 444.3(c), provides:

To prevent these unfair or deceptive acts or practices, a disclosure, consisting of a separate document that shall contain the following statement and no other, shall be given to the cosigner prior to becoming obligated, which in the case of open end credit shall mean prior to the time that the agreement creating the cosigner's liability for future charges is executed:

Notice to Cosigner

You are being asked to guarantee this debt. Think carefully before you do. If the borrower doesn't pay the debt, you will have to. Be sure you can afford to pay if you have to, and that you want to accept this responsibility.

You may have to pay up to the full amount of the debt if the borrower does not pay. You may also have to pay late fees or collection costs, which increase this amount.

The creditor can collect this debt from you without first trying to collect from the borrower. The creditor can use the same collection methods against you that can be used against the borrower, such as suing you, garnishing your wages, etc. If this debt is ever in default, that fact may become a part of your credit record.

This notice is not the contract that makes you liable for the debt.

Here is another way the transaction could be structured:

- Peter promises to repay Creditor, and
- Paul grants Creditor a security interest in collateral that Paul owns.

Because this transaction involves the grant of a security interest, it is governed by Article 9. Let's look at the designations that Article 9 gives the parties in this situation, starting with *debtor*. *Debtor* is defined in § 9-102(a)(28):

> (28) "Debtor" means:
>
> (A) a person having an interest, other than a security interest or other lien, in the collateral, whether or not the person is an obligor.

Who is the debtor in this example? Be careful. Note that for Article 9 purposes, *debtor* has a more limited definition than it has in common usage. The narrower usage is suggested by the language "whether or not the person is an obligor"; in other words, not all Article 9 debtors are obligors. What is an *obligor*? *Obligor* is defined in § 9-102(a)(59):

> (59) "Obligor" means a person that, with respect to an obligation secured by a security interest in or an agricultural lien on the collateral, (i) owes payment or other performance of the obligation, (ii) has provided property other than the collateral to secure payment or other performance of the obligation, or (iii) is otherwise accountable in whole or in part for payment or other performance of the obligation.

So it now appears that Peter is an obligor, because he owes payment of the obligation, and Paul is a debtor, because he has an interest in the collateral.

To complicate matters, Article 9 also characterizes some parties as *secondary obligors* and defines *secondary obligor* in § 9-102(a)(72) as follows:

> (72) "Secondary obligor" means an obligor to the extent that:
>   (A) the obligor's obligation is secondary; or
>   (B) the obligor has a right of recourse with respect to an obligation secured by collateral against the debtor, another obligor, or property of either.

What it means for an obligation to be *secondary* is not explained in the Code, but *Restatement (Third) of Suretyship and Guaranty* § 1 Comment d has a useful explanation:

> d. [T]his Restatement avoids use of the terms "guarantor" and "surety." Rather, it refers to the "secondary obligor" who has liability to the "obligee" on the "secondary obligation" and the "principal obligor" whose liability to the obligee is based on the "underlying obligation."
>
>   The obligation of the principal obligor is always the "underlying obligation"; similarly, the obligation of the secondary obligor is always the "secondary obligation." This means that when the principal obligor and the secondary obligor are both liable on the same contract (as is the case, for example, when the secondary obligor "cosigns" for the principal obligor) that contract creates both the underlying obligation and the secondary obligation.

To illustrate this concept, let's look at another way the transaction could be structured:

- Peter promises to repay Creditor; and
- Paul promises to repay Creditor, and Paul grants Creditor a security interest in collateral that Paul owns.

Now Paul is a secondary obligor as well as a debtor. He is a debtor because he has an interest in the collateral. And he is a secondary obligor because he has assumed liability for Peter's obligation. You will often see a party who has agreed to be liable for the debt of another described as a "guarantor" or "surety." There is a lot of confusion about these terms in credit transactions, particularly about whether it is a condition of the guarantor's or surety's liability that the creditor be unable to recover from the principal obligor. The *Restatement (Third) of Suretyship and Guaranty* and Article 9 avoid these problems by not using the terms. Instead, they use the term *secondary obligor*. This does not mean that the obligor is secondary in the sense of being inferior or conditional. Rather, it means there is a second obligation.

In spite of this modern trend, you will frequently encounter the words *guaranty* and *surety* to describe the secondary obligation and *guarantor* and *surety* to describe the secondary obligor. In general, these terms indicate that there is an agreement to perform the obligation of another. The scope of that obligation, however, may be hard to determine based on the word used, so the scope is usually clarified in the contract. For example, contracts traditionally state that the guarantor is "unconditionally liable," to make clear that the creditor need not pursue the principal obligor as a condition precedent to pursuing the guarantor. For an example of this language, see the first paragraph of the Letter of Guaranty in part D of this chapter.

Question 1. Olivia borrows $5,000 from Bank and executes a promissory note. Sabrina cosigns the note and also grants Bank a security interest in her car. Which of the following statements is true under Article 9?

A. Only Olivia is a debtor, and only Sabrina is an obligor.
B. Only Sabrina is a debtor, and only Olivia is an obligor.
C. Only Olivia is a debtor, and both Olivia and Sabrina are obligors.
D. Only Sabrina is a debtor, and both Olivia and Sabrina are obligors.

Analysis.   As defined in § 9-102(a)(59), an *obligor* is one who owes payment, while a *debtor* is defined in § 9-102(a)(28) as one who has an interest in the collateral. Here, both owe payment because both signed the note, but only Sabrina has granted an interest in property to secure the payment of the debt. Therefore, both Olivia and Sabrina are obligors, but only Sabrina is a debtor, so **D** is the correct response. Note that Sabrina is also a *secondary obligor*.

Question 2. Patterson wants to buy a new computer, but he doesn't have enough money, and the bank will not loan it to him because of his bad credit history. However, the bank will loan him the money if Corbett pledges his Ted Williams baseball card as collateral. After the agreement is made, Patterson defaults, and the bank exercises its rights in Corbett's card. Corbett claims that his grant of a security interest is not enforceable. Is he correct?

A. Yes, there is no consideration for Corbett's pledge of the collateral.
B. Yes, the Law of Guaranty provides that the promise of a guarantor is enforceable without consideration.
C. No, the loan to Patterson is consideration for Corbett's pledge of the collateral.
D. No, while there is no consideration at common law for Corbett's pledge of the collateral, Article 9 contains a statutory exception making the contract enforceable without consideration.

Analysis. This question clarifies an important point. The party borrowing the money (the *obligor* under Article 9) is not always the same as the party putting up the collateral (the *debtor* under Article 9). In common law contracts, the consideration need not flow to the promisor. See *Restatement (Second) of Contracts* § 71(4). There is an enforceable contract because Corbett bargained for the bank to loan the money to Patterson in return for Corbett's promise to provide collateral. Therefore, the correct response is C.

B. Notice to Secondary Obligors

Secondary obligors are frequently involved in a secured transaction when a partnership or a close corporation seeks credit and the creditor requires that the partners or officers and directors agree to be personally liable for the debt. This often occurs when the organization is thinly capitalized or has few assets. Also, as we have seen in Chapter 8.C, if the loan is secured by the organization's assets as well as by the individuals' personal property, then the individuals have an incentive to see that the organization pays the obligation or turns over the collateral in the event of default. By doing so, the individuals reduce their personal liability for any deficiency.

Under former Article 9, there was an issue as to whether parties who agreed to be liable for the debt of another were entitled to notice of disposition of the collateral after default and repossession. The problem arose because the Code required a secured party to give notice to "debtors." For example, assume ABC Corporation borrowed money from Creditor. ABC Corporation granted Creditor a security interest in its personal property, and Directors A, B, and C promised to be personally liable for the debt. ABC Corporation defaulted, and Creditor repossessed the collateral. The Code required that secured parties give notice of resale to debtors, but Creditor could argue that it did not have to give notice to A, B, and C because they were not debtors as defined in the Code. Recall that a debtor is one with an interest in the collateral; here, A, B, and C are only liable to pay the obligation, so they are obligors but not debtors. On the other hand, it makes good policy sense to require the secured party to notify them. Secondary obligors have a strong interest in seeing that the sale is effective, because as obligors they will be personally liable for any deficiency after the sale proceeds are applied to the debt.

That issue was resolved in Revised § 9-611(c), which provides in relevant part:

§ 9-611. Notification Before Disposition of Collateral.

(c) [**Persons to be notified.**] To comply with subsection (b), the secured party shall send an authenticated notification of disposition to:

(1) the debtor;

(2) any secondary obligor; and . . .

Under the situation described in our hypothetical, it is clear from this provision that Creditor is required to send notice to ABC Corporation because it is the debtor, and to A, B, and C individually because they are secondary obligors. The creditor's obligation to give notice is another obligation that can't be waived under § 9-602. However, some flexibility is restored by § 9-624(a), which provides that the right to notice may be waived by an agreement authenticated after default.

Question 3. *Statute reader.* Creditor is drafting the documents for a transaction in which (1) ABC Corporation will borrow money from Creditor, (2) ABC Corporation will grant Creditor a security interest in its personal property, and (3) Directors A, B, and C will promise to be personally liable for the debt. Can Creditor include a term stating that A, B, and C waive their right to notice of disposition of collateral in the event of default? Consider the following Code sections:

§ 1-302. Variation by Agreement.
    (a) Except as otherwise provided in subsection (b) or elsewhere in [the Uniform Commercial Code], the effect of provisions of [the Uniform Commercial Code] may be varied by agreement.

§ 9-602. Waiver and Variance of Rights and Duties. Except as otherwise provided in Section 9-624, to the extent that they give rights to a debtor or obligor and impose duties on a secured party, the debtor or obligor may not waive or vary the rules stated in the following listed sections: . . .
    (7) Sections 9-610(b), 9-611, 9-613, and 9-614, which deal with disposition of collateral.

§ 9-624. Waiver.
    (a) **Waiver of disposition notification.** A debtor or secondary obligor may waive the right to notification of disposition of collateral under Section 9-611 only by an agreement to that effect entered into and authenticated after default.

A. Yes, under the general freedom of contract rule of § 1-302.
B. Yes, because the Code specifically permits waiver of notice of disposition.
C. No, because, although not specifically mentioned in the Code, public policy would prohibit the waiver.
D. No, because the Code specifically prohibits waiver of the notice rules prior to default.

Analysis.   As secondary obligors, A, B, and C have a right to notice under § 9-611(c)(2). The general rule of § 1-302 is that provisions of the Code may be varied by agreement. However, that general rule is applicable "[e]xcept as otherwise provided . . . elsewhere in [the Uniform Commercial Code]." A list of rules that cannot be varied is found in § 9-602, which includes in subsection (7) the rules in § 9-611. That exception is clarified by § 9-624, which provides that the secondary obligor can waive the right, but only in an agreement authenticated *after default*. Therefore, Creditor cannot put in the initial agreement that the secondary obligors waive their rights, so **D** is the correct response.

C.   Contract Law Issues

When a corporation or partnership goes down the tubes and the creditor goes after individuals who have agreed to be personally liable, the individuals frequently come up with all sorts of defenses to payment, many of which are rooted in old-fashioned contract law. I realize this is a book about secured transactions, but since a secured transaction involves a contract, it is helpful to see how the concepts apply in this context. We will look at three of those defenses involving consideration, modification, and the parol evidence rule.

Assume the creditor loans money to ABC Corporation and Directors A, B, and C agree to be personally liable for the obligation. Director C was not able to attend the closing when the loan documents were signed, but she signed a few days later. We have seen that there is consideration for the promises by A and B, even though the loan went to the corporation rather than to them. One is free to bargain for a benefit to be conferred upon another. But what about C? C has an argument that there is no consideration for her promise because the exchange had already been made at the time C made the promise. Under the doctrine sometimes called *past consideration*, it is not consideration when a party merely promises to do what it has already bound itself to do. Here, the bank had already bound itself to make the loan by the time C signed the contract. Some courts might excuse C on this ground, while others would rule that C's obligation is deemed to have been made at the same time as the others.

Secondary obligors sometimes claim that although they agreed to be liable for the principal's obligation, the bank later modified that obligation and they are not liable for the obligation as modified. For example, if the principal obligor has difficulty repaying the loan, the creditor might extend the time for payment. The older rule held that any material change in the principal obligor's obligation discharged the secondary obligors. This rule had its foundation in formalistic contract law: the changed obligation was simply different from the one the secondary obligor had agreed to. In fact, carried to its logical conclusion, the rule was sometimes invoked even when the change was beneficial to the secondary obligor! The modern rule states the more reasonable position that a secondary obligor is discharged only when the change materially increases the risk that the secondary obligor will suffer a loss. See *Restatement (Third) of Suretyship and Guaranty* § 37.

The careful drafter will finesse this issue by including in the contract that the secondary obligor consents to modifications by the lender. For an example, see the third paragraph of the Letter of Guaranty in part D of this chapter.

Another claim made by some secondary obligors is that oral representations were made to them at the time they were negotiating the loan. They claim that the creditor promised to go after them only after exhausting its remedies against the principal, that the creditor promised to go after them only for a certain portion of the debt, or that some event had to occur before their obligation would become effective. These claims raise issues under our old friend the parol evidence rule. That rule provides that if a written agreement is intended to be final and complete, then evidence of prior oral terms or representations are not admissible to supplement or contradict it. However, many courts find an exception to the parol evidence rule if a party alleges that the parties orally agreed that performance of the agreement was subject to the occurrence of a condition.

Question 4. First Bank entered into a transaction in which it agreed to loan AB, Inc., $100,000 and took a security interest in the equipment of AB, Inc. As part of the transaction, A individually agreed to pay First Bank if AB, Inc., did not. AB, Inc., defaulted when a payment was due, and First Bank gave AB, Inc., an additional 60 days to pay. The contract is silent on the effect of modifications. If AB, Inc., defaults after the 60 days are up, is A still liable to pay First Bank under the modern rule?

A. No, because a modification discharges a party in A's situation.
B. No, because consent to a modification is required, and First Bank did not obtain A's consent.
C. Yes, unless the modification materially increases A's risk.
D. Yes, a party in A's situation always remains liable after a modification is made.

Analysis. Response **A** represents the "old rule," and the question asked for the answer under "the modern rule." That rule is correctly stated in response **C**.

Note on test-taking. Response **D** uses the word "always." This is law, so a response is rarely *always* true. You should be skeptical of a response that is phrased in absolute terms.

Question 5. First Bank entered into a transaction in which it agreed to loan the AB Partnership $100,000 and took a security interest in the equipment of the partnership. As part of the transaction, A, one of the partners, agreed to pay First Bank if the AB Partnership did not. The AB Partnership defaulted, and the bank sued A. A defended on the ground that before signing, the bank's loan officer told him that the bank would also obtain a guaranty from B, the other partner, and that A's guaranty would not be effective unless and until the bank obtained a guaranty from B. There is no guaranty from B, and the loan documentation contains a merger clause stating that "there are no terms, promises, or representations other than those stated in the writing." Will A be able to offer evidence of this alleged promise?

A. Yes, because A's performance is subject to the occurrence of a condition.

B. Yes, because A is offering evidence on an issue of interpretation, which is not barred by the parol evidence rule.

C. No, because the agreement is fully integrated, so the parol evidence rule bars the evidence.

D. No, because the offered evidence contradicts the written terms.

Analysis. We can eliminate response **B**, because the issue is not the interpretation of contract language but whether a term should be admitted. We can also eliminate **D**, because the offered evidence supplements rather than contradicts the agreement. As between **A** and **C**, it is a tough call, and probably not all courts would agree. But the key fact is that since "A's guaranty would not be effective unless and until the bank obtained a guaranty from B," then B's guaranty was a condition to A's performance. Most courts admit evidence of an oral condition to performance of the written agreement as an exception to the parol evidence rule. See *Restatement (Second) of Contracts* § 217 and *United States v. Hub City Volkswagen, Inc.*, 625 F.2d 213 (9th Cir. 1980). Therefore, the best choice is **A**.

D. Closers

The questions that follow are based on the following Letter of Guaranty sent by Alvin Bright to Smith & Co., Inc. The letter was requested by Smith & Co. as part of a transaction in which Smith & Co. is selling inventory to The Blank Corporation on credit and taking a security interest in that inventory.

Smith & Company, Inc.
400 Sixth Avenue
New York, NY 10020

Gentlemen:

To induce you to extend credit to The Blank Corporation of 1 Duane Street, New York, NY, 10001, and in consideration thereof, the undersigned hereby unconditionally guarantees the payment when due of any and all indebtedness which may at any time and from time to time be owing to you by the said corporation or by any successor thereof.

All prior notice of default and demand for payment are hereby waived.

You shall have the unrestricted right to renew, extend, modify and/or compromise any indebtedness and to accept, substitute, surrender or otherwise deal with any collateral security or guaranties, without notice to the undersigned and without in any wise affecting the obligation of the undersigned hereunder.

This guaranty shall continue in full force and effect until such time as you shall have received from the undersigned written notice of revocation by registered or certified mail. Such notice of revocation shall be ineffective as to any existing indebtedness or as to any transaction or commitment previously undertaken by you.

Notice of acceptance of this guaranty is hereby waived.

Very truly yours,

Alvin Bright

Question 6. Who is the secondary obligor in this transaction?

A. Alvin Bright.
B. The Blank Corp.
C. Smith & Co., Inc.
D. None of the above.

Analysis.   Smith & Co. is a secured party and also a creditor extending credit. The one who is obligated on the debt is The Blank Corp., which is known as an obligor for purposes of Article 9. Note that The Blank Corp. is also a debtor in Article 9. The party the letter calls the guarantor, or one who is promising to pay if the obligor does not, is called a secondary obligor in Article 9. That party is Alvin Bright, so **A** is the correct response.

Question 7. After default, Smith & Co. tries to recover from Bright, who defends on grounds that Smith & Co. did not inform him that his offer to be liable for the debt was accepted. Is the defense good?

A. Yes, because the offer was to be accepted by performance, and the offeror would not reasonably know that performance had been given.
B. Yes, because in a unilateral contract, the offeree must always inform the offeror of acceptance.
C. No, because the offer was accepted by a return promise, thus binding both parties.
D. No, because notice of acceptance was expressly waived.

Analysis.   Isn't this a great review of Contracts? The guarantor is making an offer to be accepted by the performance of extending credit. So **B** is an incorrect response, since this is not a bilateral contract. When an offer is to be accepted by performance (sometimes called a *unilateral contract*), the rule is that if the offeree has reason to know that the offeror has no adequate means of learning of the performance, then the duty of the offeror may be discharged if notice is not given. See *Restatement (Second) of Contracts* § 54. Thus, **A** is a good statement of this rule, but **B** is not a good statement, because it uses that overly encompassing word "always." **A** is not applicable here, however, because the offer specifically states in the last paragraph, "Notice of acceptance of this guaranty is hereby waived." Therefore, the correct response is **D**.

Note on test-taking. Read the facts carefully. This is a good example of a fact (the paragraph in the letter) that changes the correct response from the general rule to the exception.

Question 8. Bright claims that Smith & Co., Inc., violated FTC Credit Practice Rule § 444.3 by failing to provide him with the Notice to Cosigner. Did the creditor violate the rule?

A. Yes, because Bright is a cosigner.
B. No, because the FTC Rule does not apply to Article 9 transactions.
C. No, because Bright is a guarantor and not a cosigner.
D. No, because this is not a consumer transaction.

Analysis.   The FTC rule applies to all consumer credit transactions, not just to Article 9 transactions, so **B** is an incorrect response. For purposes of the rule, § 444.1(k) defines *cosigner* as "[a] natural person who renders himself or herself liable for the obligation of another person without compensation." That description would fit Bright, so the statement in **A** is correct, and the statement in **C** is not correct. However, even though Bright is a cosigner, the rule only applies to *consumer* credit transactions. Since this is a commercial transaction, the rule would not apply, so **D** is the correct response.

 # Burnham's Picks

Question 1	**D**
Question 2	**C**
Question 3	**D**
Question 4	**C**
Question 5	**A**
Question 6	**A**
Question 7	**D**
Question 8	**D**

12

Perfection by Filing—the Initial Financing Statement

CHAPTER OVERVIEW

A. **Introduction**
B. **Who Can File a Financing Statement?**
C. **Contents of the Financing Statement**
   1. **Introduction**
   2. **The Debtor's Name: § 9-502(a)(1)**
   3. **Cutting the Filer Some Slack: § 9-506**
   4. **Identification of the Collateral: § 9-502(a)(3)**
D. **Where Is It Filed?**
   1. **Choice of Law**
   2. **In What State Is the Debtor Located?**
   3. **Where Is It Filed in That State?**
E. **When Is It Filed?**
F. **Closers**
   ✦ **Burnham's Picks**

A. Introduction

Although *perfection* is not defined in the Code, we have seen in Chapter 4.A that perfection can be thought of as giving notice of the security interest to third parties. Perfection is important in priority disputes because the general rule is that, between two security interests, priority goes to the first to file or perfect. See § 9-322(a). We are therefore examining perfection before we examine priority disputes. Note that in Chapter 8, "Secured Party v. Debtor," we made no mention of perfection. Although you are likely to forget it from time to time, this was because perfection is not relevant to the transaction between the secured party and the debtor.

According to § 9-308(a), a security interest is perfected if "it has attached and all of the applicable requirements for perfection . . . have been satisfied."

Because perfection requires attachment, a party can prevail in a priority dispute either by showing that the security interest hasn't attached or that it hasn't been otherwise perfected. You might want to review the requirements for attachment in § 9-203 in Chapter 6.A.

If the security interest has attached, then in order to determine whether it is perfected we look to see whether "all of the applicable requirements for perfection . . . have been satisfied." The most common form of perfection is the filing of a financing statement. See § 9-310(a). By the way, don't confuse the *financing statement* used in Article 9 transactions with the *financial statement* used in corporate finance—they have nothing to do with each other. We will examine perfection by the filing of a financing statement in this chapter and perfection by other methods in Chapter 14.

Part 5 of Article 9 is called "Filing," so we will find most of the relevant rules there. A standard form financing statement, reproduced on the next page, is found in § 9-521.

It is not necessary that a filer use this standard form, which is often referred to as Form UCC1. However, because the standard form allows the filing office to record the information on the financing statement more efficiently, many states provide an incentive, such as a lower filing fee, to filers who use the standard form.

You will sometimes be in the position of a party trying to file an effective financing statement and sometimes in the position of a party trying to determine whether a filed financing statement is effective, that is, whether it properly perfects the security interest. We will generally refer to the secured creditor who files a financing statement as the "filing creditor" or the filer, and to the creditor who searches for financing statements as the "searching creditor" or the searcher.

Imagine that you are in the position of a creditor who has been asked to extend credit to a debtor. As a *searching creditor,* you want to know whether the debtor has any other obligations that are secured by the collateral in which you are planning to take a security interest. Assume that you have located a financing statement filed against the debtor. What does that financing statement tell you? Official Comment 2 to § 9-502 describes the system as "notice filing." All the filing tells you, in the words of the Official Comment, is "that a person may have a security interest in the collateral indicated":

> The notice itself indicates merely that a person may have a security interest
> in the collateral indicated. Further inquiry from the parties concerned will be
> necessary to disclose the complete state of affairs.

Now that you have been put on notice, you need to gather more information. You might think you could contact the filing creditor to obtain it, but because you have no relationship with the filing creditor, the creditor has no obligation to respond to your request. Instead, you have to ask the debtor to request further information from the secured party with which it has a relationship. Section 9-210(b) provides as follows:

UCC FINANCING STATEMENT
FOLLOW INSTRUCTIONS

A. NAME & PHONE OF CONTACT AT FILER (optional)

B. E-MAIL CONTACT AT FILER (optional)

C. SEND ACKNOWLEDGMENT TO: (Name and Address)

[Print]   [Reset]

THE ABOVE SPACE IS FOR FILING OFFICE USE ONLY

1. DEBTOR'S NAME: Provide only one Debtor name (1a or 1b) (use exact, full name; do not omit, modify, or abbreviate any part of the Debtor's name); if any part of the Individual Debtor's name will not fit in line 1b, leave all of item 1 blank, check here ☐ and provide the Individual Debtor information in item 10 of the Financing Statement Addendum (Form UCC1Ad)

1a. ORGANIZATION'S NAME			
1b. INDIVIDUAL'S SURNAME	FIRST PERSONAL NAME	ADDITIONAL NAME(S)/INITIAL(S)	SUFFIX
1c. MAILING ADDRESS	CITY	STATE	POSTAL CODE	COUNTRY

2. DEBTOR'S NAME: Provide only one Debtor name (2a or 2b) (use exact, full name; do not omit, modify, or abbreviate any part of the Debtor's name); if any part of the Individual Debtor's name will not fit in line 2b, leave all of item 2 blank, check here ☐ and provide the Individual Debtor information in item 10 of the Financing Statement Addendum (Form UCC1Ad)

2a. ORGANIZATION'S NAME			
2b. INDIVIDUAL'S SURNAME	FIRST PERSONAL NAME	ADDITIONAL NAME(S)/INITIAL(S)	SUFFIX
2c. MAILING ADDRESS	CITY	STATE	POSTAL CODE	COUNTRY

3. SECURED PARTY'S NAME (or NAME of ASSIGNEE of ASSIGNOR SECURED PARTY): Provide only one Secured Party name (3a or 3b)

3a. ORGANIZATION'S NAME			
3b. INDIVIDUAL'S SURNAME	FIRST PERSONAL NAME	ADDITIONAL NAME(S)/INITIAL(S)	SUFFIX
3c. MAILING ADDRESS	CITY	STATE	POSTAL CODE	COUNTRY

4. COLLATERAL: This financing statement covers the following collateral:

5. Check only if applicable and check only one box: Collateral is ☐ held in a Trust (see UCC1Ad, item 17 and instructions)   ☐ being administered by a Decedent's Personal Representative

6a. Check only if applicable and check only one box:
☐ Public-Finance Transaction   ☐ Manufactured-Home Transaction   ☐ A Debtor is a Transmitting Utility

6b. Check only if applicable and check only one box:
☐ Agricultural Lien   ☐ Non-UCC Filing

7. ALTERNATIVE DESIGNATION (if applicable):   ☐ Lessee/Lessor   ☐ Consignee/Consignor   ☐ Seller/Buyer   ☐ Bailee/Bailor   ☐ Licensee/Licensor

8. OPTIONAL FILER REFERENCE DATA:

FILING OFFICE COPY — UCC FINANCING STATEMENT (Form UCC1) (Rev. 04/20/11)   International Association of Commercial Administrators (IACA)

(b) **Duty to respond to requests.** Subject to subsections (c), (d), (e), and (f), a secured party, other than a buyer of accounts, chattel paper, payment intangibles, or promissory notes or a consignor, shall comply with a request within 14 days after receipt:

(1) in the case of a request for an accounting, by authenticating and sending to the debtor an accounting; and

(2) in the case of a request regarding a list of collateral or a request regarding a statement of account, by authenticating and sending to the debtor an approval or correction.

Once you have sufficient information regarding the "complete state of affairs," you will be in a position to determine whether the filed financing statement is effective. Again, note the importance of this inquiry. Priority generally goes to the first secured creditor to effectively file or perfect. If you find an earlier filing but that filing is ineffective, your filing will have priority over it. A financing statement can be ineffective for a number of reasons, including the following:

- It was not filed by an authorized person.
- It does not contain the required information.
- It was not filed in the right place.
- It was not filed in a timely manner.

We will examine each of these topics in turn, keeping in mind the converse: if we understand what makes a financing statement ineffective, we will also understand what we need to do as a filing creditor to make a filing effective.

Question 1. You are a creditor contemplating entering into a security agreement with a law firm. You plan to take a security interest in the debtor's office furniture. You conduct a search of the filings, and you find that a creditor has filed a financing statement against that debtor. Part 4 of that financing statement has been filled in as follows: "4. This FINANCING STATEMENT covers the following collateral: equipment." What should you do at this point?

A. Don't go ahead with the transaction because there is no way you can obtain priority.

B. Go ahead with the transaction because this filing was not effective.

C. Go ahead with the transaction because even if the other creditor has made an effective filing with respect to equipment, you would be the first to file with respect to office furniture.

D. Ask the debtor to contact the creditor to request more information.

Analysis.   **B** is not correct because there is nothing on its face that indicates that this filing was not effective. **C** is not correct because the office furniture is equipment, and § 9-504(1) permits "a description of the collateral pursuant to Section 9-108," and § 9-108(b)(3) permits as a description "a type of collateral defined in the Uniform Commercial Code." **A** is not correct because it is overly broad. While you might eventually decide not to go ahead with the transaction, you should first gather more information. Therefore, **D** is the best response. Under § 9-210, the debtor may request this information from the creditor.

We will return to this problem at the end of the chapter after we have gathered more information.

B.   Who Can File a Financing Statement?

Section 9-510(a) provides that "[a] filed record is effective only to the extent that it was filed by a person that may file it under Section 9-509." A person who is not authorized to file may be subject to damages under § 9-625. Section 9-509 provides that a person may file a financing statement if the debtor (1) authorizes the filing in an authenticated record or (2) authenticates a security agreement. For example, on February 1, a bank files a financing statement covering a debtor's inventory, and, on March 1, the debtor signs a security agreement granting the bank a security interest in inventory. The filing on February 1 was not authorized, but it became authorized on March 1 when the debtor signed the security agreement.

Incidentally, you may be wondering why the bank would file on February 1, since perfection requires attachment and there could be no attachment until the security interest was granted on March 1. The answer is that priority generally goes to the first party to file *or* perfect. See § 9-322. For priority purposes, it may be important to be first to *file*, even if perfection comes later. If the bank waited until March 1 to file, it is possible that another secured party could file on February 28 and be first to file. Even if the bank checked the filings on March 1, that February 28 filing might not show up on the records. Therefore, to be assured that it will get priority, a creditor should make an authorized filing and then wait until that filing shows up in the records. This practice is sometimes called *pre-filing*. If at that time there are no earlier filings, then the creditor can enter into the security agreement with the assurance that it has priority. The Official Comments to §§ 9-509, 9-502, and 9-322 make clear that if the filing is subsequently authorized, then the prior unauthorized act of the filer is ratified, making the earlier filing date the date that is used for purposes of establishing priority.

Question 2. On March 1, a debtor signed a security agreement granting a bank a security interest in inventory. On March 3, the bank filed a financing statement covering debtor's inventory and accounts. To what extent is the financing statement effective?

A. It is an effective filing in inventory and accounts as of March 1.
B. It is an effective filing in inventory and accounts as of March 3.
C. It is an effective filing in inventory as of March 1.
D. It is an effective filing in inventory as of March 3.

Analysis.   There was no filing until March 3, so **A** and **C** cannot be correct. The debtor did not affirmatively authorize any filing. However, by entering into a security agreement, the debtor implicitly authorized the bank to file a financing statement, but only with respect to the collateral covered in the security agreement. See § 9-509. Since the security agreement only covered inventory, the correct response is **D**. Note that it would be unwise for the creditor to wait until March 3 to file, because it could lose priority to a creditor who filed earlier.

Question 3. On February 1, without authorization from the debtor, a bank filed a financing statement covering the debtor's inventory and accounts. On March 1, the debtor signed a security agreement granting a bank a security interest in inventory. To what extent is the financing statement effective?

A. It was an effective filing in inventory and accounts when made on February 1.
B. On March 1, it became an effective filing in inventory and accounts as of February 1.
C. It was an effective filing in inventory when made on February 1.
D. On March 1, it became an effective filing in inventory as of February 1.

Analysis.   The filing was not authorized until the debtor authenticated the security agreement on March 1, so **A** and **C** cannot be correct. However, by entering into a security agreement on March 1, the debtor implicitly authorized the bank to file a financing statement and thereby ratified the unauthorized filing on February 1. However, the debtor only authorized a filing with respect to the collateral covered in the security agreement. See § 9-509. Since the security agreement only covered inventory, the correct response is **D**.

C. Contents of the Financing Statement

1. Introduction

You would think it would be easy to discover what information is required to make a financing statement effective. Article 9 does not make it so easy, however. We begin with § 9-502, which lulls us with the caption "Contents of Financing Statement":

> **§ 9-502. Contents of Financing Statement.**
>
> (a) Subject to subsection (b) [extracted collateral timber, fixture filings], a financing statement is sufficient only if it:
>
> (1) provides the name of the debtor;
>
> (2) provides the name of the secured party or a representative of the secured party; and
>
> (3) indicates the collateral covered by the financing statement.

Our initial thought that only these three items of information are required may be shaken, however, when we read Official Comment 4 to § 9-502, which is ominously captioned, "Certain Other Requirements":

> In addition, the filing office must reject a financing statement lacking certain other information formerly required as a condition for perfection (e.g. an address for the debtor or secured party). See Sections 9-516(b), 9-520(a).

As instructed, we look at those sections:

> **§ 9-516. What Constitutes Filing; Effectiveness of Filing. . . .**
>
> (b) Refusal to accept record; filing does not occur. Filing does not occur with respect to a record that a filing office refuses to accept because:
>
> (1) the record is not communicated by a method or medium of communication authorized by the filing office;
>
> (2) an amount equal to or greater than the applicable filing fee is not tendered;
>
> (3) the filing office is unable to index the record because:
>
> (A) in the case of an initial financing statement, the record does not provide a name for the debtor;
>
> (B) in the case of an amendment or information statement, the record:
>
> (i) does not identify the initial financing statement as required by Section 9-512 or 9-518, as applicable; or
>
> (ii) identifies an initial financing statement whose effectiveness has lapsed under Section 9-515;
>
> (C) in the case of an initial financing statement that provides the name of a debtor identified as an individual or an

amendment that provides a name of a debtor identified as an individual which was not previously provided in the financing statement to which the record relates, the record does not identify the debtor's surname; or

(D) in the case of a record filed [or recorded] in the filing office described in Section 9-501(a)(1), the record does not provide a sufficient description of the real property to which it relates;

(4) in the case of an initial financing statement or an amendment that adds a secured party of record, the record does not provide a name and mailing address for the secured party of record;

(5) in the case of an initial financing statement or an amendment that provides a name of a debtor which was not previously provided in the financing statement to which the amendment relates, the record does not:

(A) provide a mailing address for the debtor; or

(B) indicate whether the name provided as the name of the debtor is the name of an individual or an organization;

(6) in the case of an assignment reflected in an initial financing statement under Section 9-514(a) or an amendment filed under Section 9-514(b), the record does not provide a name and mailing address for the assignee; or

(7) in the case of a continuation statement, the record is not filed within the six-month period prescribed by Section 9-515(d).

§ 9-520. Acceptance and Refusal to Accept Record.

(a) Mandatory refusal to accept record. A filing office shall refuse to accept a record for filing for a reason set forth in Section 9-516(b) and may refuse to accept a record for filing only for a reason set forth in Section 9-516(b).

These sections alert us to the fact that the filing office requires more information than we suspected when we first read § 9-502. Note that § 9-502 provides that a financing statement is "sufficient" if it contains those three bits of information. Section 9-520 provides that the filing office "shall refuse to accept a record for filing" for a reason set forth in § 9-516 but "may refuse to accept a record for filing only for a reason set forth in Section 9-516(b)." Finally, § 9-516(b) states that "filing does not occur" if the filing office refuses to accept a record because the filer did not follow the requirements of that section.

Let's see if we can reconcile these various provisions. It may be helpful to keep in mind that one of the goals of the drafters of Revised Article 9 was to limit the discretion of the filing office; the office is to mechanically check the filing but to exercise little judgment. For example, a filer presents a financing statement that lacks the mailing address of the debtor. Does the filing office have an obligation to reject this filing? Yes. This information is required by

§ 9-516(b)(5)(A), and § 9-520 provides that "[a] filing office *shall* refuse to accept a record for filing for a reason set forth in Section 9-516(b)" (emphasis added). Assume, however, that the filing office nevertheless accepts this filing. Is it an effective filing? Yes! This is where § 9-502 kicks in. Even though the filing office had an obligation to refuse it, once the filing office accepts it, it is an effective filing because it satisfies the minimum requirements of a "sufficient" filing.

Now comes the hard part. Assume in the same hypothetical that the filing office properly rejects the filing because it lacks the mailing address of the debtor. In a hurry to get the statement filed, the filer makes up an address and resubmits the filing. The clerk knows this is not a real address and refuses to accept the filing. Is this an effective filing? Surprisingly, the answer is yes! This is where it becomes important that the filing office "may refuse to accept a record for filing *only* for a reason set forth in Section 9-516(b)" (emphasis added). The filing office abused its discretion. Because the filing did "provide a mailing address for the debtor," this filing was not rejected for "a reason set forth in 9-516(b)." Therefore, it was an effective filing. In their own strange way, these rules seem to make sense.

Question 4. *Statute reader.* In anticipation of an agreement with a debtor, a creditor prepares a security agreement and a financing statement. What authentications (in this case, signatures) are required on these documents?

A. Both parties must authenticate both documents.
B. Both parties must authenticate the security agreement, but only the creditor must authenticate the financing statement.
C. Only the debtor must authenticate the security agreement, and only the creditor must authenticate the financing statement.
D. Only the debtor must authenticate the security agreement, and no one must authenticate the financing statement.

Analysis. We discussed the requirements for attachment in Chapter 6.A. Section 9-203(b)(3) provides that, for a security agreement to attach, "the debtor has authenticated a security agreement," so we need the debtor's authentication on the security agreement. However, the requirements for a financing statement in §§ 9-502 and 9-516 make no mention of authentication. Official Comment 3 to § 9-502 states in part:

> Whereas former Section 9-402(1) required the debtor's signature to appear on a financing statement, this Article contains no signature requirement.

The Code now uses the terms *authentication* and *authenticate* instead of *signature* and *sign* to accommodate electronic filing. Because no authentication is required on the financing statement, the correct response is **D**. Note that there is no signature line on the UCC Form 1 in part A of this chapter.

Question 5. A creditor presents a financing statement for filing that contains the name of the debtor and the name of the secured party and that indicates the collateral covered. The financing statement, however, lacks the mailing address of the debtor. The clerk in the filing office nevertheless accepts the financing statement. Is there an effective filing?

A. Yes, because the financing statement contains sufficient information under § 9-502.

B. Yes, because all financing statements accepted by the filing office are effective.

C. No, because the financing statement does not contain information required by § 9-516(b)(5)(A).

D. No, because the financing statement does not contain sufficient information under § 9-502.

Analysis.   A financing statement is sufficient under § 9-502 only if it contains these three items of information: the name of the debtor, the name of the secured party, and the collateral covered. Here, the financing statement contains these three items of information, so it is effective. The correct response is **A**.

_____

An awkward situation is created when, under § 9-516(b), the filing office refuses to accept a filing but it is nevertheless deemed to be an effective filing. How can a filing be effective if it does not notify third parties of the existence of the security interest? The answer, found in § 9-516(d), is that the filing is effective against some third parties but not against all third parties. That section provides:

> (d) **Refusal to accept record; record effective as filed record.** A record that is communicated to the filing office with tender of the filing fee, but which the filing office refuses to accept for a reason other than one set forth in subsection (b), is effective as a filed record except as against a purchaser of the collateral which gives value in reasonable reliance upon the absence of the record from the files.

This rule creates an important exception to the effectiveness of the filing: the filing is ineffective against a "purchaser" of the collateral, but it is not ineffective against all purchasers; it is ineffective only against purchasers who actually relied on a search of the files. Let's look at the definition of *purchaser*. According to § 1-201(b)(30), a *purchaser* is "a person that takes by purchase," and § 1-201(b)(29) provides:

> (29) "Purchase" means taking by sale, lease, discount, negotiation, mortgage, pledge, lien, security interest, issue or reissue, gift, or any other voluntary transaction creating an interest in property.

Note that the definition of *purchase* not only includes the obvious—a taking by sale—it also includes a taking by "security interest." So if another secured party searches the filings and does not find the filing, that filing is not effective against the searching creditor. The message to the filer is clear: to get protection against other creditors, comply with the changes requested by the filing office and refile.

Question 6. On March 1, First Bank presented a financing statement that had all the information required by § 9-516(b) along with the filing fee, but the clerk in the filing office refused to accept it. The financing statement indicated that the collateral was a certain piece of equipment belonging to the debtor. On March 10, Second Bank was planning to loan money to the same debtor. Before it did so, Second Bank checked the filing system and found nothing. It therefore concluded that it would have priority, so it took a security interest in the same piece of equipment and filed. Does First Bank have priority over Second Bank in the piece of equipment?

A. Yes, because First Bank's filing was effective, it was first to file.
B. Yes, because First Bank's filing is not effective against a purchaser that gave value in reliance on the absence of a filing, but Second Bank is not a purchaser.
C. No, because First Bank's filing was not effective.
D. No, because First Bank's filing is not effective against a purchaser that gave value after reliance on the absence of a filing, and Second Bank is a purchaser.

Analysis.   Let's start by asking whether First Bank made an effective filing. The general rule of § 9-516(d) is that a filing is effective if the filing office refuses to accept it for a reason other than one set out in § 9-516(b). Under the facts, the filing complied with § 9-516(b). So it must have been refused for some other reason. Therefore, the filing is effective. But it does not seem fair that a filing should be effective as against another party, such as Second Bank, who could not find it. The last part of § 9-516(d) covers this possibility, stating that the filing is effective "except as against a purchaser of the collateral which gives value in reasonable reliance upon the absence of the record from the files." Under our facts, Second Bank gave value when it made a loan to the debtor, and it did so in reasonable reliance on the absence of the record from the files, for it thought it would have priority. So the only remaining issue is whether Second Bank is a "purchaser." According to §§ 1-201(b)(29) and (30), a secured party is a purchaser. Second Bank satisfies all the requirements for the exception, and the filing by First Bank is not effective against Second Bank. The correct response is **D**.

Before you conclude that the exception to § 9-516(d) swallows up the rule, let me point out that there are significant parties who do not fall under the exception. There is protection for the filer against parties who do not acquire their interest in a "voluntary transaction," such as a judgment lien creditor. Most importantly, there is protection for the filer against the bankruptcy trustee. Recall that a creditor must perfect a security interest in order to have priority over the bankruptcy trustee. Under the definition of *purchaser*, the bankruptcy trustee is not a purchaser. Therefore, a creditor who makes an effective filing, even when the record cannot be found by a third party, is protected if the debtor declares bankruptcy.

Let us switch now from the unlikely situation in which a filing is deemed effective even though it does not end up in the filing system, to the more significant situation in which the filing is actually made but a searcher claims it is not effective. Sometimes the claim that a filing is not effective is made by a searcher. But to make matters worse for filing creditors, the claim that the filing was misleading can be made by a bankruptcy trustee who did not even conduct a search. As we will see in Chapter 19, under the powers granted by § 544(a) of the Bankruptcy Code, the trustee in bankruptcy acts as a *hypothetical* claimant who searched the records. The trustee can deem a security interest to be unperfected on grounds that the filing was not effective even if no one was actually misled by the filing.

The requirements for a sufficient financing statement in § 9-502 seem very simple. Yet, in an incredible number of cases, the filing creditor has not followed the requirements. We will examine two areas in which filers frequently err: (1) the debtor's name and (2) identification of the collateral.

2. The Debtor's Name: § 9-502(a)(1)

Why is the name so important? Financing statements must be placed in a database that is searchable, either by a human or by a computer. Section 9-519(c)(1) provides that "the filing office shall . . . index an initial financing statement according to the name of the debtor." Because filings are indexed by name, it is crucial for both the filer and the searcher to get the name right. For example, Creditor 2 searches the database and concludes that no financing statement was filed against the debtor. It therefore completes the transaction and files its own financing statement. After debtor defaults, another creditor, Creditor 1, surfaces. Creditor 1 claims that it filed before Creditor 2 and listed the name of the debtor as one that a reasonable searcher should have found. The battle is joined. If the court determines that Creditor 1 did not get the name right, Creditor 1's security interest is declared to be unperfected, and it loses priority to Creditor 2's perfected security interest. But if the court determines that Creditor 1 did get the name right, Creditor 1 has priority over Creditor 2.

A proposed draft of the standard form financing statement we looked at in part A of this chapter cautioned the filer entering the debtor's name to "use exact, full name; do not omit, modify, or abbreviate any word in the Debtor's name." This language was ultimately omitted from the form because it is not found in the Code itself. Nevertheless, it exemplifies the principle that guided the drafters of Revised Article 9—the filer need file under only one name and the searcher need search under only one name. But what is that name for a particular debtor? For purposes of filing under Article 9, we need to be concerned about three types of debtors: a registered organization, an individual, and an organization. Let's look at each of these in turn.

a. A Registered Organization

The thinking with respect to registered organizations was that since each state requires a registered organization to have a different name, there would be a unique name for every such organization in a state. Revised Article 9 directed the filer to look to the "public record" of that jurisdiction to find the name. Experience, however, has shown that there may be different names in different public records. Therefore, Amended Article 9 used a narrower approach when it revised the definition of "registered organization" in § 9-102(a)(71) as follows:

> (71) "Registered organization" means an organization formed or organized solely under the law of a single State or the United States by the filing of a public organic record with, the issuance of a public organic record by, or the enactment of legislation by the State or the United States. The term includes a business trust that is formed or organized under the law of a single State if a statute of the State governing business trusts requires that the business trust's organic record be filed with the State.

A "registered organization," therefore, includes such entities as corporations, limited liability companies (LLCs), and certain partnerships, such as limited liability partnerships (LLPs). Section 9-503(a)(1) provides:

> A financing statement sufficiently provides the name of the debtor:
>
> (1) except as otherwise provided in paragraph (3), if the debtor is a registered organization or the collateral is held in a trust that is a registered organization, only if the financing statement provides the name that is stated to be the registered organization's name on the public organic record most recently filed with or issued or enacted by the registered organization's jurisdiction of organization which purports to state, amend, or restate the registered organization's name;

According to this scheme, the "public organic record" is the single document that the filer or searcher needs to look to in order to find the name of the registered organization. Amended Article 9 added this definition in § 9-102(a)(68):

> (68) "Public organic record" means a record that is available to the public for inspection and is:
>
> (A) a record consisting of the record initially filed with or issued by a State or the United States to form or organize an

organization and any record filed with or issued by the State or the United States which amends or restates the initial record;

    (B) an organic record of a business trust consisting of the record initially filed with a State and any record filed with the State which amends or restates the initial record, if a statute of the State governing business trusts requires that the record be filed with the State; or

    (C) a record consisting of legislation enacted by the legislature of a State or the Congress of the United States which forms or organizes an organization, any record amending the legislation, and any record filed with or issued by the State or the United States which amends or restates the name of the organization.

Both the filer and the searcher, therefore, must acquire the public organic record and use the name on that record. Trade names should never be used.

b. An Individual

Filing with respect to the name of an individual proved to be problematic under Revised Article 9, for an individual may have more than one name. An individual sometimes uses one name in personal life and another in professional life. An individual might sometimes use a maiden name or a married name. Or an individual might through usage have made a common law change to his or her name. Unfortunately, the drafters of Amended Article 9 could not agree on a single solution to this problem that would work for all jurisdictions. They therefore proposed two uniform versions of the subsections of § 9-503 that relate to individual names, leaving it up to each jurisdiction to decide which one to adopt. Those Alternatives are as follows:

[Alternative A]

    (4) subject to subsection (g), if the debtor is an individual to whom this State has issued a [driver's license] that has not expired, only if the financing statement provides the name of the individual which is indicated on the [driver's license];

    (5) if the debtor is an individual to whom paragraph (4) does not apply, only if the financing statement provides the individual name of the debtor or the surname and first personal name of the debtor; and

[Alternative B]

    (4) if the debtor is an individual, only if the financing statement:

    (A) provides the individual name of the debtor;

    (B) provides the surname and first personal name of the debtor; or

    (C) subject to subsection (g), provides the name of the individual which is indicated on a [driver's license] that this State has issued to the individual and which has not expired; and . . .

The alternatives recognize the same three categories of individual names but give them different weight. Alternative A, which is called the "only if" rule, gives more weight to the name on the driver's license (or other term used by the state to describe a state-issued form of identification). If the debtor has an unexpired driver's license, then under that alternative, the name on the license must be used. If the debtor does not have a license, then the creditor may use either the "individual name" of the debtor, or the debtor's surname and first personal name. While this sounds like an easy-to-apply rule, it assumes that the name on the driver's license will be accepted by the UCC filing office. This is not always the case because punctuation issues or space limitations may not permit the same name to be used for both purposes. Alternative B, known as the "safe harbor" rule, gives less weight to the driver's license and permits the filing creditor to use any of the three categories of individual names.

Because of the uncertainty of filing and searching for an individual name, contrary to the practice for a registered organization, a filer may consider filing in more than one name and a searcher may consider searching for more than one name. Nicknames, however, should not be used.

c. An Organization

Finally, let's look at how to deal with an organization which is an entity that is not a registered organization and not an individual. An example of such an organization in the United States is a general partnership. Finding the name of an organization that is not registered may be problematic. If two people form a general partnership, the organization may not be known by a single name. Lenny Burnham and Trevor Burnham may call themselves "The Burnham Group" without even realizing they are a partnership. Subsection (6) of Alternative A and subsection (5) of Alternative B provide the rule in this case:

[A financing statement sufficiently provides the name of the debtor:] in other cases:

(A) if the debtor has a name, only if the financing statement provides the organizational name of the debtor; and

(B) if the debtor does not have a name, only if the financing statement provides the names of the partners, members, associates, or other persons comprising the debtor, in a manner that each name provided would be sufficient if the person named were the debtor.

In our example, if the organization has the name "The Burnham Group," the creditor should use that name. If it does not have a name, then the individual names found pursuant to the appropriate Alternative should be used.

Note that the definition of "registered organization" includes only those organizations that are organized under the law of a state or of the United States. If an organization is organized outside of the United States, even if it is incorporated, for purposes of § 9-502 it is an organization rather than a registered organization.

Question 7. Nguyen Tan Dung applies for a secured loan in a state that has enacted Alternative A. He introduces himself as "Mr. Dung," and produces a driver's license that provides the name Nguyen Tan Dung without any indication as to which name is the surname. Mr. Dung is culturally Vietnamese and unknown to the creditor, in Vietnamese culture the first name in a person's name is their family name or surname. In completing the financing statement, which name should the filer put in the box "individual's surname"?

A. Dung, because that is the last component of the name on the driver's license.

B. Nguyen, because that is the surname indicated on the driver's license, in spite of the fact that it appears as the first component.

C. Nguyen, because under subsection (5), that is the surname of the debtor.

D. Either Dung or Nguyen.

Analysis. The Official Comment to § 9-503 advises: "Determining the name that should be provided on the financing statement must not be done mechanically. The order in which the components of an individual's name appear on a driver's license differs among the States. . . . Regardless of the order on the driver's license, the debtor's surname must be provided in the part of the financing statement designated for the surname." Here, the last component of the name on the driver's license is not the surname, which is Nguyen. That is the name that should be used as a surname in the filing. As between the two responses indicating that name, **B** and **C**, **B** is the better choice because subsection (5) applies only when the person does not have a driver's license. Because this debtor has a driver's license, the best choice is **B**. This might be a case where the filer would file in both names. However, in order to do that, the creditor would have to become aware that the last component of the name is not necessarily the surname. If the driver's license does not indicate the surname, a prudent creditor might ask the debtor.

3. Cutting the Filer Some Slack: § 9-506

Article 9 does cut the filer some slack. According to § 9-506(a), a filing with errors is still effective as long as the errors are not "seriously misleading." What does that mean? Under former Article 9, the rule of thumb was whether a reasonable searcher would have found the filing in spite of the error. But we don't have many human searchers anymore; they have been replaced by computerized searches. Revised Article 9 provides in § 9-506(c) that the filing is not seriously misleading if the filing office's "standard search logic" would find the filing. So in order to determine whether a filing is seriously misleading, you would need to be familiar with the search logic in your jurisdiction.

For example, if the name of an entity is "Safe Harbor Filings, Inc.," a filing under the name of "Safe Harbour Filings, Inc." would not have been misleading under the former system, because a human searcher would probably have found it. However, in a jurisdiction in which the search logic looks only for exact match, which is the usual case, this filing would be seriously misleading because the search logic would not find it. It would therefore not be an effective filing. Note that the search logic may vary from one jurisdiction to another. You can usually find the rules on the website of the entity, such as the Secretary of State, with which financing statements are filed. However, different programmers may follow the rules in different ways. As a practical matter, the filer should conduct a search after the financing statement has been filed to be sure that the standard search logic of that jurisdiction will find the filing.

> **Question 8.** Grace Elizabeth Prouty lives in a state that has enacted Alternative A. Prouty operates an accounting business called GEP Accounting as a sole proprietorship. Prouty bought a new computer system for her business on credit from Purple Cow Computer Co. and granted Purple Cow a security interest in the computer system. Prouty's driver's license uses her married name, which is Grace Elizabeth Clarke. In completing the financing statement, how should Purple Cow list the debtor's name?
>
> **A.** Grace Elizabeth Prouty.
> **B.** Grace Elizabeth Clarke.
> **C.** Either Grace Elizabeth Prouty or Grace Elizabeth Clarke.
> **D.** GEP Accounting.

Analysis. Begin your analysis by asking whether the debtor is an individual, a registered organization, or an organization. Here the debtor is an individual; a sole proprietorship is simply an individual doing business under a trade name. Section 9-503(c) makes clear that "a financing statement that provides only the debtor's trade name does not sufficiently provide the name of the debtor." Therefore, **D** is not correct. If the debtor is an individual, that name should be provided on the financing statement. In a jurisdiction that has enacted Alternative A, the financing statement sufficiently provides the name of the debtor "only if the financing statement provides the name of the individual which is indicated on the driver's license." Here, that name is Grace Elizabeth Clarke, so **B** is correct. See § 9-503(a) Alternative A (4).

> **Question 9.** Grace Elizabeth Prouty moved to a state that has enacted Alternative B and obtained a driver's license in that state that uses her married name, which is Grace Elizabeth Clarke. Prouty operates an accounting business called GEP Accounting as a sole proprietorship.

> Prouty bought a new computer system for her business on credit from
> Purple Cow Computer Co. and granted Purple Cow a security interest in
> the computer system. In completing the financing statement, how should
> Purple Cow list the debtor's name?
>
> **A.** Grace Elizabeth Prouty.
> **B.** Grace Elizabeth Clarke.
> **C.** Either Grace Elizabeth Prouty or Grace Elizabeth Clarke.
> **D.** GEP Accounting.

Analysis.   *Note on test-taking.* The facts are the same as in the previous question, except that the transaction is now governed by Alternative B to § 9-503(a) instead of Alternative A. That is a tip that the answer will turn on the difference between the two alternatives.

Under Alternative B, the financing statement sufficiently provides the name of the debtor only if the financing statement uses the individual name, the surname and first personal name, or the name indicated on the driver's license of the debtor. Therefore, the filer may use either Grace Elizabeth Prouty or Grace Elizabeth Clarke, so **C** is correct. See § 9-503(a) Alternative B (4).

> **Question 10.** In the jurisdiction in which a financing statement is filed,
> the search logic of the filing system looks for "an exact match of the name
> requested; 'the' and words and abbreviations that indicate the existence
> of an entity are disregarded." The name of a debtor on its public organic
> record is "Able Persons of America Inc." A number of filings have been
> made against this debtor, using the names below. Which of these filings
> will be found by a searcher who uses the debtor's name?
>
> **A.** Able Person of America Inc.
> **B.** Able Persons USA Inc.
> **C.** Able Persons of America.
> **D.** Abel Persons of America Inc.

Analysis.   Section 9-506(c) provides that "[i]f a search of the records of the filing office under the debtor's correct name, using the filing office's standard search logic, if any, would disclose a financing statement that fails sufficiently to provide the name of the debtor in accordance with Section 9-503(a), the name provided does not make the financing statement seriously misleading." Under the facts you were given regarding the search logic in this particular jurisdiction, there must be an exact match, except that the entity abbreviation is disregarded. Here, only response **C** would be found by the search logic; the other choices would not be disclosed by the search. Therefore, only the filing that uses the name in **C** is an effective filing.

4. *Identification of the Collateral: § 9-502(a)(3)*

Other than the debtor's name, the most frequent source of problems with financing statements is the requirement that it "indicates the collateral covered by the financing statement." Review the discussion of collateral description for purposes of the security agreement in Chapter 6.D. The rules are different for the description of collateral in the financing statement, because the financing statement serves a different purpose. The purpose of the description in the security agreement is for purposes of attachment: as a matter of contract, the security interest only attaches to the collateral described in the agreement. The purpose of the financing statement is merely to give inquiry notice to a searcher. Once a party has found the financing statement, they have other ways to discover exactly what is covered by the security agreement. See § 9-210.

Therefore, the description in the financing statement can generally be broader than the description in the security agreement. Note that while many drafters include it, there is no need to mention after-acquired collateral in the financing statement. We saw in Chapter 7.D that the prudent creditor taking a security interest in collateral that frequently turns over, such as accounts or inventory, will make clear in the security agreement that the security interest attaches to after-acquired accounts or inventory. But for purposes of the financing statement, it is sufficient to identify the collateral merely as "accounts" or "inventory." Some drafters include in the financing statement a reference to the "proceeds or products" of collateral, but this language is also unnecessary.

However, § 9-504 provides that "[a] financing statement sufficiently indicates the collateral that it covers if the financing statement provides . . . a description of the collateral pursuant to Section 9-108." Therefore, when describing collateral, the same rules apply. We saw in Chapter 6.D that § 9-108(e), provides that "[a] description only by type of collateral defined in [the Uniform Commercial Code] is an insufficient description of: (1) a commercial tort claim; or (2) in a consumer transaction, consumer goods, a security entitlement, a securities account, or a commodity account." So for purposes of both the security agreement and the financing statement, the particular collateral must be identified in these two situations.

Unlike the description for purposes of the security agreement, however, § 9-504(2) permits a supergeneric description in the financing statement. As an alternative to the § 9-108 description of the collateral, the financing statement may contain "an indication that the financing statement covers all assets or all personal property." Therefore, the financing statement, unlike the security agreement, may contain a description such as "all personal property of debtor."

Some commentators talk about a "double filter" test to determine whether the security interest has attached to the collateral and whether the security interest is perfected. Under this test, only the narrowest description in both the security agreement and the financing statement passes through both filters, resulting in both attachment and perfection only with respect to that collateral. Let's look at some examples.

Question 11. At the time the security agreement is executed, a debtor owns an X-10 copy machine. The security agreement describes the collateral as "all of debtor's equipment," and the financing statement describes the collateral as "X-10 copy machine." To what collateral does the creditor's security interest attach, and in what collateral is the security interest perfected?

A. Attached in all equipment and perfected in all equipment.
B. Attached in the X-10 copy machine and perfected in all equipment.
C. Attached in the X-10 copy machine and perfected only in the X-10 copy machine.
D. Attached in all equipment and perfected only in the X-10 copy machine.

Analysis.   Recall from Chapter 6.A that the security interest attaches to collateral described in the security agreement. Here, that is "all of debtor's equipment." Therefore, responses **B** and **C** must be incorrect. However, only the X-10 copy machine passes through the filter of the financing statement, so the security interest is perfected only as to it. Therefore, **A** is incorrect, and **D** is correct. Obviously this is not how a creditor should complete a financing statement; in order to perfect all of the collateral, the scope of the collateral described in the financing statement should be the same or larger than that described in the security agreement.

Question 12. At the time the security agreement is executed, a debtor owns an X-10 copy machine. The security agreement describes the collateral as "X-10 copy machine," and the financing statement describes the collateral as "equipment." To what collateral does the creditor's security interest attach, and in what collateral is the security interest perfected?

A. Attached in all equipment and perfected in all equipment.
B. Attached in the X-10 copy machine and perfected in all equipment.
C. Attached in the X-10 copy machine and perfected only in the X-10 copy machine.
D. Attached in all equipment and perfected only in the X-10 copy machine.

Analysis.   Recall from Chapter 6.A that the security interest attaches to collateral described in the security agreement. Here, that is "X-10 copy machine." Therefore, responses **A** and **D** must be incorrect. "Equipment" is a proper category to use in a financing statement to put searchers on inquiry notice that there may be a security interest in equipment. However, in order to be perfected, a security interest must attach. Here, only the X-10 copy machine passes through the filter of attachment and perfection, so the security interest is perfected only as to it. Therefore, **B** is incorrect, and **C** is correct. This is a proper way for a creditor to describe the collateral in a financing statement, especially if the creditor contemplates more transactions with the debtor. Since it is already perfected with respect to equipment, the creditor would not have to file each time debtor granted a security agreement in another piece of equipment. If this is a one-shot deal, however, and the creditor does not contemplate further dealings with this debtor, it might consider limiting the description in the financing statement to the same collateral described in the security agreement.

D. Where Is It Filed?

1. *Choice of Law*

Once the filing creditor has properly completed the financing statement, it must determine where to file it. Let's first review choice of law. Recall that the parties to a UCC transaction are generally free to choose the law that will govern their transaction. See § 1-301. However, if parties could choose where to file financing statements, the result would be a logistical nightmare, because third parties wouldn't have a clue where to search for the filings. It won't surprise you, then, that perfection represents an exception to the parties' usual freedom to choose the applicable law. Section 1-301(g) provides:

> Where one of the following provisions of this Act specifies the applicable law, that provision governs and a contrary agreement is effective only to the extent permitted by the law (including the conflict of laws rules) so specified:
>
> . . .
>
> Law governing perfection, the effect of perfection or nonperfection, and the priority of security interests and agricultural liens. Sections 9-301 through 9-307.

2. *In What State Is the Debtor Located?*

In order to determine the law that governs perfection, let's look at the sections to which § 1-301 referred us:

> **§ 9-301. Law Governing Perfection and Priority of Security Interests.**
> Except as otherwise provided in Sections 9-303 through 9-306, the following rules determine the law governing perfection, the effect of perfection or nonperfection, and the priority of a security interest in collateral:
> (1) Except as otherwise provided in this section, while a debtor is located in a jurisdiction, the local law of that jurisdiction governs perfection, the effect of perfection or nonperfection, and the priority of a security interest in collateral.

(2) While collateral is located in a jurisdiction, the local law of that jurisdiction governs perfection, the effect of perfection or nonperfection, and the priority of a possessory security interest in that collateral.

You have to read subsections (1) and (2) very carefully to determine whether perfection is governed by the jurisdiction where the debtor is located or where the collateral is located. The key is the word *possessory* in subsection (2): the jurisdiction where the collateral is located is the relevant jurisdiction only when the security interest is possessory, that is, when the creditor has possession of the collateral. In all other cases, we need to look at the rules in the jurisdiction where the debtor is located.

We determine the location of a debtor by looking to § 9-307:

§ 9-307. Location of Debtor.

(a) **"Place of business."** In this section, "place of business" means a place where a debtor conducts its affairs.

(b) **Debtor's location: general rules.** Except as otherwise provided in this section, the following rules determine a debtor's location:

(1) A debtor who is an individual is located at the individual's principal residence.

(2) A debtor that is an organization and has only one place of business is located at its place of business.

(3) A debtor that is an organization and has more than one place of business is located at its chief executive office.

(c) **Limitation of applicability of subsection (b).** Subsection (b) applies only if a debtor's residence, place of business, or chief executive office, as applicable, is located in a jurisdiction whose law generally requires information concerning the existence of a nonpossessory security interest to be made generally available in a filing, recording, or registration system as a condition or result of the security interest's obtaining priority over the rights of a lien creditor with respect to the collateral. If subsection (b) does not apply, the debtor is located in the District of Columbia.

(d) **Continuation of location: cessation of existence, etc.** A person that ceases to exist, have a residence, or have a place of business continues to be located in the jurisdiction specified by subsections (b) and (c).

(e) **Location of registered organization organized under State law.** A registered organization that is organized under the law of a State is located in that State.

(f) **Location of registered organization organized under federal law; bank branches and agencies.** Except as otherwise provided in subsection (i), a registered organization that is organized under the law of the United States and a branch or agency of a bank that is not organized under the law of the United States or a State are located:

(1) in the State that the law of the United States designates, if the law designates a State of location;

(2) in the State that the registered organization, branch, or agency designates, if the law of the United States authorizes the registered organization, branch, or agency to designate its State of location, including by designating its main office, home office, or other comparable office; or

(3) in the District of Columbia, if neither paragraph (1) nor paragraph (2) applies.

(g) **Continuation of location: change in status of registered organization.** A registered organization continues to be located in the jurisdiction specified by subsection (e) or (f) notwithstanding:

(1) the suspension, revocation, forfeiture, or lapse of the registered organization's status as such in its jurisdiction of organization; or

(2) the dissolution, winding up, or cancellation of the existence of the registered organization.

(h) **Location of United States.** The United States is located in the District of Columbia.

(i) **Location of foreign bank branch or agency if licensed in only one state.** A branch or agency of a bank that is not organized under the law of the United States or a State is located in the State in which the branch or agency is licensed, if all branches and agencies of the bank are licensed in only one State.

(j) **Location of foreign air carrier.** A foreign air carrier under the Federal Aviation Act of 1958, as amended, is located at the designated office of the agent upon which service of process may be made on behalf of the carrier.

(k) **Section applies only to this part.** This section applies only for purposes of this part.

As we saw earlier, for purposes of filing, §§ 9-307(b) and (e) enumerate three categories of debtors: an individual, an organization, and a registered organization. Once we understand which category a debtor falls into, it is easy to determine the jurisdiction in which to look for the rules on perfection. For individuals, § 9-307(b)(1) provides that it is the state in which the individual has his or her principal residence; for registered organizations, § 9-307(e) provides that it is the state under which they are organized; for other organizations, §§ 9-307(b)(2) and (3) provide that if it has only one place of business, it is the state in which it has that place of business, and if it has more than one place of business, it is where it has its chief executive office. Note that the prudent creditor will ask the debtor to provide the creditor with documentation that indicates where it is located.

Question 13. Tom Joad, a resident of Oklahoma, entered into a security agreement by pledging his wedding ring at a pawnshop in Las Vegas, Nevada, that is owned by a California corporation. Which state's laws govern whether the security interest is perfected?

A. Oklahoma.
B. California.
C. Nevada, because it is the state in which the security agreement was made.
D. Nevada, because it is the state in which the collateral is located.

Analysis. The key to this question is to note that because the debtor has pledged the collateral, it is in the *possession* of the creditor, so the security is possessory. Section § 9-301(2) provides:

> (2) While collateral is located in a jurisdiction, the local law of that jurisdiction governs perfection, the effect of perfection or nonperfection, and the priority of a possessory security interest in that collateral.

Since the law of the jurisdiction where the collateral is located governs the place of filing, that jurisdiction is Nevada. The correct response is **D.**

Question 14. Donald R. Willett lives in Williamstown, Massachusetts. Willett, who is known in the business community as "Don," operates an accounting business called DRW Accounting as a sole proprietorship across the state line in Vermont. Willett bought a new computer system for his business on credit from Purple Cow Computer Co. of Troy, New York, and granted Purple Cow a security interest in the computer system. To perfect its security interest, where should Purple Cow file its financing statement?

A. Massachusetts.
B. Vermont.
C. New York.
D. Washington, D.C.

Analysis. Under the general rule of § 9-301, a security interest is filed where the debtor is located. In order to determine where the debtor is located, we must determine whether the debtor is an individual, an organization, or a registered organization. This debtor is doing business as DRW Accounting, but the legal entity is an individual. Section 9-307(b)(1) provides that "a debtor who is an individual is located at the individual's principal residence." Here, the debtor's principal residence is in Massachusetts. Therefore, the correct response is **A.**

Question 15. Able, who lives in Massachusetts, and Baker, who lives in New York, form a general partnership, called AB Services, that has its only office in Vermont. First Bank takes a security interest in assets of AB Services. Where should First Bank file the financing statement?

A. Massachusetts.
B. New York.
C. Both Massachusetts and New York.
D. Vermont.

Analysis.   Under the general rule of § 9-301, a security interest is filed where the debtor is located. In order to determine where the debtor is located, we must determine whether the debtor is an individual, an organization, or a registered organization. AB Services is a general partnership; since states do not require this kind of organization to be registered, it is an organization for purposes of § 9-301. Section 9-307(b)(2) provides that if an organization is not a registered organization, then "a debtor that is an organization and has only one place of business is located at its place of business." Here, AB Services has only one place of business. It is in Vermont, so the debtor is located in Vermont, and **D** is the correct response.

Question 16. Big Sky Baking, Inc., is a Wyoming corporation with its only place of business in Fort Mercy, Colorado. First Bank of New York, a Delaware corporation that has its principal office in New York, and Big Sky enter into a security agreement that has a choice of law provision that states, "This agreement shall be governed by the law of New York." In which state should First Bank file the financing statement?

A. Wyoming.
B. Colorado.
C. Delaware.
D. New York.

Analysis.   According to § 1-301, choice of law clauses do not apply to the law governing perfection. Under the general rule of § 9-301, a security interest is filed where the debtor is located. Under § 9-307(e), "a registered organization that is organized under the law of a State is located in that State." Since Big Sky Baking, Inc. is a registered organization organized under the law of Wyoming, it is located in Wyoming, so that is where First Bank should file the financing statement. The correct response is **A**.

You may wonder why the parties included a choice of law provision if it was not effective under the Code. The answer is that the choice of law provision is not effective for the purpose of determining the place for perfection, but it is effective for other purposes. For example, if a question arose involving a contract issue, such as parol evidence or interpretation, that issue would be resolved using the chosen law, the law of New York.

Question 17. *Statute reader.* An American bank took a security interest in property of Offshore Gambling, Ltd., a corporation that is incorporated in Antigua, has its chief executive office in Antigua, and has its only American office in Connecticut. The security agreement provides that financing statements are effective if filed in New York. The bank has discovered that there is no office in Antigua designated for filing financing statements, but there is an office for filing real estate records. Where should the bank file the financing statement? (One benefit of reading § 9-307 is that it also tells you where Elvis is located.)

A. Connecticut.
B. New York.
C. The office designated for the filing of real estate records in Antigua.
D. Washington, D.C.

Analysis.   This question shows that the drafters of Article 9 tried to supply an answer for every question. Section 1-301 provides that a choice of law provision is not effective if sections 9-301 through 9-307 apply, and here they do, so response **B** is not correct. This organization is not a registered organization that is organized under the law of a State, so § 9-307(e) does not apply. Since the debtor is an organization, we would look to § 9-307(b) and find that its chief executive office is in Antigua. However, § 9-307(c) provides that subsection (b) applies only if that place has a filing office. If it does not, and you are told in the facts that Antigua does not, then the debtor is located in Washington, D.C. Therefore, **D** is the correct response.

Did you also discover where Elvis is? Section 9-307(d) provides that "A person that ceases to exist . . . continues to be located in the jurisdiction specified by subsections (b) and (c)." Subsection (b)(1) provides that "an individual is located at the individual's principal residence." Therefore, Elvis must still be located at Graceland in Tennessee!

3.   *Where Is It Filed in That State?*

Once we have found which jurisdiction's rules govern perfection, finding the right place to file in that jurisdiction is simple. Section 9-501 provides as follows:

§ **9-501. Filing Office.**

(a) **Filing offices.** Except as otherwise provided in subsection (b), if the local law of this State governs perfection of a security interest or agricultural lien, the office in which to file a financing statement to perfect the security interest or agricultural lien is:

> (1) the office designated for the filing or recording of a record of a mortgage on the related real property, if:
>
> > (A) the collateral is as-extracted collateral or timber to be cut; or
> >
> > (B) the financing statement is filed as a fixture filing and the collateral is goods that are or are to become fixtures; or
>
> (2) the office of [ ] [or any office duly authorized by [ ]], in all other cases, including a case in which the collateral is goods that are or are to become fixtures and the financing statement is not filed as a fixture filing.

In most jurisdictions, the brackets in § 9-501(a)(2) are filled in with the words "the Secretary of State." So you file with the Secretary of State, except that you file where real property records are filed if the collateral closely resembles real property, such as minerals in the ground, standing timber, or fixtures. In most jurisdictions, real property records are filed in the county where the real property is located.

Question 18. Financing statements as described below need to be filed in Arizona. In Arizona, the brackets in § 9-501(a)(2) are filled in with "Secretary of State." Below is the description of collateral in four financing statements. Which one of these financing statements would *not* be filed in the office of the Secretary of State?

A. The furniture of John McCain, whose principal residence is in Phoenix, Arizona, but who keeps the furniture at his residence in Virginia while he works in Washington, D.C.

B. The inventory of Arizona Farm Machinery Sales and Service, Inc., an Arizona corporation with its principal place of business in Sedona, Arizona.

C. The crops and farm equipment of James Murnion, who lives in Gila County, Arizona.

D. Timber to be cut from property in Long Valley, Arizona, belonging to Oak Creek Inc., an Arizona Corporation.

Analysis. According to § 9-501(a)(2), filings are generally made in the office of the Secretary of State. There is an exception for "timber to be cut" in § 9-501(a)(1)(A), so the correct response is **D**. Because timber to be cut is affixed to real property, that filing is made where an interest in real property would be filed, which in Arizona, like most jurisdictions, is the county.

Note on test-taking. You had to carefully read this question to see that it asked you which financing statement would *not* be filed in the office of the Secretary of State; it was testing for the exception to the general rule.

E.   When Is It Filed?

A financing statement can be initially filed at any time—*before or after the security interest comes into existence.* See § 9-502(d). Because the time of filing controls a number of possible priority contests, a secured party should file its financing statement as soon as possible. Recall from part B of this chapter that to secure priority, a creditor may file a financing statement even before the security agreement has been signed. In that event, however, recall that the creditor should obtain the debtor's authenticated authorization. If the creditor does not, and later enters into a security agreement with the debtor, then the debtor will be deemed to have ratified the earlier filing.

Question 19. On October 1, Creditor 1 signed a security agreement with Debtor. Creditor 1 brought its financing statement and filing fee to the clerk, who accepted it but then inadvertently misplaced it. On October 2, Creditor 2 signed a security agreement with Debtor. That same day, Creditor 2 brought its financing statement and filing fee to the clerk, who accepted and indexed it. On October 3, the clerk found Creditor 1's financing statement and indexed it. Assuming (as we will see later) that the first secured party to file or perfect has priority, which creditor has priority?

A. Creditor 1, because it was first to file.
B. Creditor 2, because it was first to file.
C. Creditor 1, because its financing statement was first to be indexed and appear in the filings.
D. Creditor 2, because its financing statement was first to be indexed and appear in the filings.

Analysis.   Section 9-516(a) provides:

What Constitutes Filing; Effectiveness of Filing.
        (a) **What constitutes filing.** Except as otherwise provided in subsection (b), communication of a record to a filing office and tender of the filing fee or acceptance of the record by the filing office constitutes filing.

According to this rule, Creditor 1 filed on October 1, and Creditor 2 filed on October 2. Under § 9-322(a)(1), the first to file or perfect has priority. Since Creditor 1 was the first to file, **A** is the correct response.

> **Question 20**. On October 1, Creditor 1 signed a security agreement with Debtor and brought its financing statement and filing fee to the clerk, who accepted it. On October 2, with knowledge that Debtor had a security agreement with Creditor 1, Creditor 2 checked the index for filings against Debtor, found nothing, signed a security agreement with Debtor, and filed a financing statement. On October 3, Creditor 1's financing statement was indexed and appeared in the filings. On October 4, Creditor 2's financing statement was indexed and appeared in the filings. On November 1, Debtor defaulted as to both creditors. Which creditor has priority?
>
> **A.** Creditor 1, because it was first to file.
> **B.** Creditor 1, because it was first to be indexed and appear in the filings.
> **C.** Creditor 1, because Creditor 2 had knowledge of its security interest when it filed.
> **D.** Creditor 2, because it reasonably relied on the absence of any filings.

Analysis. According to the rule of § 9-516(a) and the priority rule of § 9-322(a)(1), the outcome is the same as in the previous question: the first secured creditor to file or perfect has priority. Since Creditor 1 was the first to file, **A** is the correct response.

 This outcome may not seem fair to Creditor 2, who made a reasonable effort to search the records before filing. What should Creditor 2 do next time to keep this from happening? Recall that the financing statement may be filed at any time. See Official Comment 2 to § 9-502, which provides as follows:

> 2. **"Notice Filing."** This section adopts the system of "notice filing." . . . The financing statement may be filed before the security interest attaches or thereafter. See subsection (d). See also Section 9-308(a) (contemplating situations in which a financing statement is filed before a security interest attaches).

With authorization from the debtor, Creditor 2 could "pre-file" weeks before it planned to enter the security agreement. If on the day for the signing of the security agreement, its financing statement and no other filing showed up, it could still be assured of priority; if another filing showed up, it could determine the priority before it proceeded.

F.   Closers

> **Question 21.** On February 1, without authorization from the debtor, a bank filed a financing statement covering debtor's inventory and accounts. On March 1, the debtor and the bank were unable to agree to

the terms of a security agreement, and they walked away from the deal. What is the consequence of the bank filing the financing statement?

A. It is not an effective filing, so there are no consequences.
B. It is an effective filing in inventory and accounts as of February 1.
C. The filing was not authorized, but because the creditor acted in good faith, the debtor has no remedies.
D. The filing was not authorized, so the debtor has the remedies provided in § 9-625.

Analysis.   The filing was not authorized since it was not affirmatively authorized by the debtor and the parties did not enter into a security agreement. See § 9-509(a). Because it was not filed by a person authorized to file it, the filing is not effective. See § 9-510(a). Under § 9-625, a debtor may secure remedies against a party who does not comply with Article 9. This includes any actual losses under § 9-625(b) and statutory damages under § 9-625(e). The correct response is **D.** The creditor should have obtained authorization to file. To prevent harm after the deal fell through, the creditor could file the termination statement that will be discussed in Chapter 13.B.

Question 22. You are a creditor contemplating entering into a security agreement with a law firm. You plan to take a security interest in the debtor's office furniture. You conduct a search of the filings, and you find that a creditor has filed a financing statement against that debtor. Part 4 of that financing statement has been filled in as follows: "4. This FINANCING STATEMENT covers the following collateral: equipment." You ask the debtor to contact the creditor to request a list of collateral. The other creditor furnishes a security agreement showing that it has taken a security interest in a copy machine. If you are a prudent creditor who wants to be sure it has priority in collateral, should you go ahead with the transaction?

A. Yes, because even if the other creditor's filing is effective, you would be the first to file with respect to office furniture.
B. Yes, because the other filing is not effective since "equipment" is too broad a description of the collateral.
C. No, because at the present time, a filing would not give you priority with respect to office furniture.
D. No, because at some future time you might not have priority with respect to office furniture.

Analysis.   In Question 1, we had this same question, but only up to the point that we requested further information. Now we have the information that the other creditor took a security interest in a copy machine but in its filed financing statement described the collateral as "equipment." What is the effect of that? The description of the collateral was appropriate under § 9-502(a)(3), because it put you on notice that the creditor may have a security agreement. Therefore, **B** cannot be correct, because the filing was effective. However, because perfection requires attachment, the other creditor's financing statement perfected an interest only in the copy machine and not in any other equipment; the copy machine is the only collateral to pass through the "double filter" of attachment and perfection. Therefore, **C** is not correct because a present filing would give you priority with respect to office furniture.

Before you conclude that **A** is correct, let's time travel. Suppose, in the future, the law firm grants the other creditor a security interest in office furniture. What is the effect of that? Its security interest would then attach to furniture. And recall that under § 9-502(d) a financing statement may be filed at any time, even before attachment. Because furniture is equipment, that creditor has already filed with respect to furniture when it filed describing the collateral as "equipment." Even though the security interest was not perfected until that later date of attachment, it was *filed* earlier, and priority goes to the first to perfect *or* file. Therefore, since the other creditor would be the first to perfect or file with respect to equipment, you would not have priority in the office furniture under that scenario. So **D** is the correct response. In Chapter 16, we will see what a secured creditor can do to protect itself when it finds an earlier filing in the same collateral.

Burnham's Picks

Question 1	D
Question 2	D
Question 3	D
Question 4	D
Question 5	A
Question 6	D
Question 7	B
Question 8	B
Question 9	C
Question 10	C
Question 11	D
Question 12	C
Question 13	D
Question 14	A
Question 15	D
Question 16	A

Question 17	**D**
Question 18	**D**
Question 19	**A**
Question 20	**A**
Question 21	**D**
Question 22	**D**

13

Amendments to the Initial Filing

A. Introduction

Recall that, using the vocabulary introduced in Chapter 12, we generally refer to the secured creditor who files a financing statement as the *filing creditor* or the *filer* and to the creditor who searches for financing statements as the *searching creditor* or the *searcher*. When a certain period of time has passed, or when circumstances change, the filing creditor must amend the filed financing statement to inform the searching creditor of any changes. Changes to a financing statement are called *amendments*. See § 9-512. The most significant amendments are made for the following purposes:

- Termination (terminating the effectiveness of the filing)
- Continuation (continuing the term of the filing)
- Changing the name of the debtor
- Adding or deleting collateral

B.   Termination

The filing of a Termination Statement, just as it sounds, terminates the effectiveness of a financing statement. See Line 2 of the UCC Financing Statement Amendment Model Form in § 9-521(b), which provides, "TERMINATION: Effectiveness of the Financing Statement identified above is terminated with respect to security interest(s) of the Secured Party authorizing this Termination Statement." If the obligation has been satisfied, the creditor must file a Termination Statement within one month when the collateral is consumer goods and within 20 days of demand in all other cases. See § 9-513. Do you see why different rules are applied to consumer and commercial transactions? A consumer transaction is likely to be a one-shot deal; if the obligation has been paid, the consumer doesn't need to have a filed financing statement hanging over his or her head. On the other hand, a commercial lender and a debtor may have a continuing relationship. If one obligation is paid off, another may follow, and the filed financing statement will give the creditor priority in the later transaction. If the creditor does not comply with the termination requirements, the debtor is authorized to make the filing. See § 9-509(d).

The ease with which filings can be made may lead to unauthorized filings, called *bogus* filings in the Official Comments. Recall that § 9-509(a) provides that before filing a financing statement, the secured party must obtain authorization from the debtor in an authenticated record and that § 9-509(b) provides that authentication of the security agreement authorizes the secured party to file a financing statement covering the collateral described in the security agreement. If an unauthorized filing is made, § 9-510(a) provides that the financing statement is not effective to the extent that it is unauthorized.

A bogus filing might be made by a purported creditor. For example, a student could file a financing statement listing Scott J. Burnham as the name of the debtor and "all personal property" as the description of the collateral. While that would not give that purported creditor any rights against the debtor, it might have the practical effect of blocking the debtor from obtaining additional secured credit if creditors from which he sought credit searched the records and found the filing. What can the debtor do to convince those creditors that the filing is not effective? First, he can request that the creditor file a termination statement and, if it is not forthcoming, file it himself. See § 9-513 and Official Comment 3. Second, he may file an information statement, formerly known as a correction statement. See § 9-518. Third, he may attempt to recover actual damages caused by the purported creditor's failure to comply with Article 9 under § 9-625(b) and, in addition, $500 statutory damages under § 9-625(e).

The fact that the debtor can make such filings suggests how easy it is for the debtor to make a bogus filing. For example, First Bank has a security interest in all the assets of the John Smith law firm. Other creditors find First

Bank's filing and refuse to extend credit to Smith because they would not have priority. Desperate for credit, Smith files a termination statement purportedly terminating the effectiveness of First Bank's filing. Is the perfection of First Bank's security interest terminated? The answer is no. Section 9-513(d) provides that "[e]xcept as otherwise provided in Section 9-510," the financing statement ceases to be effective upon the filing of a termination statement. But § 9-510(a) provides that "a filed record is effective only to the extent that it was filed by a person that may file it under Section 9-509." And § 9-509(d) (2) provides that the debtor is entitled to file a termination statement only if the secured party has failed to do so under § 9-513. So while the termination statement is not effective under Article 9, the practical problem is that searching creditors will find it difficult to determine whether it is effective or not.

In either of these cases of bogus filing, if the party who was injured was able to demonstrate to the filing clerk that the filing was bogus (which shouldn't be very hard to do), should the clerk remove the bogus filing? The answer in the official text of Article 9 is no. See §§ 9-520(a), 9-516(b), 9-519(g), and Official Comment 6. The clerks are supposed to be passive and simply put whatever is filed into an "open drawer;" the searcher can open the drawer and try to make sense of all the filings found in it. In some jurisdictions, clerks who were concerned about this restriction on their authority got their legislatures to pass nonuniform amendments to Article 9. An example of one of these nonuniform Article 9 provisions is Montana Code Annotated § 30-9A-420, which provides as follows:

30-9A-420. Removal of improper or fraudulent liens.

> (1) If a filing officer receives a complaint or has reason to believe that a lien submitted or filed with the filing officer's office is improper or fraudulent, the filing officer may reject the submission or remove the filing from existing files after giving notice and an opportunity to respond to the secured party.

> (2) A person adversely affected by a lien that is determined to be improper or fraudulent by the filing officer may recover treble damages from the person responsible for submitting the lien.

Abuses of the filing system can also be dealt with outside of Article 9. See Official Comment 3 to § 9-518, which disapproves of the nonuniform provisions. It provides:

> 3. **Resort to Other Law**. This Article cannot provide a satisfactory or complete solution to problems caused by misuse of the public records. The problem of "bogus" filings is not limited to the UCC filing system but extends to the real-property records, as well. A summary judicial procedure for correcting the public records and criminal penalties for those who misuse the filing and recording systems are likely to be more effective and put less strain on the filing system than provisions authorizing or requiring action by filing and recording offices.

You may have noticed, by the way, that no signatures (I mean "authentications") are required on a financing statement. Some people think a signature requirement would deter bogus filers, but others think the bogus filer would just use a false signature. Again, the drafters of Article 9 believe the filing clerks should not get involved in this issue. See Official Comment 3 to § 9-502, which concludes, "the filing office is neither obligated nor permitted to inquire into issues of authorization. See Section 9-520(a)."

Question 1. On February 1, Creditor 1 files a financing statement that it is authorized to file against Debtor. On March 1, Debtor wrongfully files a Termination Statement terminating Creditor 1's financing statement. On March 3, seeing that a termination statement has been filed, the clerk in the recording office removes Creditor 1's financing statement and the termination statement from the file. On April 1, Creditor 2 conducts a search under the name of Debtor, finds nothing, enters into a security agreement, and files a financing statement. Assuming the official text of Article 9 is the law of the state, who has priority as between Creditor 1 and Creditor 2?

A. Creditor 1, because it was first to file a financing statement.
B. Creditor 1, because its claim is more equitable under the circumstances.
C. Creditor 2, because a filed termination statement is presumed to be effective.
D. Creditor 2, because it reasonably relied on the absence of other filings when it filed.

Analysis.   Debtor was not authorized to file a termination statement, so that filing is of no effect. Under the "open drawer" policy, the clerk should have made both filings available for Creditor 2 to determine which filings were effective. Because Creditor 1 complied with the filing requirements and its filing was not effectively terminated, its filing is effective. **A** is therefore the best response.

In these circumstances, Creditor 2 might have a claim against the state. Some states have a fund or self-insure to cover these claims. Note that if the jurisdiction has enacted a nonuniform amendment such as Montana § 30-9A-420, the result would be the same. That provision gives the clerk authority to remove a bogus termination statement, such as the one Debtor filed, but it does not give the clerk authority to remove a filing that, like Creditor 1's, was not bogus.

C.   Continuation

Subject to very limited exceptions, § 9-515(a) provides that "a filed financing statement is effective for a period of five years after the date of filing." Note that the Code does not establish the date of filing itself. This is established by the administrative regulations of each state, which can often be found at the website of the department where filings are made. To continue perfection, § 9-515(d) provides that "[a] continuation statement may be filed only within six months before the expiration of the five year period." The same Amendment form is filed for Continuation as for Termination. See Line 4 of the UCC Financing Statement Amendment Model Form in § 9-521(b), which provides, "CONTINUATION: Effectiveness of the Financing Statement identified above with respect to security interest(s) of the Secured Party authorizing this Continuation Statement is continued for the additional period provided by applicable law."

Like attorneys, creditors should have a good system to remind them when to file documents such as a continuation statement (such a system is often referred to as a "tickler"). After the continuation statement is effectively filed, perfection is continued for another five years from the end of the original five-year period. If it is not effectively filed, § 9-510(c) provides that the filing is ineffective. This means that it does not have the effect of a financing statement.

Question 2. A creditor files a financing statement on July 1, 2017. On June 30, 2021, the creditor files a continuation statement. On what date does the effectiveness of the financing statement terminate?

A. Five years from July 1, 2017.
B. Five years from June 30, 2021.
C. Five years from July 1, 2022.
D. It remains effective until a termination statement is filed.

Analysis.   Under § 9-515, the initial filing is effective for five years, so its effectiveness would terminate five years from July 1, 2017. To be effective, a continuation statement may be filed "only within six months before the expiration of the five-year period." Here, the continuation was not timely filed, for it was filed 12 months before the expiration of the five-year period. Therefore, it does not effectively continue the effectiveness of the financing statement. The effectiveness of the original filing terminates five years from July 1, 2017. So the correct response is **A.**

Question 3. A creditor files a financing statement on July 1, 2017. On August 1, 2022, the creditor files a continuation statement. What is the status of perfection of the security interest after that filing?

A. The security interest was perfected for five years from July 1, 2017, at which time perfection lapsed.
B. The security interest was perfected for five years from July 1, 2017, at which time perfection was terminated.

> **C.** The security interest was perfected for five years from July 1, 2017 and continues for another five years because the continuation statement was filed within six months from the expiration of the five-year period.
>
> **D.** The security interest was perfected for five years from July 1, 2017 and is perfected for another five years beginning August 1, 2022 because the improperly filed continuation statement acts like a new filing.

Analysis.   Section 9-515(d) provides that "[a] continuation statement may be filed only within six months *before* the expiration of the five year period." Since this continuation statement was filed *after* the expiration of the five-year period, it is not timely filed. **C** is incorrect. According to § 9-510(c), a continuation statement that is not timely filed is ineffective. Therefore, **D** is incorrect. The perfection therefore ended five years after the initial filing. The correct vocabulary here is that it lapsed, since termination requires an affirmative act. The correct response is **A**.

D.   Other Amendments

Sometimes a refiling is necessary other than for the purpose of continuation. A number of changes can occur during the five-year period, including:

1. change in the debtor's location
2. change in the debtor's name
3. transfer of the collateral to a new location
4. transfer of the collateral to a new debtor
5. change in the characterization of the collateral
6. exchange of the collateral for proceeds with a different characterization

If the policy was to require refiling for every change, then secured parties would have to monitor their debtors' every activity. The expense of such policing could be staggering. On the other hand, if refiling is not required, third parties cannot rely on the accuracy of the information in the filing system. The Code tries to balance these interests of filing creditors and searching creditors. Let's look at each of these situations in turn.

1.   Change of Debtor's Location

When a debtor moves to a new jurisdiction, new creditors conducting a search may not be aware of where they need to look to find filings. Under § 9-316(a)(2), the interests of both the filing creditor and the searching creditor are balanced when the debtor's location changes:

§ 9-316. Effect of Change in Governing Law.

(a) **General rule: effect on perfection of change in governing law.** A security interest perfected pursuant to the law of the jurisdiction designated in Section 9-301(1) or 9-305(c) remains perfected until the earliest of:

> (1) the time perfection would have ceased under the law of that jurisdiction;

> (2) the expiration of four months after a change of the debtor's location to another jurisdiction.

Under this rule, the filing creditor has four months after the change in location to discover that the debtor has relocated and to refile in the new location to continue the perfection of security interests perfected in the "old" location. Note, however, that filings in the old jurisdiction made during the four-month grace period are not effective. As a practical matter, existing creditors should monitor their debtors to the extent of knowing where they are located at least every four months; prospective creditors should ask their debtors if they have been located in the jurisdiction for at least four months.

This rule addresses only a security interest that was perfected *before* the debtor changed its location. A security interest in after-acquired property that attached in the new jurisdiction would not be perfected because it was not perfected pursuant to the law of the original jurisdiction. This issue was addressed in Amended Article 9, which provides in § 9-316(h)(1):

> (h) [**Effect on filed financing statement of change in governing law.**] The following rules apply to collateral to which a security interest attaches within four months after the debtor changes its location to another jurisdiction:

> > (1) A financing statement filed before the change pursuant to the law of the jurisdiction designated in Section 9-301(1) or 9-305(c) is effective to perfect a security interest in the collateral if the financing statement would have been effective to perfect a security interest in the collateral had the debtor not changed its location.

Pursuant to the amendment, a security interest in after-acquired property also continues for the four-month period after the debtor changes its location. Thus, if the creditor files during the four-month period, perfection continues both in collateral that existed prior to the relocation and in collateral to which the security interest attached after the relocation.

What happens if the creditor fails to file during the four-month period? That is a bit tricky. Section 9-316(b) provides:

> If the security interest does not become perfected under the law of the other jurisdiction before the earliest time or event, it becomes unperfected and is deemed never to have been perfected as against a purchaser of the collateral for value.

So the answer depends on whether the other party claiming the collateral is a "purchaser" for value. The definition of "purchaser" in § 1-201(b)(30) refers us to the definition of "purchase" in § 1-201(b)(29). This definition takes us a bit by surprise:

> (29) "Purchase" means taking by sale, lease, discount, negotiation, mortgage, pledge, lien, security interest, issue or re-issue, gift, or any other voluntary transaction creating an interest in property.

Under this definition, a party is a *purchaser* of the collateral if they take a security interest in the collateral. Therefore, if the original secured party fails to perfect during the four-month period, as against a secured party who took a security interest in the collateral during the four-month period, the security interest never would have been perfected. In other words, the perfection is retroactively lost if not perfected during that four-month period. However, as against a party who is not a purchaser, such as a bankruptcy trustee, the perfection continues during the four-month period and is lost only prospectively at the end of that period.

Question 4. On July 1, 2017, a secured creditor properly filed a financing statement against an individual debtor, Joseph Smith, in Ohio, the state in which Smith resided. On July 1, 2018, Smith moved to Utah. Which of the following statements is true?

A. The creditor has until four months from July 1, 2018, to file in Utah or the creditor loses its security interest.
B. The creditor has until four months from July 1, 2018, to file in Utah or the security interest becomes unperfected.
C. The security interest in the existing collateral will remain perfected even if the creditor does not refile in Utah.
D. The creditor has five years from July 1, 2017, to refile in Utah or the security interest becomes unperfected.

Analysis.   Under § 9-316, the security interest "remains perfected until the earliest of . . . the expiration of four months after a change of the debtor's location to another jurisdiction." Here, it remains perfected until four months from July 1, 2018, the time of the debtor's change of location. The correct response is **B.** It is important to note that **A** is not correct because even if perfection is lost, the security interest remains attached. Recall that outside of bankruptcy, filing and perfection are not relevant as between the creditor and the debtor, so the security interest remains good as against the debtor even if the creditor does not timely refile. It is only third parties who would be prejudiced by the change in location.

> **Question 5.** *Statute reader.* On July 1, 2017, a secured creditor properly filed a financing statement against an individual debtor, Joseph Smith, in Ohio, the state in which Smith resided. On May 1, 2022, Smith moved to Utah. For how long is perfection in Utah effective under § 9-316?
>
> **A.** Until five years from July 1, 2017.
> **B.** Until May 1, 2022.
> **C.** Until four months after May 1, 2022.
> **D.** It depends on what the law of Utah provides.

Analysis.   Note that § 9-316 provides that perfection is effective until "the earliest of: (1) the time perfection would have ceased under the law of that jurisdiction; (2) the expiration of four months after a change of the debtor's location to another jurisdiction."

This is careful drafting, for if the creditor always had four months to file, that might extend the effectiveness of the initial filing beyond five years. The language in § 9-316(a)(1) prevents that from happening. Under our facts, the time under subsection (1) is five years from July 1, 2017; the time under subsection (2) is four months after May 1, 2022. If the creditor had until four months from May 1 to file, that would extend the time of perfection to five years and two months. Under the statute, the creditor has until the *earliest* of those times, which is five years from July 1, 2017. Therefore, the correct response is **A.**

2. *Change of Debtor's Name*

We are here referring to a change in name only, and not to a transfer of the collateral. Because filing offices file financing statements in the debtor's name, creditors search by name. When Archie Leach becomes Cary Grant, financing statements indexed under "Archie Leach" will not be found by a creditor searching for "Cary Grant." When New Haven Growers Corp. becomes Yale Fruits Inc., financing statements indexed under "New Haven Growers" will not be found by a person searching for "Yale Fruits." Should the filing creditor be required to monitor the debtor and refile in the new name, or should the searching creditor be required to discover earlier names for the debtor?

Section 9-507(c) attempts to balance the competing interests and needs of filers and searchers. It provides:

§ 9-507. Effect of Certain Events on Effectiveness of Financing Statement.
    (a) **Disposition.** A filed financing statement remains effective with respect to collateral that is sold, exchanged, leased, licensed, or otherwise disposed of and in which a security interest or agricultural lien continues, even if the secured party knows of or consents to the disposition.

(b) **Information becoming seriously misleading.** Except as otherwise provided in subsection (c) and Section 9-508, a financing statement is not rendered ineffective if, after the financing statement is filed, the information provided in the financing statement becomes seriously misleading under Section 9-506.

(c) **Change in debtor's name.** If the name that a filed financing statement provides for a debtor becomes insufficient as the name of the debtor under Section 9-503(a) so that the financing statement becomes seriously misleading under Section 9-506:

> (1) the financing statement is effective to perfect a security interest in collateral acquired by the debtor before, or within four months after, the filed financing statement becomes seriously misleading; and

> (2) the financing statement is not effective to perfect a security interest in collateral acquired by the debtor more than four months after the filed financing statement becomes seriously misleading, unless an amendment to the financing statement which renders the financing statement not seriously misleading is filed within four months after the financing statement became seriously misleading.

Under this provision, action is required by the filing creditor only if the filing "becomes seriously misleading." What does that mean? Recall from Chapter 12.C.3 that § 9-506(c) provides that the filing is not seriously misleading if the filing office's "standard search logic" would find the filing. If the filing cannot be found because of a name change, and the filing creditor takes no action, then the original filing protects only (1) collateral existing at the time of the name change, and (2) after-acquired collateral acquired within four months of the name change. But the original filing is not effective to protect collateral acquired more than four months after the change. To perfect that collateral, the filing creditor must file an amendment to the financing statement within the four months.

Note that unlike the rule for the change of debtor's location discussed in Chapter 13.D.1, if the original creditor fails to file during the four-month period after a name change, perfection is not lost retroactively. Perfection continues both in existing collateral and collateral acquired after the name change for the four months after the name change, and is lost only prospectively at the end of the four-month period.

Question 6. On January 1, 2017, Creditor 1 obtains a security interest in the equipment and after-acquired equipment of Adams Corp. and perfects its security interest by filing. On January 1, 2018, Adams Corp. changes its name to Baker Corp. On January 1, 2019, Creditor 2 does a search of the appropriate filing system, finds no filings against Baker

> Corp., and files to perfect its security interest in the equipment and after-acquired equipment of Baker Corp. On January 1, 2020, Baker Corp. declares bankruptcy. What are the respective rights of Creditor 1 and Creditor 2 in the equipment of Baker Corp.?
>
> **A.** Creditor 1 has priority in the original and after-acquired equipment.
> **B.** Creditor 1 has priority in the original equipment, and Creditor 2 has priority in the after-acquired equipment.
> **C.** Creditor 1 has priority in the original equipment and equipment acquired within four months from January 1, 2018, and Creditor 2 has priority in equipment acquired after that.
> **D.** Creditor 1 has priority in the original equipment and equipment acquired until January 1, 2019, and Creditor 2 has priority in equipment acquired after January 1, 2019.

Analysis.   The answer is found in § 9-507(c), which provides:

> **Effect of Certain Events on Effectiveness of Financing Statement....**
>
>   (c) **Change in debtor's name**. If the name that a filed financing statement provides for a debtor becomes insufficient as the name of the debtor under Section 9-503(a) so that the financing statement becomes seriously misleading under Section 9-506:
>
>   (1) the financing statement is effective to perfect a security interest in collateral acquired by the debtor before, or within four months after, the filed financing statement becomes seriously misleading; and
>
>   (2) the financing statement is not effective to perfect a security interest in collateral acquired by the debtor more than four months after the filed financing statement becomes seriously misleading, unless an amendment to the financing statement which renders the financing statement not seriously misleading is filed within four months after the financing statement became seriously misleading.

Under our facts, there was a name change that became seriously misleading because the search logic of the filing system would be unable to find it. In that case, under subsection (c)(1), the original filing is effective as to collateral acquired by the debtor before or within four months after the name change. Those facts are reflected in **C**, so **C** is the correct response. Note that under subsection (c)(2), Creditor 1 could have continued the effectiveness of its filing as to collateral acquired more than four months after the name change by making an amended filing within that time. So as a practical matter, the filing creditor should check whether the debtor has changed its name during the preceding four months.

> **Question 7.** I take a security interest in a Rembrandt painting owned by Archie Leach and perfect using Archie Leach as the name of the debtor. On April 1, Archie Leach changes his name to Cary Grant. What do I need to do?
>
> **A.** File an amendment within four months or perfection will be lost.
> **B.** File an amendment within four months or the security interest will be lost.
> **C.** Nothing, because the change is not seriously misleading.
> **D.** Nothing, because the filing is effective as to the collateral acquired before the name change.

Analysis. This does not seem intuitive, but the statute is clear. The name change did make the filing seriously misleading, so response **C** is not correct. But even if the name change makes the filing seriously misleading, the filing creditor does not have to file an amendment with respect to "collateral acquired by the debtor before, or within four months after, the change." Section 9-507(c)(1). Therefore, the correct response is **D**.

As a practical matter, the searching creditor should check whether the debtor has changed its name during the preceding five years, since five years is the term of effectiveness of a financing statement under § 9-515(a).

3. *Transfer of Collateral*

The default rule with respect to a transfer of collateral is that the security interest remains attached despite the transfer. See § 9-201. Perfection continues as well under § 9-507(a). Perfection, however, can be lost if the transfer is to a debtor who is located in another jurisdiction. Recall that § 9-102(a)(28) defines "debtor" as any person having an interest in the collateral, so the transferee automatically becomes a debtor. Because of the difficulty of tracking down collateral that is now owned by a transferee located in a new jurisdiction, § 9-316(a)(3) gives the creditor one year to file in the new jurisdiction in order to continue perfection:

§ 9-316. Effect of Change in Governing Law.
(a) **General rule: effect on perfection of change in governing law.** A security interest perfected pursuant to the law of the jurisdiction designated in Section 9-301(1) or 9-305(c) remains perfected until the earliest of: . . .
(3) the expiration of one year after a transfer of collateral to a person that thereby becomes a debtor and is located in another jurisdiction.

As with the relocation of the debtor, if the creditor does not timely refile when the collateral is transferred, then perfection is retroactively lost against purchasers for value. See § 9-316(b). Frequently, the transfer of collateral occurs in connection with a merger or acquisition, as we shall see next.

4. Transfer to a "New Debtor"

The process of balancing the interests of filers and searchers becomes even more complex when there is what Article 9 calls a "new debtor." According to § 9-102(a)(56), *new debtor* means "a person that becomes bound as debtor under Section 9-203(d) by a security agreement previously entered into by another person." Section 9-203, which you will recall from Chapter 6.A is the basic provision governing the attachment of a security interest, provides in subsection (d):

> (d) **When person becomes bound by another person's security agreement.** A person becomes bound as debtor by a security agreement entered into by another person if, by operation of law other than this article or by contract:
>
>> (1) the security agreement becomes effective to create a security interest in the person's property; or
>>
>> (2) the person becomes generally obligated for the obligations of the other person, including the obligation secured under the security agreement, and acquires or succeeds to all or substantially all of the assets of the other person.

This situation frequently arises when one party acquires rights to the property of another party, such as through incorporation of a sole proprietorship or through merger or acquisition, and the acquiring party also becomes obligated under any security agreements with respect to that property. The party who acquires the rights and obligations is the *new debtor*. For example, assume First Bank has a security interest in the assets of Homebrew Software and has properly filed a financing statement. Homebrew Software is the original debtor. If Megasoft Inc. acquires the assets and liabilities of Homebrew Software, then Megasoft is the *new debtor* and is bound under the security agreement.

As to existing collateral, the rules of § 9-316(a) and (b) as described in D.2 determine whether the security interest remains perfected. Amended Article 9 added a new § 9-316(i) to clarify what happens with respect to after-acquired property when the new debtor is located in a different jurisdiction from the original debtor. It provides:

> (i) [**Effect of change in governing law on financing statement filed against original debtor.**] If a financing statement naming an original debtor is filed pursuant to the law of the jurisdiction designated in Section 9-301(1) or 9-305(c) and the new debtor is located in another jurisdiction, the following rules apply:
>
>> (1) The financing statement is effective to perfect a security interest in collateral acquired by the new debtor before, and within four months after, the new debtor becomes bound under Section

9-203(d), if the financing statement would have been effective to perfect a security interest in the collateral had the collateral been acquired by the original debtor.

(2) A security interest perfected by the financing statement and which becomes perfected under the law of the other jurisdiction before the earlier of the time the financing statement would have become ineffective under the law of the jurisdiction designated in Section 9-301(1) or 9-305(c) or the expiration of the four-month period remains perfected thereafter. A security interest that is perfected by the financing statement but which does not become perfected under the law of the other jurisdiction before the earlier time or event becomes unperfected and is deemed never to have been perfected as against a purchaser of the collateral for value.

As with the rule on the debtor changing its location discussed in part D.1, when a new debtor in another jurisdiction becomes bound to the secured party, the secured creditor has four months in which to file in the new jurisdiction in order to continue perfection. Failure to file during that time results in retroactive loss of perfection as against purchasers for value.

Question 8. First Bank has a security interest in certain equipment of Homebrew Software Inc., which is incorporated in Arizona. Sixteen months after First Bank perfected its security interest by filing in Arizona, all the assets and liabilities of Homebrew Software were acquired by Megasoft Inc., which is incorporated in the state of Washington. What does First Bank have to do to continue perfection in the equipment?

A. Nothing, for the perfection continues automatically until the financing statement needs to be continued.
B. Refile in Arizona within one year, indicating the name of Megasoft Inc. as the new debtor.
C. File in Washington within four months, indicating the name of Megasoft Inc. as the new debtor.
D. File in Washington within one year, indicating the name of Megasoft Inc. as the new debtor.

Analysis. This is a *new debtor* situation, in which Megasoft has become bound as a new debtor under § 9-203(d) by a security agreement previously entered into by Homebrew. The name of the debtor has become seriously misleading under § 9-508(b). Refiling is not required for the existing collateral merely because of the name change. See § 9-508(b). However, in this case, the new debtor is located in a different jurisdiction. Therefore, since under § 9-316(a)(3) perfection in Arizona lapses within one year after the relocation, First Bank must refile in Washington to continue perfection. **D** is the correct response.

5. *Change in the Characterization of the Collateral*

Collateral can be chameleon-like in its ability to change its characterization. For example, debtor is a lawyer who is a sole practitioner. Creditor 1 takes a security interest in debtor's "equipment," which includes a painting that hangs in the lawyer's office. The creditor files a financing statement identifying the collateral as "equipment." The lawyer then takes the painting home to hang in the living room. Creditor 2 now wants to take a security interest in the painting. It appears to Creditor 2 that the painting is consumer goods, but there are no financing statements listing the painting as collateral. (Recall from Chapter 6.D and Chapter 12.C.3 that §§ 9-108(e)(2) and 9-504 provide that the filing creditor must not describe consumer goods by type but must specify the goods.) Should the responsibility fall on Creditor 1 to monitor the use of the collateral and refile when it changes? Or does the responsibility fall on Creditor 2 to determine whether the debtor has used the collateral for some other purpose in the past? In this case, the responsibility falls on Creditor 2, the new creditor. We know this from a provision we have already looked at, § 9-507(b):

> (b) **Information becoming seriously misleading.** Except as otherwise provided in subsection (c) and Section 9-508, a financing statement is not rendered ineffective if, after the financing statement is filed, the information provided in the financing statement becomes seriously misleading under Section 9-506.

In the case of our painting, has the financing statement become seriously misleading under § 9-506? That section, along with §§ 9-507(c) and 9-508, makes clear that it is the change in name of the debtor that makes a financing statement seriously misleading. Therefore, the financing statement did not become seriously misleading when the use changed. The responsibility is not on the filing creditor to monitor the use but on the searching creditor to discover the changed use.

Question 9. GMAC has a properly perfected security interest in the inventory of Lundegaard Motors, an automobile dealership. On April 1, Jerry Lundegaard takes a van out of inventory to use as a courtesy van for Lundegaard Motors' pick-up and drop-off service. Is GMAC's financing statement effective with respect to that van?

A. No, because the financing statement became seriously misleading when the characterization of the collateral changed.

B. No, because a prospective creditor thinks the collateral is inventory and not equipment.

C. Yes, but only for four months from April 1.

D. Yes, because amendment is not necessary when the debtor's use of the collateral changes.

Analysis. The financing statement did not become seriously misleading, since that only applies to a name change. Therefore, response **A** is incorrect. It is true that the characterization of the collateral changed, in this case from inventory to equipment. That might mislead a prospective creditor who was thinking of taking a security interest in equipment and concluded from an examination of the title that no one had a perfected security interest in the courtesy van. Nevertheless, Article 9 puts the burden in this case on the searching creditor to discover the changed use. Therefore, response **D** is correct.

6. Exchange of Collateral for Proceeds with a Different Characterization

We have seen that amendment of the financing statement is not necessary when the collateral changes use so that it has a different characterization. The burden is on the searching creditor to discover the history of the collateral. The situation is more complex when the collateral becomes proceeds that have a different characterization. In that case, it is harder for the searching creditor to discover the history. The searcher must discover not whether an item was used differently in the past but whether it is the proceeds of an item that were used differently. An example of the former is a work of art that changes from consumer goods to office equipment. An example of the latter is an item of inventory that is sold, with the proceeds of the sale then used to purchase an item of equipment.

We know from Chapter 7.C that the security interest continues to *attach* to proceeds; the issue now is whether *perfection* continues. In our first hypothetical, Creditor 1 has a perfected security interest in Debtor's inventory. Debtor takes an item from inventory and trades it with a customer for an item that Debtor uses as equipment. We know that Creditor 1's security interest attaches to the piece of equipment, because it is the identifiable proceeds of collateral. See § 9-315(a)(2). But is the security interest in the proceeds perfected? The concern is with Creditor 2, who is thinking of taking a security interest in Debtor's equipment and who believes, based on the security agreement and the filed financing statement, that no other creditor has a claim to the equipment of Debtor. The answer is found in § 9-315(d), which is a good provision for working on statute-reading skills:

> **§ 9-315(d) Continuation of perfection.** A perfected security interest in proceeds becomes unperfected on the 21st day after the security interest attaches to the proceeds unless:
>> (1) the following conditions are satisfied:
>>> (A) a filed financing statement covers the original collateral;
>>> (B) the proceeds are collateral in which a security interest may be perfected by filing in the office in which the financing statement has been filed; and
>>> (C) the proceeds are not acquired with cash proceeds;

(2) the proceeds are identifiable cash proceeds; or

(3) the security interest in the proceeds is perfected other than under subsection (c) when the security interest attaches to the proceeds or within 20 days thereafter.

The filing creditor has continuing perfection under three circumstances. The first, in subsection (d)(3), gives the creditor 20 days to perfect. In other words, in our example, Creditor 1 could file with respect to the piece of equipment. This will rarely happen, because it requires the creditor to rigorously monitor the collateral. The second, in subsection (d)(2), applies only to identifiable cash proceeds.

The remaining circumstance, subsection (d)(1), requires the filing creditor to satisfy three conditions in order that perfection continue beyond 20 days. Let's apply them to our hypothetical, noting that under these facts the original collateral is inventory and the proceeds are equipment. We ask:

(A) Did a filed financing statement cover the original collateral?

(B) Are the proceeds collateral in which a security interest may be perfected by filing in the office in which the financing statement has been filed?

(C) Are the proceeds *not* acquired with cash proceeds?

Questions (A) and (C) are straightforward, but (B) may require some explanation. Ask in what office the financing statement was filed for the original collateral. Then ask in what office the financing statement for the proceeds would be filed. If the answer to both questions is the same, we have satisfied that condition. Here, for example, the financing statement for the original collateral—inventory—would be filed in the office of the Secretary of State. See Chapter 12.D. The financing statement for the proceeds—equipment—would also be filed in the office of the Secretary of State. See Chapter 12.D. Therefore, the answer to this question is yes.

So in our hypothetical, the answer to all three questions is yes. We have therefore satisfied the three conditions, and the security interest remains perfected. What does this mean to Creditor 2, who is thinking of taking a security interest in Debtor's equipment? It means that when Creditor 2 finds the financing statement with respect to inventory, it must inquire of the debtor where the equipment came from. The honest debtor will show that he traded inventory for it. Creditor 2 will realize that the equipment is proceeds of the inventory, that the security interest is perfected, and that it will not have priority in the equipment.

Let's try a second hypothetical using the same facts, except in this case Debtor sells the item of inventory for cash and uses the cash proceeds to buy the piece of equipment (a more realistic scenario). We again apply subsection (d)(1) to our hypothetical. The original collateral is inventory, and the proceeds are equipment. We ask:

(A) Did a filed financing statement cover the original collateral?

(B) Are the proceeds collateral in which a security interest may be perfected by filing in the office in which the financing statement has been filed?

(C) Are the proceeds *not* acquired with cash proceeds?

The answer to the first two questions is yes, but the answer to the third is no. We have therefore not satisfied the conditions, so Creditor 1's security interest in the equipment is *not* perfected. What does this mean to Creditor 2, who is thinking of taking a security interest in Debtor's equipment? It means that Creditor 2 finds the financing statement with respect to inventory and must inquire of Debtor where the equipment came from. The honest Debtor says that he bought it with cash. It is too hard for Creditor 2 to trace where the cash came from, so Creditor 2 can assume there is no perfected security interest in it and can use it as collateral. Alternately, if Creditor 1 filed a financing statement under (d)(3) listing the collateral as equipment, Creditor 2 has notice of that filing. Note that this rule gives the creditor an incentive to be overly broad in listing (with the consent of the debtor) the collateral on the financing statement.

Question 10. First Bank has taken a security interest in the inventory of Bitterroot Motors and has properly filed a financing statement with the central filing office listing the collateral as "inventory." Bitterroot Motors sells a car and obtains from the buyer a Windstar as a trade-in that it decides to use for its customer shuttle service. That car is titled in the name of Bitterroot Motors. When Bitterroot needs money, it borrows from Title Loan Company. Title Loan Company, after checking that the title is clear, takes a security interest in the Windstar and properly perfects the security interest on the title through the Department of Motor Vehicles, as required by state law. A month after this transaction, a dispute arises as to whether First Bank or Title Loan Co. has priority in the Windstar. Which party has priority in the Windstar?

A. First Bank, because a security interest continues when collateral becomes proceeds.

B. First Bank, because all of the conditions of § 9-315(d) were satisfied: a filed financing statement covers the original collateral, the proceeds are collateral in which a security interest may be perfected by filing in the office in which the financing statement has been filed, and the proceeds are not acquired with cash proceeds.

C. Title Loan Co., because a security interest does not continue when collateral becomes proceeds.

> **D.** Title Loan Co., because all of the conditions of § 9-315(d) were not satisfied: a filed financing statement covers the original collateral, the proceeds are collateral in which a security interest may be perfected by filing in the office in which the financing statement has been filed, and the proceeds are not acquired with cash proceeds.

Analysis. We can eliminate responses **A** and **C** because we know that whether a security interest continues when collateral becomes proceeds depends on the three circumstances in § 9-315. We know that First Bank, which has a security interest in the original collateral, did not perfect its security interest in the proceeds, so we know subsection (d)(3) is not relevant. We know that the proceeds are a Windstar and not cash, so subsection (d)(2) is not relevant. The choices come down to whether all of the conditions of § 9-315(d)(1) are satisfied. If they are, **B** is the correct response; if they are not, **D** is the correct response.

Let's work through the three conditions. A filed financing statement covers the original collateral, and the proceeds are not acquired with cash proceeds. A security interest in inventory is filed with the central filing office, but a security interest in a titled vehicle is filed with the Department of Motor Vehicles. Therefore, the second condition is not satisfied: the proceeds are not collateral in which a security interest may be perfected by filing in the office in which the financing statement has been filed. Therefore, all of the conditions of § 9-315(d)(1) are not satisfied, so the correct response is **D**. The practical reason for this answer is that the searching creditor, Title Loan Co., is not reasonably expected to search for filings in offices other than the office in which financing statements for the original collateral (inventory) are filed.

E.   Closers

> **Question 11.** A lender is considering lending money to an individual who moved to State A from State B 18 months ago. Both states in § 9-501(a)(2) provide that filings are made with the Secretary of State and both have adopted § 9-503(a) Alternative A. The name on the driver's license is "Jonathan Smith." A search of records in both sates reveal no filings under "Jonathan Smith" but reveals a filing in State A for a person at the same address named "Jon Smith." Which of the following advice would you give to the lender?
>
> **A.** There may be an effective filing against the individual in another state.

> **B.** There may be an effective filing against the individual in another county in State A.
> **C.** The filing under Jon Smith is effective.
> **D.** If the lender files under Jonathan Smith, it will be an effective filing.

Analysis. Section 9-316(a) provides that to continue perfection, a creditor has four months to file after a change of the debtor's location. Since the debtor has been in State A for more than four months, a filing in another state would not be effective, so **A** is not correct. Because § 9-501(a)(2) provides that filings are made with the Secretary of State, a filing against an individual in a county would not be effective, so **B** is not correct. Because the state has enacted the "only if" alternative to § 9-503(a), a filing that does not use the name on the driver's license does not sufficiently provide the name of the debtor. Therefore, response **C** is not correct. Because a filing under Jonathan Smith will be an effective filing, the correct response is **D**. Since it does not appear that there are any other security interests perfected by filing, you can advise the lender that it will likely have priority in those assets of the debtor. As we will see in the next chapter, however, there are exceptions to perfection by filing.

> **Question 12.** First Bank has a security interest in equipment and after-acquired equipment of Homebrew Software Inc., which is incorporated in Arizona. Sixteen months after First Bank perfected its security interest by filing in Arizona, all the assets and liabilities of Homebrew Software were acquired by Megasoft Inc., which is incorporated in the state of Washington. What does First Bank have to do to continue perfection in the after-acquired equipment?
>
> **A.** Nothing, for the perfection continues automatically until the financing statement needs to be continued.
> **B.** Refile in Arizona within one year, indicating the name of Megasoft Inc. as the new debtor.
> **C.** File in Washington within four months, indicating the name of Megasoft Inc. as the new debtor.
> **D.** File in Washington within one year, indicating the name of Megasoft Inc. as the new debtor.

Analysis. *Note on test-taking.* This question is very similar to Question 8. When questions are similar, look for a different fact that may suggest a different answer. The difference is that the previous question asked about perfection in equipment that was perfected in the original jurisdiction, while this question asks about the after-acquired equipment to which the security interest attached in the new jurisdiction. Under § 9-316(i), the secured party must file in the new jurisdiction during the four months after the transfer of the collateral in order to continue perfection. Therefore, First Bank must refile in Washington within four months to continue perfection. **C** is the correct response.

Question 13. Bitterroot Motors has granted Bank One a security interest in its inventory of cars that is properly perfected by a filing that lists the collateral as "inventory." Bitterroot sells a car for (1) a cash down payment, part of which is used to buy a floor waxer, (2) a trade-in car, (3) chattel paper, and (4) a set of socket wrenches that Bitterroot gives to its mechanics to use. In which of these items does Bank One's security interest *not* continue to be perfected beyond 20 days if Bank One takes no action?

A. The floor waxer.
B. The trade-in car.
C. The chattel paper.
D. The socket wrenches.

Analysis.   Bank One did not perfect its security interest in the proceeds, so we know subsection 9-315(d)(3) is not relevant. We are not asked about the remaining cash proceeds, but it is worth noting that under subsection (d)(2), perfection does continue in identifiable cash proceeds. That leaves § 9-315(d)(1), which provides that the security interest in the proceeds becomes unperfected unless the three conditions are satisfied. Let's work through the three conditions to see if they are satisfied. In all four cases, a filed financing statement covers the original collateral, so A is satisfied. The proceeds would all be filed in the same office as the original collateral (the office of the Secretary of State), so B is satisfied. All are not acquired with cash proceeds, except for the floor waxer, which is acquired with cash proceeds. The condition in subsection C is not satisfied with respect to the floor waxer. Therefore, the security interest becomes unperfected with respect to the floor waxer, so **A** is the correct response.

 # Burnham's Picks

Question 1	**A**
Question 2	**A**
Question 3	**A**
Question 4	**B**
Question 5	**A**

Question 6 **C**
Question 7 **D**
Question 8 **D**
Question 9 **D**
Question 10 **D**
Question 11 **D**
Question 12 **C**
Question 13 **A**

14

Exceptions to Perfection by Filing

A.   Introduction

We have seen that the principal method of perfection is filing. However, recall that § 9-308(a) provides that a security interest is perfected if "all of the applicable requirements for perfection . . . have been satisfied." Filing in the location designated in Article 9 is only one of the methods available to perfect a security interest. This chapter looks at some of those other methods.

Section 9-310(a) states the general rule that "[e]xcept as otherwise provided . . . a financing statement must be filed to perfect all security interests and agricultural liens." We will look at just a few of the many exceptions under which the filing of a financing statement is not necessary to perfect a security interest. See § 9-310(b). These exceptions include:

- possession
- control
- other filing systems
- automatic perfection

This topic will have greater significance when we study the priority among secured creditors in Chapter 16. There we will see that some forms of collateral may be perfected by different methods. When that is the case, there must be a rule to determine which method has priority over another.

B.   Possession

Recall that a security interest may *attach* to collateral by the secured party's taking possession of the property. See § 9-203(b)(3). A security interest may also be *perfected* by the creditor's possession of the property. Section 9-310(b)(6) provides that "[t]he filing of a financing statement is not necessary to perfect a security interest . . . in collateral in the secured party's possession under Section 9-313." Section 9-313 provides:

When Possession by or Delivery to Secured Party Perfects Security Interest Without Filing.
　　(a) **Perfection by possession or delivery.** Except as otherwise provided in subsection (b), a secured party may perfect a security interest in tangible negotiable documents, goods, instruments, money, or tangible chattel paper by taking possession of the collateral. A secured party may perfect a security interest in certificated securities by taking delivery of the certificated securities under Section 8-301.
　　(b) **Goods covered by certificate of title.** With respect to goods covered by a certificate of title issued by this State, a secured party may perfect a security interest in the goods by taking possession of the goods only in the circumstances described in Section 9-316(d).
　　(c) **Collateral in possession of person other than debtor.** With respect to collateral other than certificated securities and goods covered by a document, a secured party takes possession of collateral in the possession of a person other than the debtor, the secured party, or a lessee of the collateral from the debtor in the ordinary course of the debtor's business, when:
　　　　(1) the person in possession authenticates a record acknowledging that it holds possession of the collateral for the secured party's benefit; or
　　　　(2) the person takes possession of the collateral after having authenticated a record acknowledging that it will hold possession of collateral for the secured party's benefit.
　　(d) **Time of perfection by possession; continuation of perfection.** If perfection of a security interest depends upon possession of the collateral by a secured party, perfection occurs no earlier than the time the

secured party takes possession and continues only while the secured party retains possession.

(e) **Time of perfection by delivery; continuation of perfection.** A security interest in a certificated security in registered form is perfected by delivery when delivery of the certificated security occurs under Section 8-301 and remains perfected by delivery until the debtor obtains possession of the security certificate.

(f) **Acknowledgment not required.** A person in possession of collateral is not required to acknowledge that it holds possession for a secured party's benefit.

(g) **Effectiveness of acknowledgment; no duties or confirmation.** If a person acknowledges that it holds possession for the secured party's benefit:

    (1) the acknowledgment is effective under subsection (c) or Section 8-301(a), even if the acknowledgment violates the rights of a debtor; and

    (2) unless the person otherwise agrees or law other than this article otherwise provides, the person does not owe any duty to the secured party and is not required to confirm the acknowledgment to another person.

(h) **Secured party's delivery to person other than debtor.** A secured party having possession of collateral does not relinquish possession by delivering the collateral to a person other than the debtor or a lessee of the collateral from the debtor in the ordinary course of the debtor's business if the person was instructed before the delivery or is instructed contemporaneously with the delivery:

    (1) to hold possession of the collateral for the secured party's benefit; or

    (2) to redeliver the collateral to the secured party.

(i) **Effect of delivery under subsection (h); no duties or confirmation.** A secured party does not relinquish possession, even if a delivery under subsection (h) violates the rights of a debtor. A person to which collateral is delivered under subsection (h) does not owe any duty to the secured party and is not required to confirm the delivery to another person unless the person otherwise agrees or law other than this article otherwise provides.

You may wonder why possession constitutes perfection. Recall that perfection means putting third parties on notice that there may be a security interest in the property. How does the creditor's possession inform a third party of the security interest? The prudent creditor will want to see the collateral, to make sure it exists and to determine its value. If the debtor explains that someone else is holding the collateral, this fact should tip the prospective creditor to make further inquiry about how a third party came to be holding the property of the debtor.

If the idea behind perfection by possession is that the collateral can be found in only one place, then it is obvious that only tangible personal property can be possessed. Section 9-313(a) provides that the types of collateral that can be perfected by possession are tangible negotiable documents, goods, instruments, money, and tangible chattel paper. See Chapter 4.B for a description of each of these collateral types. Certificated securities can also be perfected by delivery, which, according to § 8-301(a), includes both delivery to the secured party or to a third party on behalf of the secured party if certain requirements are complied with.

Possession is not defined in the Code. See Official Comment 3 to § 9-313, which provides in part:

> This section does not define "possession." It adopts the general concept as it developed under former Article 9. As under former Article 9, in determining whether a particular person has possession, the principles of agency apply.

Possession is clear in the case of a creditor such as a pawnbroker, whose business involves holding on to the goods. But actual possession is rare because it is expensive for the creditor and impractical for many debtors, who need the collateral to run their homes and businesses. For example, it would make little sense for a secured party to take possession of the inventory or equipment of a business, or the car of a consumer. Therefore, many situations arise in which the creditor does not have actual possession but claims perfection because a party designated by the creditor has possession.

The issue of whether possession by a party other than the secured creditor constitutes possession under the Code can often be resolved by determining whether that party is an agent of the creditor. For example, First Bank has an unperfected security interest in the inventory of Lundegaard Motors. First Bank and Jerry Lundegaard agree that the night watchman of Lundegaard Motors will watch the cars on behalf of First Bank. First Bank also puts a sign on the lot stating, "These cars are in the possession of First Bank." Do these acts constitute possession by First Bank? The answer is probably no. The cars are being watched by an agent of the debtor (Lundegaard Motors), not an agent of the creditor (First Bank). And the sign does not seem meaningful when there is no other act indicating possession.

As indicated by § 9-313(c), however, it is possible for the secured party to have possession when the property is in the possession of someone other than the creditor or the debtor. This is accomplished through the possessor giving notice that it holds the collateral for the benefit of the secured party. The statute explains the steps that must be taken:

> (c) **Collateral in possession of person other than debtor.** With respect to collateral other than certificated securities and goods covered by a document, a secured party takes possession of collateral in the possession of a person other than the debtor, the secured party, or a lessee of the collateral from the debtor in the ordinary course of the debtor's business, when:

> (1) the person in possession authenticates a record acknowledging that it holds possession of the collateral for the secured party's benefit; or
>
> (2) the person takes possession of the collateral after having authenticated a record acknowledging that it will hold possession of collateral for the secured party's benefit.

Question 1. First Bank takes a security interest in Debtor's equipment but does not file a financing statement. Debtor defaults, and First Bank repossesses a piece of equipment. Second Bank then takes a security interest in Debtor's equipment and properly files. First Bank then announces a sale of the repossessed collateral. Second Bank objects on the grounds that it has a priority security interest in the collateral. Which creditor has priority at the time of the sale?

A. First Bank, because its security interest was the first to attach.
B. First Bank, because it was first to file or perfect.
C. Second Bank, because it was first to file.
D. Second Bank, because even though First Bank's security interest was first to attach, it never filed a financing statement.

Analysis. Even though Second Bank filed when First Bank had not filed, in fact First Bank was perfected at that time. First Bank did not perfect by filing, but when it repossessed collateral characterized as goods, it was then perfected by possession under § 9-313. Because First Bank was first "in time of filing or perfection" under § 9-322(a)(1), the correct response is **B**. The lesson here is that Second Bank should examine the collateral in which it is taking a security interest. If the debtor cannot produce it, the creditor should be suspicious. The plot of one of the best movies about secured transactions, *Fargo*, turns on a creditor (GMAC) that wants to verify what collateral is in the hands of the debtor (Lundegaard Motors).

Question 2. First Bank takes a security interest in a Picasso painting owned by Gonzalez that Gonzalez intends to have displayed at the Museum of the Arts. Which of the following would *not* constitute perfection by possession once the painting is hung in the museum?

A. After the painting is hung in the museum, the museum sends First Bank a letter acknowledging that it holds possession of the painting for First Bank's benefit.
B. Before the painting is hung in the museum, the museum sends First Bank an e-mail stating that it will hold possession of the painting for First Bank's benefit.

> C. First Bank hires a guard to stand near the painting during the hours
>   the museum is open and to patrol the museum when it is closed.
> D. First Bank puts a conspicuous sign next to the painting stating:
>   "Notice. First Bank has a possessory security interest in this painting."

Analysis.   Under the facts of **C,** if the guards are paid by First Bank and not
by the museum, they are agents of First Bank; this is probably enough to constitute possession by the creditor and further steps under § 9-313(c) would
not be required. The steps in **A** and **B** satisfy the requirements for possession
by First Bank under §§ 9-313(c)(1) and (2), for both the letter and the e-mail
constitute authenticated records. Under the facts in **D,** there is neither actual
possession by First Bank or its agents nor compliance with the requirements of
§ 9-313(c). Since you were asked which response would *not* constitute perfection by possession, the correct response is **D.**

C.   Control

According to § 9-313(a), perfection by possession is effective only if the collateral is "tangible negotiable documents, goods, instruments, money, or tangible
chattel paper." However, many types of collateral may take an intangible form
and are therefore difficult to possess. How does one obtain the equivalence of
possession of such collateral? The answer is that some forms of intangible collateral may be perfected by *control.* Section 9-314(a) provides:

> (a) [**Perfection by control.**] A security interest in investment prop-
>   erty, deposit accounts, letter-of-credit rights, electronic chattel paper, or
>   electronic documents may be perfected by control of the collateral under
>   Section 7-106, 9-104, 9-105, 9-106, or 9-107.

The idea is to design a system that provides the equivalent of possession, so
that even though the property is intangible, one person can be identified who
is in control of it. We will look at how perfection by control is accomplished
in the case of:

- investment property
- deposit accounts
- electronic chattel paper and electronic documents

1.   *Control of Investment Property: § 9-106*

Section 9-102(a)(49) defines "investment property" as "a security, whether
certificated or uncertificated, security entitlement, securities account, commodity contract, or commodity account." To further define *security,* we would

have to explore Article 8 of the UCC, which deals with investment securities and is generally beyond our scope, but the intention of the drafters of Articles 8 and 9 was to modernize the kinds of investments beyond what we think of as stocks and bonds. Not only have the types of investment property been modernized, but so have the ways of handling them. In the old days, buyers of stock obtained certificates, making it easy to transfer or pledge the stock by transferring the piece of paper. This may still work for shares of close corporations that are rarely traded, but for stock that is traded we generally use "uncertificated securities," with ownership indicated by an electronic entry on the part of the "securities intermediary," usually a broker.

A security interest in investment property may be perfected by filing. See § 9-312(a). However, a security interest in investment property may also be perfected by control. See § 9-314. Section 9-106 provides that control is obtained "as provided in Section 8-106." Under that provision, the debtor, the secured party, and the broker (called a "securities intermediary") can all agree that the broker will honor the instructions of the secured party. Finally, § 9-328(1) provides that a secured party with control over investment property has priority over a secured party who has filed with respect to investment property.

> **Question 3.** Debtor grants Creditor a security interest in Debtor's shares in Cisco Systems. Debtor does not have the certificates, but Debtor's ownership is recorded with its broker. What is the best way for Creditor to perfect its security interest?
>
> **A.** File a financing statement.
> **B.** Take possession of the shares.
> **C.** Make an agreement among the debtor, the secured party, and the broker regarding the secured party's control of the shares.
> **D.** Make an agreement among the debtor, the secured party, and Cisco Systems regarding the secured party's control of the shares.

Analysis.   Under § 9-313(a), "a secured party may perfect a security interest in negotiable documents, goods, instruments, money, or tangible chattel paper by taking possession of the collateral." Since shares of stock are "investment property" and "investment property" is not on that list, it appears that perfection may not be by possession. Under § 9-312(a), a security interest in investment property may be perfected by filing, so response A does not appear to be incorrect. However, under § 9-314(a), "a security interest in investment property . . . may be perfected by control of the collateral." Section 9-106 refers us to § 8-106 for the methods of control of securities. If the shares are certificated, then the secured party may take possession as a form of control under § 8-301. However, under our facts, the securities are not certificated, so response **B** cannot be correct. If the shares are uncertificated, then the parties may make an agreement regarding control. The agreement is with the broker rather than the issuer, however, so **D** is not correct. It therefore appears that both **A** and **C** are correct responses. However, § 9-328(1) provides that a secured party with control has priority over a secured party that does not have control. Therefore, response **C** is a better answer than response **A**.

2.   *Control of Deposit Accounts: § 9-104*

What is a *deposit account*? Section 9-102(a)(29) provides that "'[d]eposit account' means a demand, time, savings, passbook, or similar account maintained with a bank." If a creditor has a security interest in the debtor's bank account, how can it get control of that account in order to perfect its security interest? It is important to first determine whether the secured creditor is the bank in which the deposit account is maintained. It is quite common for a bank to take a security interest in the debtor's funds that are deposited in that bank. If the secured party is the bank, then control is automatic. See § 9-104(a)(1). If it is not, then there are two methods for the secured party to obtain control. One is for the debtor, the secured party, and the bank to agree that the bank will allow access by the secured party. See § 9-104(a)(2). Such an agreement is often called, appropriately enough, a Deposit Account Control Agreement. The other method is for the secured party to become the bank's customer on the account with the debtor. See § 9-104(a)(3). The latter is a powerful weapon in the hands of the secured party, for the secured party is entitled to operate the debtor's account.

To understand why a secured creditor would prefer to use one of these methods of gaining control over another method, it is necessary to discuss the priority rules between secured creditors found in § 9-327. That section first provides that a secured creditor who has control has priority over a secured party that does not have control. Initially, one might wonder how a secured party could have a perfected security interest other than through control, for § 9-312(b)(1) provides that a security interest in a deposit account may be perfected only by control. The answer is that cash proceeds are frequently placed in a deposit account and, as we have seen in Chapter 13.D, perfection often continues in the proceeds. Section 9-327 then provides that a security interest held by the bank in which the deposit account is maintained has priority over other secured creditors. Finally, it provides that if the secured creditor who is not the bank perfects by control under § 9-104(a)(3) by becoming the bank's customer on the account, then that secured creditor has priority over the bank. This priority scheme — and not greed — explains why a secured party would wish to gain control by becoming a party to the account.

> **Question 4.** Debtor grants Creditor a security interest in Debtor's checking account. What is the best way for Creditor to perfect its security interest?
>
> A. File a financing statement.
> B. Take possession of the bank account.
> C. Make an agreement among the debtor, the secured party, and the bank that the bank will comply with the secured party's directions.
> D. Become the bank's customer with respect to the bank account.

Analysis.   Under § 9-313(a), "a secured party may perfect a security interest in negotiable documents, goods, instruments, money, or tangible chattel paper by taking possession of the collateral." Since a checking account is a deposit account, and "deposit account" is not on that list, perfection may not be by possession. Therefore, response **B** must be incorrect. Under § 9-312(b) (1), a security interest in a deposit account may be perfected only by control. Therefore, response **A** must be incorrect. While both **C** and **D** describe methods of control under § 9-104, § 9-327 provides that when the creditor becomes the bank's customer with respect to the bank account, the creditor has priority over a security interest held by the bank. Therefore, response **D** describes the best way for the creditor to perfect its security interest.

3. Control of Electronic Chattel Paper and Electronic Documents: §§ 9-105 and 7-106

Recall from Chapter 4.B that § 9-102(a)(11) defines chattel paper as "a record or records that evidence both a monetary obligation and a security interest in specific goods." For example, if I buy a car and give the car dealer a promissory note and a security interest in the car, then the car dealer has chattel paper that it can use as collateral when it seeks a secured loan from the bank. That chattel paper may take electronic form, in which case it is "electronic chattel paper" as defined in § 9-102(a)(31). It is impossible for the bank to possess electronic chattel paper, but the bank may control it if it jumps through the right hoops as described in § 9-105. Just as with a paper version, a party has control of an electronic version if, according to § 9-105(1), "a single authoritative copy of the record or records exists which is unique identifiable and . . . unalterable."

The rules for control of electronic documents of title are similar, but they are found in Article 7, specifically § 7-106. The Code leaves it to the market to develop systems that will satisfy the requirement of identifying a "single authoritative copy" of the document or chattel paper. Official Comment 3 provides an example of how such a system might work:

> Of great importance to the functioning of the control concept is to be able to demonstrate, at any point in time, the one person entitled under the

electronic document. For example, a carrier may issue an electronic bill of lading by having the required information in a database that is encrypted and accessible by virtue of a password. If the computer system in which the required information is maintained identifies the person as the person to which the electronic bill of lading was issued or transferred, that person has control of the electronic document of title. That identification may be by virtue of passwords or other encryption methods. Registry systems may satisfy this test. This Article leaves to the market place the development of sufficient technologies and business practices that will meet the test.

Question 5. Farmer Wicks stores his grain in the Shelby Elevator and receives an electronic warehouse receipt. Wicks then grants First Bank a security interest in the warehouse receipt. Wicks transfers the electronic warehouse receipt to First Bank according to the rules of the electronic warehouse receipt system in effect that identifies First Bank as the party to whom the warehouse receipt was transferred. The security agreement between Wicks and First Bank also provides that First Bank has control of the warehouse receipt. Does First Bank have perfection in the electronic warehouse receipt by control?

A. Yes, because the security agreement provides that it does.
B. Yes, because the system identifies First Bank as the person to which the electronic document was transferred.
C. No, because multiple copies of the electronic warehouse receipt could be issued.
D. No, because there is no Control Agreement between Wicks, First Bank, and Shelby Elevator.

Analysis. To solve this problem we must first classify the collateral. A warehouse receipt is a "document of title" according to § 1-201(b)(16). Under § 9-314(a), "electronic documents may be perfected by control of the collateral under Section 7-106." Section 7-106(a) provides that "[a] person has control of an electronic document of title if a system employed for evidencing the transfer of interests in the electronic document reliably establishes that person as the person to which the electronic document was issued or transferred." Here, the system established does provide that First Bank is the person to which the document was transferred. Therefore, the correct response is **B**. Because the system is designed to identify only one party who has control, **C** is not correct. **A** is not correct because the test looks at the actual situation, not the parties' intent. As explained by Official Comment 4 to § 7-106:

> Parties may not by contract provide that control exists. The test for control is a factual test that depends upon whether the general test in subsection (a) or the safe harbor in subsection (b) is satisfied.

If you chose **D**, then you confused control of a deposit account with control of electronic documents.

D.   Other Filing Systems

1. Federal Filing

Filing a financing statement under Article 9 is not "necessary or effective" to perfect a security interest when federal law has established a filing system that preempts the Article 9 system. See § 9-311(a)(1). For example, federal law has expressly established a filing system for security interests in aircraft engines, railroad rolling stock, ships, and certain motor vehicles operated by interstate common carriers. The place of filing for patents and copyrights is somewhat cloudy, for although statutes have established federal filing systems, those statutes are silent on whether those systems preempt Article 9, and case law is divided. The prudent creditor might be wise to file in both places.

> **Question 6.** Teresa Bodwell is the author of the book *Loving Mercy*. The book is published by Kensington Press, but Bodwell has kept the copyright, which is registered with the Copyright Office of the Library of Congress. She borrows money from a bank and grants the bank a security interest in the book. How should the bank perfect its security interest?
>
> **A.** Enter into an agreement with the author and publisher to perfect by control.
> **B.** File with the Secretary of State.
> **C.** File with the Copyright Office.
> **D.** File with both the Secretary of State and the Copyright Office.

Analysis.   Like many perfection problems, this one turns on characterization of the collateral. When an author grants a creditor its interest in a book, that interest is the author's copyright in the book. Note that an author might also grant a creditor an interest in the royalty stream from the book, but that is not the case here. Response **A** would apply if the collateral were deposit accounts or investment property, but it is not. According to the characterization scheme we studied in Chapter 4.B, a copyright would be a general intangible as defined in § 9-102(a)(42). The general rule under Article 9 is that security interests in general intangibles are filed with the office of the Secretary of State. See Chapter 12.D.3. However, this particular intangible is a copyright, which may be registered with the Copyright Office. According to § 9-311(a)(1), when there is a federal scheme for filing that preempts the state scheme, the state filing is not effective. Here, although there is a federal filing scheme, it does not necessarily preempt the state scheme, so the prudent creditor will file in both places. Therefore, while **C** and **D** are not wrong answers, for multiple-choice purposes, you should choose the *best* answer, which is **D**.

2. State Certificate of Title Laws

In many jurisdictions, the owner of property such as a motor vehicle, boat, mobile home, or farm tractor is issued a Certificate of Title. In a title jurisdiction, filing under Article 9 is not effective to perfect a security interest in that property. Instead, the lien must be noted on the Certificate of Title. The uniform version of § 9-311(a)(2) instructs each state to list statutes that require certain property to be titled. For example, if a state has enacted the Uniform Certificate of Title Law, it might provide as follows:

§ 9-311. Perfection of security interests in property subject to certain statutes, regulations, and treaties.

(a) Except as otherwise provided in subsection (d), the filing of a financing statement is not necessary or effective to perfect a security interest in property subject to: . . .

(2) a certificate of title issued pursuant to the Certificate of Title Law.

The Uniform Certificate of Title Law provides in part:

§ 25. Effectiveness of Security-Interest Statement.

(a) A security-interest statement is sufficient if it includes the name of the debtor, the name of the secured party or a representative of the secured party, and a description of the vehicle and it is delivered by a person authorized to file an initial financing statement covering the vehicle pursuant to [Uniform Commercial Code Section 9-509]. A description of the vehicle is sufficient if it reasonably identifies the vehicle and is not seriously misleading under Section 20.

(b) A security-interest statement that is sufficient under subsection (a) is effective upon receipt by the office.

§ 26. Perfection of Security Interest.

(a) Except as otherwise provided in subsection (b), (d), or (e), a security interest in a vehicle may be perfected only by a security-interest statement that is effective under Section 25. The security interest is perfected upon the later of receipt of the security-interest statement under Section 25 or attachment of the security interest under [Uniform Commercial Code Section 9-203].

(b) If the office creates a certificate of title naming a lessor, consignor, bailor, or secured party as owner and the interest of the person named as owner is a security interest, the certificate of title serves as a security-interest statement that provides the name of the person as secured party. If the interest of the person named as owner in an application for a certificate of title delivered to the office in accordance with Section 9 is a security interest, the application is a security-interest statement that provides the name of the person as secured party. The naming of the person as owner on the application or certificate of title is not of itself a factor in determining whether the interest is a security interest.

(c) If a secured party assigns a perfected security interest in a vehicle, the receipt by the office of a security-interest statement providing the name of the transferee or its representative as secured party is not required in order to continue the perfected status of the security interest against creditors of and transferees from the original debtor. However, a purchaser of a vehicle subject to a security interest which obtains a release from the secured party indicated in the files of the office or on the certificate of title takes free of the security interest and of the rights of a transferee if the transfer is not indicated in the files of the office and on the certificate of title.

(d) This section does not apply to a security interest in a vehicle created by a person during any period in which the vehicle is inventory held for sale or lease by the person or is leased by the person as lessor if the person is in the business of selling goods of that kind.

Question 7. Assume that Springfield Imports does business in a state that has enacted the Uniform Certificate of Title Act and defines the "office" in § 25(b) as the Department of Motor Vehicles. Springfield Imports sells a new car on credit to a consumer buyer and takes a security interest in the car. How does Springfield Imports perfect its security interest?

A. The security interest is automatically perfected.
B. It files a financing statement with the Secretary of State.
C. It files a financing statement with the county in which the debtor resides.
D. It sends a statement to the Department of Motor Vehicles.

Analysis. Under these facts, the collateral is consumer goods. Even though this transaction involves a PMSI in consumer goods, § 9-309(1) provides that automatic perfection applies "except as otherwise provided in Section 9-311(b) with respect to consumer goods that are subject to a statute or treaty described in Section 9-311(a)." Because under this state's version of § 9-311(a) an automobile is subject to the certificate of title laws, automatic perfection does not apply, so response **A** is not correct. Uniform Certificate of Title Act § 26(a) provides that "a security interest in a vehicle may be perfected only by a security-interest statement that is effective under Section 25." Therefore, responses **B** and **C** are not correct (and in any event, **C** is way off, because if there were filing, it would be with the Secretary of State). Therefore, the correct response is **D**, because there is a statute providing for the security interest to be filed with the Department of Motor Vehicles.

> **Question 8.** Assume that Springfield Imports does business in a state that has enacted the Uniform Certificate of Title Act and defines the "office" in § 25(b) as the Department of Motor Vehicles. First Bank loans money to Springfield Imports and takes a security interest in Springfield Imports' inventory of new cars. How does First Bank perfect its security interest?
>
> **A.** The security interest is automatically perfected.
> **B.** It files a financing statement with the Secretary of State.
> **C.** It files a financing statement with the county in which the debtor resides.
> **D.** It sends a statement to the Department of Motor Vehicles.

Analysis.   *Note on test-taking.* The responses here are the same as in the previous question. It is likely that the answer is going to be different due to a change in the facts. If you spot that change in the facts, you should be able to determine why the answer is different.

Recall that we always characterize the collateral from the point of view of the debtor. Here, the collateral is inventory. Section 9-311 as enacted in this state led us to the Uniform Certificate of Title Act, which provides in § 26(d) that "[t]his section does not apply to a security interest in a vehicle created by a person during any period in which the vehicle is inventory held for sale or lease by the person or is leased by the person as lessor if the person is in the business of selling goods of that kind." In other words, even though the collateral is motor vehicles, when motor vehicles are held as inventory, the special rule on certificate of titles does not apply and the security interest is perfected in accordance with the provisions of Article 9. As we know from Chapter 12.D.3, § 9-501 provides that when the collateral is inventory, the financing statement is filed with the Secretary of State, so response **B** is correct.

E.   Automatic Perfection

Section 9-309 contains a list of various interests that are "automatically perfected" on attachment. Let that sink in — the secured party does not have to affirmatively do anything in order for its security interest to be perfected. We will focus on § 9-309(1), which provides:

> **Security Interest Perfected upon Attachment.** The following security interests are perfected when they attach:
>> (1) a purchase-money security interest in consumer goods, except as otherwise provided in Section 9-311(b) with respect to consumer goods that are subject to a statute or treaty described in Section 9-311(a).

This provision, while relatively unimportant in the world of commerce, seems to show up frequently on law school exams and bar exams. It is a good provision for practicing our code methodology, for we have to look carefully at which security interests are automatically perfected. The rule (subject to an important exception we will examine shortly) applies only to "a purchase-money security interest in consumer goods."

Let's review those concepts. In Chapter 4.D, we introduced the concept of the PMSI. We saw that § 9-103(a)(2) provides this definition:

> "purchase-money obligation" means an obligation of an obligor incurred as all or part of the price of the collateral or for value given to enable the debtor to acquire rights in or the use of the collateral if the value is in fact so used.

In other words, a security interest in collateral is a PMSI if either (1) a seller sold the debtor the collateral in which it took a security interest, or (2) a lender loaned the debtor the money that the debtor used to buy the collateral. We also saw in Chapter 4.C that § 9-102(a)(23) defines "consumer goods" as "goods that are used or bought for use primarily for personal, family, or household purposes." So putting that together, there is automatic perfection only if the debtor purchased the goods constituting the collateral for personal, family, or household purposes and only if the secured party is the seller or financer.

The exception is for "consumer goods that are subject to a statute or treaty described in Section 9-311(a)." As explained in section D of this chapter, the principal statutes that govern the perfection of consumer goods are certificate-of-title laws that require the security interest in property such as an automobile, boat, or mobile home to be perfected by an indication on the title. In that event, there is no automatic perfection. The seller or financer taking a security interest in those consumer goods must comply with the certificate of title statute to perfect the security interest. The policy seems to be that the secured party does not have to go to the expense of filing a financing statement for what is usually a minor purchase. See, for example, the security interest in a purchase from Sears in Chapter 6.B. However, note that the statute does not limit automatic perfection to minor purchases.

Question 9. A department store sells a customer a pair of socks for $8.99. The customer uses his store credit card, and the receipt signed by the customer states that the store takes a security interest in the socks. See Chapter 6.B. Which of the following advice would you give to the department store?

A. To perfect the security interest, it must file in the central filing office.
B. To perfect the security interest, it must file in the county in which the customer resides.
C. The security interest is automatically perfected because it is a purchase-money security interest in consumer goods.
D. The security interest is automatically perfected because the value of the goods is less than $10.00.

Analysis.   Section 9-309(1) provides that a purchase-money security interest in consumer goods is automatically perfected. Does this transaction involve consumer goods? According to § 9-102(a)(23), consumer goods are purchased "primarily for personal, family, or household purposes." It seems likely that a pair of socks is bought for personal purposes. Does this transaction involve a PMSI? It is a PMSI if the seller takes a security interest in the goods that the seller sells to the buyer on credit. See § 9-103. Here the department store as seller is taking a security interest in the goods (the socks) that it sells to the customer. Since all the elements of automatic perfection are satisfied, **C** is the correct response. Note that the size of the transaction is irrelevant, so **D** is not a correct response. It should be mentioned, by the way, that most credit card purchases do not involve the grant of a security interest.

Question 10. A local attorney who collects sports memorabilia as a hobby bought a Ted Williams autographed baseball on credit from the Sports Memorabilia Store. The store took a security interest in the ball but did not file. After the ball sat in his home for the weekend, the attorney took it to his law office, where he displayed it to clients. Six months later, the attorney was negotiating with a bank for a loan. The bank searched the filings and found no filed financing statement naming the attorney as debtor. The bank then took a security interest in the attorney's office equipment and filed. The attorney then defaulted on his security agreement with the bank. Assuming (see § 9-322(a)(1)) that priority goes to the first secured creditor to file or perfect, which creditor has priority in the baseball?

A. The store, because it was first to file or perfect.

B. The bank, because it was first to file or perfect.

C. The bank, because it relied on the absence of filings before it entered into a security agreement with the attorney.

D. The bank because, even though the store was first to file or perfect, the store failed to timely file when the collateral changed its characterization.

Analysis.   There is a lot going on in this problem. We are getting a preview of Chapter 16, because even though the subject of this chapter is perfection, the significance of perfection is in priority contests such as this one. We know that the bank's security interest is perfected by filing. Is the store's security interest perfected? It is not filed, but it may fall under the automatic perfection exception if it qualifies as a PMSI in consumer goods. Here it qualifies, because the baseball purchased as a hobby is consumer goods, and the seller took the security interest in it. Therefore, the store was the first to file or perfect, since its interest was perfected by automatic perfection. Was it necessary for the store to monitor the collateral and take any action when the baseball became re-characterized as office equipment? We saw in Chapter 13.D.5 that there is no responsibility for a creditor to monitor the collateral for changed use, so response **D** is not correct. It is the responsibility of the searching creditor to discover the changed use, so response **C** is not correct. Therefore, response **A** is correct, because the store was first to file or perfect when it perfected by automatic perfection.

F.   Closers

> **Question 11.** John's Art Gallery sold a Renoir painting for $2 million to Winston, a local art collector, on credit and retained a security interest in the painting. Winston stated that he was buying the Renoir to hang in his living room. A year later, a museum is considering buying the painting from Winston. If the museum asked you to determine whether there are any security interests in the painting, what would you advise?
>
> **A.** Check the filings against John's Art Gallery, and if there are none, then the painting is free of security interests.
> **B.** Check the filings against Winston, and if there are none, then the painting is free of security interests.
> **C.** There may be an unrecorded security interest, which could only be determined by obtaining the documentation of the previous sales of the painting.
> **D.** There may be an unrecorded security interest, but the general rule is that transferees take free of security interests.

Analysis.   Is John's security interest in the painting automatically perfected? Yes, the transaction is a PMSI, and the collateral is consumer goods. The policy behind automatic perfection is that filing is not cost effective in consumer transactions, because these transactions tend to be small. However, even if that is the policy, the rule is the same even if the transaction is not a small transaction; the fact that here it is a $2 million transaction is irrelevant. Therefore, checking the filings will not be the only way to discover a security interest, so responses **A** and **B** are not correct (and in any event, filings are in the name of the debtor, so **A** is way off). There may be an unrecorded security interest, and we learned in Chapter 7.B that the general rule is that a security agreement is effective against purchasers of the collateral. Therefore, **D** is not a correct response. The correct response is **C**. A prudent purchaser of a big-ticket item will research the circumstances under which the consumer goods were purchased to determine whether there may be a security interest that was automatically perfected.

> **Question 12.** Assume that the only secured creditor with a security interest in the debtor's property did not properly perfect its security interest. If the debtor defaults, can the creditor repossess the collateral from the debtor?
>
> A. Yes, because perfection is not relevant as between the creditor and the debtor.
> B. Yes, because as between the creditor and the debtor, the creditor need only make a good faith effort to perfect.
> C. No, because the security interest is not effective if it is not perfected.
> D. No, because without perfection third parties lack notice of the security interest.

Analysis.   Recall that in Chapter 8 we discussed the secured creditor's right to repossess the collateral on default with no mention of perfection. We began Chapter 12 by stating that the purpose of perfection is to give notice of the security interest to third parties. This question is a final reminder that perfection is not relevant as between the creditor and the debtor, so the correct response is **A**. In the next chapter we will look at priority disputes between multiple creditors, where perfection will assume great significance.

 Burnham's Picks

Question 1	**B**
Question 2	**D**
Question 3	**C**
Question 4	**D**
Question 5	**B**
Question 6	**D**
Question 7	**D**
Question 8	**B**
Question 9	**C**
Question 10	**A**
Question 11	**C**
Question 12	**A**

15

Secured Party v. Buyer

CHAPTER OVERVIEW

A. **Introduction**
B. **Unperfected Security Interests**
C. **Perfected Security Interests**
  1. **Introduction**
  2. **Section 9-320(a)**
  3. **Section 9-320(b)**
  4. **The Farm Products Exception to § 9-320(a)**
D. **Closers**
✦ **Burnham's Picks**

A. Introduction

In Chapters 15 through 18, we will be dealing with various parties competing for the collateral. To solve the problem of which party prevails, we will use the following methodology:

1. Characterize the parties.
2. Classify the collateral.
3. Determine whether the security interest is perfected or unperfected.
4. Find the Code section that contains the appropriate rule.
5. Apply the facts to the rule to obtain the result.

We begin in this chapter with disputes between the secured party and a party who obtains the collateral when the debtor disposes of it. In the typical situation, we characterize that party as a buyer of the collateral. Recall that in Chapter 7.B we looked briefly at the issue of whether the security interest continues upon the disposition of the collateral. We looked at the rule of § 9-315(a)(1), which provides in part:

Except as otherwise provided in this article and in Section 2-403(2):

(1) a security interest or agricultural lien continues in collateral notwithstanding sale, lease, license, exchange, or other disposition thereof

unless the secured party authorized the disposition free of the security interest or agricultural lien.

We used this hypothetical:

Farmer Brown buys a "Model A irrigation system" and finances $100,000 of the purchase price with First Bank, giving the bank a security interest in the irrigation system. Two years later, Brown trades his Model A system to Farmer Smith for a cheaper Model B system plus $10,000 in cash. After the sale, Farmer Brown stops making his payments to First Bank. Under the general rule, can the bank repossess the Model A system, which is now owned by Farmer Smith?

The general rule says the answer is *yes*! The secured party (First Bank) can take the collateral out of the hands of the buyer (Smith), because the security interest, in the words of § 9-315(a)(1), "continues in collateral notwithstanding sale." Does this seem fair to the buyer? We noted that there are exceptions to the general rule. We looked at the exception expressly stated in § 9-315(a)(1): *"unless the secured party authorized the disposition,"* and concluded that it was unlikely that First Bank authorized the sale of the irrigation equipment in the security agreement.

The more general exception, stated at the beginning of § 9-315(a), is *"Except as otherwise provided in this Article."* We saw that Official Comment 2 to § 9-315 gave us a hint as to where we might look in Article 9 to find those other exceptions. We didn't take the journey at that time, leaving you in suspense. I know it has been tough to wait, but we're about to embark on a great voyage of discovery as we explore the other exceptions to the general rule that the security interest continues in the collateral after disposition by the debtor. These exceptions involve the following transactions:

- sale when the security interest is unperfected;
- sale of inventory;
- sale of seller's consumer goods to a consumer buyer; and
- sale of farm products.

B.   Unperfected Security Interests

Let's use our methodology to solve the problem that arose when Brown sold his irrigation system to Smith. In the Official Comment to § 9-315, we find the three variables that lead us to the Code section that contains the appropriate rule: the party, the status of the security interest as perfected or not, and the collateral:

Section 9-317 states when transferees take free of unperfected security interests; Sections 9-320 and 9-321 on goods, 9-321 on general intangibles, 9-330 on chattel paper and instruments, and 9-331 on negotiable instruments, negotiable documents and securities state when purchasers of such collateral take free of a security interest, even though perfected and even though the disposition was not authorized.

Let's identify the variables in our problem. (1) *The party:* Because he is a buyer, we identify Smith as a *transferee.* (2) *The status of the security interest:* We classify the security interest as *unperfected* because we have not been told that it was filed or otherwise perfected. The Comment tell us that "[s]ection 9-317 states when transferees take free of unperfected security interests," so we go to that section. The subsection that concerns buyers is § 9-317(b), which provides:

> **(b) Buyers that receive delivery.** Except as otherwise provided in subsection (e), a buyer, other than a secured party, of tangible chattel paper, documents, goods, instruments, or a certificated security takes free of a security interest or agricultural lien if the buyer gives value and receives delivery of the collateral without knowledge of the security interest or agricultural lien and before it is perfected.
>
> (3) *The collateral:* Since this rule refers to a buyer of "tangible chattel paper, documents, goods, instruments, or a certificated security," we must classify the collateral in order to determine whether this is the applicable rule. Do you think irrigation equipment is included within "tangible chattel paper, documents, goods, instruments, or a security certificate?" Sure. It is *goods.* See § 9-102(a)(44).

Now that we have found the appropriate rule, § 9-317(b), let's apply the facts to the rule to obtain the result. A buyer (that is Smith) of goods (that is the irrigation system) "takes free of a security interest . . . if the buyer gives value and receives delivery of the collateral without knowledge of the security interest . . . and before it is perfected." Did Smith give value? Yes, he paid for the goods. Did Smith take delivery without knowledge of the security interest? Yes. Did Smith take delivery before the security interest was perfected? Yes. Therefore, we conclude that Smith, the buyer, takes free of the Bank's security interest.

Let's review the methodology we used to solve this problem:

Characterize the parties: secured party and buyer
Classify the collateral: goods
SI perfected or unperfected: unperfected
Rule: § 9-317(b)
Result: buyer takes free (if gives value and receives delivery of the collateral without knowledge of the security interest)

Do you see the logic of the rule of § 9-317(b)? In the transaction between the debtor and the secured party, the buyer is a third party. If the third party has no notice of the security interest, either because the buyer lacked knowledge (lack of actual notice) or the security interest is unperfected (lack of constructive notice), then the third party should take free of it. In other words, a prospective buyer who is not informed of the security interest and who would find no notice of it in the filings takes free of it.

> **Question 1.** Farmer Brown buys a "Model A irrigation system" and finances $100,000 of the purchase price with First Bank, giving the bank a security interest in the irrigation system. The bank does not file a financing statement. Two years later, Brown trades his Model A system to Farmer Smith for a cheaper Model B system plus $10,000 in cash. During the negotiations for the sale, Smith asked Brown if the system had any liens on it. Brown replied, "Yes, the bank took a security interest in it, but those fools were asleep in their Secured Transactions class, and they neglected to file a financing statement to perfect it." After the sale, Farmer Brown stops making his payments to First Bank. Can the bank repossess the Model A system, which is now owned by Farmer Smith?
>
> **A.** Yes, because a security interest is effective as against purchasers.
> **B.** Yes, because the purchaser had knowledge of the security interest.
> **C.** No, because the bank did not perfect the security interest.
> **D.** No, because Smith is not the debtor.

Analysis.   Using our methodology, we see that we are again led to § 9-317(b). Applying the facts to the rule, we see that the facts have changed from our original hypothetical: here, Smith purchased with knowledge of the security interest. One of the conditions for a buyer to take free is that the buyer "receives delivery of the collateral without knowledge of the security interest." Since Farmer Smith had knowledge, the buyer does not take free. So **B** is the correct response.

We will now change the variable from an unperfected security interest to a perfected security interest.

C.   Perfected Security Interests

1. Introduction

According to Official Comment 2 to § 9-315, in a priority dispute between a secured creditor and a buyer, if the security interest is in *goods* and is *perfected*, we look to § 9-320 for the rules. Section 9-320 provides in principal part:

§ **9-320. Buyer of Goods**.

(a) **Buyer in ordinary course of business.** Except as otherwise provided in subsection (e), a buyer in ordinary course of business, other than a person buying farm products from a person engaged in farming operations, takes free of a security interest created by the buyer's seller, even if the security interest is perfected and the buyer knows of its existence.

(b) **Buyer of consumer goods.** Except as otherwise provided in subsection (e), a buyer of goods from a person who used or bought the goods for use primarily for personal, family, or household purposes takes free of a security interest, even if perfected, if the buyer buys:

(1) without knowledge of the security interest;

(2) for value;

(3) primarily for the buyer's personal, family, or household purposes; and

(4) before the filing of a financing statement covering the goods.

In order to apply our methodology to solve problems involving buyers of goods, we must determine whether the party is a "buyer in ordinary course of business," in which event, § 9-320(a) will apply, or a "buyer of consumer goods," in which case § 9-320(b) will apply.

Section 1-201(b)(9) contains a definition of "buyer in ordinary course of business" that is both important and complex:

(9) "Buyer in ordinary course of business" means a person that buys goods in good faith, without knowledge that the sale violates the rights of another person in the goods, and in the ordinary course from a person, other than a pawnbroker, in the business of selling goods of that kind. A person buys goods in the ordinary course if the sale to the person comports with the usual or customary practices in the kind of business in which the seller is engaged or with the seller's own usual or customary practices. A person that sells oil, gas, or other minerals at the wellhead or minehead is a person in the business of selling goods of that kind. A buyer in ordinary course of business may buy for cash, by exchange of other property, or on secured or unsecured credit, and may acquire goods or documents of title under a pre-existing contract for sale. Only a buyer that takes possession of the goods or has a right to recover the goods from the seller under Article 2 may be a buyer in ordinary course of business. A person that acquires goods in a transfer in bulk or as security for or in total or partial satisfaction of a money debt is not a buyer in ordinary course of business.

For purposes of § 9-320(a), the most important part of that definition describes the buyer as buying "from a person . . . in the business of selling goods of that kind." When a seller is in the business of selling a certain kind of goods, it is selling from its inventory. Therefore, read the "buyer in ordinary course of business" rule of § 9-320(a) as applying to a buyer of inventory in the hands of the seller. For example, when you buy a TV from Best Buy, you are a § 9-320(a) buyer.

Let us now return to the "buyer of consumer goods" rule of § 9-320(b). That section concerns a buyer who buys from a person "who used or bought the goods for use primarily for personal, family, or household purposes." Whenever you see that a person bought goods "primarily for personal, family, or household purposes," you are reminded of the definition of "consumer" in § 1-201(b)(11):

"Consumer" means an individual who enters into a transaction primarily for personal, family, or household purposes.

Therefore, § 9-320(b) applies to a buyer from a consumer seller. Furthermore, § 9-320(b)(3) provides that the buyer buys the goods "primarily for the buyer's personal, family, or household purposes." The goods must therefore be "consumer goods" as defined in § 9-102(a)(23):

"Consumer goods" means goods that are used or bought for use primarily for personal, family, or household purposes.

So we know that the buyer is a consumer buying consumer goods in the hands of the seller. Remember that we always characterize collateral from the point of view of the debtor. For Article 9 purposes, a store that has granted a security interest in its stock of dishwashers is not selling consumer goods; it is selling inventory. Therefore, "consumer goods in the hands of the seller" must refer to the consumer who has bought the dishwasher on credit and granted a security interest in it. When does § 9-320(b) apply? Think of it as the "yard sale" rule, for that is a typical place where consumer buyers meet with consumer sellers, although, of course, the yard sale is not the only transaction covered by the rule.

Question 2. *Statute reader.* First Bank took a security interest in the inventory of Sound City and perfected the security interest by filing. Tony is a lawyer who has been representing Sound City for several years. Sound City owed Tony $16,500 for legal services rendered in two employment discrimination suits. Tony agreed to accept a $14,000 sound system as partial payment, and Sound City installed the sound system in his home. On Sound City's default, is First Bank entitled to repossess the sound system from Tony?

A. Yes, because Tony is not a buyer in ordinary course.
B. Yes, because Tony did not act in good faith.
C. No, because the goods are consumer goods in the hands of Tony.
D. No, because Tony is a buyer from inventory.

Analysis. Since Tony obtained the goods from inventory, he would be a § 9-320(a) buyer if he is a "buyer in ordinary course of business." If you made it all the way through the definition of "buyer in ordinary course of business" in § 1-201(b)(9), you saw that "[a] person that acquires goods in a transfer in bulk or as security for or in total or partial satisfaction of a money debt is not a buyer in ordinary course of business." Since Tony acquired the goods in satisfaction of a money debt, Tony is not a buyer in ordinary course of business. Tony is not a consumer buyer of consumer goods, for the goods are not consumer goods in the hands of the seller: they are inventory. Furthermore, because the security interest is perfected by filing, Tony cannot be a § 9-317(b) buyer. Therefore, under the general rule of § 9-315, the security interest continues notwithstanding the disposition, so **A** is the correct response.

Question 3. First Bank has a perfected security interest in the inventory of Bitterroot Motors. Mary purchases a car for her personal use from Bitterroot Motors on credit, and Bitterroot Motors takes a security interest in the car. Which of the following statements is true?

A. First Bank is a § 9-320(a) buyer because it has a security interest in inventory.

B. Mary is a § 9-320(a) buyer because she is buying from inventory.

C. Mary is a § 9-320(b) buyer because she is buying for personal use.

D. Bitterroot Motors is a § 9-320(b) buyer because it has a security interest in consumer goods.

Analysis. First, let's characterize the parties. In the First Bank–Bitterroot Motors transaction, First Bank is a secured party, not a buyer. Therefore, **A** cannot be a correct response. Similarly, in the Bitterroot Motors–Mary transaction, Bitterroot Motors is a secured party, not a buyer. Therefore, **D** cannot be a correct response. It is true that Mary is buying for personal use. But a § 9-320(b) buyer must also be buying from a seller who uses the goods as consumer goods, and that is not true of Mary's seller, Bitterroot Motors, so **C** is not a correct response. In the hands of Bitterroot Motors, the goods are inventory. Therefore, response **B** is correct.

Now that we understand the vocabulary, let's take a closer look at these sections.

2. Section 9-320(a)

Section 9-320(a) provides:

> (a) **Buyer in ordinary course of business.** Except as otherwise provided in subsection (e), a buyer in ordinary course of business, other than a person buying farm products from a person engaged in farming operations, takes free of a security interest created by the buyer's seller, even if the security interest is perfected and the buyer knows of its existence.

As we saw in the introduction, this subsection applies to a "buyer in ordinary course of business," who is a buyer from inventory. According to the subsection, such a buyer "takes free of a security interest created by the buyer's seller, even if the security interest is perfected and the buyer knows of its existence." Why should a buyer from inventory take free of a security interest? For example, First Bank has a perfected security interest in the inventory of Bitterroot Motors, and Mary purchases a car from Bitterroot Motors. Should Mary take the car subject to the bank's security interest? Of course not. The bank *wants* Bitterroot Motors to sell the cars, because that is how Bitterroot Motors gets the money to pay off the debt.

Note that under this provision, the buyer takes free "even if the security interest is perfected and the buyer knows of its existence." So if the salesperson at Bitterroot Motors tells Mary, "We just want you to know that First Bank has a perfected security interest in this car," Mary can tell the salesperson, "Ha! Ha! I don't care because I am a § 9-320(a) buyer!"

Question 4. *Statute reader.* Holland, a resident of Florida, purchased a mechanical harvester. The purchase was financed by Exchange Bank, which took a security interest in the harvester and properly filed. Holland, without the permission of the bank and in violation of the security agreement, sold the harvester to CB&O Equipment in Iowa, which is in the business of selling farm equipment. Jarrett purchased the harvester from CB&O and took it to Montana. The bank discovered these facts. Can the bank repossess the harvester from Jarrett? (Hint: Note that this question is a statute reader. Read § 9-320(a) carefully before you answer.)

A. No, because Jarrett is a § 9-320(a) buyer.
B. No, because the bank's security interest was not perfected, since it did not file in Iowa.
C. Yes, because the security interest was not created by Jarrett's seller.
D. No, because a reasonable buyer could not have checked the filings and found the security interest.

Analysis. Section 9-320(a) provides:

Buyer of Goods.

(a) **Buyer in ordinary course of business.** Except as otherwise provided in subsection (e), a buyer in ordinary course of business, other than a person buying farm products from a person engaged in farming operations, takes free of a security interest created by the buyer's seller, even if the security interest is perfected and the buyer knows of its existence.

Response **B** raises a review question. Does a filing creditor have to monitor the collateral and refile when the collateral changes its location? No. We saw in Chapter 12.D that a financing statement is filed where the debtor is located, not where the collateral is located. So response **B** is not correct. We know that normally a buyer in ordinary course of business (that is, a buyer from inventory) takes free of a security interest; but note that the rule only applies to a security interest "created by the buyer's seller." Here, the security interest was not created by CB&O, which was Jarrett's seller; it was created by Holland. Therefore, response **A** is not correct. This can be a harsh rule, as there is little Jarrett could have done to find the security interest. So the bad news for Jarrett is that **D** is not correct either: **C** is correct. See *Exchange Bank of Osceola v. Jarrett*, 588 P.2d 1006 (Mont. 1979) (decided under former Article 9). Incidentally, in its opinion, the court stated, "It may be that legislative action is necessary to prevent such results in the future." However, no action was taken in Revised Article 9 to change this result.

Question 5. Holland, a resident of Florida, purchased a mechanical harvester. The purchase was financed by Exchange Bank, which took a security interest in the harvester and properly filed. Holland, without the permission of the bank and in violation of the security agreement, sold the harvester to CB&O Equipment in Iowa, which is in the business of selling farm equipment. Jarrett purchased the harvester from CB&O and took it to Montana. The bank discovered these facts and repossessed the harvester from Jarrett. Does Jarrett have any recourse?

A. Yes, against Holland for breaching his security agreement.
B. Yes, against the bank for not monitoring its collateral.
C. Yes, against CB&O for breach of the warranty of good title.
D. No, Jarrett has no recourse.

Analysis. This question provides an opportunity to review (I hope it is review!) your knowledge of Article 2. Section 2-312(1)(b) provides:

> **§ 2-312. Warranty of Title and Against Infringement.**
>   (1) Subject to subsection (2), there is in a contract for sale a warranty by the seller that: . . .
>   (b) the goods shall be delivered free from any security interest or other lien or encumbrance of which the buyer at the time of contracting has no knowledge.

The correct response is **C.** Jarrett would have a claim against the seller for breach of the warranty of good title, which is found in every contract for the sale of goods. We often think of that warranty as providing that the seller promises that it is the owner of the goods, but the seller also promises that no undisclosed security interests are attached to the goods. You probably also remember that while a seller may disclaim that warranty, the general disclaimer of implied warranties under § 2-316 does not do the job; according to § 2-312(2), it may be disclaimed only by specific language.

3. *Section 9-320(b)*

Section 9-320(b) provides:

> **(b) Buyer of consumer goods.** Except as otherwise provided in subsection (e), a buyer of goods from a person who used or bought the goods

for use primarily for personal, family, or household purposes takes free of a security interest, even if perfected, if the buyer buys:

> (1) without knowledge of the security interest;
>
> (2) for value;
>
> (3) primarily for the buyer's personal, family, or household purposes; and
>
>> (4) before the filing of a financing statement covering the goods.

As a practical matter, most buyers aren't expected to check the filings before making a purchase. As we have seen, if the purchase is from inventory, there is generally no need to check the filings. And with respect to the consumer buyer of consumer goods, usually the secured party who takes a security interest in consumer goods doesn't file anyway. Do you remember why? See Chapter 14.E. Right! Most security interests in consumer goods are purchase money security interests (see § 9-103), and they are automatically perfected (see § 9-309(1)). Therefore, under § 9-320(b), the qualified buyer takes free of the security interest "even if perfected." For example, assume I buy a washer from Sears for my home on credit and grant Sears a security interest in it. I then sell it to you to use in your home. You take the dishwasher free of Sears' security interest, even though that security interest was perfected by automatic perfection.

There are, however, a couple of catches. Subsection 9-302(b)(1) provides that the buyer takes free only if the buyer buys "without knowledge of the security interest." For example, assume I tell you, "Sears took a security interest in this washer, but they never bothered to file it!" Because of your knowledge of the security interest, you have lost your status as a § 9-320(b) buyer. Most importantly, subsection (b)(4) provides that the buyer takes free only if the buyer buys "before the filing of a financing statement covering the goods." Under this provision, if the secured party perfects by filing rather than by relying on automatic perfection, the buyer loses his or her status as a § 9-320(b) buyer.

Why would a secured party bother to file to perfect a security interest in consumer goods? The designation "consumer goods" refers to the debtor's use of the goods, not to the value of the item. Recall our $2 million painting. If I buy a Renoir for $2 million to hang in my living room and the gallery finances the purchase, taking a security interest in the Renoir, then the Renoir is consumer goods. It would be prudent for the gallery to spring for the filing fee to give the world notice of its interest. So the next time you are thinking of buying a "big ticket" item from a consumer, a light should go on, and you should say, "Hold on while I check the filings! I want to be sure I am a § 9-320(b) buyer."

Question 6. Deborah bought furniture for her home on credit from Friendly Furniture and granted Friendly a security interest in the furniture. Friendly did not file a financing statement, but its security agreement expressly prohibited Deborah from disposing of the furniture while it was subject to the security interest. Several months later, without Friendly's permission, Deborah sold the furniture at a yard sale to Brenda, who planned to use the furniture in her home. Friendly discovered these facts and insisted that Brenda surrender the furniture. Brenda refused. In a dispute between Friendly and Brenda, does Brenda take free of Friendly's security interest?

A. Yes, because Friendly's security interest was not perfected.
B. Yes, even though Friendly's security interest was perfected.
C. No, because Friendly's security interest was automatically perfected.
D. No, because Deborah's sale violated the terms of her security agreement with Friendly.

Analysis. Section 9-320(b) provides:

> (b) **Buyer of consumer goods.** Except as otherwise provided in subsection (e), a buyer of goods from a person who used or bought the goods for use primarily for personal, family, or household purposes takes free of a security interest, even if perfected, if the buyer buys:
>> (1) without knowledge of the security interest;
>> (2) for value;
>> (3) primarily for the buyer's personal, family, or household purposes; and
>> (4) before the filing of a financing statement covering the goods.

All of the elements of this provision are satisfied by the facts. Friendly's security interest was automatically perfected under § 9-309(1), but it was not perfected by filing, which would have prevented this consumer buyer from taking free of it. Therefore, Brenda takes free and the correct response is **B.**

What about the language in the contract that prohibited Deborah from disposing of the furniture? The sale would constitute a breach of contract by Deborah, but would have no effect on Brenda.

Question 7. Deborah bought furniture for her home on credit from Friendly Furniture and granted Friendly a security interest in the furniture. Friendly did not file a financing statement, but its security agreement expressly prohibited Deborah from disposing of the furniture while it was subject to the security interest. Several months later, without Friendly's permission, Deborah sold the furniture at a yard sale to Brenda, who planned to use the furniture in her home. At the time of the sale, Deborah said to Brenda, "Friendly Furniture took a security interest in this furniture, but I checked, and they never filed it." Friendly discovered these facts and insisted that Brenda surrender the furniture. Brenda refused. In a dispute

> between Friendly and Brenda, would you advise Brenda that she bought
> the furniture subject to Friendly's security interest?
>
> A. Yes, because she bought with knowledge of it.
> B. Yes, because she did not buy for value.
> C. Yes, because she did not buy primarily for personal, family, or
>   household purposes.
> D. No, even though it remained perfected after the sale.

Analysis.   The correct response is **A.** According to § 9-320(b)(1), the buyer
takes free if the buyer buys "without knowledge of the security interest." So
even though Brenda satisfies the other elements of § 9-320(b), she did not
satisfy that one. Brenda does not take free because she bought with knowledge
of the security interest.

> **Question 8.** Farmer Brown buys a "Model A irrigation system" and
> finances $100,000 of the purchase price with First Bank, giving the bank
> a security interest in the irrigation system. First Bank files a financing
> statement. Two years later, Brown trades his Model A system to Farmer
> Smith for a cheaper Model B system plus $10,000 in cash. After the sale,
> Farmer Brown stops making his payments to First Bank. Can the bank
> repossess the Model A system, which is now owned by Farmer Smith?
>
> A. Yes, because a security interest is effective as against purchasers.
> B. Yes, because the purchaser had actual knowledge of the security
>   interest.
> C. No, because the bank did not perfect the security interest.
> D. No, because Smith is not the debtor.

Analysis.   Let us take a final look at this hypothetical. Using our methodology, we (1) characterize the parties as secured party and buyer; (2) classify
the collateral as equipment; and (3) determine that the security interest is
perfected.

Since the goods are neither inventory nor consumer goods in the hands
of the seller, neither of the § 9-320 exceptions applies. Because the security
interested is perfected, the § 9-317(b) rule does not apply. Therefore, in the
absence of any exceptions, we go back to the general rule of § 9-315(a)(1): the
security interest "continues in collateral notwithstanding sale." Therefore, **A** is
the correct response.

Does this result make sense? Yes. If a buyer is making a purchase from a
seller who doesn't usually sell goods of that kind (that is, they are not inventory in the hands of that seller), then the prudent buyer should check the filings. If the security interest is not perfected by filing, the buyer takes free of
the security interest; if it is filed, the buyer takes subject to the security interest.

4. The Farm Products Exception to § 9-320(a)

We saw in part C.2 of this chapter that, under § 9-320(a), a buyer from inventory takes free of a security interest created by the buyer's seller. We did not, however, deal with the exception stated in § 9-320(a): "other than a person buying farm products from a person engaged in farming operations." See the definition of "farm products" in § 9-102(a)(34). Our analysis of this exception starts out easy but quickly becomes complex because of an applicable federal statute.

> **Question 9.** First Bank takes a security interest in the crops of a farmer and files in the office of the Secretary of State. A representative from General Mills buys 50,000 bushels of wheat from the farmer. Under the uniform version of the UCC, does General Mills take free of First Bank's security interest?
>
> A. Yes, because General Mills is a buyer in ordinary course of business.
> B. Yes, because General Mills is buying the wheat to turn it into consumer goods.
> C. No, because First Bank did not properly perfect.
> D. No, because General Mills is buying farm products from a person engaged in farming operations.

Analysis. We saw in Chapter 12.D.3 that, in most jurisdictions, § 9-501 (a)(2) provides that the proper place for filing financing statements is the office of the Secretary of State, so First Bank properly perfected. Therefore, **C** is not correct. The use General Mills will make of the wheat is not relevant; it is classified as "farm products" (see § 9-102(a)(34)) in the hands of the debtor, so **B** is not correct. We know from § 9-320(a) that, in general, a buyer in ordinary course of business takes free of a perfected security interest. However, the exception tells us that this rule does not apply to "a person buying farm products from a person engaged in farming operations." Since the farmer is engaged in farming operations, and General Mills is buying farm products, it appears that the exception applies. Therefore, response **A** is incorrect, and response **D** is correct. General Mills does not take free of the security interest.

To complicate matters, the exception stated in § 9-320(a) is the subject of a federal statute, the Food Security Act of 1985. Section 1631(d) of the Act (7 U.S.C. § 1631(d)) provides:

> **(d) Purchases free of security interest.** Except as provided in subsection (e) of this section and notwithstanding any other provision of Federal, State, or local law, a buyer who in the ordinary course of business buys a farm product from a seller engaged in farming operations shall take free of a security interest created by the seller, even though the security interest is perfected; and the buyer knows of the existence of such interest.

Question 10. First Bank takes a security interest in the crops of a farmer and files in the office of the Secretary of State. A representative from General Mills buys 50,000 bushels of wheat from the farmer. Based on the language of UCC § 9-320(a) and 7 U.S.C. § 1631(d), does General Mills take free of First Bank's security interest?

A. Yes, because the Food Security Act so provides, and in a conflict between the Food Security Act and the UCC, the Food Security Act governs.

B. Yes, because the UCC so provides, and in a conflict between the Food Security Act and the UCC, the UCC governs.

C. No, because the UCC so provides, and in a conflict between the Food Security Act and the UCC, the UCC governs.

D. No, because the Food Security Act so provides, and in a conflict between the Food Security Act and the UCC, the Food Security Act governs.

Analysis.   We have already seen that under the UCC, General Mills does not take free of the security interest. Under Food Security Act § 1631(d), however, General Mills does take free of the security interest. So which one governs? As a general rule, when both a federal and a state statute govern the same transaction, the federal law preempts the state law. This preemption is made explicit by this federal statute, which provides that it is the rule "notwithstanding any other provision of Federal, State, or local law." Therefore, response **A** is correct when we consider just those statutes. There are, however, exceptions.

Having completed that analysis, we note that the rule of § 1631(d) applies "[e]xcept as provided in subsection (e)." There are two principal parts to subsection (e). They make sense in the context that one of the principal reasons Congress enacted the Food Security Act is that many states had either no filing system or a filing system for farm products under which the financing statement had to be filed in the county where the farmer resided. We will call this "local" filing. It was a hardship for buyers, who were often multistate or international corporations, to discover the existence of the security interest. So Congress made it easier for them to find the filings by setting up two schemes, one in § 1631(e)(1) for states that have local filing and one in § 1631(e)(2) for states that have central filing with the Secretary of State. Beware, however—the rule does not apply to all states with central filing for farm products, but as defined in § 1631(c)(2), only to states with central filing systems that have been certified by the Department of Agriculture. While most states now have central filing for farm products, most have not been certified.

If there is local filing or non-certified central filing, then for the secured party to prevail over the buyer, it must give actual notice to the buyer of the farm products in which it has a security interest. If there is certified central filing, then for the secured party to prevail over the buyer, it must file what the statute describes as an "effective financing statement," which unfortunately differs a bit from an effective financing statement under Article 9. If the secured party makes an effective filing, and the buyer registers with the Secretary of State so that it obtains notice of the filings, then the buyer takes subject to the security interest. In most cases, then, the buyer becomes informed of the security interest in one of these ways and obtains a release of the security interest from the secured party before it purchases the farm products.

Question 11. In a state that has certified central filing of farm products, First Bank took a security interest in the wheat crop of McDonald, a farmer in Cascade County, and filed in the county. McDonald truthfully told First Bank that he had always sold his crop to Cargill, and First Bank duly notified Cargill of the security interest. McDonald then sold his wheat to General Mills. Did General Mills take the crop free of the security interest?

A. No, because under § 9-320(a), a buyer in ordinary course of business, *other than a person buying farm products from a person engaged in farming operations*, takes free of a security interest created by the buyer's seller.

B. No, because First Bank made a good faith effort to notify buyers of wheat from McDonald of its security interest.

C. Yes, because First Bank did not send proper notice to General Mills.

D. Yes, because First Bank did not properly file with the central filing system.

Analysis.   The federal Food Security Act preempts Article 9. If the state has certified central filing, then, under Food Security Act § 1631(e)(2), the buyer takes subject to a security interest if the buyer has failed to register with the central filing office and the secured party has filed an effective financing statement. Here, the secured party did not file an effective financing statement, so the buyer takes free of the security interest. The correct response is **D.**

Question 12. In a state where notice of security interests in farm products is filed in the county where the farmer resides, First Bank took a security interest in the wheat crop of Farmer McDonald and filed in the county. McDonald truthfully told First Bank that he had always sold his crop to Cargill, and First Bank duly notified Cargill of the security interest. McDonald then sold his wheat to General Mills. Did General Mills take the crop free of the bank's security interest?

A. No, because, under § 9-320(a), a buyer in ordinary course of business, *other than a person buying farm products from a person engaged in farming operations*, takes free of a security interest created by the buyer's seller.
B. No, because First Bank properly filed in the county.
C. Yes, because First Bank did not send proper notice to General Mills.
D. Yes, because First Bank did not properly file with the central filing system.

Analysis. Because this state does not have certified central filing, the applicable rule is found in Food Security Act § 1631(e)(1). Even though First Bank properly filed, the buyer does not have to search for local filings but looks to notice from the secured party. Here, the bank did not give notice to General Mills, so the correct response is **C.** First Bank's claim is against the farmer. Since the scheme is dependent on the farmer telling the buyer to whom it should give notice, there is a sanction in § 1631(h)(3) if the farmer violates this provision.

D. Closers

Question 13. Bank has a perfected security interest in Jeweler's inventory, which consists of a few items of high value. The security agreement provides that Bank must consent to any sale by Jeweler, and Bank has never waived this right. Jeweler tells a buyer that Bank "has a security interest" in an item that the buyer is planning to wear on special occasions. Jeweler sells the item to the buyer without obtaining the consent of Bank. Does the security interest continue in the item?

A. Yes, because the sale violated a term of the security agreement.
B. Yes, because the buyer knew that there was a security interest in the item.
C. No, because the buyer was a buyer in ordinary course of business.
D. No, because the buyer bought for personal, family, or household purposes.

Analysis. The facts that the sale violated the security agreement and that the buyer knew Bank had a security interest do not change the rule of § 9-320(a) that the buyer in ordinary course of business takes free even if the buyer knows of the existence of the security interest. Therefore, the correct answer is **C**. However, if the buyer knew that the sale violated the terms of the security agreement, then the buyer would not be a "buyer in ordinary course of business" under § 1-201(b)(9), because he would not be "without knowledge that the sale violates the rights of another person in the goods." In that event, he would buy subject to the security interest. In other words, there is a difference between mere knowledge that the seller has a security interest and knowledge that the sale violates the terms of a security agreement.

Question 14. On April 1, AP Furniture sold a reclining chair for $500 to Homer Simpson on credit, took a security interest in the chair, and delivered it to Simpson's house, where he used it in his living room. AP did not file a financing statement. On April 7, Simpson's neighbor Ned Flanders offered Simpson a box of donuts for the chair, which Flanders planned to use in his rec room, and Simpson accepted. On Simpson's default, can AP enforce its security interest in the chair against Flanders?

A. No, because the security interest was not perfected.
B. No, because AP did not file a financing statement.
C. Yes, because Flanders did not give value for the chair.
D. Yes, because under the general rule, a security interest remains notwithstanding sale.

Analysis.   This question invokes the "yard sale" exception of § 9-320(b), where a person who bought goods for consumer purposes sells them to a consumer buyer. The rule is that the buyer takes free of the security interest if the buyer buys (1) without knowledge; (2) for value; (3) for personal, family, or household purposes; and (4) before a financing statement was filed. Here, elements (1), (3), and (4) are clearly satisfied. **A** is not correct because the security interest was perfected—it was automatically perfected under § 9-309(1). The question of whether value was given is answered by the definition of "value" in § 1-204(4): "a person gives value for rights if the person acquires them . . . in return for any consideration sufficient to support a simple contract." As you recall from Contracts, the law does not inquire into the adequacy of consideration. As long as there was a bargain, there was consideration. Since Flanders gave value, **C** is not correct. With that element satisfied, all the elements of § 9-320(b) are satisfied, so **D** is wrong because an exception to the general rule has been established. Under the rule of § 9-320(b), a creditor has to file to prevail over this buyer. Since AP did not file, **B** is the correct response.

Burnham's Picks

Question 1	**B**
Question 2	**A**
Question 3	**B**
Question 4	**C**
Question 5	**C**
Question 6	**B**
Question 7	**A**
Question 8	**A**
Question 9	**D**
Question 10	**A**
Question 11	**D**
Question 12	**C**
Question 13	**C**
Question 14	**B**

16

Secured Party v. Secured Party

A. The General Rules of Priority: § 9-322

1. Introduction

Determining priority between secured creditors is like playing poker. You first have to read the hands by determining the nature of each party's holding—what is their interest in the collateral? Then you have to rank the hands by applying the appropriate rule to determine which holding prevails over another.

To solve priority problems, we will continue to use the following methodology:

1. Characterize the parties.
2. Classify the collateral.
3. Determine whether the security interest is perfected or unperfected.
4. Find the Code sections that contain the appropriate rule.
5. Apply the facts to the rule to obtain the result.

For this chapter, assume that we have characterized the parties competing for priority in the collateral and we have determined that each is a secured creditor with a security interest in the same collateral. The general rule for resolving a priority contest among secured parties is found in § 9-322:

§ **9-322. Priorities among Conflicting Security Interests in and Agricultural Liens on Same Collateral.**

(a) **General priority rules.** Except as otherwise provided in this section, priority among conflicting security interests and agricultural liens in the same collateral is determined according to the following rules:

(1) Conflicting perfected security interests and agricultural liens rank according to priority in time of filing or perfection. Priority dates from the earlier of the time a filing covering the collateral is first made or the security interest or agricultural lien is first perfected, if there is no period thereafter when there is neither filing nor perfection.

(2) A perfected security interest or agricultural lien has priority over a conflicting unperfected security interest or agricultural lien.

(3) The first security interest or agricultural lien to attach or become effective has priority if conflicting security interests and agricultural liens are unperfected.

(b) **Time of perfection: proceeds and supporting obligations.** For the purposes subsection (a)(1):

(1) the time of filing or perfection as to a security interest in collateral is also the time of filing or perfection as to a security interest in proceeds; and

(2) the time of filing or perfection as to a security interest in collateral supported by a supporting obligation is also the time of filing or perfection as to a security interest in the supporting obligation.

Subject of course to exceptions, the basic rule of § 9-322(a)(1) is that "conflicting perfected security interests . . . rank according to priority in time of filing or perfection." Recall that § 9-308(a) provides that a security interest is perfected if "it has attached and all of the applicable requirements for perfection have been satisfied." Therefore, perfection requires attachment. Filing, however, does not require attachment. Recall that § 9-502(d) provides that an effective filing can be made at any time, even before attachment, as long as it is authorized. Therefore, in order to resolve priority disputes, we must look for (1) effective filings, and (2) perfection by means other than filing.

2. Methods of Perfection

If each secured party has used the same method of filing or perfection, then priority generally goes to the first in time. But as we saw in Chapters 13 and 14, there are many different methods of perfection, and sometimes a certain type of collateral can be perfected in different ways. If each secured party has used a different method of perfection, then we have to look at Article 9 rules that may give a priority to one method of perfection over another method. The four principal methods of perfection are filing, possession, control, and automatic perfection.

Filing. The general rule is that collateral may be perfected by an Article 9 filing. See § 9-310(a). The exceptions are enumerated in § 9-310(b). The exceptions include deposit accounts, letter of credit rights, money, and property subject to a statutory system, such as titled goods and property subject to a federal filing system. Deposit accounts and letter of credit rights may be perfected only by control. Money may be perfected only by possession. Goods that must be perfected by notation on the title vary from state to state. Federal filing schemes exist for such property as aircraft, ships, and intellectual property.

Possession. Types of collateral that can be perfected by possession are enumerated in § 9-313. These include tangible chattel paper, tangible documents, goods, instruments, and money.

Control. Types of collateral that can be perfected by control are enumerated in § 9-314. These include investment property, deposit accounts, letter of credit rights, electronic chattel paper, and electronic documents. As noted above, deposit accounts and letter of credit rights may be perfected only by control.

Automatic perfection. Many types of collateral are temporarily automatically perfected or automatically perfected under narrow circumstances. See § 9-309 for these rules. The principal one that we are concerned with is automatic perfection of a PMSI in consumer goods (other than titled goods). See § 9-309(1) and Chapter 14.E.

3. Priority

Now that we have a sense of the different methods of perfection, let's look at the priority rules for different types of collateral.

Deposit accounts. These rules are found in § 9-327, and give priority to the party with control. However, a security interest held by the bank with which the deposit account is maintained has priority over a conflicting interest held by another secured party. The secured party, may, however, gain priority over the bank by becoming the bank's customer with respect to the deposit account under § 9-104(a)(3).

Investment property. These rules are found in § 9-328. A secured party with control of investment property has priority over a secured party that does not have control. The priority as between two parties with control is not merely based on first in time, however. See the Official Comments to that section to see how it is worked out.

Letter of credit rights. The rules are found in § 9-329. They are similar to the rules for investment property, except that the security interests perfected by control rank according to priority in time of obtaining control.

Chattel paper and documents. The rules are found in § 9-330. Recall that chattel paper and documents can be perfected by filing, possession, or control. Another complication is that the priority rules for chattel paper may depend on whether the secured party claims the chattel paper as original collateral or as proceeds. The rules operate to permit a purchaser (which you recall includes a secured party) of chattel paper and instruments that has perfection by possession to have priority over a secured party who is perfected in another manner. Fortunately, the working out of these details is beyond our scope.

> **Question 1.** *Statute reader.* Farmer Wicks took his wheat crop to the Chester Co-op Grain Elevator, which gave him a negotiable warehouse receipt. Farmer Wicks then agreed with First Bank that in consideration of a loan, Wicks granted First Bank a security interest in the wheat he has stored in the warehouse, and he gave First Bank the warehouse receipt. Wicks then asked Second Bank for a loan, offering as collateral the wheat that is stored in the warehouse. Second Bank checked the filings and found no financing statement indicating an interest in the wheat. Second Bank loaned the money to Wicks, and Wicks granted a security interest in the wheat, which Second Bank then filed. Which bank has priority in the wheat in the Grain Elevator?
>
> See §§ 1-201(b)(16), 1-201(b)(42), 7(yes, 7)-106, 9-102(a)(30), 9-312(c), 9-313(a).
>
> A. First Bank, because while both security interests were perfected, First Bank was first to file or perfect.
>
> B. First Bank, because its perfected security interest in the warehouse receipt has priority over Second Bank's perfected security interest in the wheat.
>
> C. Second Bank, because First Bank's security interest was unperfected.
>
> D. Second Bank, because First Bank did not have the Chester Co-op authenticate a record acknowledging that it holds possession of the collateral for the secured party's benefit.

Analysis.   A good place to start is to characterize the collateral held by First Bank. It is a *document*, which is defined in § 9-102(a)(30) as a "document of title." That is the subject matter of Article 7. The term *document of title* is defined in § 1-201(b)(16) as including a *warehouse receipt*, which is defined in § 1-201(b)(42) as "a document of title issued by a person engaged in the business of storing goods for hire." This describes the document that Farmer Wicks obtained from the Co-op. It enables him to obtain the wheat, and since it is described as a "negotiable" document, it can be transferred from one person to another, giving the recipient the right to delivery of the goods. See § 7-104. It should be apparent that the negotiable document is a valuable item of personal property, but the complication is that a security interest could be obtained in either the underlying goods, the wheat, or in the document that allows one to obtain those goods from the warehouse. The question then becomes which security interest and method of perfection would give a secured party priority.

Response **D** is not correct, because § 9-313(c) provides that this method of possession applies only "to collateral other than certificated securities and goods covered by a document." Here, we are dealing with goods covered by a document. Section 9-312(a) provides that "a security interest in documents . . . may be perfected by filing." However, filing is not the exclusive method of perfection. Section 9-313(a) provides that "a secured party may perfect a security interest in tangible negotiable documents . . . by taking possession of the collateral." Here, First Bank took possession when it obtained the document from Farmer Wicks. Therefore, First Bank was perfected by possession. A security interest in goods such as the wheat may be perfected by filing. See § 9-310(a). Therefore, Second Bank was also perfected.

The conflict between these two perfected security interests is resolved by § 9-312(c). It provides:

> (c) [**Goods covered by negotiable document.**] While goods are in the possession of a bailee that has issued a negotiable document covering the goods:
>> (1) a security interest in the goods may be perfected by perfecting a security interest in the document; and
>> (2) a security interest perfected in the document has priority over any security interest that becomes perfected in the goods by another method during that time.

Here, the security interest perfected in the document (First Bank's security interest) has priority over a security interest perfected by another method during that time. Second Bank's security interest was perfected during the time the goods were in the possession of the bailee (Chester Co-op Grain Elevator). Therefore, First Bank has priority over Second Bank. **B** is the correct response. Note that if Second Bank had perfected its security interest before the wheat was delivered to the warehouse, then Second Bank would have priority.

B. The Rules of Priority Between Parties Who Perfected by Filing

We will now focus on perfection by filing. We're going to do something different in this part of the book. There is little I can tell you about solving these problems other than to read and apply the statute. So let's get right into the questions, each one of which requires you to read the indicated statute and use our methodology to answer them.

1. Unperfected Security Interests: § 9-322(a)(3)

Question 2. On January 1, Creditor 1 sells Consumer a car. Consumer promises to pay Creditor 1 installments of $300 per month for five years. Creditor 1 takes a security interest in the car but does not perfect. On February 1, Creditor 2 loans Consumer $10,000 and takes a security interest in the car. Creditor 2 does not perfect. On March 1, Consumer defaults as to both creditors. Whose claim to the car has priority?

A. Creditor 1, because its security interest was first to attach.
B. Creditor 2, because Creditor 1's failure to file misled Creditor 2 into thinking there were no security interests in the car.
C. Both have a claim that is prorated according to the amount of the debt.
D. Neither has an enforceable security interest because they both failed to perfect.

Analysis. Creditor 1 is a secured party with a security interest that attached on January 1, but it is not perfected. Creditor 2 is a secured party with a security interest that attached on February 1, but it is not perfected. Section 9-322(a)(3) provides that as between two unperfected security interests, the first to attach has priority. That is Creditor 1, so the correct response is **A**.

As a practical matter, you may wonder how this could happen. Once the facts were discovered, wouldn't the secured parties file immediately? Where this situation has come up, each secured party had thought it was perfected, but the court determined it was unperfected; the filing was deemed not effective because it had been filed in the wrong place or under the wrong name or for some other reason. These, of course, are things that you will never do.

2. *Perfected Security Interests: §§ 9-322(a)(1) and (a)(2)*

Question 3. On February 2, Creditor 1 lends D $2,000 and obtains a security interest in D's existing equipment. On March 2, D seeks a loan from Creditor 2. Creditor 2 asks D if he has granted anyone a security interest, and D responds, "Yes. I granted Creditor 1 a security interest in equipment." Creditor 2 nevertheless lends D $2,000 and obtains a security interest in the same equipment. Creditor 2 files a financing statement on March 3. Creditor 1 files its financing statement on April 2. Whose claim has priority?

A. Creditor 1, because its security interest was first to attach.
B. Creditor 1, because Creditor 2 had actual knowledge of the security interest of Creditor 1.
C. Creditor 2, because it was first to file or perfect.
D. Both have a claim that is prorated according to the amount of the debt.

Analysis.   Creditor 1 has a security interest that was perfected by filing on April 2. Creditor 2 has a security interest that was perfected by filing on March 3. Section 9-322(a)(1) provides that "[c]onflicting perfected security interests . . . rank according to priority in time of filing or perfection. Priority dates from the earlier of the time a filing covering the collateral is first made or the security interest or agricultural lien is first perfected." Therefore, Creditor 2's security interest has priority over Creditor 1's, because it was the first to be filed. The correct response is **C.** Note that the fact that Creditor 2 had actual knowledge of Creditor 1's security interest is irrelevant; the rule that only constructive knowledge by filing is significant protects the integrity of the filing system and prevents factual disputes.

Question 4. On January 1, Creditor 1 sells D on credit a $1,000 washer for her home laundry and obtains a security interest in the washer. Creditor 1 does not file a financing statement. On February 1, Creditor 2 lends D $1,000 and obtains a security interest in D's washer. Creditor 2 files a financing statement. On June 1, D defaults as to both creditors. Which security interest has priority?

A. Creditor 1, because it was first to file or perfect.
B. Creditor 2, because it was first to file or perfect.
C. Creditor 1 because PMSIs are entitled to a superpriority over regular security interests.
D. Creditor 1 because a PMSI seller has priority over a PMSI financer.

Analysis. This is a tricky application of the same rule. What you need to notice is that Creditor 1 is a secured party whose interest is *perfected* on January 1. This is because Creditor 1 has a PMSI in consumer goods that was automatically perfected under § 9-309(1). Review Chapter 4.D on PMSIs, and Chapter 14.E on automatic perfection.

Creditor 2 is a secured party whose interest was perfected by filing on February 1. We then apply the rule of § 9-322(a)(1) that provides that "[c]onflicting perfected security interests . . . rank according to priority in time of filing or perfection." Here, Creditor 1 has priority because it was first to file or perfect. Therefore, the correct response is **A.**

Question 5. D is seeking a $40,000 loan from Creditor 1. In the course of the negotiations, with D's consent, Creditor 1 files a financing statement on January 4, 2015, indicating D's accounts as collateral. Creditor 1 and D are unable to agree on terms, and no loan is made. On February 2, 2018, Creditor 2 lends D $50,000 and obtains and perfects a security interest in D's accounts. On March 1, 2018, Creditor 1 lends D $40,000 and obtains a security interest in D's accounts. Which claim has priority?

A. Creditor 1, because it was first to file or perfect.
B. Creditor 2, because it was first to file or perfect.
C. Creditor 2, because there was no other creditor with a security interest in D's accounts at the time of its transaction with D.
D. Creditor 2, because Creditor 1 failed to file after the March 1, 2018, transaction.

Analysis. This is just another tricky application of the same rule. Creditor 1 is a secured party whose interest was filed on January 4, 2015. Creditor 2 is a secured party whose interest was filed on February 2, 2018. We then apply the rule of § 9-322(a)(1) that provides that "[c]onflicting perfected security interests . . . rank according to priority in time of filing or perfection." Here, Creditor 1 has priority because it was first to file or perfect. Therefore, the correct response is **A.** Creditor 2 found Creditor 1's filing, and even though there had been no loan at that time, Creditor 2 was on notice that Creditor 1 would enjoy priority if a loan was made. With the debtor's authorization, a party is free to file any time before the security interest attaches (see Chapter 12.B) and the filing is good for five years (see Chapter 13.C). Creditor 2 could have taken steps such as having Creditor 1 file a termination statement (see Chapter 13.B) or enter into a subordination agreement (see part C of this chapter).

3.   The Last Clause of § 9-322(a)(1): "if there is no period thereafter when there is neither filing nor perfection"

Question 6. Creditor 1 obtains and perfects by filing a security interest in equipment and after-acquired equipment used in Marion Morrison's law practice. On January 15, Morrison legally changes his name to John Wayne. On June 13, Creditor 2 obtains and perfects a security interest in John Wayne's equipment and after-acquired equipment. On July 7, Creditor 1 amends its financing statement to reflect the change of name. On August 28, John Wayne acquires a Picasso to hang in his law office. Which creditor has priority in the Picasso?

A. Creditor 1, because it was first to file or perfect.

B. Creditor 2, because it was first to file or perfect.

C. Creditor 2, because there was a period during which Creditor 1 was not filed or perfected.

D. Creditor 2, because Creditor 1 lost its security interest when it did not timely file after a change in the debtor's name.

Analysis.   This question requires us to review § 9-507(c), which we discussed in Chapter 13.D.2. It provides:

> **§ 9-507. Effect of Certain Events on Effectiveness of Financing Statement.**
>
> . . .
>
> (c) **Change in debtor's name.** If the name that a filed financing statement provides for a debtor becomes insufficient as the name of the debtor under Section 9-503(a) so that the financing statement becomes seriously misleading under Section 9-506:
>
> > (1) the financing statement is effective to perfect a security interest in collateral acquired by the debtor before, or within four months after, the filed financing statement becomes seriously misleading; and
>
> > (2) the financing statement is not effective to perfect a security interest in collateral acquired by the debtor more than four months after the filed financing statement becomes seriously misleading, unless an amendment to the financing statement which renders the financing statement not seriously misleading is filed within four months after the financing statement became seriously misleading.

Under our facts, the debtor so changed his name on January 15 that the filed financing statement became seriously misleading. Creditor 1 then had four months to amend the financing statement in order to perfect an interest in after-acquired collateral. Creditor 1 filed the amendment on July 7, which was not within the four months, so a gap was created in perfection. Because of that gap, the original financing statement was not effective to perfect collateral acquired more than four months after the change, which included the Picasso. Section 9-322(a)(1) provides that "[p]riority dates from the earlier of the time a filing covering the collateral is first made or the security interest or agricultural lien is first perfected, *if there is no period thereafter when there is neither filing nor perfection*." Here, even though Creditor 1 made the first filing, there was a period thereafter when there was neither filing nor perfection as to collateral acquired by the debtor more than four months after the change, such as the Picasso. Therefore, Creditor 1 lost priority in that property to Creditor 2, who filed on June 13. Therefore, **C** is the best response. Note that **D** is not correct, because failure to file leads to loss of perfection, but not to loss of the security interest. In other words, if Creditor 1 did not timely file but had priority over any other secured creditors, it would have all of the rights of a secured party against the debtor.

4. Future Advances: § 9-322(a)(1)

In Chapter 7.F we were introduced to the concept of the future advances clause. A security interest can secure not only the payment of antecedent or present debts but also the payment of future debts. Section 9-204(c) provides:

> (c) **Future advances and other value.** A security agreement may provide that collateral secures, or that accounts, chattel paper, payment intangibles, or promissory notes are sold in connection with, future advances or other value, whether or not the advances or value are given pursuant to commitment.

The issue now is determining, for purposes of priority, the date on which the future advance is perfected. The answer is found in the same place, § 9-322(a)(1).

Question 7. On January 1, Creditor 1 made a loan to D and took a security interest in D's equipment. The security agreement had a future advances clause. Creditor 1 properly filed a financing statement. In March, D completely repaid the loan. On May 1, Creditor 2 made a loan to D and took a security interest in D's equipment. Creditor 2 properly filed a financing statement. On July 1, D borrowed money from Creditor 1, but Creditor 1 did not have D execute a security agreement to secure that loan. Who has priority in D's equipment?

A. Creditor 1, because its filing covering the collateral was made before Creditor 2's filing.

B. Creditor 1, because its second loan was made pursuant to commitment.

C. Creditor 2, because the original loan from Creditor 1 had been repaid at the time it took its security interest.

D. Creditor 2, because the second loan from Creditor 1 was unsecured.

Analysis.   Because of the future advances clause, the collateral secures the July 1 loan. According to § 9-322(a)(1), "[p]riority dates from . . . the time a filing covering the collateral is first made." That date is January 1, and it does not matter that the first loan was repaid. There remains an effective filing covering that collateral. Therefore, the correct response is **A.**

Question 8. On January 1, Creditor 1 made a loan to D and took a security interest in D's equipment. The security agreement did *not* have a future advances clause. Creditor 1 properly filed a financing statement. In March, D completely repaid the loan. On May 1, Creditor 2 made a loan to D and took a security interest in D's equipment. Creditor 2 properly filed a financing statement. On July 1, D borrowed money from Creditor 1. Creditor 1 had D execute a security agreement granting Creditor 1 a security interest in equipment to secure that loan, but Creditor 1 did not file a financing statement. Who has priority in D's equipment?

A. A. Creditor 1, because its filing covering the collateral was made before Creditor 2's filing.

B. Creditor 1, because its second loan was not made pursuant to a future advances clause.

C. Creditor 2, because the original loan from Creditor 1 had been repaid at the time it took its security interest.

D. Creditor 2, because Creditor 1 did not file a financing statement when it made the second loan.

Analysis.   *Note on test-taking.* This question is very similar to the previous one, so it is important to focus on the changed facts. In this question, (1) there is no future advances clause, and (2) Creditor 1 took a security interest when making the second loan. Since in the previous question Creditor 1 prevailed because the agreement had a future advances clause, we might think that the absence of a future advances clause would be fatal to Creditor 1's claim. But before coming to that conclusion, we must consider the effect of the other changed fact.

Under these facts, Creditor 1 entered into a security agreement covering equipment on July 1, and it had filed with respect to that collateral on the previous January 1. Creditor 2 has a security agreement covering equipment, and it filed with respect to that collateral on May 1. Therefore, under the basic rule of § 9-322(a)(1), Creditor 1 was first to file or perfect, so **A** remains the correct response.

The fact of repayment of the loan and the fact that there was no future advances clause are both red herrings. The important fact is the date of filing, which can be prior to the date the security agreement is executed. So putting these two questions together, note that a secured party who has filed can maintain priority as to a future advance either by having a future advances clause or by executing a security agreement at the time of the future advance.

Section § 9-323(a) has additional priority rules concerning future advances, but these apply only rarely. Official Comment 3 states:

> Subsection (a) of this section states the only other instance when the time of an advance figures in the priority scheme in Section 9-322: when the security interest is perfected only automatically under Section 9-309 or temporarily under Section 9-312(e), (f), or (g), and the advance is not made pursuant to a commitment entered into while the security interest was perfected by another method. Thus, an advance has priority from the date it is made only in the rare case in which it is made without commitment and while the security interest is perfected only temporarily under Section 9-312.

We will return to § 9-323 in the next chapter when we discuss priority disputes between secured creditors and lien creditors.

5. Proceeds: § 9-322(b)

In Chapter 7.C we were introduced to the concept of proceeds, and we saw that under § 9-315(a)(2) a security interest attaches automatically to proceeds. Then in Chapter 13.D.4 we examined whether a perfected security interest in collateral remained perfected in the proceeds of the collateral when it changed use. Assume now that both the collateral and the proceeds are perfected. The issue now is to determine, for purposes of priority, the date on which the security interest in the proceeds is perfected. For example, Creditor 1 has a perfected security interest in D's inventory. Creditor 2 has a perfected security interest in D's accounts. D takes an item from inventory and sells it to a customer on credit. The inventory has become an account. Who has priority? Creditor 1, claiming the accounts as proceeds of collateral, or Creditor 2, claiming the accounts as collateral? The answer is found in § 9-322(b)(1):

> (b) **Time of perfection: proceeds and supporting obligations.** For the purposes of subsection (a)(1):
>> (1) the time of filing or perfection as to a security interest in collateral is also the time of filing or perfection as to a security interest in proceeds.

Question 9. On January 15, Creditor 1 obtains a security interest in D's inventory and after-acquired inventory. On March 15, D approaches Creditor 2 about obtaining financing secured by D's accounts. D's accounts result from credit sales of her inventory. Creditor 2 searches the filings and finds that Creditor 1 has filed a financing statement indicating the collateral as D's "inventory now owned and after-acquired." No one has filed a financing statement covering D's accounts. Creditor 2 loans money to D secured by D's accounts and files. D declares bankruptcy and both Creditor 1 and Creditor 2 claim the accounts. Which claim has priority?

A. Creditor 1, because it was first to file with respect to the accounts.
B. Creditor 2, because it was first to file with respect to the accounts.
C. Creditor 2, because Creditor 1 is not perfected with respect to accounts since its financing statement indicated only inventory.
D. Creditor 1, because at the time Creditor 2 filed, it had knowledge of Creditor 1's security interest.

Analysis. Section 9-322(b)(1) provides that "the time of filing or perfection as to a security interest in collateral is also the time of filing or perfection as to a security interest in proceeds." Creditor 1 filed with respect to inventory on January 15. The time of filing in collateral is also the time of filing in proceeds, and the accounts are the proceeds of inventory. Perfection in the proceeds continues under § 9-315(d). So Creditor 1 filed with respect to the accounts as proceeds on January 15, and Creditor 2 filed with respect to the accounts on March 15. According to the basic rule of § 9-322(a)(1), Creditor 1 was the first to file or perfect with respect to that collateral, so the correct response is **A**.

Question 10. On January 1, Creditor A obtains a security interest in D's accounts (including after-acquired accounts) and properly perfects its security interest. On February 2, Creditor I obtains a security interest in D's inventory and properly perfects. On March 3, D sells inventory for cash and accounts. Which creditor has priority in the accounts D acquired on March 3?

A. A, because it was the first to file in the accounts.
B. A, because accounts receivable financing is more important to the credit economy.
C. I, because it was the first to file in inventory, and the time of filing in collateral is also the time of filing in proceeds.
D. I, because inventory turns into accounts, so it is not fair that another creditor can gain priority in its collateral.

Analysis. Section 9-322(b)(1) provides that "the time of filing or perfection as to a security interest in collateral is also the time of filing or perfection as to a security interest in proceeds." The time of filing in collateral is also the time of filing in proceeds, and the accounts are the proceeds of inventory. Perfection in the proceeds continues under § 9-315(d). So Creditor A filed with respect to the accounts on January 1, and Creditor I filed with respect to the accounts as proceeds on February 2. According to the basic rule of § 9-322(a)(1), Creditor A was the first to file or perfect with respect to that collateral, so the correct response is **A**.

C. The Relationship Between Priority and Default

Once it has been determined that one secured party has priority over another, it does not mean that the "junior" secured party has no rights. The senior secured party can only recover the amount of its debt (plus certain other expenses, as we saw in Chapter 10.A) from the debtor, so anything left can be claimed by the junior secured party. Furthermore, § 9-609(a)(1) states on its face that "[a]fter default, a secured party . . . may take possession of the collateral." It does not say that only the senior secured party may repossess the collateral. Official Comment 5, however, makes clear that as a practical matter, a junior party will usually allow a senior party to take over a sale:

> 5. **Multiple Secured Parties.** More than one secured party may be entitled to take possession of collateral under this section. Conflicting rights to possession among secured parties are resolved by the priority rules of this Article. Thus, a senior secured party is entitled to possession as against a junior claimant. Non-UCC law governs whether a junior secured party in possession of collateral is liable to the senior in conversion. Normally, a junior who refuses to relinquish possession of collateral upon the demand of a secured party having a superior possessory right to the collateral would be liable in conversion.

Another reason a subordinate security interest is unlikely to repossess is that the sale will not discharge the senior security interest. You may recall from Chapter 10.A that, under § 9-617(a), the sale pursuant to a repossession discharges the security interest under which the disposition was made as well as any subordinate security interest. But it does not discharge senior security interests.

Question 11. On January 15, Bank 1 obtains and by filing perfects a security interest in D's farm equipment. On April 5, Bank 2 obtains and by filing perfects a security interest in the same farm equipment. Later, D defaulted on her loan from Bank 2. Bank 2 repossesses the farm equipment and sells it to a buyer. Which of the following statements best describes the situation?

A. Bank 2 had no right under the Code to conduct a sale, so Bank 1 can obtain sanctions.
B. Bank 1 may have claims outside the Code against Bank 2 and may repossess the collateral from the buyer under the Code.
C. Bank 1 may have claims outside the Code against Bank 2 but may not repossess the collateral from the buyer, who is an innocent party.
D. Bank 1 has no claims against Bank 2 or the buyer.

Analysis. According to § 9-609, a secured party may take possession of the collateral after default. Since the Code does not prohibit a junior secured party from exercising its remedies, response **A** is not correct. Bank 1 may have claims against Bank 2 outside the Code, however, such as the common law claim of conversion. Furthermore, under § 9-617(a), the sale pursuant to a repossession discharges the security interest under which the disposition was made as well as any subordinate security interest. But it does not discharge senior security interests. Therefore, Bank 1's security interest remains effective after the sale to the buyer, so Bank 1 may pursue Article 9 remedies against the buyer as a transferee. Therefore, **B** is the correct response.

The priorities we have discussed are those provided by application of the Code rules. As with many other Code provisions, these rules are default rules that may be changed by agreement of the parties. Subordination agreements in which the secured parties agree to alter the priorities are expressly permitted by § 9-339, which provides:

> **Priority Subject to Subordination.** This article does not preclude subordination by agreement by a person entitled to priority.

Question 12. On January 1, A loans D $50,000, takes a security interest in D's equipment, and files. On February 2, B loans D $70,000, takes a security interest in D's equipment, and files. A agrees with B that A's security interest will be subordinate to B's. On March 3, C loans D $30,000, takes a security interest in D's equipment, and files. On D's default, D has equipment worth $100,000. According to the priority among creditors, how much does each creditor recover?

A. A $50,000; B $70,000; C $30,000.
B. A $50,000; B $50,000; C $0.
C. A $30,000; B $70,000; C $0.
D. A $0; B $70,000; C $30,000.

Analysis. Each party has a perfected security interest. A filed on January 1, B on February 2, and C on March 3. According to the default rule of § 9-322(a)

(1), the priorities would be A, B, C. Of the $100,000 available, A would first recover $50,000, and B would then recover $50,000; C would recover $0. But by agreement authorized by § 9-339, A has agreed to be subordinate to B, so the priorities are B, A, C. After B claims $70,000, there remains only $30,000 for A and $0 for C. Therefore, **C** is the correct response.

D.   The Superpriority Exceptions to § 9-322

Additional exceptions to the general rules of § 9-322(a) are found in § 9-324. This section protects holders of PMSIs. Review § 9-103, discussed in Chapter 4.D. The exceptions describe situations in which a PMSI takes priority over an earlier non-PMSI even though the non-PMSI was first filed or perfected. These priorities are called *superpriorities* because they allow a later perfected security interest to obtain priority over an earlier perfected security interest. The section provides:

§ 9-324. Priority of Purchase-Money Security Interests.

(a) **General rule: purchase-money priority.** Except as otherwise provided in subsection (g), a perfected purchase-money security interest in goods other than inventory or livestock has priority over a conflicting security interest in the same goods, and, except as otherwise provided in Section 9-327, a perfected security interest in its identifiable proceeds also has priority, if the purchase-money security interest is perfected when the debtor receives possession of the collateral or within 20 days thereafter.

(b) **Inventory purchase-money priority.** Subject to subsection (c) and except as otherwise provided in subsection (g), a perfected purchase-money security interest in inventory has priority over a conflicting security interest in the same inventory, has priority over a conflicting security interest in chattel paper or an instrument constituting proceeds of the inventory and in proceeds of the chattel paper, if so provided in Section 9-330, and, except as otherwise provided in Section 9-327, also has priority in identifiable cash proceeds of the inventory to the extent the identifiable cash proceeds are received on or before the delivery of the inventory to a buyer, if:

(1) the purchase-money security interest is perfected when the debtor receives possession of the inventory;

(2) the purchase-money secured party sends an authenticated notification to the holder of the conflicting security interest;

(3) the holder of the conflicting security interest receives the notification within five years before the debtor receives possession of the inventory; and

(4) the notification states that the person sending the notification has or expects to acquire a purchase-money security interest in inventory of the debtor and describes the inventory.

(g) **Conflicting purchase-money security interests.** If more than one security interest qualifies for priority in the same collateral under subsection (a), (b), (d), or (f):

(1) a security interest securing an obligation incurred as all or part of the price of the collateral has priority over a security interest securing an obligation incurred for value given to enable the debtor to acquire rights in or the use of collateral; and

(2) in all other cases, Section 9-322(a) applies to the qualifying security interests.

We will first examine the § 9-324(a) superpriority in collateral other than inventory or livestock and then the § 9-324(b) superpriority in inventory. We will not cover the § 9-324(d) superpriority in livestock, but it parallels the superpriority in inventory. In the unusual situation in which there are two PMSIs in the same collateral, the priority between the two PMSIs is resolved under § 9-324(g).

1. *Collateral Other Than Inventory or Livestock: § 9-324(a)*

The § 9-324(a) superpriority applies only if:

1. the collateral is "other than inventory or livestock";
2. there are at least two security interests in the same collateral;
3. one of the security interests is a PMSI; and
4. the PMSI was perfected when "the debtor receives possession of the collateral or within 20 days thereafter."

Let's apply this provision to a series of problems.

Question 13. On January 15, Creditor 1 loans money to D and takes a security interest in all of D's equipment, now owned and after acquired. Creditor 1 immediately files. On February 1, Creditor 2 sells D on credit an X1 copier that D will use in its office and takes a security interest in the X1. Creditor 2 checks the filing system, finds the filing by Creditor 1, and immediately files. Which secured party has priority in the X1 copier?

A. Creditor 1, because it was first to file or perfect.
B. Creditor 1, because Creditor 2 had knowledge of its security interest in equipment.
C. Creditor 2, because it was first to file or perfect.
D. Creditor 2, because it has a PMSI that has obtained a superpriority.

Analysis. Under the general rule of § 9-322(a)(1), Creditor 1 would have priority as first to file or perfect. However, Creditor 2 has satisfied all the requirements to obtain a superpriority under § 9-324(a): the collateral is equipment, so it is collateral "other than inventory or livestock"; it is a PMSI, since it was obtained by the seller of the collateral; and the creditor timely filed within 20 days of the debtor's possession. Therefore, the correct response is **D**.

Note that Creditor 2 enjoys this superpriority only with respect to the X1 copier, which is the collateral that it allowed the debtor to obtain. So in theory, this exception allows the debtor to obtain additional credit without hurting Creditor 1, since Creditor 2 is taking nothing from the debtor except the item it provided to the debtor.

Question 14. On January 15, D buys an item of equipment from Creditor 1 on credit and grants Creditor 1 a security interest in this equipment. Creditor 1 delivers the equipment on January 18. Creditor 1, however, delays filing a financing statement until January 27. Meanwhile on January 22, D borrows from Creditor 2, which obtains a security interest in the same equipment. Creditor 2 perfects by filing a financing statement on January 22. Which security interest has priority in this item of equipment?

A. Creditor 1, because it was first to file or perfect.
B. Creditor 2, because it was first to file or perfect.
C. Creditor 1 because it has a PMSI that has obtained a superpriority.
D. Creditor 2 because Creditor 1 did not timely file to obtain a superpriority.

Analysis.   This example may illustrate the "dark side" of § 9-324(a). As illustrated in the previous question, most of the time the superpriority will be used to allow a debtor to obtain additional credit without harming the underlying creditor. Here, however, Creditor 1 has satisfied all the elements of a superpriority and will be able to prevent Creditor 2 from obtaining priority in the same collateral. The correct response is **C**. This result occurred because of the 20 days a creditor with a PMSI is given to file. A prudent creditor in the position of Creditor 2 would have to check the transaction by which the debtor obtained the collateral. If it came into the debtor's possession more than 20 days earlier and there is no filing, then Creditor 2 is assured of priority.

Question 15. D borrows $20,000 from Creditor 1 to use as a down payment on new farm machinery. D grants Creditor 1 a security interest in "all farm machinery, now owned or later acquired." Creditor 1 files its financing statement on January 15. On January 17, D buys new farm machinery from Creditor 2 for $35,000. D uses the $20,000 it obtained from Creditor 1 as a down payment and finances the balance with Creditor 2, which obtains a security interest in the new farm machinery and files a financing statement on January 27. Which security interest will have priority as to the new farm equipment?

A. Creditor 1, because it was first to file or perfect.
B. Creditor 1, because PMSIs are entitled to a superpriority over regular security interests.
C. Creditor 2, because PMSIs are entitled to a superpriority over regular security interests.
D. Creditor 2 because a PMSI seller has priority over a PMSI financer.

Analysis.   This is a tricky one. The key to solving this problem is to note that Creditor 1 has a PMSI because it loaned the debtor the money that was used to purchase the collateral. But Creditor 2 also has a PMSI because it sold the debtor the item in which it took a security interest. Article 9 provides a way to resolve the priority between two PMSIs in § 9-324(g), which provides:

> (g) **Conflicting purchase-money security interests.** If more than one security interest qualifies for priority in the same collateral under subsection (a), (b), (d), or (f):
>
> > (1) a security interest securing an obligation incurred as all or part of the price of the collateral has priority over a security interest securing an obligation incurred for value given to enable the debtor to acquire rights in or the use of collateral; and
> >
> > (2) in all other cases, Section 9-322(a) applies to the qualifying security interests.

Both Creditor 1 and Creditor 2 have a PMSI under subsection (a). Subsection (g) provides that the seller (the party securing an obligation as part of the price) has priority over the financer (the party who gave value to enable the debtor to acquire rights in the collateral). Therefore, Creditor 2 has priority as a seller, so response **D** is correct. Note that if both parties had loaned money to the debtor, subsection (g)(2) provides that the rule of § 9-322(a) (first to file or perfect) would apply.

2. Inventory: § 9-324(b)

Section 9-324(b) provides an important exception to the general rule that gives priority to the first secured party to file or perfect. This section applies to a creditor with a PMSI in inventory. Notice the difference between the requirements of § 9-324(b) and those of § 9-324(a) considered in part D.1, which applies to collateral other than inventory or livestock. Section 9-324(b) applies if:

1. the collateral is inventory;
2. there are at least two security interests in the same inventory;
3. one of the security interests is a PMSI;
4. the PMSI was perfected "when the debtor receives possession of the inventory"; and

5. the purchase money secured party sends notice within five years before the debtor receives possession of the collateral to all other holders of perfected security interests in the inventory who earlier filed.

Let's apply this provision to a series of problems.

Question 16. On January 15, Creditor 1 loans money to D and takes a security interest in all of D's inventory, now owned and after acquired. Creditor 1 immediately files. On February 1, Creditor 2 sells D on credit an item that D puts in its inventory and takes a security interest in the item. After the sale, Creditor 2 checks the filing system, finds the filing by Creditor 1, and immediately files. Which secured party has priority in the item?

A. Creditor 1, because it was first to file or perfect.
B. Creditor 1, because Creditor 2 had knowledge of its security interest in equipment.
C. Creditor 2, because it was first to file or perfect.
D. Creditor 2, because it has a PMSI that has obtained a superpriority.

Analysis.   Under the general rule of § 9-322(a)(1), Creditor 1 would have priority as first to file or perfect. You may note that this is the same question we had earlier, except that the item is inventory rather than equipment. There are additional requirements that the creditor who obtains a PMSI in inventory must satisfy to obtain a superpriority. Creditor 2 has not satisfied two of these: (1) it did not perfect when the debtor received possession of the inventory, and (2) it did not send notice to Creditor 1. Therefore, the superpriority rule does not come into play, and under the general rule of § 9-322(a)(1), Creditor 1 has priority, so the correct response is **A**.

Question 17. Your client, Confections Inc., is a wholesaler who sells goods to convenience stores on terms that require payment within 30 days from delivery. Every once in a while, one of the stores goes bankrupt, and there always seems to be a bank with a security interest in the inventory of the store that has a claim to the goods delivered by Confections that haven't been paid for. Confections asks whether there is an inexpensive way it can recover something in the event of its customer's bankruptcy.

A. Confections can take a security interest in inventory and file before delivery.
B. Confections can take a security interest in inventory, file before delivery, and send notice to the bank.
C. Confections can take a security interest in equipment and file within 20 days.
D. There is no way Confections can obtain priority over the bank.

Analysis. This question represents the kind of problem that § 9-324(b) can solve. The goods are inventory, and there is an existing security interest in the inventory. If it took a security interest, Confections would have a PMSI in the goods, since it is the seller of the goods. Under § 9-324(a), in order to obtain a superpriority over the bank, Confections has to file before delivery and send notice to the bank. The notice provision in § 9-324(a)(3) is a bit awkward. It states that "the holder of the conflicting security interest receives the notification within five years before the debtor receives possession of the inventory." All that means is that once given, the notice is good for five years. In other words, if the notice was sent today, then for all deliveries for the next five years, the bank will have received the notification within five years before the debtor receives possession. Therefore, the correct response is **B**.

You may wonder why § 9-324 treats PMSIs in inventory differently from other PMSIs. The answer has to do with commercial practices. Official Comment 4 to § 9-324 states:

> The arrangement between an inventory secured party and its debtor typically requires the secured party to make periodic advances against incoming inventory or periodic releases of old inventory as new inventory is received. A fraudulent debtor may apply to the secured party for advances even though it has already given a purchase-money security interest in the inventory to another secured party. For this reason, subsections (b)(2) through (4) and (c) impose a second condition for the purchase-money security interest's achieving priority: the purchase-money secured party must give notification to the holder of a conflicting security interest who filed against the same item or type of inventory before the purchase-money secured party filed or its security interest became perfected temporarily under Section 9-312(e) or (f). The notification requirement protects the non-purchase-money inventory secured party in such a situation: if the inventory secured party has received notification, it presumably will not make an advance; if it has not received notification (or if the other security interest does not qualify as purchase-money), any advance the inventory secured party may make ordinarily will have priority under Section 9-322. Inasmuch as an arrangement for periodic advances against incoming goods is unusual outside the inventory field, subsection (a) does not contain a notification requirement.

E. The "Double Debtor" Problem: § 9-325

1. Sale of the Collateral

Occasionally, the provisions of the Code will create a problem that can be resolved only by the creation of a new Code provision. Such is the case with the superpriority rules. The policy of the superpriority is that the creditor with the underlying security interest is not hurt by the creditor who is given a superpriority. Because the creditor with a superpriority has a PMSI, it only has a security interest in the collateral that it allowed the debtor to obtain; thus, nothing is taken away from the underlying creditor.

But suppose a creditor takes a security interest in the debtor's equipment and properly files. The debtor then sells the equipment to another person, who finances the purchase by taking out a loan, and that lender takes a security interest in the equipment. At first blush, it appears that the lender qualifies for a superpriority under § 9-324(a). But that would not be fair to the underlying creditor, for that creditor would lose its collateral if the lender repossessed it. To create an exception to the superpriority rules, the drafters of the Code came up with the "double debtor" rule of § 9-325:

§ 9-325. Priority of Security Interests in Transferred Collateral.

(a) **Subordination of security interest in transferred collateral.** Except as otherwise provided in subsection (b), a security interest created by a debtor is subordinate to a security interest in the same collateral created by another person if:

(1) the debtor acquired the collateral subject to the security interest created by the other person;

(2) the security interest created by the other person was perfected when the debtor acquired the collateral; and

(3) there is no period thereafter when the security interest is unperfected.

(b) **Limitation of subsection (a) subordination.** Subsection (a) subordinates a security interest only if the security interest:

(1) otherwise would have priority solely under Section 9-322 (a) or 9-324; or

(2) arose solely under Section 2-711(3) or 2A-508(5).

Question 18. Bethany owns a portable cart used to sell coffee beverages. In return for a loan to expand her business, Bethany granted Al a security interest in the cart, which Al immediately perfected. Without Al's consent, Bethany then sold the cart to Chris, who borrowed $10,000 from Doug to finance the purchase. As part of the loan agreement, Chris granted Doug a security interest in the cart, which Doug properly perfected. Chris then defaults, and both Al and Doug claim the cart. Which of them has priority?

A. Al, because he was first to file or perfect.

B. Al, because even though Doug has a PMSI, Doug's security interest is subordinate to Al's.

C. Doug, because he was first to file or perfect.

D. Doug, because he has a PMSI that has obtained a superpriority.

Analysis. It appears that Doug has satisfied all of the requirements for a superpriority in equipment under § 9-324(a). However, it does not seem correct to apply that policy in a situation in which a debtor acquires property that is subject to a security interest created by another debtor. Subsection (b) of the "double debtor" rule of § 9-325 provides that subsection (a) applies only if the security interest would have had priority under § 9-324. Here, Doug's security interest would have had priority. Let's then apply subsection (a), filling in the names of the parties:

> A security interest created by a debtor [Chris] is subordinate to a security interest in the same collateral created by another person [Bethany] if:
>
> 1. the debtor [Chris] acquired the collateral subject to the security interest created by the other person [Bethany];
> 2. the security interest created by the other person [Bethany] was perfected when the debtor [Chris] acquired the collateral; and
> 3. there is no period thereafter when the security interest is unperfected.

The first requirement is satisfied because, when the cart was sold to Chris, it was subject to the security interest. The second requirement is satisfied because Al immediately perfected the security interest in Bethany's cart. And the third requirement is satisfied because it remained perfected. Therefore, the security interest created by Chris and granted to Doug is subordinate to the security interest in the same collateral created by Bethany and granted to Al. Therefore, Al continues to enjoy priority. The correct response is **B.** This appears to be a correct result, for Chris was purchasing equipment, and, as we learned in Chapter 15.A, the general rule is that a buyer of equipment is subject to a security interest in the equipment. Before he became a secured creditor, Doug should have checked the filings for any previously perfected security interests in this equipment.

2. Transfer to a "New Debtor"

In Chapter 13.D.4, we examined whether a security interest remained perfected when the collateral was acquired by a "new debtor"—an entity that assumed the obligation. We saw that different rules apply in this situation depending on whether the name of the debtor became seriously misleading (see § 9-508) and whether the new debtor was located in located in another jurisdiction (see § 9-316). Now, assuming the secured parties have taken all steps to continue perfection in the collateral, the issue is which secured party has priority in the collateral—the secured party of the original debtor or the secured party of the new debtor.

For example, Bank One has a perfected security interest in the equipment and after-acquired equipment of Homebrew Software, an Arizona corporation. Bank Two has a perfected security interest in the equipment and after-acquired equipment of Megasoft, a Washington corporation. Megasoft acquires Homebrew and assumes all obligations of Homebrew. Bank One filed a financing statement naming Megasoft as the debtor in Washington within four months of Megasoft's acquisition of Homebrew. That filing is effective to continue perfection of Bank One's security interest in the existing equipment and in the after-acquired equipment.

To resolve the priority contest in the equipment between Bank One and Bank Two, we have to distinguish between the equipment existing at the time of Megasoft's acquisition of Homebrew ("the acquisition") and the equipment that was acquired by Megasoft after that. As to the equipment that was existing at the time of the acquisition, because each secured party claims it, we might expect to resolve the dispute under the general rule of § 9-322. But instead we have a double-debtor problem, because Megasoft is a debtor that has acquired property that is subject to a security interest created by another debtor, Homebrew. We therefore look to the double-debtor rule of § 9-325, which tells us that the security interest created by Megasoft is subordinate to the security interest created by Homebrew because (1) Megasoft acquired the collateral subject to the security interest created by Homebrew, (2) the security interest created by Homebrew was perfected when Megasoft acquired the collateral, and (3) the security interest created by Homebrew was continually perfected.

For the rules with respect to the collateral acquired by Megasoft after the acquisition of Homebrew, we look to § 9-326, which provides:

§ 9-326. Priority of Security Interests Created by New Debtor.

(a) [**Subordination of security interest created by new debtor.**] Subject to subsection (b), a security interest that is created by a new debtor in collateral in which the new debtor has or acquires rights and is perfected solely by a filed financing statement that would be ineffective to perfect the security interest but for the application of Section 9-316(i)(1) or 9-508 is subordinate to a security interest in the same collateral which is perfected other than by such a filed financing statement.

(b) [**Priority under other provisions; multiple original debtors.**] The other provisions of this part determine the priority among conflicting security interests in the same collateral perfected by filed financing statements described in subsection (a). However, if the security agreements to which a new debtor became bound as debtor were not entered into by the same original debtor, the conflicting security interests rank according to priority in time of the new debtor's having become bound.

In order to apply these provisions, we have to ask whether Bank One's filed financing statement would have been ineffective but for § 9-508 or § 9-316(i) (1). These rules affect only the property acquired after Megasoft's acquisition of Homebrew, for the effectiveness of Bank One's filed financing statement in the property existing at the time of the acquisition is not affected by those provisions. Because perfection of Bank One's security interest in the equipment acquired after the acquisition was effective solely because of § 9-508, § 9-326(a) provides that Bank Two prevails with respect to property acquired after the acquisition irrespective of when the financing statements were filed.

Question 19. First Bank has a security interest in the inventory and after-acquired inventory of Homebrew Software, an Arizona corporation, that was properly perfected by filing on February 1, 2020. In July, 2020, Megasoft, a Washington corporation, purchased the assets of Homebrew and agreed to be responsible for Homebrew's obligations, including its security agreements. Second Bank had taken a security interest in Megasoft's inventory and after-acquired inventory on March 1, 2020 and properly perfected by filing. First Bank filed a financing statement in Washington naming Megasoft as debtor in July, 2020. Which bank has priority in the inventory of Megasoft?

A. First Bank has priority in all the inventory because it was first to file or perfect.

B. First Bank has priority in the inventory acquired by Megasoft from Homebrew; Second Bank has priority in the inventory acquired after the acquisition.

C. Second Bank has priority in all the inventory because First Bank's security interest is subordinate to Second Bank's security interest.

D. First Bank has priority in all the inventory because Second Bank is a new debtor.

Analysis.   To review perfection, the collateral was acquired by a new debtor in another jurisdiction and the name of the debtor became seriously misleading under § 9-508. First Bank timely filed in the new jurisdiction. Therefore, under § 9-316(a) and (b), the security interest remained perfected in the collateral that was acquired, and under § 9-316(i), the security interest is perfected in collateral that is acquired by Megasoft after its acquisition of Homebrew. Second Bank, however, has a competing interest in the same collateral that is properly perfected.

With respect to priority in the collateral that was existing at the time of the acquisition, the double-debtor rule of § 9-325 tells us that the security interest of Megasoft is subordinated to the interest of Homebrew. With respect to the collateral acquired by Megasoft after the acquisition of Homebrew, First Bank's financing statement would have been ineffective to perfect the security interest but for the application of § 9-316(i)(1). Therefore, under § 9-326(a), First Bank's security interest is subordinate to the security interest in the same collateral perfected by Second Bank. Note that this priority contest is not resolved by the time of filing; therefore it does not matter that First Bank was first to file or perfect. The correct response is **B**.

This situation looks bad for First Bank, because within a short time the inventory acquired by Megasoft will be used up and there will be no collateral to secure the debt. That, however, is an academic result that is unlikely to occur in the real world. For one thing, Homebrew's agreement to sell the assets is likely to be an event of default in its security agreement with First Bank. But even that consequence is likely academic. More likely, in doing its due diligence prior to the acquisition, Megasoft will discover the security interest of First Bank and will work with First Bank to resolve the problem prior to the purchase.

F.   Closers

> **Question 20.** First Bank has a security interest in the equipment and after-acquired equipment of Store that is properly perfected. Later, Second Bank took a security interest in an item of Store's equipment and properly perfected within 20 days of Store's possession of the item. In order for Second Bank to have priority in that item, which of the following facts must be true?
>
> **A.** Second Bank's security interest is a PMSI.
> **B.** Second Bank perfected before Store got possession.
> **C.** Second Bank gave notice to First Bank before Store got possession.
> **D.** All of the above.

Analysis.   This question reviews the general rule and the exception. Under the general rule of § 9-322(a)(1), priority goes to the first secured party to file or perfect. Here that would be First Bank. Since the collateral is equipment, Second Bank would be entitled to a superpriority if it complied with all the requirements of § 9-324(a). Those requirements are that one of the security interests is a PMSI and that the PMSI is perfected within 20 days of debtor's possession. We are told in the facts that this second requirement is satisfied. Therefore, the only additional requirement is that it is a PMSI, which is satisfied by response **A**.

> **Question 21.** First Bank has a security interest in the inventory and after-acquired inventory of Store that is properly perfected. Later, Second Bank took a security interest in an item of Store's inventory and properly perfected within 20 days of Store's possession of the item. In order for Second Bank to have priority in that item, which of the following facts must be true?

> **A.** Second Bank's security interest is a PMSI.
> **B.** Second Bank perfected before Store got possession.
> **C.** Second Bank gave notice to First Bank before Store got possession.
> **D.** All of the above.

Analysis. This question reviews the general rule and the exception and contrasts the rule for inventory with the rule for equipment. Under the general rule of § 9-322(a)(1), priority goes to the first secured party to file or perfect. Here that would be First Bank. Since the collateral is inventory, Second Bank would be entitled to a superpriority if it complied with all the requirements of § 9-324(b). Those requirements are that one of the security interests is a PMSI, that the PMSI is perfected when the debtor receives possession, and that the other secured party got notice before debtor got possession. Therefore, the requirements of responses **A, B,** and **C** would have to be satisfied, so **D** is the correct response.

 # Burnham's Picks

Question 1	B
Question 2	A
Question 3	C
Question 4	A
Question 5	A
Question 6	C
Question 7	A
Question 8	A
Question 9	A
Question 10	A
Question 11	B
Question 12	C
Question 13	D
Question 14	C
Question 15	D
Question 16	A
Question 17	B
Question 18	B
Question 19	B
Question 20	A
Question 21	D

17

Secured Party v. Other Creditors

A. Introduction

In Chapter 16, we characterized the competing creditors and determined that each was a secured creditor. In this chapter, one of the creditors is characterized as a secured creditor and the other is not. The other may be one of the following:

- An unsecured creditor (§§ 9-201 and 9-317(a)(2)).
- A creditor with a lien arising by operation of law (§ 9-333).
- A creditor with an agricultural lien.
- The IRS with a tax lien.

B. An Unsecured Creditor: §§ 9-201 and 9-317(a)(2)

1. *Secured Party v. Lien Creditor*

Unsecured creditors are generally out of luck when competing with secured creditors. Unlike secured creditors, unsecured creditors have no claim to particular property of the debtor. The unsecured creditor must first obtain a judgment against the debtor and then obtain a writ of execution directing the sheriff to levy on property of the debtor. The lien attaches to particular property only at the moment that the sheriff levies on the property. The sheriff seizes the property, sells it, and then pays off the creditor.

If the sheriff seizes property in which there is a security interest, does the secured party or the lien creditor have priority? As stated in § 9-201, the secured party generally has priority over other creditors. However, there is an exception to this rule. Under § 9-317(a)(2), "a security interest . . . is subordinate to the rights of . . . a person that becomes a lien creditor before . . . the security interest is . . . perfected" as to that item of property. So a lien creditor may prevail if the secured party has not perfected the security interest in the collateral.

What is a "lien creditor"? Not every creditor with a lien is a "lien creditor," which is a defined term in Article 9. Section 9-102(a)(52) provides:

> (52) "Lien creditor" means:
> (A) a creditor that has acquired a lien on the property involved by attachment, levy, or the like;
> (B) an assignee for benefit of creditors from the time of assignment;
> (C) a trustee in bankruptcy from the date of the filing of the petition; or
> (D) a receiver in equity from the time of appointment.

To distinguish this creditor from other creditors with liens, the lien creditor in § 9-102(a)(52)(A) is often referred to as a "*judicial* lien creditor" because this creditor generally has to go to court to obtain the lien. In general, in a competition between a judicial lien creditor and a secured creditor, if the sheriff levies on the property before the secured creditor perfects its security interest, the judicial lien creditor has priority as to that item of property. This is the rule of § 9-317(a)(2), which provides:

> **Interests That Take Priority over or Take Free of Unperfected Security Interest or Agricultural Lien.**
> (a) **Conflicting security interests and rights of lien creditors.** An unperfected security interest or agricultural lien is subordinate to the rights of:
> . . .

(2) a person that becomes a lien creditor before the earlier of the time the security interest or agricultural lien is perfected or a financing statement covering the collateral is filed.

. . .

(e) **Purchase-money security interest.** Except as otherwise provided in Sections 9-320 and 9-321, if a person files a financing statement with respect to a purchase-money security interest before or within 20 days after the debtor receives delivery of the collateral, the security interest takes priority over the rights of a buyer, lessee, or lien creditor which arise between the time the security interest attaches and the time of filing.

Since the statute provides that an unperfected security interest is subordinate to the rights of a subsequent lien creditor, we can read in the implication that a *perfected* security interest prevails over a subsequent lien creditor. Once again, we see the importance of perfection to a secured creditor. There is an exception in § 9-317(e), however. If the secured creditor has a purchase money security interest in the collateral, and the security interest is unperfected at the time the interest of the lien creditor arose, the secured creditor can still obtain priority over a buyer, lessee, or lien creditor if it files within 20 days after the debtor receives delivery of the collateral.

Note that a practical effect of this rule is that the sheriff will be reluctant to levy on property on which there is a security interest. In many jurisdictions, there is a statutory scheme that requires the judgment lien creditor to post a bond before the sheriff executes on the property. The sheriff then uses the bond to pay the secured creditor.

Another significance of § 9-317(a)(2) will be revealed when we study the impact of bankruptcy on secured creditors in Chapter 19. Note that the definition of *lien creditor* in § 9-102(a)(52)(C) includes "a trustee in bankruptcy from the date of the filing of the petition." We will discover that Bankruptcy Code § 544 (known as the "strong arm clause") permits the trustee acting on behalf of unsecured creditors to avoid an unperfected security interest. This is another reason proper perfection is important. If the secured party files in the wrong name, for example, the security interest is unperfected, and the bankruptcy trustee as a hypothetical judicial lien creditor can avoid it.

Question 1. On January 15, L obtains a $40,000 judgment against D Co. On February 2, S lends D Co. $20,000 and obtains a nonpurchase money security interest in D Co.'s office equipment. On February 5, L tries to collect her $40,000 judgment against D Co. by having the sheriff levy on D Co.'s office equipment. S perfects its security interest by filing on February 7. Which party has priority?

A. S, because a security interest always has priority over an execution lien.
B. S, because a secured creditor with a PMSI has 20 days after the debtor receives delivery of the collateral to file.
C. L, because an execution lien always has priority over a security interest.
D. L, because S's security interest was unperfected at the time of execution.

Analysis.   Section 9-317(a)(2) provides that "a security interest . . . is subordinate to the rights of . . . a person that becomes a lien creditor before . . . the security interest is . . . perfected" as to that item of property. Note that the judgment itself is not a lien because it does not attach to any particular personal property of the debtor. Under the facts, L became a lien creditor on February 5, when the sheriff levied on particular property, the office equipment. S obtained a security interest on February 2, but did not perfect until February 7. Therefore, L became a lien creditor before S's security interest was perfected, so S's lien is subordinate to L's. **D** is the correct response. Note that **B** is not the correct response because S did not have a PMSI under these facts.

Question 2. On January 15, L obtains a $40,000 judgment against D Co. On February 2, S lends D Co. $20,000 to buy a computer and obtains a security interest in the computer. D Co. purchased the computer with S's money on that day. On February 5, L tries to collect her $40,000 judgment against D Co. by having the sheriff levy on D Co.'s computer. S perfects its security interest on February 17. Which party has priority?

A. S, because a security interest always has priority over an execution lien.
B. S, because a secured creditor with a PMSI has 20 days after the debtor receives delivery of the collateral to file.
C. L, because an execution lien always has priority over a security interest.
D. L, because S's security interest was unperfected at the time of execution.

Analysis.   Section 9-317(a)(2) provides that "a security interest . . . is subordinate to the rights of . . . a person that becomes a lien creditor before . . . the security interest is . . . perfected" as to that item of property. Under the facts, L became a lien creditor on February 5, when the sheriff levied on the property. Note that the judgment itself is not a lien because it does not attach to any particular property of the debtor. S obtained a security interest on February 2, but did not perfect until February 17. Therefore, L became a lien creditor before S's security interest was perfected, so under § 9-317(a)(2), S's lien is subordinate to L's.

Note on test-taking. If that were all there was to this question, it would be the same as the previous question. It is unlikely that the assessor would test you twice on the same point, so check the facts to see if there is any difference. You notice that in this question, "S lends D Co. $20,000 to buy a computer." Because S loaned the money to the debtor that the debtor used to buy the collateral, S is a secured party with a PMSI under § 9-103 (see Chapter 4.D). Therefore, we should check to see whether the exception in § 9-317(e) is satisfied by our facts:

> (e) **Purchase-money security interest.** Except as otherwise provided in Sections 9-320 and 9-321, if a person files a financing statement with respect to a purchase-money security interest before or within 20 days after the debtor receives delivery of the collateral, the security interest takes priority over the rights of a buyer, lessee, or lien creditor which arise between the time the security interest attaches and the time of filing.

We now see that the computer was delivered on February 2, and S filed its financing statement on February 17, so since S had a PMSI and filed within 20 days of debtor's possession, it takes priority over the rights of L, the lien creditor, which arose on February 5. The statute says that a secured creditor with a PMSI prevails over the rights of a lien creditor "which arise between the time the security interest attaches and the time of filing." Here, the date on which the rights of L arose (February 5) is between the time of attachment (February 2) and the time of filing (February 17). Therefore, the correct response is **B**. Note that while in this question the secured party with a PMSI gets priority over a lien creditor, § 9-317(e) also gives the secured party with a PMSI priority over a buyer.

Question 3. On January 15, L obtains a $400 judgment against D, an individual. On February 2, D buys a computer on credit from S for use by her children as an educational toy, and S retains a security interest. On February 5, L tries to collect its judgment against D by having the sheriff levy on D's new computer. S does not file a financing statement until February 25. Which party has priority?

A. S, because it was perfected at the time of execution.
B. S, because a secured creditor with a PMSI has 20 days after the debtor receives delivery of the collateral to file.
C. L, because an execution lien always has priority over a security interest.
D. L, because S's security interest was unperfected at the time of execution.

Analysis. Let's carefully apply our methodology to solve this one:

1. Characterize the parties.
2. Classify the collateral.
3. Determine whether the security interest is perfected or unperfected.
4. Find the Code section that contains the appropriate rule.
5. Apply the facts to the rule to obtain the result.

Here, the parties are a secured creditor and a judicial lien creditor. The collateral is consumer goods. The security interest is perfected, because S took a PMSI in consumer goods, which is automatically perfected under § 9-309(1). Did you notice that important fact? If not, you might want to review Chapter 14.E. The appropriate rule for priority disputes between a secured creditor and a judicial lien creditor is § 9-317(a)(2), which provides that "a security interest . . . is subordinate to the rights of . . . a person that becomes a lien creditor before . . . the security interest is . . . perfected" as to that item of property. Under the facts, L became a lien creditor on February 5, when the sheriff levied on the property. Note that the judgment itself is not a lien because it does not attach to any particular property of the debtor. S obtained a security interest on February 2, and it was perfected automatically on February 2. S's later filing is irrelevant. Therefore, L did not become a lien creditor before S's security interest was perfected, so under § 9-317(a)(2), L's lien is subordinate to S's. The correct response is **A.**

2. Secured Party Making a Future Advance v. Lien Creditor

We saw in Chapter 16.A that, for purposes of priority, a future advance made pursuant to a future advance clause is perfected on the date of the filing as to the collateral. We noted that we would return to the discussion of priority in future advances as against judicial lien creditors. There is a complex statute on that issue, and the statute seems to appear frequently on Article 9 examinations, so we had better take a look at it. Section 9-323(b) provides:

> (b) **Lien creditor.** Except as otherwise provided in subsection (c), a security interest is subordinate to the rights of a person that becomes a lien creditor while the security interest is perfected only to the extent that it secures advances made more than 45 days after the person becomes a lien creditor unless the advance is made:
> (1) without knowledge of the lien; or
> (2) pursuant to a commitment entered into without knowledge of the lien.

This is a good provision for practicing statute-reading skills, so let's leap into some questions.

Question 4. On January 1, S lends D $10,000 and obtains a security interest in D's equipment. The security agreement contains a future advances clause. S perfects its security agreement by filing on January 5. On February 1, X has the sheriff execute on the same equipment to satisfy a $15,000 judgment against D. On March 1, D asks S to lend D an additional $5,000. S is hesitant to make the loan because S knows of X's lien and believes that the equipment is worth no more than $20,000. S seeks your advice as to the consequences of loaning D an additional $5,000. Will S have priority over X in the $5,000 loan?

A. Yes, because the loan is a future advance made within 45 days after X became a lien creditor.
B. Yes, because future advances always have priority over judicial liens.
C. No, because X became a lien creditor before the future advance was made.
D. No, because S had knowledge of X's lien.

Analysis. According to § 9-323(b), "a security interest is subordinate to the rights of a person that becomes a lien creditor while the security interest is perfected only to the extent that it secures advances made more than 45 days after the person becomes a lien creditor." Under our facts, X became a lien creditor on February 1, and the advance would be made on March 1, which is approximately 30 days after X became a lien creditor. Since a security interest is subordinate to a lien creditor only when the advance is made more than 45 days after the person becomes a lien creditor, the security interest is not subordinate when it is made in less than 45 days. Therefore, the correct answer is **A.**

Note on test-taking. Watch out for distractors, such as **B,** that contain the word "always." Since law is full of exceptions, a response that is stated in absolute terms is rarely correct.

Question 5. On January 1, S lends D $10,000 and obtains a security interest in D's equipment. The security agreement contains a future advances clause. S perfects its security agreement by filing on January 5. On February 1, X has the sheriff execute on the same equipment to satisfy a $15,000 judgment against D. On July 1, D asks S to lend D an additional $5,000. S is hesitant to make the loan because S knows of X's lien and believes that the equipment is worth no more than $20,000. S seeks your advice as to the consequences of loaning D an additional $5,000. Will S have priority over X in the $5,000 loan?

A. Yes, because the loan is a future advance made within 45 days after X became a lien creditor.

B. Yes, because future advances always have priority over judicial liens.

C. No, because X became a lien creditor before the future advance was made.

D. No, because S had knowledge of X's lien.

Analysis. *Note on test-taking.* This question appears similar to the previous question, so look for differences and determine whether the different fact leads to a different result. The change in facts is that the future advance would be made on July 1 rather than March 1.

According to § 9-323(b), "a security interest is subordinate to the rights of a person that becomes a lien creditor while the security interest is perfected only to the extent that it secures advances made more than 45 days after the person becomes a lien creditor." Under our facts, X became a lien creditor on February 1 and the advance would be made on July 1, which is approximately 90 days after X became a lien creditor. Since a security interest is subordinate to a lien creditor only when the advance is made more than 45 days after the person becomes a lien creditor, here it looks like the security interest is subordinate. However, there are two exceptions. If they apply, then the advance is not subordinate even if made after 45 days. To apply, the advance must be made, according to § 9-323(b)(1) and (2):

(1) without knowledge of the lien; or

(2) pursuant to a commitment entered into without knowledge of the lien.

Here, the advance was made with knowledge of the lien, and the facts do not say it was made pursuant to a commitment, so it appears that the exceptions do not apply. Therefore, the correct response is **D.** You may be wondering about the meaning of the second exception, "made . . . pursuant to a commitment entered into without knowledge of the lien." That would arise if back when the agreement was made on January 1, S made a commitment to lend D another $5,000 on July 1. You would then have a future advance made pursuant to a commitment, and if S made the commitment without knowledge of the lien, which would have been the facts under our case, then the exception would apply.

Additional note on test-taking. Note that response **C** does not initially appear to be incorrect. It gives the correct conclusion, which is no. It also states a correct fact: "X became a lien creditor before the future advance was made." The problem is that a causal connection is lacking. The reason the answer is no is not for the reason stated, "because X became a lien creditor before the future advance was made."

C.   A Creditor with a Lien Arising by Operation of Law: § 9-333

Liens arising by operation of law are statutory liens. They differ from Article 9 security interests in that they are not consensual, and they differ from judicial liens in that they require no judicial proceedings. For example, many jurisdictions have enacted a statutory "mechanic's lien." Such a statute may, for example, give an automobile repair shop a lien on an automobile in its possession until the repairs are paid for. To obtain this lien, the creditor does not have to obtain the consent of the debtor and does not have to go to court. That is why it is said to arise "by operation of law." Disputes between these lien creditors and secured parties are resolved by § 9-333, which provides:

> **Priority of Certain Liens Arising by Operation of Law.**
>   (a) **"Possessory lien."** In this section, "possessory lien" means an interest, other than a security interest or an agricultural lien:
>   (1) which secures payment or performance of an obligation for services or materials furnished with respect to goods by a person in the ordinary course of the person's business;
>   (2) which is created by statute or rule of law in favor of the person; and
>   (3) whose effectiveness depends on the person's possession of the goods.
>   (b) **Priority of possessory lien.** A possessory lien on goods has priority over a security interest in the goods unless the lien is created by a statute that expressly provides otherwise.

Note that the lien arising by operation of law (I wish there were an easier way of saying that) has priority under the Code only if:

- it is possessory;
- it secures payment for services or materials furnished with respect to goods;
- it is created by statute; and
- the statute does not provide for a different priority scheme.

The general rule of § 9-333(b) is that a creditor with a lien arising by operation of law "has priority over a security interest in the goods." The policy behind giving this lien a priority is that the creditor with a lien arising by operation of law has added value to the goods, which benefits the secured party as well. For example, in the case of the automobile repair shop, the repair is for the benefit of a party with a security interest in the car as well as for the benefit of the owner. Note the exception: the Code gives the creditor with a lien arising by operation of law priority "unless the lien is created by a statute that expressly provides otherwise." Always examine the lien statute to see if it creates its own priority rules.

Question 6. Bank takes a security interest in Rancher's cattle. Bank files on January 1. On May 1, Rancher asks Neighbor to allow 100 head of cattle to graze on Neighbor's property for six months for $1,200 per month. On September 1, Rancher defaults as to Bank and Neighbor. A statute in the jurisdiction provides for the following "agister's lien":

> If there is an express or implied contract for keeping, feeding, herding, pasturing, or ranching stock, a ranchman, farmer, agister, herder, hotelkeeper, livery, or stablekeeper to whom any horses, mules, cattle, sheep, hogs, or other stock are entrusted has a lien upon the stock for the amount due for keeping, feeding, herding, pasturing, or ranching the stock and may retain possession of the stock until the sum due is paid.

Who has priority in the cattle between Bank and Neighbor?

A. Bank, because Article 9 provides that secured creditors have priority over creditors with liens arising by operation of law.

B. Neighbor, because Article 9 provides that creditors with liens arising by operation of law have priority over secured creditors unless the lien statute provides otherwise, and here it is silent.

C. Bank, because Article 9 provides that liens arising by operation of law have priority unless the lien statute provides otherwise, and here it provides otherwise.

D. Neighbor, because public policy favors the creditor with a lien arising by operation of law, whose efforts made the collateral more valuable to the secured party.

Analysis. Section 9-333 provides that "[a] possessory lien on goods has priority over a security interest in the goods unless the lien is created by a statute that expressly provides otherwise." Here, Bank has a security interest in the cattle, and Neighbor has a lien arising by operation of law. According to § 9-333, the lien arising by operation of law has priority, unless the lien statute provides otherwise, and here it does not. Therefore, **B** is the correct response.

Question 7. Creditor has a perfected security interest in ABC Co.'s computer. ABC takes the computer to ER Computers for repair. When ABC does not pay ER, ER says it is going to hold on to the computer under a state statute that provides for the following "mechanic's lien":

> Every person who, while lawfully in possession of an article of personal property, renders any service to the owner or lawful claimant of the article by labor or skill employed for the making, repairing, protection, improvement, safekeeping, carriage, towing,

> or storage of the article or tows or stores the article as directed under authority of law has a special lien on it. The lien is dependent on possession and is for the compensation, if any, that is due to the person from the owner or lawful claimant for the service and for material, if any, furnished in connection with the service. The lien hereby created shall not take precedence over perfected security interests under the Uniform Commercial Code—Secured Transactions.

While ER is holding the computer, ABC defaults as to Creditor. Who has priority as between Creditor and ER?

A. Creditor, because Article 9 provides that secured creditors have priority over creditors with liens arising by operation of law.

B. ER, because Article 9 provides that creditors with liens arising by operation of law have priority over secured creditors unless the lien statute provides otherwise, and here it is silent.

C. Creditor, because Article 9 provides that liens arising by operation of law have priority unless the lien statute provides otherwise, and here it provides otherwise.

D. ER, because public policy favors the creditor with a lien arising by operation of law, whose efforts made the collateral more valuable to the secured party.

Analysis. Section 9-333 provides that "[a] possessory lien on goods has priority over a security interest in the goods unless the lien is created by a statute that expressly provides otherwise." Here, the Bank has a security interest in the computer, and ER has a lien arising by operation of law. According to § 9-333(b), the lien arising by operation of law has priority unless the lien statute provides otherwise. This statute provides that "[t]he lien hereby created shall not take precedence over perfected security interests under the Uniform Commercial Code—Secured Transactions," thereby bringing it under the exception of § 9-333(b). Therefore, **C** is the correct response.

D. A Creditor with an Agricultural Lien

You may recall from Chapter 5.D that Revised Article 9 brought agricultural liens within the scope of Article 9. The definition in § 9-102(a)(5) provides: "Agricultural lien" means an interest in farm products:

> (A) which secures payment or performance of an obligation for:
> > (i) goods or services furnished in connection with a debtor's farming operation; or
> > (ii) rent on real property leased by a debtor in connection with its farming operation;

(B) which is created by statute in favor of a person that:

    (i) in the ordinary course of its business furnished goods or services to a debtor in connection with a debtor's farming operation; or

    (ii) leased real property to a debtor in connection with the debtor's farming operation; and

(C) whose effectiveness does not depend on the person's possession of the personal property.

The theory of the Code is that the same rules as to filing, priority, and default that apply to security interests should apply to agricultural liens. Recall that while an agricultural lien is not an Article 9 security interest, it is brought within the scope of Article 9 by § 9-109(a)(2). It is, like the liens arising by operation of law, a statutory lien, but it does not require possession to be effective. In most states, agricultural liens operate like the § 9-324(a) and (b) liens we looked at in Chapter 16.D that give a later secured party a "superpriority" over an earlier secured party. They are designed to enable a farmer who has already given one creditor a lien on the crop to obtain credit with which to purchase additional goods and services essential to the debtor's farming operation. For example, typical agricultural lien statutes cover the purchase of seed or grain, crop-dusting, hail insurance, threshing services, and farm labor. They give the creditor who supplies those goods and services a superpriority over the underlying creditor's security interest in the crops. A few states have adopted an optional Article 9 provision, § 9-324a, that expressly codifies such a scheme in Article 9. Most states, however, rely on separate agricultural lien statutes, which become governed by Article 9 through the operation of the following statutes:

§ 9-302. Law Governing Perfection and Priority of Agricultural Liens. While farm products are located in a jurisdiction, the local law of that jurisdiction governs perfection, the effect of perfection or nonperfection, and the priority of an agricultural lien on the farm products.

§ 9-308. When Security Interest or Agricultural Lien Is Perfected; Continuity of Perfection.

    . . .

    (b) **Perfection of agricultural lien.** An agricultural lien is perfected if it has become effective and all of the applicable requirements for perfection in Section 9-310 have been satisfied. An agricultural lien is perfected when it becomes effective if the applicable requirements are satisfied before the agricultural lien becomes effective.

§ 9-310. When Filing Required to Perfect Security Interest or Agricultural Lien.

    (a) **General rule: perfection by filing.** Except as otherwise provided in subsection (b) and Section 9-312(b), a financing statement must be filed to perfect all security interests and agricultural liens.

Putting those sections together, the jurisdiction where the farm products are located governs perfection and priority of an agricultural lien on the farm products. The lien is then perfected according to § 9-310, which requires filing for perfection. For example, a farm located in California is owned by MegaAgra, a Delaware corporation. Recall that in Chapter 12.D we learned that a security interest in a corporation's personal property, such as MegaAgra's interest in the crops growing on this farm, would be filed in the debtor's state of incorporation, in this case, Delaware. But if a creditor obtains an agricultural lien pursuant to a California statute on the crop, then it must perfect according to the rules for filing in California, where the farm products are located.

Question 8. On February 2, a bank takes a security interest in a farmer's wheat crop and files with the Secretary of State of the jurisdiction in which the farm is located. On May 5, Seedco sells seed to the farmer on credit, with payment due September 1, and files with the Secretary of State of the jurisdiction in which the farm is located. On September 1, the farmer defaults as to the bank and Seedco. Seedco consults you. Your research uncovers the following statutes in the jurisdiction:

§ 71-3-701. Lien for seed or grain.
Any person, company, association, or corporation who furnishes to another seed to be sown or planted or funds or means with which to purchase seed to be sown or planted or to be used in the production or cultivation of a crop or crops on the lands owned or contracted to be purchased, used, leased, occupied, or rented by him or held under government entry, upon filing a UCC-1 financing statement, has a lien not exceeding the purchase price of the seed or grain furnished upon the crop produced from the seed or grain furnished, or any part thereof, and upon the seed or grain threshed from the crop to secure the payment of the amount or the value of the seed or grain furnished or the funds or means advanced to purchase the seed or grain.

§ 71-3-702. Priority.
The lien provided by 71-3-701 shall, as to the crop covered thereby, have priority over all other liens and encumbrances thereon.

A. Does Seedco have an interest in the crop that has a priority over the bank's interest?
B. Yes, because Seedco complied with the agricultural lien laws of the jurisdiction.
C. Yes, because Seedco has a security interest that is entitled to a superpriority.
D. No, because Seedco filed in the wrong jurisdiction.
E. No, because the bank has priority since it was first to file or perfect.

Analysis.   The governing jurisdiction under § 9-302 is the one in which the farm is located. Seedco satisfies the requirements for an agricultural lien under § 9-102(a)(5) because its lien is created under a statute in that jurisdiction, § 71-3-701. Note that an agricultural lien, according to the definition, is not a security interest, so **B** cannot be a correct response. According to §§ 9-308 and 9-310, an agricultural lien must be perfected by the filing of a financing statement, and this was done, so **C** cannot be a correct response. Under the general rule of § 9-322(a)(1), the bank would have priority because it was the first to file, so **D** would be the correct response if there is no exception to the general rule. But § 9-302 provides that "the local law of that jurisdiction governs . . . the priority of an agricultural lien on the farm products." Such a local law is found in § 71-3-702, which provides that "[t]he lien provided by 71-3-701 shall, as to the crop covered thereby, have priority over all other liens and encumbrances thereon." Therefore, Seedco's agricultural lien has priority over the bank's security interest, and **A** is the correct response.

E.   Federal Tax Liens

Creditors frequently find that they are competing with the federal and state governments for the assets of their debtors. The principal reason this competition arises is that it is easy for business debtors to "borrow" from the government. Businesses are required to withhold a portion of employees' wages and to remit the withheld amounts at periodic intervals to the tax authorities. While employees think of these amounts as "taken out" of their wages, employers often see withholding as a payment obligation to a creditor that they can choose not to fulfill if they lack other resources or have other, more compelling obligations. In other words, the Internal Revenue Service (IRS) is just another creditor competing for payment by the business.

One significant consequence that arises if a business does not pay money to the IRS is that the IRS may impose the "100 percent penalty" under Internal Revenue Code § 6672:

> **§ 6672. Failure to collect and pay over tax, or attempt to evade or defeat tax**
>
>   (a) General rule — Any person required to collect, truthfully account for, and pay over any tax imposed by this title who willfully fails to collect such tax, or truthfully account for and pay over such tax, or willfully attempts in any manner to evade or defeat any such tax or the payment thereof, shall, in addition to other penalties provided by law, be liable to a penalty equal to the total amount of the tax evaded, or not collected, or not accounted for and paid over.

In other words, not only is the taxpayer—the business entity—liable for payment of the tax, but so are those individuals in the business who actively participated in the decision not to pay the IRS. The following case excerpt indicates a typical understanding of who is liable under this statute:

In determining whether a person is a "responsible person" within the meaning of the statute imposing a penalty based on a corporate employer's failure to pay over withholding taxes, a court should consider whether such a person: is an officer or member of the board of directors; owns a substantial amount of stock in the company; manages day-to-day operations of the business; has authority to hire or fire employees; makes decisions as to disbursement of funds and payment of creditors; and possesses authority to sign company checks.

Barnett v. I.R.S., 988 F.2d 1449 (5th Cir. 1993).

Once it decides to pursue a taxpayer or other person for nonpayment of taxes, the IRS proceeds by assessment. The assessment is a lien that attaches to all property of the debtor. According to IRC § 6323(a), however, the IRS must file the tax lien, and it loses priority to an earlier filed security interest. The IRS has also ruled that a later PMSI that would have priority over a security interest also has priority over a tax lien. Most jurisdictions have enacted a "Uniform Federal Lien Registration Act" that provides for the place of filing. Unfortunately, this uniform act has not been coordinated with Revised Article 9, so a searcher may have to search in more than one place to find the filed liens. For example, the Act provides that "[i]f the person against whose interest the lien applies is a corporation or partnership whose principal executive office is in this State," then the federal lien is filed "in the office of the Secretary of State." You recall from Chapter 12.D that a financing statement naming a corporation as debtor is filed in the office of the Secretary of State in the jurisdiction where the corporation is incorporated, not where its principal executive office is found. See § 9-307(e). Furthermore, since the filing is not made pursuant to Article 9, the IRS may file in a name that would not be effective for an Article 9 filing. So the searcher for tax liens must look in different places and under different names than those used by the searcher for security interests.

Question 9. S has a security interest in the equipment of D Inc. D Inc. has been erratic in making payments, and S has threatened to repossess the equipment if D Inc. is late in making the next payment. Without equipment, D Inc. can't make any money. P, the President of D Inc., determines that the company could get by in the short run by sending money to S and not to the IRS for withholding. P instructs C, the clerk in the payroll department, to send money to S and not to the IRS. In addition to D Inc., against whom is the IRS likely to make an assessment for unpaid taxes?

A. P and C.

B. P only.

C. C only.

D. Neither P nor C, because only D Inc. is the taxpayer liable for D Inc.'s taxes.

Analysis. This isn't technically an Article 9 question, but it is something very important to know in practice. Don't let your clients do this! While it is true that only D Inc. is liable for payment of D Inc.'s taxes, others may be liable for nonpayment of D Inc.'s taxes. That is the point of the penalty in Internal Revenue Code § 6672. So **D** is not a correct response. It is unlikely that the IRS would impose the penalty against **C,** who was merely "obeying orders" and did not participate in the decision-making, so **A** and **C** are not correct responses. Since P is the person with decision-making power, the best response is **B.**

Question 10. On February 1, Bank loans D Inc. $10,000 and takes a security interest in D Inc.'s personal property. On March 1, the IRS files a tax lien against D Inc.'s personal property and files notice in the proper place. On April 1, Bank files a financing statement in the proper place. Who has priority?

A. Bank, because security interests always have priority over tax liens.
B. IRS, because tax liens always have priority over security interests.
C. Bank, because it was first to file.
D. IRS, because it was first to file.

Analysis. The correct response is **D.** The authority is Internal Revenue Code § 6323(a), which is an incomprehensible statute, but it essentially fits tax liens into the Article 9 scheme, with priority between a secured party and the IRS going to the first party to file.

F.   Closers

Question 11. On August 1, First Bank (FB) loaned a Kansas lawyer $5,000 and took a security interest in the professional books that were in the lawyer's office. On August 10, a former client (JC) got a judgment against the lawyer for $5,000 and immediately had the sheriff levy on the lawyer's professional books. FB filed on August 15. Who has the best claim to the books? Hint: Review Chapter 3.A.

A. FB, because it has a PMSI and effectively filed.
B. JC, because the sheriff levied before FB effectively filed.
C. FB, because the property is exempt from execution but subject to a valid security interest.
D. The lawyer, because the property is exempt from execution.

Analysis.   Here, FB does not have a PMSI, so it does not have priority over a judgment creditor, since it was not perfected at the time of the levy. It might therefore appear that the correct response is **B**, but I made the debtor a Kansas lawyer in hopes that you would recall the Kansas exemption statutes in Chapter 3.A, which provide that the books of a professional are exempt from execution up to a value of $7,500. Therefore, **B** is not correct. However, the lawyer does not prevail either, because even though the property is exempt from execution, it is still subject to a security interest. So **C** is the correct response.

Question 12. On December 20, F Finance Co. loans money to D to purchase inventory and takes a security interest in inventory. On January 1, D acquires the inventory with F's money. On January 5, C Judgment Creditor has the sheriff levy on the inventory. On January 6, B Bank takes a nonpurchase money security interest in D's inventory and properly files. On January 7, F Finance Co. files its financing statement. Who has priority in the inventory?

(Suggestion: Use the Secured Transactions methodology, which is:

1. Characterize the parties.
2. Classify the collateral.
3. Determine whether the security interest is perfected or unperfected.
4. Find the Code section that contains the appropriate rule.
5. Apply the facts to the rule to obtain the result.

Work through the three possible priority contests: F v. C, B v. C, and F v. B.)

A. B.
B. C.
C. F.
D. None of the parties clearly has priority.

Analysis.   This problem passes for a joke among fans of secured transactions (and I am sure you are one of them).

Let's start with *F v. C.* The parties are secured creditor v. judgment lien creditor. Also note that F has a PMSI, since it loaned the debtor the money used to purchase the collateral in which it took a security interest. The collateral is inventory. F perfected on January 7; C levied on January 5. The general rule for priority disputes between a secured party and a judgment lien creditor is found in § 9-317(a)(2). (See part B of this chapter.) Under the general rule, the lien creditor prevails over a secured party if the secured party is not perfected at the time of the levy. Under that rule, C would prevail. But the exception in § 9-317(e) applies if the secured creditor has a PMSI, and the financing statement is filed within 20 days after D's possession. Under our facts, D acquired the inventory on January 1, and F filed on January 7, so F qualifies under the exception. So F has priority over C.

B v. C. The parties are secured creditor v. judgment lien creditor. The collateral is inventory. B perfected on January 6; C levied on January 5. The general rule for priority disputes between a secured party and a judgment lien creditor is found in § 9-317(a)(2). (See part B of this chapter.) Under the general rule, the lien creditor prevails over a secured party if the secured party is not perfected at the time of the levy. Under that rule, C would prevail. The exception in § 9-317(e) does not apply because B does not have a PMSI. So C has priority over B.

F v. B. The parties are secured creditor v. secured creditor. Also note that F has a PMSI, since it loaned the debtor the money used to purchase the collateral in which it took a security interest. The collateral is inventory. F perfected on January 7; B perfected on January 6. The general rule for priority disputes between two perfected secured creditors is found in § 9-322(a). (See Chapter 16.A.) Under the general rule, the first to file or perfect has priority. Under that rule, B would prevail. But the exception in § 9-324(b) applies if the secured creditor has a PMSI in inventory, the financing statement is filed at the time of D's possession, and notice is given to the underlying secured creditor. (See Chapter 16.D.) Under our facts, F did not timely perfect or give notice, so F does not qualify for the exception. So under the general rule, B has priority over F.

The bottom line is that the priorities are F over C, C over B, and B over F. Ha! Ha! This is a case of circular priority, so the correct response is **D**, "none of the above."

 # Burnham's Picks

Question 1	D
Question 2	B
Question 3	A
Question 4	A
Question 5	D
Question 6	B
Question 7	C
Question 8	A
Question 9	B
Question 10	D
Question 11	C
Question 12	D

Secured Party v. Party with an Interest in Fixtures, Accessions, or Commingled Goods

CHAPTER OVERVIEW

A. The Definition of Fixtures

What is a fixture? On the continuum from personal property to real property, fixtures are the gray area in the middle. Fixtures are items of personal property that have become attached to the real property; they are sometimes treated as personal property, sometimes as real property. For example, a buyer makes an offer to buy a house. At the time of the offer, the house is fully furnished. If the sellers accept the offer, what can they legally take away, and what must they leave behind? The buyer purchased real property but not (unless otherwise agreed) personal property, so the sellers retain the personal property. If an item is a fixture, it goes to the buyer, who purchased the real property. For this purpose, fixtures are treated as real property.

When we looked at the scope of Article 9 in Chapter 5.C, we saw that § 9-109(a)(1) provides that Article 9 applies to "a transaction . . . that creates a security interest in personal property or fixtures." Section 9-334(a) states that "a security interest under this Article may be created in goods that are fixtures or may continue in goods that become fixtures." However, while Article 9 applies to fixtures, Article 9 does not define *fixtures*. Although § 9-102(a) (41) contains a definition of fixtures, in fact the definition refers us to "real property law," which is found in the law of each state:

> (41) "Fixtures" means goods that have become so related to particular real property that an interest in them arises under real property law.

Many jurisdictions apply a three-part test, as stated in this old New York case:

> The true criterion of a fixture is the united application of these requisites: (1) Actual annexation to the realty or something appurtenant thereto; (2) application to the use or purpose to which that part of the realty with which it is connected is appropriated; (3) the intention of the party making the annexation to make a permanent accession to the freehold.

McRea v. Central National Bank, 66 N.Y. 489 (1876).

Frustrated by the inconsistent application of these tests, White and Summers suggested this tongue-in-cheek approach:

> If one lets his imagination fly, he can easily devise objective standards for determining what is and what is not a fixture. An excellent candidate for a certain rule is the half-inch formula. Under this formula anything which could be moved more than a half inch by one blow with a hammer weighing not more than five pounds and swung by a man weighing not more than 250 pounds would not be a fixture. Another formula might be the screwdriver-crescent-wrench-one-hour rule. Under such a rule anything affixed to the realty would be regarded as a fixture unless one man with a screwdriver and a crescent wrench could loosen it from the floor or wall within one hour. Of course, even our objective standards would meet difficulty in real life (would the item remain a fixture if after removal by the screwdriver and wrench there was no door large enough to allow it to exit from the building?).

White and Summers, *Uniform Commercial Code* 1056 (2d ed., 1980).

We will not explore further whether an item is a fixture, although this is a frequently disputed issue. We will take the easy route of stating in the facts that an item is a fixture, and we will then explore the legal ramifications of that determination. For example, Creditor takes a security interest in all personal property and fixtures of Debtor Law Firm. As against Debtor, Creditor has a security interest in its personal property and the fixtures.

But frequently there is a competing interest: the debtor may have a debt secured by real estate. For example, Debtor Law Firm owns its own building.

First Bank has a mortgage on the building. Second Bank has a security interest in all the personal property. The firm defaults as to both creditors, and the banks go in to carve up the collateral. Who gets the land and building? The conference room table and chairs? The wall-to-wall carpeting? The furnace? Clearly the building goes to First Bank, and the table and chairs go to Second Bank. The carpeting and furnace may well be fixtures. The general rule in a priority contest between a personal property secured creditor and a real property secured creditor is that the real property secured creditor has priority in fixtures. Section 9-334(c) provides:

§ 9-334. Priority of Security Interests in Fixtures and Crops.

. . .

(c) **General rule: subordination of security interest in fixtures.** In cases not governed by subsections (d) through (h), a security interest in fixtures is subordinate to a conflicting interest of an encumbrancer or owner of the related real property other than the debtor.

Question 1. An automobile dealership in a certain state has a Quonset hut–type building that it uses to store vehicles. The building is made of corrugated metal pieces bolted to a wooden framework. Is this building a fixture?

A. Yes, under the Article 9 definition.
B. No, under the Article 9 definition.
C. It depends on the property law of the state.
D. It depends on whether the automobile dealership considers it to be a fixture.

Analysis.   Section 9-102(a)(41) leaves the definition of fixture to state property law. In many jurisdictions, the intent of the parties may be a factor, but this is not always the case. Therefore, the best response is **C**.

Question 2. An automobile dealership in a certain state has a Quonset hut–type building that it uses to store vehicles. In this state, the building is a fixture. Bank 1 has loaned money to the dealership secured by the real property. Bank 2 has loaned money to the dealership secured by the personal property. Which bank is entitled to the building?

A. Bank 1, because a building is real property.
B. Bank 1, because fixtures go with the real property interest.
C. Bank 2, because Article 9 gives a creditor an interest in personal property and fixtures.
D. It depends whether the building is a fixture.

Analysis. *Note on test-taking.* You are told in the facts that "the building is a fixture." Don't fight the facts. Therefore, response **D** must not be correct.

Response **A** is not correct, because in this case the building is a fixture, not real property. While it is true that the scope of Article 9 includes security interests in fixtures, you are not told in the facts that Bank 2 has a security interest in fixtures. And even if Bank 2 did have a security interest in fixtures, the general rule of § 9-334(c) is that "a security interest in fixtures is subordinate to a conflicting interest of an encumbrancer or owner of the related real property." Therefore, **C** is not correct. The best response is **B,** because in the absence of another applicable rule, fixtures go with the real property interest, even if there is a security interest in fixtures.

B.   Priorities in Fixtures

As we have seen, the general rule is that in a priority contest between a personal property secured party and a real property secured party, the fixture goes to the real property interest. But this is Article 9, so there are, of course, exceptions where the personal property secured party has priority in fixtures over the real property secured party. We are told in § 9-334(c) that the general rule applies only "[i]n cases not governed by subsections (d) through (h)." Those exceptions provide:

(d) **Fixtures purchase-money priority.** Except as otherwise provided in subsection (h), a perfected security interest in fixtures has priority over a conflicting interest of an encumbrancer or owner of the real property if the debtor has an interest of record in or is in possession of the real property and:

(1) the security interest is a purchase-money security interest;

(2) the interest of the encumbrancer or owner arises before the goods become fixtures; and

(3) the security interest is perfected by a fixture filing before the goods become fixtures or within 20 days thereafter.

(e) **Priority of security interest in fixtures over interests in real property.** A perfected security interest in fixtures has priority over a conflicting interest of an encumbrancer or owner of the real property if:

(1) the debtor has an interest of record in the real property or is in possession of the real property and the security interest:

(A) is perfected by a fixture filing before the interest of the encumbrancer or owner is of record; and

(B) has priority over any conflicting interest of a predecessor in title of the encumbrancer or owner;

(2) before the goods become fixtures, the security interest is perfected by any method permitted by this article and the fixtures are readily removable:

(A) factory or office machines;

(B) equipment that is not primarily used or leased for use in the operation of the real property; or

(C) replacements of domestic appliances that are consumer goods;

(3) the conflicting interest is a lien on the real property obtained by legal or equitable proceedings after the security interest was perfected by any method permitted by this article; or

(4) the security interest is:

(A) created in a manufactured home in a manufactured-home transaction; and

(B) perfected pursuant to a statute described in Section 9-311(a)(2).

(f) **Priority based on consent, disclaimer, or right to remove.** A security interest in fixtures, whether or not perfected, has priority over a conflicting interest of an encumbrancer or owner of the real property if:

(1) the encumbrancer or owner has, in an authenticated record, consented to the security interest or disclaimed an interest in the goods as fixtures; or

(2) the debtor has a right to remove the goods as against the encumbrancer or owner.

(g) **Continuation of subsection (f) priority.** The priority of the security interest under subsection (f) continues for a reasonable time if the debtor's right to remove the goods as against the encumbrancer or owner terminates.

(h) **Priority of construction mortgage.** A mortgage is a construction mortgage to the extent that it secures an obligation incurred for the construction of an improvement on land, including the acquisition cost of the land, if a recorded record of the mortgage so indicates. Except as otherwise provided in subsections (e) and (f), a security interest in fixtures is subordinate to a construction mortgage if a record of the mortgage is recorded before the goods become fixtures and the goods become fixtures before the completion of the construction. A mortgage has this priority to the same extent as a construction mortgage to the extent that it is given to refinance a construction mortgage.

Let's take a closer look at the most significant exceptions. They are:

- consent
- first in time
- PMSI

1. Consent

The real estate interest may consent to give up its rights. See § 9-334(f)(1). This is an example of freedom of contract. We saw in Chapter 16.C that secured parties may use a subordination agreement to change the priorities that are otherwise dictated by Article 9. Similarly, the real estate encumbrancer and the secured party may agree to change their priorities in fixtures.

2. *First in Time*

A security interest in a fixture has priority over a *later* real estate interest if the secured party makes a *fixture filing* before the real property encumbrance is recorded. See § 9-334(e)(1)(A). The definition of a fixture filing is found in § 9-102(a)(40), which provides:

> (40) "Fixture filing" means the filing of a financing statement covering goods that are or are to become fixtures and satisfying Section 9-502(a) and (b). The term includes the filing of a financing statement covering goods of a transmitting utility which are or are to become fixtures.

The requirements for a fixture filing are found in § 9-502(a) and (b), which provide:

> **Contents of Financing Statement; Record of Mortgage as Financing Statement; Time of Filing Financing Statement.**
>
> (a) **Sufficiency of financing statement.** Subject to subsection (b), a financing statement is sufficient only if it:
>
> (1) provides the name of the debtor;
>
> (2) provides the name of the secured party or a representative of the secured party; and
>
> (3) indicates the collateral covered by the financing statement.
>
> (b) **Real-property-related financing statements.** Except as otherwise provided in Section 9-501(b), to be sufficient, a financing statement that covers as-extracted collateral or timber to be cut, or which is filed as a fixture filing and covers goods that are or are to become fixtures, must satisfy subsection (a) and also:
>
> (1) indicate that it covers this type of collateral;
>
> (2) indicate that it is to be filed [for record] in the real property records;
>
> (3) provide a description of the real property to which the collateral is related [sufficient to give constructive notice of a mortgage under the law of this State if the description were contained in a record of the mortgage of the real property]; and
>
> (4) if the debtor does not have an interest of record in the real property, provide the name of a record owner.

Finally, the place in which the fixture filing is filed is found in § 9-501(a) (1)(B):

> **§ 9-501. Filing Office.**
>
> (a) **Filing offices.** Except as otherwise provided in subsection (b), if the local law of this State governs perfection of a security interest or

agricultural lien, the office in which to file a financing statement to perfect the security interest or agricultural lien is:

> (1) the office designated for the filing or recording of a record of a mortgage on the related real property, if:
>
> . . .
>
> > (B) the financing statement is filed as a fixture filing and the collateral is goods that are or are to become fixtures.

Putting this all together, the usual case in which the rule of § 9-334(e)(1)(A) applies is one in which a secured creditor takes a security interest in goods that are or that become fixtures and then makes a fixture filing. In that case, the secured party has priority over a later real estate interest. It should now become clear why a fixture filing must describe the real property and why it is filed not where other financing statements are filed, but in the real property records. That way, a prospective real estate purchaser or creditor searching for all recorded interests in the real property will find the fixture filing and will have notice of the secured creditor's interest in the fixture.

3. PMSI

A purchase money security interest (PMSI) has priority over an *earlier* real estate interest if the secured party makes a timely *fixture filing*. See § 9-334(d). In this case, the secured party's interest in the fixtures comes *after* the interest of the real estate party. But if the secured party makes a fixture filing before the goods become fixtures or within 20 days thereafter, then the secured creditor is entitled to a superpriority, rather like the superpriority enjoyed by a secured party in § 9-324 that we looked at in Chapter 16.D. As with the other superpriorities, the policy is that the secured party is taking nothing other than what it enabled the debtor to obtain, so the underlying creditor is not disadvantaged.

Question 3. Debtor grants Bank a security interest in its current and after-acquired equipment. Bank intends to perfect its security interest by filing a financing statement with the applicable filing office. Bank is concerned that some of the equipment could be deemed a fixture, so Bank also intends to file a fixture filing. What additional requirement must the financing statement satisfy in order to be a fixture filing?

A. It must be authenticated by the owner of the real estate on which the fixture is or may be located.

B. It must provide a description of the real estate on which the fixture is or may be located.

C. It must summarize the secured debt.

D. It must describe, with detailed particularity, the equipment that is or may become a fixture.

Analysis. As we saw in Chapter 12.C, § 9-502(a) provides that a financing statement is sufficient only if it provides the names of the debtor and the secured party and indicates the collateral. Section 9-502(b) provides:

> a fixture filing . . . must satisfy subsection (a) and also: . . .
>   (1) indicate that it covers this type of collateral;
>   (2) indicate that it is to be filed [for record] in the real property records;
>   (3) provide a description of the real property to which the collateral is related; and
>   (4) if the debtor does not have an interest of record in the real property, provide the name of a record owner.

Of the responses you are given, the one that contains one of these additional requirements is **B,** which would satisfy the requirement in § 9-502(b)(3).

Question 4. R has a mortgage on D's office building that is properly recorded. S loans D money, takes a security interest in the central air conditioning for the office, and immediately makes a fixture filing. Who has priority?

A. R, because the general rule is that a mortgage interest has priority over a security interest in fixtures.

B. R, because in order to obtain priority, S must file before loaning the money and must notify R.

C. S, because the general rule is that a security interest in fixtures has priority over a mortgage interest.

D. S, because there is an exception for PMSIs in fixtures that are timely filed.

Analysis. The general rule of § 9-334(c) is that "a security interest in fixtures is subordinate to a conflicting interest of an encumbrancer or owner of the related real property other than the debtor." We have seen that there are exceptions for waiver by the real property encumbrancer, an interest in fixtures perfected by an earlier filed fixture filing, or a later PMSI in fixtures that is perfected by a timely fixture filing. None of the exceptions applies here, so the general rule as found in response **A** applies.

Question 5. R has a mortgage on D's office building that is properly recorded. S sells D central air conditioning for the office building on credit, takes a security interest in the air conditioning equipment, and immediately makes a fixture filing. Does S's security interest have priority over R's mortgage?

> **A.** No, because the general rule is that a mortgage interest has priority over a security interest in fixtures.
>
> **B.** No, because in order to obtain priority, S must file before loaning the money and must notify R.
>
> **C.** Yes, because the general rule is that a security interest in fixtures has priority over a mortgage interest.
>
> **D.** Yes, because the general rule that a mortgage interest has priority over a security interest in fixtures has an exception for a PMSI in fixtures that is timely filed.

Analysis.   *Note on test-taking.* This question is similar to the previous one, so you should look for different facts that may produce a different answer. Here, the key fact is that S sold on credit the air conditioning in which it took a security interest. This means that S is a secured creditor with a PMSI. Because S took all the steps required under § 9-334(d), S has a superpriority over R. The correct response is **D.**

C.   Remedies

We know that a secured party may repossess the collateral on default, but the situation is a little different with fixtures. Because fixtures are not easily removable, there may be some damage done during their removal, or they may be of little value when separated from the real property. Who is responsible for that damage? Section 9-604 provides:

§ 9-604. Procedure If Security Agreement Covers Real Property or Fixtures.

(a) **Enforcement: personal and real property.** If a security agreement covers both personal and real property, a secured party may proceed:

(1) under this part as to the personal property without prejudicing any rights with respect to the real property; or

(2) as to both the personal property and the real property in accordance with the rights with respect to the real property, in which case the other provisions of this part do not apply.

(b) **Enforcement: fixtures.** Subject to subsection (c), if a security agreement covers goods that are or become fixtures, a secured party may proceed:

(1) under this part; or

(2) in accordance with the rights with respect to real property, in which case the other provisions of this part do not apply.

(c) **Removal of fixtures.** Subject to the other provisions of this part, if a secured party holding a security interest in fixtures has priority over all owners and encumbrancers of the real property, the secured party, after default, may remove the collateral from the real property.

(d) **Injury caused by removal.** A secured party that removes collateral shall promptly reimburse any encumbrancer or owner of the real property, other than the debtor, for the cost of repair of any physical injury caused by the removal. The secured party need not reimburse the encumbrancer or owner for any diminution in value of the real property caused by the absence of the goods removed or by any necessity of replacing them. A person entitled to reimbursement may refuse permission to remove until the secured party gives adequate assurance for the performance of the obligation to reimburse.

In many cases, the value of the fixtures after removal is only a fraction of their value as part of the real property. In a famous case under former Article 9, Sears had installed built-in cabinets and appliances on credit. When the debtor defaulted, Sears wanted to recover the value added to the real estate instead of tearing out the fixtures and selling them. Sears was denied relief, but while it lost the battle, it may have won the war, for § 9-604(b) now provides that "if a security agreement covers goods that are or become fixtures, a secured party may proceed: (1) under this part; or (2) in accordance with the rights with respect to real property, in which case the other provisions of this part do not apply." In other words, the secured party with an interest in fixtures may proceed under Article 9 or under local real estate law.

> **Question 6.** R has a mortgage on D's office building that is properly recorded. S sells D central air conditioning for the office building on credit, takes a security interest in the air conditioning equipment, and immediately makes a fixture filing. D defaults, and S removes the central air conditioning, causing $10,000 worth of damage to the building and reducing its value by $100,000. How much does S have to pay to each party?
>
> A. $0 to R and $0 to D.
> B. $10,000 to R and $0 to D.
> C. $10,000 to R and $100,000 to D.
> D. $110,000 to R and $0 to D.

Analysis. This problem is easily answered by reading § 9-604(d), which provides that "[a] secured party that removes collateral shall promptly reimburse any encumbrancer or owner of the real property, other than the debtor, for the cost of repair of any physical injury caused by the removal. The secured party need not reimburse the encumbrancer or owner for any diminution in value of the real property caused by the absence of the goods removed or by any necessity of replacing them." The cost of repair, $10,000, is not to be paid to the owner if the owner is the debtor. Here, D is the owner and the debtor, so the $10,000 is to be paid only to the encumbrancer, R. Neither party is to be paid for the diminution in value. So the correct response is **B**.

D.   Accessions

What is an *accession*? *Accession* is defined in § 9-102(a)(1), which provides:

> "Accession" means goods that are physically united with other goods in such a manner that the identity of the original goods is not lost.

Question 7. Which of the following is an example of an accession?

A. Built-in bookcases that are firmly attached to the wall of a house.
B. Books that are placed in a built-in bookcase.
C. A camper top that is bolted to the back of a pickup truck.
D. A cake that is made from flour, eggs, butter, and sugar.

Analysis.   According to the definition of *accession* in § 9-102(a)(1), the goods must be physically united with other goods, so **B** does not qualify. The identity of the original goods must not be lost, so **D** does not qualify (as we shall see, these ingredients are described as *commingled goods*). The bookcases are physically united with the wall of the house, but the house is not goods. Since the house is real property, the bookcase that is attached to it is a fixture. Therefore, **A** does not qualify. Conceptually, accessions are very similar to fixtures, except that both the underlying item and the accession are goods. The camper top and the pickup would both qualify as goods, and the top is physically united with the pickup but does not lose its identity, so the best answer is **C**.

The rules governing accessions are found in § 9-335, which provides:

§ 9-335. Accessions.
  (a) **Creation of security interest in accession.** A security interest may be created in an accession and continues in collateral that becomes an accession.
  (b) **Perfection of security interest.** If a security interest is perfected when the collateral becomes an accession, the security interest remains perfected in the collateral.
  (c) **Priority of security interest.** Except as otherwise provided in subsection (d), the other provisions of this part determine the priority of a security interest in an accession.
  (d) **Compliance with certificate-of-title statute.** A security interest in an accession is subordinate to a security interest in the whole which

is perfected by compliance with the requirements of a certificate-of-title statute under Section 9-311(b).

(e) **Removal of accession after default.** After default, subject to Part 6, a secured party may remove an accession from other goods if the security interest in the accession has priority over the claims of every person having an interest in the whole.

(f) **Reimbursement following removal.** A secured party that removes an accession from other goods under subsection (e) shall promptly reimburse any encumbrancer or owner of the whole or of the other goods, other than the debtor, for the cost of repair of any physical injury to the whole or the other goods. The secured party need not reimburse the encumbrancer or owner for any diminution in value of the whole or the other goods caused by the absence of the accession removed or by any necessity for replacing it. A person entitled to reimbursement may refuse permission to remove until the secured party gives adequate assurance for the performance of the obligation to reimburse.

The general rule of § 9-335(c) is that "the other provisions of this part determine the priority of a security interest in an accession." That is, we would go to the priority rules of § 9-322. (See Chapter 16.A.) There is an exception with accessions to goods governed by a certificate of title statute, such as automobiles. According to § 9-335(d), in that case the security interest in the accession is subordinate to the security interest in the whole. The rules on repossession and reimbursement for damage in § 9-335(e) and (f) mirror the rules for fixtures.

Question 8. Creditor 1 has a perfected security interest in a computer used in the office of ABC Inc. Creditor 2 sells additional memory chips to ABC on credit, takes a security interest in the memory chips, installs the chips in the computer, and immediately files. Who has priority in the memory chips?

A. Creditor 1, because it has a security interest in the whole.
B. Creditor 1, because it was first to file.
C. Creditor 2, because it has a security interest in an accession.
D. Creditor 2, because it has a superpriority in the collateral.

Analysis. This is a bit tricky. The memory chips are accessions as defined in § 9-102(a)(1). Since computers are not titled goods, according to § 9-335(c), priority in accessions is determined by the other provisions of the Code. Under the general rule of 9-322(a), the first to file or perfect would have priority. But there is an exception in § 9-324(a), which provides for a superpriority for a PMSI in goods other than inventory or livestock if the secured party files within 20 days. Creditor 2 complied with those requirements, so it is entitled to the superpriority. See Chapter 16.D. The correct response is **D**.

> **Question 9.** Creditor 1 has a security interest in Mary's automobile, properly recorded on the title. Creditor 2 sells Mary new tires on credit, and Mary grants a security interest in the tires to Creditor 2. Creditor 2 installs the tires and immediately perfects. Who has priority in the tires?
>
> **A.** Creditor 1, because it has a security interest in the whole.
> **B.** Creditor 1, because it was first to file.
> **C.** Creditor 2, because it has a security interest in an accession.
> **D.** Creditor 2, because it has a superpriority in the collateral.

Analysis.   Under § 9-335(d), when titled goods are involved, a security interest in an accession is subordinate to a security interest in the whole. The tires are the accession, and the car is the whole. Therefore, **A** is the correct response.

> **Question 10.** Mary owns her automobile free and clear. Creditor 1 sells Mary new tires on credit, and Mary grants a security interest in the tires to Creditor 1. Creditor 1 installs the tires and immediately perfects. Mary then grants Creditor 2 a security interest in her automobile, which is properly recorded on the title. Who has priority in the tires?
>
> **A.** Creditor 1, because it was first to file.
> **B.** Creditor 1, because it has a security interest in an accession.
> **C.** Creditor 2, because it has a security interest in the whole.
> **D.** Creditor 2, because it has a superpriority in the collateral.

Analysis.   Under § 9-335(d), when titled goods are involved, a security interest in an accession is subordinate to a security interest in the whole. The tires are the accession, and the car is the whole. Therefore, **C** is the correct response.

Note that it doesn't matter that, in this case, unlike the previous question, the security interest in the car came later. The lesson here is that those who install accessions on titled goods are taking a risk. They might want to work only for cash or seek other collateral.

E.   Commingled Goods

When goods are so combined with other goods that they cannot be recovered, they are not fixtures or accessions. They are *commingled goods*. Section 9-336(a) defines *commingled goods* as "goods that are physically united with other goods in such a manner that their identity is lost in a product or mass." That section provides:

§ 9-336. Commingled Goods.

(a) **"Commingled goods."** In this section, "commingled goods" means goods that are physically united with other goods in such a manner that their identity is lost in a product or mass.

(b) **No security interest in commingled goods as such.** A security interest does not exist in commingled goods as such. However, a security interest may attach to a product or mass that results when goods become commingled goods.

(c) **Attachment of security interest to product or mass.** If collateral becomes commingled goods, a security interest attaches to the product or mass.

(d) **Perfection of security interest.** If a security interest in collateral is perfected before the collateral becomes commingled goods, the security interest that attaches to the product or mass under subsection (c) is perfected.

(e) **Priority of security interest.** Except as otherwise provided in subsection (f), the other provisions of this part determine the priority of a security interest that attaches to the product or mass under subsection (c).

(f) **Conflicting security interests in product or mass.** If more than one security interest attaches to the product or mass under subsection (c), the following rules determine priority:

(1) A security interest that is perfected under subsection (d) has priority over a security interest that is unperfected at the time the collateral becomes commingled goods.

(2) If more than one security interest is perfected under subsection (d), the security interests rank equally in proportion to value of the collateral at the time it became commingled goods.

The problem here is to trace the security interest when it becomes part of the commingled goods. For example, if Creditor 1 has a security interest in the eggs of a bakery, and the bakery uses the eggs to make cakes, then the eggs are now commingled goods. Under subsection (b), Creditor 1's security interest attaches to the cakes, and if the security interest in the eggs was perfected, then, under subsections (c) and (d), the security interest in the cakes is also perfected. Working out the priority rules in subsections (e) and (f) is a piece of cake!

Question 11. Creditor 1 has a security interest in Debtor's eggs, perfected on February 2. The eggs have a value of $300 and secure a debt of $300. Creditor 2 has a perfected security interest in Debtor's flour, perfected on February 12. The flour has a value of $100 and secures a debt of $600. Creditor 3 has a security interest in creditor's cakes, perfected on February 22 to secure a debt of $3,000. On February 24, Debtor uses the flour and eggs to make cakes, which have a value of $1,000. How much of the value can each creditor claim?

A. Creditor 1, $300; Creditor 2, $600; Creditor 3, $100.
B. Creditor 1, $0; Creditor 2, $0; Creditor 3, $1,000.
C. Creditor 1, $750; Creditor 2, $250; Creditor 3, $0.
D. Creditor 1, $300; Creditor 2, $250; Creditor 3, $450.

Analysis.   Let's start with the priorities. Section 9-336(e) tells us that other provisions of this part determine the priority. According to the general rule of § 9-322(a)(1), perfected security interests rank in order of time of filing or perfection. Here, that order is Creditor 1, Creditor 2, and Creditor 3. But both Creditor 1 and Creditor 2 had security interests that were perfected before the collateral became commingled goods. According to subsection (f)(2), those interests rank equally in proportion to the value of the collateral. The ratio of the value of the eggs to the flour is $300 to $100 or 3:1. Of the $1,000 value of the cake, this ratio would entitle Creditor 1 to $750 and Creditor 2 to $250. However, Creditor 1's debt is only $300, so that is the most it can recover. Creditor 2 can recover $250. That leaves $450 for Creditor 3. Therefore, the correct response is **D.** I told you this question would be a piece of cake!

F.   Closers

Question 12. First Bank has a mortgage on the real property of Debtor Law Firm. Second Bank took a security interest in built-in bookcases on Debtor's premises. To determine whether the bookcases are a fixture, which source in that jurisdiction should you look to first?

A. The Article 9 definition of *fixtures*.
B. The definition of *fixtures* in statutes other than Article 9.
C. Case law that defines *fixtures*.
D. A contract between the relevant parties that defines what is a *fixture*.

Analysis.   The definition of *fixtures* in § 9-102(a)(41) refers us to the "real property law" of the jurisdiction. In any jurisdiction, the courts must follow statutes enacted by the legislature, so the first place to look is a statute. The correct answer is **B.** If there is no statute, or the statute must be applied to particular facts, then cases should be consulted. The understanding of the parties is often a relevant test, but the researcher must first go to the statute and the case law to find out what the tests are in a particular jurisdiction.

Question 13. Assume in the previous question that the bookcases are fixtures and that Second Bank has priority in the bookcases over First Bank and all other creditors. On Debtor's default, can Second Bank repossess the bookcases?

A. Yes, but only if it can do so without damaging property in which First Bank has an interest.
B. Yes, but it must pay Debtor and First Bank for any damage caused.
C. Yes, but it must pay First Bank for any damage caused.
D. No, under Article 9, but it may proceed pursuant to the real estate law of the jurisdiction.

Analysis. Section 9-604(c) provides that "[s]ubject to the other provisions of this part, if a secured party holding a security interest in fixtures has priority over all owners and encumbrancers of the real property, the secured party, after default, may remove the collateral from the real property." Here, you are told that Second Bank has priority over all other creditors. It may therefore repossess the bookcases, so **D** is not a correct response. Section 9-604(d) provides that "[a] secured party that removes collateral shall promptly reimburse any encumbrancer or owner of the real property, other than the debtor, for the cost of repair of any physical injury caused by the removal. The secured party need not reimburse the encumbrancer or owner for any diminution in value of the real property caused by the absence of the goods removed or by any necessity of replacing them." Here, First Bank is an encumbrancer who is not the debtor. Therefore, Second Bank must reimburse First Bank for any damage caused, so **C** is the correct response.

 # Burnham's Picks

Question 1	C
Question 2	B
Question 3	B
Question 4	A
Question 5	D
Question 6	B
Question 7	C
Question 8	D
Question 9	A
Question 10	C
Question 11	D
Question 12	B
Question 13	C

19

The Impact of Bankruptcy on Security Interests

CHAPTER OVERVIEW

A. Introduction

Bankruptcy law is federal law, found in the Bankruptcy Code, Title 11 of the U.S. Code. Bankruptcy begins with the filing of a petition in federal bankruptcy court. The bankruptcy may be either voluntary, filed by the debtor, or involuntary, filed by the creditors. Each creditor, known in bankruptcy as the holder of a claim, may be either secured, partially secured, or unsecured. Whether a creditor is secured or unsecured is a question of state law, determined by the application of Article 9. If the creditor is partially secured, the value of the collateral that secures the debt is less than the amount of the debt. The value of the collateral is an important factor in bankruptcy. According to Bankruptcy Code § 506(a), value is determined by the court.

For example, assume a creditor has loaned a debtor $100,000, secured by equipment. If the bankruptcy court determines that the security interest is valid under state law and that the value of the equipment is $60,000, then the creditor is partially secured: secured in the amount of $60,000 and unsecured in the amount of $40,000. If the debtor owes $100,000 to a creditor lacking a security interest, the creditor is unsecured. If a creditor has a $100,000 judgment against the debtor, the creditor is also unsecured. The bankruptcy trustee, who is appointed by the court, has the initial power to make these determinations on behalf of the creditors.

Chapters 1, 3, and 5 of the Bankruptcy Code (there are no Chapters 2 and 4) contain administrative provisions applicable to all forms of bankruptcy. Chapter 7, Liquidation, is what lay persons often think of as bankruptcy. In a liquidation, some property is exempt from creditors. The rest of the debtor's property (called the debtor's "estate") is sold, and the proceeds are distributed to the creditors. However, many bankruptcies involve not the liquidation of the debtor's estate, but the reorganization or rehabilitation of the debtor. In bankruptcy under Chapters 11, 12, and 13, the debtor retains the estate and makes payments to creditors out of postbankruptcy earnings pursuant to a plan approved by the court. Chapter 11 is for the reorganization of a business; Chapter 12 is for the rehabilitation of family farmers; and Chapter 13 is for the rehabilitation of individuals with regular income.

All creditors are not treated equally in bankruptcy. Creditors with security interests valid in bankruptcy are "more equal" than other creditors. For example, in Chapter 7, secured creditors are paid first to the extent of the value of the property subject to each security interest. Unsecured creditors entitled to priority under Bankruptcy Code § 507 are paid next. Finally, a pro rata distribution of the remaining assets is made to the other unsecured creditors, often called general creditors. In reorganization and rehabilitation, as well, a secured creditor's rights are substantially greater than those of an unsecured creditor. The odd thing is that no section of the Bankruptcy Code can be cited to support this status accorded to the secured creditor. Rather, it is simply an application of the principle that, in bankruptcy, *the debtor's* interest in property is distributed to the creditors. When the debtor has granted a creditor a security interest, the secured party has an interest in that property; to that extent, it is not the debtor's property.

For example, assume B files a petition for relief under Chapter 7. B owns $50,000 of nonexempt property. B owes S $30,000, U $30,000, and other creditors $70,000. Assume that S has a security interest in property of B worth at least $30,000 and that all of B's other creditors are unsecured. Also, assume that the Chapter 7 case results in $10,000 of administrative expenses, a priority claim under the Bankruptcy Code. Under these facts, S will be paid $30,000 on its $30,000 secured claim. To compute the distribution to the holder of an unsecured claim in a Chapter 7 case, follow these steps:

1. Determine the amount available for distribution to all holders of general unsecured claims by subtracting from the nonexempt property of the debtor distributions to secured claims and to priority claims ($50,000 − $30,000 − $10,000 = $10,000);
2. Divide the amount available for distribution to holders of general unsecured claims by the total amount of unsecured claims ($10,000 divided by [$30,000 + $70,000]); and
3. Apply that ratio or fraction to the unsecured claim in question:

$$\frac{10,000}{100,000} \times \$30,000 = \$3,000$$

$$\frac{10,000}{100,000} \times \$70,000 = \$7,000$$

So S gets $30,000 on its $30,000 claim, U gets $3,000 on its $30,000 claim, and the other unsecured creditors receive "ten cents on the dollar"; that is, ten cents payment for every dollar of debt. Unsecured creditors are rarely so lucky. In fact, 80 to 90 percent of unsecured creditors receive nothing, and the other 10 to 20 percent often receive seven to ten cents on the dollar.

Question 1. D owes X $60,000 and owes Y $40,000. Both X and Y have a perfected security interest in D's equipment, but X's security interest has priority over Y's. D files a bankruptcy petition. D's equipment has a value of $50,000. How would you describe X's status as a creditor in bankruptcy?

A. Fully secured to the extent of $60,000, the total amount of the debt.
B. Partially secured to the extent of $30,000, because X has 60 percent of the secured claims.
C. Partially secured to the extent of $50,000, the value of the collateral.
D. Unsecured.

Analysis.   X has extended $60,000 to D, and this debt is secured by equipment worth only $50,000. So it is readily apparent that X is only partially secured, because the value of the collateral ($50,000) is less than the amount of the debt ($60,000). Therefore, X is unsecured to the extent of $10,000, so **C** is the correct response. We were not asked about Y, but note that Y is unsecured, because there is no remaining collateral to satisfy Y's secured claim.

Question 2. D owes X $60,000 and owes Y $40,000. Both X and Y have a security interest in D's equipment, but X's security interest has priority over Y's. D files a Chapter 7 bankruptcy petition. D's equipment has a value of $50,000. There are additional unsecured creditors whose claims amount to $50,000, and D's nonexempt assets other than the equipment have a value of $10,000. How much will X, Y, and the other creditors recover in bankruptcy?

A. X, $20,000; Y, $20,000; the others, $20,000.
B. X, $50,000; Y, $6,000; the others, $4,000.
C. X, $51,000; Y, $4,000; the others, $5,000.
D. X, $60,000; Y, $0; the others, $0.

Analysis. Let us follow the three steps we used earlier in this section. (1) Determine the amount available for distribution to all holders of general unsecured claims by subtracting from the nonexempt property of the debtor all distributions to secured claims and to priority claims. Here, the debtor has nonexempt assets worth $50,000 and $10,000. From that amount we subtract the $50,000 distributed to X for its secured claim. There is no equipment remaining to satisfy Y's claim, so Y is unsecured. That leaves $10,000 in assets. (2) Divide the amount available for distribution to holders of general unsecured claims by the total amount of unsecured claims. Here, the amount available for distribution is $10,000, and the total amount of unsecured claims is X, $10,000; Y, $40,000; and additional creditors, $50,000; the total is $100,000. Note that X was partially secured; after the $50,000 secured part of X's claim is satisfied, X still has an unsecured claim of $10,000. So the fraction is 10,000/100,000 = 1/10. (3) Apply that ratio or fraction to the unsecured claim in question: for X, 1/10×$10,000 = $1,000; for Y, 1/10 × $40,000 = $4,000; for the others, 1/10×$50,000 = $5,000. Putting it all together, X gets $51,000, Y gets $4,000, and the others get $5,000. Therefore, **C** is the correct response.

_____

It is pretty obvious that you would rather be a secured creditor than an unsecured creditor when the debtor is in bankruptcy, and you would rather be fully secured than partially secured. Things are not, however, entirely rosy for the secured creditor in bankruptcy. Bankruptcy may also cause the following:

- Delayed recovery by a secured party or alteration in a debtor's payment obligations.
- Loss of payments the secured party received prior to bankruptcy.
- Invalidation of the Article 9 security interest.

We will look at each of these issues in turn.

B. Delayed Recovery by a Secured Party or Alteration in a Debtor's Payment Obligations

According to § 362 of the Bankruptcy Code, the filing of a bankruptcy petition acts as an *automatic stay*, barring creditors from taking steps to obtain property from the debtor's estate. That section provides in part:

(a) Except as provided in subsection (b) of this section, a petition filed under section 301, 302, or 303 of this title, . . . operates as a stay, applicable to all entities, of—

(1) the commencement or continuation, including the issuance or employment of process, of a judicial, administrative, or other action or proceeding against the debtor that was or could have been commenced before the commencement of the case under this title, or to recover a claim against the debtor that arose before the commencement of the case under this title;

(2) the enforcement, against the debtor or against property of the estate, of a judgment obtained before the commencement of the case under this title;

(3) any act to obtain possession of property of the estate or of property from the estate or to exercise control over property of the estate;

(4) any act to create, perfect, or enforce any lien against property of the estate;

(5) any act to create, perfect, or enforce against property of the debtor any lien to the extent that such lien secures a claim that arose before the commencement of the case under this title;

(6) any act to collect, assess, or recover a claim against the debtor that arose before the commencement of the case under this title.

The effect of the automatic stay is quite sweeping. We are particularly interested in subsection (4), which stays "any act to create, perfect, or enforce any lien against property of the estate." Because the stay is *automatic*, it does not depend on knowledge; if the creditor acts without knowledge of the stay, then that act is of no effect and can be nullified by the bankruptcy trustee. The effect of the stay is that the debtor's status vis-à-vis creditors is essentially frozen at the moment of bankruptcy, and no creditor can improve its position at that point.

The stay also means that secured creditors cannot take steps they might have taken absent the stay, such as repossession and sale of the collateral. There are, however, exceptions, found in § 362(d), that allow a creditor to obtain relief from the automatic stay. Section 362(d) provides:

(d) On request of a party in interest and after notice and a hearing, the court shall grant relief from the stay provided under subsection (a) of this section, such as by terminating, annulling, modifying, or conditioning such stay—

(1) for cause, including the lack of adequate protection of an interest in property of such party in interest;

(2) with respect to a stay of an act against property under subsection (a) of this section, if—

> (A) the debtor does not have an equity in such property; and
>
> (B) such property is not necessary to an effective reorganization.

To understand this provision, it is helpful to explain the concept of the debtor's plan. In cases involving reorganization or rehabilitation of the debtor under Chapters 11, 12, and 13, the debtor presents the court with a plan for payment of its debts (called "claims" in the Bankruptcy Code), which may involve settling the unsecured debts by paying a portion of the debt; for example, five cents on the dollar. Secured debts, however, must be paid in full. The Bankruptcy Code provides that the court may confirm the plan over the objections of a secured creditor if the plan gives the creditor the present value equivalent of its claim. Because the creditor can be compelled to accept the plan, the statute is known as the *cram down* provision, since it can be crammed down the creditor's throat. In a Chapter 13 consumer rehabilitation, § 1325(a)(5) provides as follows:

> (a) Except as provided in subsection (b), the court shall confirm a plan if—
>
> . . .
>
> (5) with respect to each allowed secured claim provided for by the plan—
>
> > (A) the holder of such claim has accepted the plan;
> > (B)(i) the plan provides that—
> >
> > > (I) the holder of such claim retain the lien securing such claim . . . ; [and]
> > >
> > > (ii) the value, as of the effective date of the plan, of property to be distributed under the plan on account of such claim is not less than the allowed amount of such claim; . . . or
> >
> > (C) the debtor surrenders the property securing such claim to such holder.

A creditor may challenge the plan if the plan does not give the creditor the present value of its claim. Alternately, a creditor may accept the plan but seek relief from the automatic stay. If successful in obtaining relief, the creditor does not need to comply with the plan but can proceed directly against the collateral.

Under § 362(d)(1), the creditor may seek relief "for cause, including the lack of adequate protection of an interest in property." Under this provision, the secured party may seek relief if the plan does not adequately protect its interest, which is its interest in having the value of the property maintained. For example, a plan may be challenged if the payments are stretched out so that the property is depreciating in value faster than payments are being made.

Under § 362(d)(2), the creditor may seek relief if "(A) the debtor does not have an equity in such property; and (B) such property is not necessary to an effective reorganization." Showing that the debtor does not have an equity in the property means that the amount of the debt is greater than the value of the property. For example, assume the property secures a debt of $5,000. If the property has a value of $6,000, then the debtor has $1,000 of equity in the property; it has an equity because the value is more than the amount of the debt. But if the property has a value of $4,000, then the debtor has no equity in the property; the value is less than the amount of the debt. Recall that under a reorganization plan, the debtor's assets are not liquidated but are used to earn the money that will pay off the debt from future earnings. Showing that the property is not necessary to an effective reorganization means showing that the debtor will not need the property for that purpose. It may be necessary, for example, for a consumer in Chapter 13 to keep a car to commute to work, but it will not be necessary to keep an off-road vehicle used for recreation.

Question 3. Through GMAC, Debtor has financed the purchase of a car that the debtor uses to commute to work. GMAC has a security interest in the car, which is worth $8,000. The remaining principal balance on the loan, which had an agreed interest rate of 15 percent, is $7,200. Debtor files for Chapter 13 rehabilitation, and in a plan, proposes that GMAC keep its security interest and Debtor will pay GMAC $200 per month for 36 months with no interest (total of $7,200). GMAC asks the court not to confirm the plan. Is the court likely to confirm the plan?

A. Yes, because under the plan GMAC retains its lien.
B. Yes, because under the plan GMAC retains its lien and will receive $7,200, the amount of its claim.
C. No, because a plan cannot change the agreement between the parties.
D. No, because under the plan GMAC will not receive $7,200, the amount of its claim.

Analysis. This is a tricky one. Response C is not correct, because a plan can change the agreement between the parties. The plan does not have to incorporate the payment schedule and interest rate from the contract. Response A is not sufficient, because a plan requires not only that the creditor retain its lien, but also requires that, in the words of § 1325(a)(5)(B)(ii), "the value, as of the effective date of the plan, of property to be distributed under the plan on account of such claim is not less than the allowed amount of such claim." Under our facts, the value of the claim is $7,200. So the plan must provide that GMAC will receive $7,200 "as of the effective date of the plan." Does the plan do this? No; it provides that GMAC will receive $7,200 over the next three years.

Because of the time value of money, $7,200 today is not the same as $7,200 over three years. How can we make it the same? By providing for interest to be paid. A plan that involves future payments must also provide for interest, although the amount of that interest need not be the same as the amount the parties originally contracted for. Therefore, **D** is the correct answer.

In this question, the creditor is fully secured since the amount of the debt ($7,200) is less than the value of the motor vehicle ($8,000). If the creditor was only partially secured, then the facts would fall within the scope of the "hanging paragraph" that was added to § 1325 when the Bankruptcy Act was reformed in 2005. The interpretation of that provision has been the subject of numerous cases, but basically when it applies, such as to a PMSI in a motor vehicle, the secured creditor may recover the amount of the debt even if that amount exceeds the value of the vehicle. If, for example, the amount of the debt was $8,000 and the value of the motor vehicle was $7,200, then the plan would have to provide for the creditor to recover $8,000.

Question 4. D owes S $100,000. S has a security interest in D's equipment. D files a bankruptcy petition. The security agreement makes a bankruptcy filing an "event of default," allowing the creditor to repossess the collateral. Can S repossess the equipment?

A. Yes, because the automatic stay does not prevent secured parties from enforcing security interests.
B. Yes, because the parties in the security agreement contracted around the automatic stay.
C. No, because secured parties may not define the events that constitute default.
D. No, because the automatic stay prevents secured parties from enforcing security interests.

Analysis. We know from Chapter 8.B that parties may define events of default, so **C** cannot be a correct response. **A** is not correct because § 362(a)(5) provides that the petition is a stay of "any act to create, perfect, or enforce against property of the debtor any lien to the extent that such lien secures a claim that arose before the commencement of the case under this title." This rule is regulatory and cannot be contracted around, so **B** is not a correct response. Therefore, response **D** states the correct rule.

Question 5. D owes Z $300,000. Z has a security interest in D's inventory. D defaults. Z properly repossesses the inventory and sends D notice of a public sale of the inventory on April 5. On April 4, D files a bankruptcy petition. Without knowledge of the filing, Z held the sale on April 5. Is the sale effective?

A. Yes, because the automatic stay does not prevent secured parties from enforcing security interests.
B. Yes, because Z relied on being able to conduct the sale and had no knowledge of the automatic stay.
C. No, because Z did not comply with Article 9 after D's default.
D. No, because the automatic stay prevents secured parties from enforcing security interests.

Analysis. We know from Chapter 9 that the secured party may repossess and sell the collateral after default, so **C** cannot be a correct response. **A** is not correct because § 362(a)(5) provides that the petition is a stay of "any act to create, perfect, or enforce against property of the debtor any lien to the extent that such lien secures a claim that arose before the commencement of the case under this title." This rule is called the *automatic stay* because it operates irrespective of a secured party's reliance and knowledge, so **B** is not a correct response. Response **D** states the correct rule.

Question 6. M Manufacturing Co. files for relief under Chapter 11. M owes S $200,000. S has a perfected security interest in M's manufacturing equipment, which is worth $300,000 and will lose its entire value through depreciation in two years. S files a request for relief from the stay. If M's plan calls for payments to S over three years, can S seek relief from the automatic stay?

A. Yes, because M does not have an equity in the property, and the property is not necessary to an effective reorganization.
B. Yes, because S's interest in the property is not adequately protected under the plan.
C. No, because the plan qualifies for a cram down.
D. No, because S cannot show either that M does not have an equity in the property and the property is not necessary to an effective reorganization or that S's interest in the property is not adequately protected under the plan.

Analysis. Section 362(d) provides for relief from the automatic stay:

(1) for cause, including the lack of adequate protection of an interest in property of such party in interest; or

(2) with respect to a stay of an act against property under subsection (a) of this section, if —

(A) the debtor does not have an equity in such property; and

(B) such property is not necessary to an effective reorganization.

Under the facts, S cannot prove the elements of § 362(d)(2) because the debtor does have equity and the property is necessary for an effective reorganization. Therefore, response **D** is not correct. But S can prove that, under § 362(d)(1), its interest is not adequately protected, because the property will depreciate faster than payments are made. Therefore, **B** is the correct response.

Question 7. Bank One loaned Paradise Boat Leasing $175,000 and took a security interest in a 65-foot yacht worth $350,000 that Paradise leases to customers by the week. Bank One got notice that the yacht insurance had been canceled. Then Paradise filed for bankruptcy under Chapter 11. Under the security agreement, it is Paradise's responsibility to keep the yacht insured, and failure to do so is an event of default. Bank One tried to get another policy, but no one would insure a boat belonging to a party in bankruptcy. What should Bank One do?

A. Repossess the yacht, since Paradise is in default.
B. Petition the Bankruptcy Court for relief from the automatic stay on grounds that Paradise does not have equity in the yacht and it is not necessary to an effective reorganization.
C. Petition the Bankruptcy Court for relief from the automatic stay on grounds of cause, including lack of adequate protection of its interest in the yacht.
D. Petition the Bankruptcy Court to convert the Chapter 11 into a Chapter 7.

Analysis. Response **A** cannot be correct because the automatic stay bars Bank One from repossessing the collateral. Section 362(d) provides for relief from the automatic stay:

> (1) for cause, including the lack of adequate protection of an interest in property of such party in interest; or
>
> (2) with respect to a stay of an act against property under subsection (a) of this section, if—
>
>> (A) the debtor does not have an equity in such property; and
>>
>> (B) such property is not necessary to an effective reorganization.

Here, the creditor's interest is not adequately protected if the boat is uninsured. Therefore, **C** is the correct response.

C.   Loss of Payments the Secured Party Received Prior to Bankruptcy

1. Voidable Preferences: The General Rule

The Bankruptcy Code gives the trustee power to avoid as preferences certain transfers the debtor made before the filing of bankruptcy. Normally a debtor is perfectly free to pay whichever creditors it wishes. However, in bankruptcy all creditors (at least those in the same class) are treated the same. It therefore seems unfair to allow a debtor to pay off certain creditors just before bankruptcy. The trustee can avoid (that is, take back for the benefit of the bankrupt's estate) these transfers if the trustee can satisfy all five elements of a voidable preference as found in Bankruptcy Code § 547(b):

> (b) Except as provided in subsections (c) and (i) of this section, the trustee may avoid any transfer of an interest of the debtor in property—
>
> (1) to or for the benefit of a creditor;
>
> (2) for or on account of an antecedent debt owed by the debtor before such transfer was made;
>
> (3) made while the debtor was insolvent;
>
> (4) made—
>
> > (A) on or within 90 days before the date of the filing of the petition; or
> >
> > (B) between ninety days and one year before the date of the filing of the petition, if such creditor at the time of such transfer was an insider; and
>
> (5) that enables such creditor to receive more than such creditor would receive if—
>
> > (A) the case were a case under chapter 7 of this title;
> >
> > (B) the transfer had not been made; and
> >
> > (C) such creditor received payment of such debt to the extent provided by the provisions of this title.

Let's look at each of the five elements of § 547(b) more closely. Subsection (1) is pretty straightforward: the transfer must benefit a creditor. Subsection (2) is a bit tricky. We are concerned only with transfers on account of an *antecedent debt*. What does that mean? The simple approach is to (1) look at the date the debt was incurred, and (2) look at the date the transfer occurred. If the second date is the same as the first date, then the transfer is on account of a present debt. If the second date is later then the first date, then the transfer is on account of an *antecedent debt*, that is, an earlier debt.

Subsection (3) provides that the debtor must have been insolvent when the transfer was made, but § 547(f) creates a rebuttable presumption that the debtor was insolvent for the 90 days immediately preceding the filing of the bankruptcy petition. Subsection (4) reiterates the 90-day rule: we look only at transfers going back 90 days before the bankruptcy filing, except with respect to transfers to insiders, for which we go back one year. The definition of *insider* in Bankruptcy Code § 101(31) provides:

> (31) The term "insider" includes—
>> (A) if the debtor is an individual—
>>> (i) relative of the debtor or of a general partner of the debtor;
>>> (ii) partnership in which the debtor is a general partner;
>>> (iii) general partner of the debtor; or
>>> (iv) corporation of which the debtor is a director, officer, or person in control;
>> (B) if the debtor is a corporation—
>>> (i) director of the debtor;
>>> (ii) officer of the debtor;
>>> (iii) person in control of the debtor;
>>> (iv) partnership in which the debtor is a general partner;
>>> (v) general partner of the debtor; or
>>> (vi) relative of a general partner, director, officer, or person in control of the debtor;
>> (C) if the debtor is a partnership—
>>> (i) general partner in the debtor;
>>> (ii) relative of a general partner in, general partner of, or person in control of the debtor;
>>> (iii) partnership in which the debtor is a general partner;
>>> (iv) general partner of the debtor; or
>>> (v) person in control of the debtor;
>> (D) if the debtor is a municipality, elected official of the debtor or relative of an elected official of the debtor;
>> (E) affiliate, or insider of an affiliate as if such affiliate were the debtor; and
>> (F) managing agent of the debtor.

The theory here is that transfers more than 90 days before the bankruptcy were not likely to have been made in contemplation of bankruptcy. So if a payment is made to a creditor, that payment is generally not a preferential transfer if the bankruptcy came more than 90 days later. But if a payment was made to an insider, it is possible that person was in control of the transactions. For example, if the president of a corporation is a creditor of the corporation, the president could decide to pay the debt to herself and then wait 90 days before filing a bankruptcy petition on behalf of the corporation.

Subsection (5) sounds tricky, but it is pretty straightforward. The transfer must enable the creditor to receive more than the creditor would have received in a hypothetical Chapter 7 liquidation. In other words, (1) calculate how much the creditor received from the transfer, then (2) calculate how much the creditor would have received in a hypothetical Chapter 7 liquidation. If the first figure is greater than the second, then that element is satisfied. For example, a debtor owes an unsecured creditor $1,000. That creditor is paid $500 just before a petition for a Chapter 11 reorganization is filed. Under the Chapter 11 plan, unsecured creditors are paid ten cents on the dollar. The creditor received $500 but would have received $100 in Chapter 7, so the creditor received a preferential payment of $400. If the other elements of § 547(b) are satisfied, then the transfer can be avoided: the creditor has to give the money back to the bankrupt debtor's "estate." It is important to remember that to avoid a transfer, the trustee must satisfy *all five* elements.

Question 8. On May 5, Debtor, the President and sole Director of Memphis Motel Inc. borrowed $10,000 from his mother on behalf of Memphis Motel Inc. and signed a note indicating that the amount was due "on demand." On July 5, realizing that the motel was insolvent, Debtor repaid $1,000 of the loan. On December 5, Memphis Motel Inc. filed for Chapter 7 liquidation. In the liquidation, unsecured creditors receive ten cents on the dollar. Can the trustee avoid the payment by Memphis Motel Inc. of $1,000 to Debtor's mother?

A. Yes, because no demand for payment had been made.
B. Yes, because all the elements of a preferential transfer are satisfied.
C. No, because the transfer was not made within 90 days of the bankruptcy filing.
D. No, because Debtor's mother received no more than she would have received under Chapter 7.

Analysis. Let's see if all of the elements of Bankruptcy Code § 547(b) are satisfied. There was a transfer of an interest of the debtor in property: $1,000. It was to a creditor: Debtor's mother. It was on account of an antecedent debt, because the debt was incurred on May 5 and the transfer occurred on July 5. Since that date is more than 90 days before the date of the filing of the petition, there is no presumption of insolvency, but you are told in the facts that the debtor was insolvent. The transfer was not made within 90 days before the date of the filing of the petition, but here the transfer was to an insider, since the definition in § 101(31)(B)(vi) includes, if the debtor is a corporation, a "relative of a general partner, director, officer, or person in control of the debtor." Finally, the transfer must enable the creditor to receive more than it would have received under Chapter 7. Since unsecured creditors received ten cents on the dollar, and Debtor's mother received a $1,000 payment on a $10,000 loan, it initially looks like she received the same amount she would have received in Chapter 7. However, after she received the $1,000 payment, she is still owed $9,000, and she would receive $900 of that in Chapter 7, so the payment allowed her to receive $1,900 instead of the $1,000 she would have received in Chapter 7. Therefore, the transfer enabled her to receive more. Since all of the elements of § 547(b) are satisfied, **B** is the correct response.

Question 9. On January 15, D borrowed $20,000 from S and granted S a security interest in equipment worth $25,000. S properly filed. On April 5, D repaid S the full amount of the debt, $20,000. On June 6, D filed a bankruptcy petition. Can the trustee recover the April 5 payment as a voidable preference?

A. Yes, because all elements of Bankruptcy Code § 547(b) are satisfied.
B. No, because the payment was not made on account of an antecedent debt.
C. No, because the payment was not made within 90 days of the filing.
D. No, because the creditor did not receive more than it would have received under Chapter 7.

Analysis.   Let's again run through the elements of § 547(b). Here, there was a transfer of $20,000 to a creditor. It was made on account of an antecedent debt owed by the debtor before such transfer was made, because the debt was incurred on January 15 and the payment was made on April 5. It was presumptively made while the debtor was insolvent, because it was made within 90 days before the date of the filing of the petition. However, the creditor was fully secured, so under Chapter 7, it would have received $20,000. The transfer was of $20,000. Therefore, the transfer did not allow the creditor to receive more than it would have under Chapter 7. The correct response is **D.** All of the elements of § 547(b) are not satisfied, so the transfer cannot be avoided as a preference.

2. Exception: Payments Made in the Ordinary Course of Business

A number of exceptions to the voidable preference rule are found in § 547(c). One of the exceptions, found in § 547(c)(2)(A) is for payments "made in the ordinary course of business." The Bankruptcy Revision notes state that "[t]he purpose of this exception is to leave undisturbed normal financial relations, because it does not detract from the general policy of the preference section to discourage unusual action by either the debtor or his creditors during the debtor's slide into bankruptcy." For example, if debtor regularly made payments on an installment loan obligation on the first of each month, the monthly payments made within 90 days of bankruptcy would not be regarded as voidable preferences. As long as payments to creditors are not unusual, they will probably not be avoided under this rule.

Question 10. Debtor regularly buys goods from suppliers (*trade creditors*) such as ABC, who provide the goods and then bill Debtor. Although not stated on the bills, the custom is that payment is due within 30 days of delivery. Debtor has also purchased a delivery van on credit from Bank,

> and the installment loan agreement calls for payments of $400 on the first of the month. Debtor has been having financial problems and, since April 1, has been unable to make payments as they come due. Debtor does not pay any of the trade creditors or the Bank from April through June. On June 1, Debtor receives a shipment of widgets from ABC and a bill for $1,200. On June 20, Debtor pays ABC $1,200 and Bank $1,200. On June 22, Debtor declares bankruptcy. Are the payments to ABC and Bank voidable preferences?
>
> **A.** Yes as to ABC and Bank.
> **B.** Yes as to ABC, but no as to Bank.
> **C.** No as to ABC, but yes as to Bank.
> **D.** No as to ABC and Bank.

Analysis. The payments satisfy all five elements of a voidable preference under § 547(b), so the issue is whether they fall under the "ordinary course of business" exception of § 547(c). Under the facts, trade creditors are customarily paid within 30 days of delivery of the goods. Debtor paid ABC on June 20 for goods delivered June 1. Even though other creditors may not have been paid, this one does seem to be within the ordinary course of business. Debtor was supposed to pay Bank on April 1, May 1, and June 1, but missed those payments. Those payments were all made on June 20. Since the usual payment would have been monthly, that was an unusual payment and probably not within the ordinary course of business. Therefore, the best choice is **C**.

D.   Invalidation of the Article 9 Security Interest

1.   *The Strong Arm Clause: § 544(a)*

Needless to say, it is the worst nightmare of creditors (and their lawyers) that their security interests may be invalidated in bankruptcy. Loss of the security interest generally comes about because of the creditor's failure to timely perfect the security interest—the law does not like "secret" liens that other creditors don't know about.

The principal (but not only) mechanism by which the trustee invalidates security interests is Bankruptcy Code § 544(a), known in the business as the *strong arm clause*, which provides:

> **§ 544. Trustee as lien creditor and as successor to certain creditors and purchasers.**
>
>   (a) The trustee shall have, as of the commencement of the case, and without regard to any knowledge of the trustee or of any creditor, the

rights and powers of, or may avoid any transfer of property of the debtor or any obligation incurred by the debtor that is voidable by—

> (1) a creditor that extends credit to the debtor at the time of the commencement of the case, and that obtains, at such time and with respect to such credit, a judicial lien on all property on which a creditor on a simple contract could have obtained such a judicial lien, whether or not such a creditor exists.

The strong arm clause gives the trustee the avoidance powers of a hypothetical judicial lien creditor. Recall that in Chapter 17.B we analyzed the outcome of a priority dispute between a secured creditor and a judicial lien creditor under § 9-317(a)(2), which provides:

> § 9-317(a) **Conflicting security interests and rights of lien creditors.** A security interest or agricultural lien is subordinate to the rights of:
>
> . . .
>
> (2) except as otherwise provided in subsection (e), a person that becomes a lien creditor before the earlier of the time:
>> (A) the security interest or agricultural lien is perfected; or
>> (B) one of the conditions specified in Section 9-203(b)(3) is met and a financing statement covering the collateral is filed.

Putting that together, § 9-317(a)(2) makes an *unperfected* security interest subordinate to a judicial lien creditor. Section 544(a) gives the bankruptcy trustee the power to avoid a transfer that is subordinate to the interest of a hypothetical judicial lien creditor as of the date the petition is filed. So the trustee can avoid a security interest that is unperfected on the date of filing.

Question 11. The Bankruptcy Code contains what is popularly known as the *strong arm clause.* This clause permits the bankruptcy trustee to avoid:

A. An unperfected security interest.
B. A transfer made by the debtor that prefers one creditor over another.
C. Claims to property repossessed by creditors after the automatic stay was imposed.
D. A debtor's plan that does not allow the secured party to retain its interest in the value of the collateral.

Analysis.   The correct response is **A.** Bankruptcy Code § 544(a)(1) provides:

> § 544. **Trustee as lien creditor and as successor to certain creditors and purchasers.**
>
> (a) The trustee shall have, as of the commencement of the case, and without regard to any knowledge of the trustee or of any creditor, the rights and powers of, or may avoid any transfer of property of the debtor or any obligation incurred by the debtor that is voidable by—

(1) a creditor that extends credit to the debtor at the time of the commencement of the case, and that obtains, at such time and with respect to such credit, a judicial lien on all property on which a creditor on a simple contract could have obtained such a judicial lien, whether or not such a creditor exists.

Recall that, under § 9-317(a)(2), a judicial lien creditor has priority over an unperfected security interest. Putting these two provisions together, unperfected security interests are voidable in bankruptcy.

Question 12. On January 10, D Co. borrows $100,000 and grants S a security interest in D Co.'s existing inventory. Thinking it was the proper place, S files its financing statement with the county clerk; relevant state law requires that financing statements covering inventory be filed with the Secretary of State. On February 2, D Co. files a Chapter 7 bankruptcy petition. Can the bankruptcy trustee avoid S's security interest?

A. Yes, because S would have lost to a judicial lien creditor whose lien attached on February 2.
B. Yes, because all unperfected security interests are avoided in bankruptcy.
C. No, because S would have had priority over a judicial lien creditor whose lien attached on February 2.
D. No, because S made a good faith effort to file the financing statement.

Analysis. Under the strong arm clause, § 544(a), the bankruptcy trustee has the power to avoid a transfer that is voidable by a hypothetical judicial lien creditor as of the date the petition is filed. Under § 9-317(a)(2), a judicial lien creditor whose lien attached on February 2 would have had priority over an unperfected security interest. A good faith attempt to file does not change the result. Therefore, the security interest is voidable, and **A** is the correct response.

Note on test-taking. Response **B** seems correct, but you should be suspicious because it is worded in a broad fashion, using the word *always*. Legal rules often have exceptions, as we shall see in the following questions.

Question 13. On February 2, D buys a new television set for his apartment on credit from S. D signs a security agreement, granting S a security interest in the television set. Thinking it was the proper place, S files its financing statement with the county clerk; relevant state law requires that financing statements covering consumer goods be filed with the Secretary of State. On March 3, D files a Chapter 13 petition. Can the bankruptcy trustee avoid S's security interest?

A. Yes, because S would have lost to a judicial lien creditor whose lien attached on February 2.

B. Yes, because all unperfected security interests are avoided in bankruptcy.

C. No, because S would have had priority over a judicial lien creditor whose lien attached on February 2.

D. No, because S made a good faith effort to file the financing statement.

Analysis. *Note on test-taking.* When you see a question that is similar to an earlier question, always look for factual differences that may change the correct response. The important fact here is that "D buys a new television set for his apartment on credit from S." Those facts indicate that S took a PMSI in consumer goods, which is automatically perfected under § 9-309(1).

Therefore, the attempted filing is irrelevant because S is perfected. The judicial lien creditor would lose to the prior perfected security interest under § 9-317(a)(2), so the bankruptcy trustee is unable to avoid the security interest. The correct response is **C.**

Question 14. On March 3, D Inc. buys new farm equipment on credit from S. D Inc. grants S a security interest in the equipment. On March 5, before S has perfected its security interest in the equipment, D Inc. files a Chapter 12 petition. Can S do anything to prevent the bankruptcy trustee from avoiding S's security interest under the strong arm clause?

A. Yes, because S has a PMSI, S can still file to defeat the bankruptcy trustee.

B. Yes, because S is automatically perfected, S defeats the bankruptcy trustee.

C. No, because S's security interest is unperfected at the time of the filing of the petition.

D. No, because the policy is that creditor's interests are frozen in time at the time of the filing of the petition.

Analysis. The important fact here is that S has a PMSI. It is not a PMSI in consumer goods, however, so S's security interest is not automatically perfected under § 9-309(1). However, you recall § 9-317(e):

(e) **Purchase-money security interest.** Except as otherwise provided in Sections 9-320 and 9-321, if a person files a financing statement with respect to a purchase-money security interest before or within 20 days after the debtor receives delivery of the collateral, the security interest takes priority over the rights of a buyer, lessee, or lien creditor which arise between the time the security interest attaches and the time of filing.

Under this provision, a secured party with a PMSI has 20 days from the debtor's possession to perfect in order to defeat a judicial lien creditor. The Bankruptcy Code allows a similar exception, and provides that perfection of the PMSI after the filing of the bankruptcy petition does not violate the automatic stay. See §§ 546(b)(1)(a) and 362(b)(3). Therefore, the correct response is **A**.

2. Loss of Security Interest Transferred Prior to Bankruptcy

In section C of this chapter we looked at whether the payment of money is a voidable transfer under § 547(b). The definition of "transfer" in Bankruptcy Code § 101(54) is broader than that. It expressly includes "disposing of . . . an interest in property" such as granting a security interest or having the security interest attach to after-acquired property. A debtor can give one creditor an advantage over another by using one of these methods of transfer before filing bankruptcy.

Question 15. On May 5, Debtor, the President and sole Director of Memphis Motel Inc., borrowed $10,000 from his mother on behalf of Memphis Motel Inc. On July 5, realizing that the motel was insolvent, Debtor granted his mother a security interest in hotel furniture worth $12,000 as security for the loan. On December 5, Memphis Motel Inc. filed for Chapter 7 liquidation. In the liquidation, unsecured creditors receive five cents on the dollar. Can the trustee avoid the grant by Memphis Motel Inc. of a security interest to Debtor's mother?

A. Yes, because there was no consideration for the grant of a security interest.

B. Yes, because all the elements of a preferential transfer are satisfied.

C. No, because the transfer was not made within 90 days of the bankruptcy filing.

D. No, because a preferential transfer is a payment of money, not the granting of a security interest.

Analysis.   Let's see if all of the elements of Bankruptcy Code § 547(b) are satisfied. There was a transfer of an interest of the debtor in property: the security interest in the furniture. It was to a creditor: Debtor's mother. It was on account of an antecedent debt, because the debt was incurred on May 5 and the transfer occurred on July 5. Since that date is more than 90 days before the date of the filing of the petition, there is no presumption of insolvency, but you are told in the facts that the debtor was insolvent. It was not made within 90 days before the date of the filing of the petition, but here the transfer was to an insider, since the definition in § 101(31)(B)(vi) includes, if the debtor is a corporation, a "relative of a general partner, director, officer, or person in control of the debtor." Finally, the transfer must enable the creditor to receive more than it would have received under Chapter 7. If the security interest in the furniture has priority, and the furniture is worth over $10,000, then the transfer made Debtor's mother fully secured, and she will recover all of her $10,000 debt. If she were an unsecured creditor, she would only receive 5 percent of the debt, or $500. Therefore, this transfer enabled her to receive more. Since all of the elements of § 547(b) are satisfied, **B** is the correct response.

This question is important because it points out that while we usually think of a preferential transfer as a transfer of money, it can also be the transfer of a security interest. But we conveniently omitted from the question any mention of the filing of the financing statement, which we address in the next subsection.

3. Loss of Security Interest If Not Timely Filed: § 547(e)

Assume that on May 5 D borrows $50,000 from S and grants S a security interest in equipment. On December 29, S files a financing statement. On December 30, D files a bankruptcy petition. Can the bankruptcy trustee avoid S's security interest under the strong arm clause, § 544(a)? The answer is no, because the security interest was perfected at the time the petition was filed. Since it could not be defeated by a hypothetical judicial lien creditor on that date, it cannot be defeated by the trustee in bankruptcy. Can the trustee avoid S's security interest under § 547(b)? Again the answer is no, because the transfer of the security interest was not on account of an antecedent debt; it was transferred at the same time.

The Bankruptcy Code, however, is concerned with unfiled security interests because potential creditors do not have a fair picture of a debtor's financial condition if there are "secret liens" outstanding that could be effectively filed just before bankruptcy. Therefore, the Bankruptcy Code gives the trustee yet another power to avoid preferential transfers: § 547(e). Recall that § 547(b) allows the trustee to avoid preferential transfers. We have seen that the definition of "transfers" includes granting security interests. Section 547(e) avoids some security interests by defining the *time* of the transfer, rendering them unperfected if not timely filed. It provides in part:

> (2) For the purposes of this section, except as provided in paragraph (3) of this subsection, a transfer is made—
> > (A) at the time such transfer takes effect between the transferor and the transferee, if such transfer is perfected at, or within 30 days after, such time, except as provided in subsection (c)(3)(B);
> > (B) at the time such transfer is perfected, if such transfer is perfected after such 30 days; or

(C) immediately before the date of the filing of the petition, if such transfer is not perfected at the later of —

(i) the commencement of the case; or

(ii) 30 days after such transfer takes effect between the transferor and the transferee.

(3) For the purposes of this section, a transfer is not made until the debtor has acquired rights in the property transferred.

So when is the transfer made under the facts of the hypothetical that begins this section? It might be clearer if we substitute the terms *security interest* for the term *transfer* and *debtor* and *creditor* for *transferor* and *transferee*, where appropriate:

(2) For the purposes of this section, except as provided in paragraph (3) of this subsection, a transfer is made —

(A) at the time such *security interest* takes effect between the *debtor* and the *creditor*, if such *security interest* is perfected at, or within 30 days after, such time, except as provided in subsection (c)(3)(B);

(B) at the time such *security interest* is perfected, if such *security interest* is perfected after such 30 days; or

(C) immediately before the date of the filing of the petition, if such *security interest* is not perfected at the later of —

(i) the commencement of the case; or

(ii) 30 days after such transfer takes effect between the *debtor* and the *creditor*.

Debtor D granted the security interest on May 5. Was it perfected within 30 days? No, it was perfected on December 29. Therefore, according to § 547(e)(2) (B), the transfer was made on December 29. Now apply the five elements under § 547(b). Is the transfer of a security interest on December 29 a voidable preference? Yes. It is a transfer for the benefit of a creditor, on account of an antecedent debt, made within 90 days of the filing of the petition that enables the creditor to receive more than the creditor would have received in a Chapter 7 liquidation. Once again, the lesson is to perfect early. Section 547(e) does not require immediate perfection, however. It provides a 30-day "grace period" for perfection.

Question 16. On January 15, D borrows $10,000 from C and grants C a security interest in equipment. C perfects its security interest by filing on January 19. D files a bankruptcy petition on February 2. Can the trustee avoid the security interest under § 547(b)?

A. Yes, because the filing four days after the grant is a transfer on account of an antecedent debt.

B. Yes, because the trustee has the power of a judicial lien creditor to avoid security interests.

C. No, because the security interest was perfected within 30 days of the grant.

D. No, because the bankruptcy petition was filed within 30 days of the grant.

Analysis.   Bankruptcy Code § 547(e)(2) provides:

> (2) For the purposes of this section, except as provided in paragraph (3) of this subsection, a transfer is made —
>
> > (A) at the time such transfer takes effect between the transferor and the transferee, if such transfer is perfected at, or within 30 days after, such time, except as provided in subsection (c)(3)(B);
> >
> > (B) at the time such transfer is perfected, if such transfer is perfected after such 30 days; or
> >
> > (C) immediately before the date of the filing of the petition, if such transfer is not perfected at the later of —
> >
> > > (i) the commencement of the case; or
> > >
> > > (ii) 30 days after such transfer takes effect between the transferor and the transferee.

Under § 547(e)(2)(A), if the security interest is perfected within 30 days of the grant of the security interest, then the transfer is deemed made at the time of the transfer. Here, the grant was on January 15 and the filing was on January 19, which is within the 30-day grace period. Therefore, the transfer is deemed to have occurred at the time of the grant, January 15. Since the debt was incurred on January 15 and the transfer was made on January 15, there is no transfer on account of an antecedent debt under § 547(b)(2). Since one of the elements is not satisfied, there is no preferential transfer. The correct response is **C**.

Question 17. On January 15, D borrows $10,000 from C and grants C a security interest in equipment. C perfects its security interest on March 2. D files a bankruptcy petition on June 30. Can the trustee avoid the security under § 547(b)?

A. Yes, because a filing more than 30 days after the grant is a transfer on account of an antecedent debt.

B. Yes, because the trustee has the power of a judicial lien creditor to avoid security interests.

C. No, because the security interest was perfected within 30 days of the grant.

D. No, because the bankruptcy petition was filed more than 90 days after the transfer.

Analysis.   This is a bit tricky. For purposes of § 547, the transfer is deemed to have taken place on March 2, because it is outside the 30-day grace period of § 547(e)(2)(B). Here there is a transfer to a creditor that is on account of an antecedent debt, since the debt was incurred on January 15 and the transfer was made on March 2. For a transfer to be voided as a preference, however, all the elements of § 547(b) must be satisfied. Even if made on March 2, the transfer was not made within 90 days before the date of the filing of the petition. The transfer was made on March 2 and the petition was filed on June 30, which is more than 90 days later. Therefore, all the elements of § 547(b) are not satisfied. Since one of the elements is not satisfied, there is no preferential transfer. The correct response is **D**.

4. *Exception to the Voidable Preference Rule: Replacement of Inventory and Accounts*

Another exception to the voidable preference rule relates to the replacement of accounts and inventory during the 90 days prior to bankruptcy. Recall that inventory and accounts are constantly rolling over and that under an after-acquired property clause, the security interest attaches to new inventory and accounts as the debtor acquires them. If § 547(b) was followed, then the attachment of a security interest to the after-acquired property would be voidable as a preference. It would not be fair to the inventory financier if its security interest in all inventory acquired by the debtor during the 90 days prior to the filing of the bankruptcy petition was voided by the trustee. On the other hand, it wouldn't be fair to the other creditors if a debtor sold all its other assets for the purpose of acquiring more inventory before filing the petition.

To balance these two concerns, the drafters of the Bankruptcy Code came up with § 547(c)(5), which essentially freezes the positions of the inventory and accounts financiers 90 days prior to the filing of the petition and avoids as a preference only any *improvement* in their position during that 90 days.

There are seven steps involved in applying the "two-point" test of § 547(c)(5):

1. Determine the amount of the debt on the date of the bankruptcy petition.
2. Determine the value of the collateral on the date of the bankruptcy petition.
3. Subtract the value determined in 2 from the amount determined in 1.
4. Determine the amount of the debt 90 days before the petition.
5. Determine the value of the collateral 90 days before the petition.
6. Subtract the value in 5 from the amount in 4.
7. Subtract the answer in 3 from the answer in 6. This is the amount of the preference.

For example, assume that D's indebtedness remained at $100,000 throughout the 90-day period prior to bankruptcy and that at the date of bankruptcy there were $75,000 of accounts securing the $100,000 of debts. C files a secured claim for $75,000 and an unsecured claim for $25,000. Assume also that 90 days before bankruptcy, the $100,000 debt was secured by accounts with a value of only $60,000. Under these facts, C's collateral position improved by $15,000 within 90 days of bankruptcy. C has realized a $15,000 preference. The bankruptcy trustee can use § 547(b) to reduce C's secured claim by $15,000, making it $60,000.

Question 18. Ninety days before bankruptcy, D owed C $100,000 secured by inventory with a value of $60,000. During the 90 days prior to filing for bankruptcy, D sold all of that inventory and bought new inventory. On the date D filed for bankruptcy, D owed C $100,000 secured by inventory with a value of $75,000. How much of D's secured claim of $75,000 can the trustee avoid as a preference?

A. $75,000.
B. $60,000.
C. $15,000.
D. $0.

Analysis.   Bankruptcy Code § 547(c)(5) allows the trustee to avoid a secured claim in inventory or accounts to the extent the creditor improved its position during the 90 days prior to bankruptcy. Let's apply the facts to the seven-step approach:

1. Determine the amount of the debt on the date of the bankruptcy petition: $100,000.
2. Determine the value of the collateral on the date of the bankruptcy petition: $75,000.
3. Subtract the value determined in 2 from the amount determined in 1: $25,000.
4. Determine the amount of the debt 90 days before the petition: $100,000.
5. Determine the value of the collateral 90 days before the petition: $60,000.
6. Subtract the value in 5 from the amount in 4: $40,000.
7. Subtract the answer in 3 from the answer in 6 for the amount of the preference: $15,000.

So $15,000 is the amount the creditor's position has improved and therefore the amount of the voidable preference. Response **C** is correct.

E.   Closer

Analysis.   Bankruptcy Code § 547(e)(2) provides:

> (2) For the purposes of this section, except as provided in paragraph (3) of this subsection, a transfer is made —
>
>> (A) at the time such transfer takes effect between the transferor and the transferee, if such transfer is perfected at, or within 30 days after, such time, except as provided in subsection (c)(3)(B);
>>
>> (B) at the time such transfer is perfected, if such transfer is perfected after such 30 days; or
>>
>> (C) immediately before the date of the filing of the petition, if such transfer is not perfected at the later of —
>>
>>> (i) the commencement of the case; or
>>>
>>> (ii) 30 days after such transfer takes effect between the transferor and the transferee.

The security interest is in "existing equipment"; since it cannot be a PMSI, response **C** is incorrect. Under § 547(e)(2)(A), if the security interest is perfected within 30 days of the grant of the security interest, then the transfer is deemed made at the time of the transfer. The grant was on February 1 and the filing was on March 15, which is not within the 30-day grace period. Therefore, under § 547(e)(2)(B) the transfer is deemed to have occurred at the time of the perfection, March 15. Since the debt was incurred on February 1 and the transfer was made on March 15, there is a transfer on account of an antecedent debt under § 547(b)(2). The other elements of § 547(b) are also satisfied; response **D** is not correct, because the transfer was made within 90 days of bankruptcy, so insolvency is presumed. Therefore, there is a preferential transfer, making the correct response **A**.

Burnham's Picks

Question 1	C
Question 2	C
Question 3	D
Question 4	D
Question 5	D
Question 6	B
Question 7	C
Question 8	B
Question 9	D
Question 10	C
Question 11	A
Question 12	A
Question 13	C
Question 14	A
Question 15	B
Question 16	C
Question 17	D
Question 18	C
Question 19	A

20

Closing Closers: Some Practice Questions

This chapter is different from the others. It consists of 64 practice questions. There is no text or black-letter law in this chapter, so you have an opportunity to try to spot the issues. The questions are not in any particular order, so the issues could come from any chapter; questions may even contain multiple issues. The chapter thus provides both a review of the issues covered and an opportunity to test your understanding of how the different concepts in Secured Transactions fit together.

I have included at the end of the chapter my picks for the best responses to each question, but to get full value from your review, first analyze the questions completely yourself before looking at my comments. My analysis will also point you toward the section of the book in which the topic is treated, should you desire further review of the topic.

Finally, you might want to use these questions as an opportunity to practice the skill of taking multiple-choice examinations. Here is a summary of the notes on test-taking we have considered:

- Carefully read the "call of the question" and answer the question you are asked.
- Answer the question based on the facts you are given; do not read into questions facts that are not there.
- If the facts of one question are similar to the facts of another question, the assessor is probably trying to determine whether you can spot the distinction and determine whether it makes a difference in the outcome.
- Pay close attention to the facts. Often the difference between a correct and an incorrect response turns on a fact that points to a different rule or to an exception to the rule.
- Watch for unusual or inverted phrasing or emphasis in questions, such as a question that asks for the response that is *not* true.
- Most of the time there will be only one correct response to a question, but be alert to a different question type in which one or more responses may be correct. In that event, it is important to examine each response to determine whether it is correct.

- Be skeptical of responses that are stated in terms of absolutes, that is, that use words such as *always* or *never*.
- To be correct, all parts of the response must be correct. Many of the responses in this book take the form "Yes, because . . ." or "No, because . . . ." For a response to be correct, it must not only indicate *yes* or *no* correctly, it must also state the correct reason.

Good luck! And, as with the rest of the material in the book, be sure to let me know if you have any questions or comments.

Question 1. A homeowner who was renovating her kitchen bought cabinets on credit from a store. The store took a security interest in the cabinets and made a fixture filing 15 days after the sale. Assuming the cabinets are fixtures, does the store have priority in the cabinets over a bank that had a mortgage on the homeowner's house at the time of the transaction?

A. Yes, because the store had a security interest that was perfected by a fixture filing before the interest of the bank was of record.

B. Yes, because the cabinets were readily removable domestic appliances.

C. Yes, because the store had a purchase money security interest in fixtures that was properly filed.

D. No, because no exception applies, and under the general rule, the security interest in the fixtures is subordinate to the real property interest of the bank.

Question 2. First Bank entered into a transaction in which it agreed to loan AB Inc. $100,000 and took a security interest in the equipment of AB Inc. A and B are the sole shareholders and directors of AB Inc. As part of the transaction, A agreed to pay First Bank if AB Inc. did not, and B agreed to grant First Bank a security interest in his baseball-card collection as additional collateral. Under Article 9, who is a secondary obligor?

A. A.

B. B.

C. A and B.

D. Neither A nor B.

Question 3. Debtor is in default under its security agreement. Creditor hired a Repo Man to repossess the collateral, a car. The Repo Man saw the car parked in Debtor's driveway at 4 A.M.; no lights were on in the house. Using a key obtained by Creditor, the Repo Man entered the car, backed it out of the driveway, and was driving down the street when Debtor came running out of the house waving his arms. The Repo Man sped away leaving behind Debtor, who thought his car had been stolen. However, when he called the police, Debtor was told that the Repo Man had notified them that a repossession was in progress. Would a judge likely conclude there was a breach of the peace?

A. Yes, because the Repo Man had to walk onto Debtor's property to get the car.
B. Yes, because Debtor appeared on the scene during the repossession.
C. Yes, because both A and B are breaches of the peace.
D. No, because neither A nor B are breaches of the peace.

Question 4. Following a repossession and sale, after all lawful expenses are paid, a secured creditor is left with $70,000 from the sale. One of the creditors of Debtor, Auto Parts Co., properly notifies the secured creditor that it has a judgment against Debtor for $4,000. The amount of the debt owed by Debtor to the secured creditor is $60,000. Which of the following distributions should the secured creditor make?

A. $60,000 to itself, $4,000 to Auto Parts, $6,000 to Debtor.
B. $60,000 to itself, $10,000 to Debtor.
C. $70,000 to itself.
D. $70,000 to Debtor.

Question 5. A creditor entered into a security agreement with a consumer that described the collateral as "all personal property of debtor." What is the consequence of this description?

A. The agreement is not enforceable under Article 9.
B. The agreement violates the FTC Credit Practices Rules.
C. Both A and B.
D. Neither A nor B.

Question 6. Juan Valdez, a Colombian immigrant, worked for three years at Starbucks to save enough money to buy a coffee cart from Mark Foster, another street vendor, for $2,000. Unknown to Valdez, Foster had granted Finance Company a security interest in the cart, and the security interest was properly perfected. Finance Company is now demanding the cart, because selling it was an act of default under its security agreement with Foster. Which statement best describes the legal situation?

A. The security interest did not attach to the cart because Foster sold it to Valdez with an implied warranty of good title.
B. The security interest may have attached, but the courts are generally sympathetic to someone like Valdez who could not be expected to understand secured transactions.
C. Because he bought the cart as a buyer in ordinary course from the owner of the cart, Valdez takes free of the security interest.
D. Finance Company is entitled to the cart.

Question 7. First Bank filed a financing statement in the appropriate place under the debtor name "James Bond Stirred Martinis Inc." The legal name of the debtor is "James Bond Shaken Martinis Inc." When the debtor declared bankruptcy, the trustee claimed that the security interest of First Bank is unperfected. This issue would be resolved by determining which of the following?

A. Whether the trustee actually found the filing.
B. Whether a reasonable searcher would have found the filing.
C. Whether the filing office's standard search logic would have found the filing.
D. Whether First Bank used the debtor's exact full legal name on the filing.

Question 8. A student decided to interfere with his professor's credit by filing an unauthorized financing statement listing the professor as the debtor and various items of the professor's personal property as collateral. The professor learned about the bogus filing when he was turned down for a loan by a bank, which found the filing and didn't want to get involved in a priority dispute. Denied secured credit, the professor was forced to borrow from a payday lender at a higher rate. What is the professor entitled to recover from the student who made the bogus filing?

A. Actual damages.
B. Statutory damages.
C. Both A and B.
D. Neither A nor B.

Question 9. First Bank took a security interest in Debtor's baseball-card collection and properly filed. Debtor defaulted, and First Bank repossessed the collateral. First Bank then properly filed a Termination Statement. Second Bank then took a security interest in Debtor's baseball-card collection and properly filed. First Bank then announced a sale of the repossessed collateral. Second Bank objected to the sale on the grounds that it had a priority security interest in the collateral. Does Second Bank have priority at the time of the sale?

A. No, because First Bank was first to file even though it filed a termination statement.
B. No, because First Bank was first to file, and there is no period thereafter when there was neither filing nor perfection.
C. Yes, because Second Bank was first to file.
D. Yes, because even though First Bank was first to file, there is a period thereafter when there was neither filing nor perfection of its security interest.

Question 10. Debtor granted Creditor 1 a security interest in accounts, which Creditor 1 properly filed on April 26, 2015. Debtor granted Creditor 2 a security interest in accounts, which Creditor 2 properly filed on June 14, 2019. Creditor 1 and Creditor 2 agreed that Creditor 2's security interest would be subordinate to Creditor 1's security interest. On July 8, 2019, Creditor 1 filed a continuation statement in the proper place. On January 25, 2021, Debtor petitioned for bankruptcy. Which party has priority in the accounts?

A. Creditor 1, because it was first to file or perfect.
B. Creditor 1, because Creditor 2 agreed that its security interest would be subordinate to Creditor 1's.
C. Creditor 1, because of both A and B.
D. Creditor 2, because Creditor 1 was not properly perfected at the time of bankruptcy.

Question 11. On January 1, First Bank took a security interest in the equipment and after-acquired equipment of "James Bond Stirred Martinis Inc." and properly filed. On February 1, the debtor changed its name to "James Bond Shaken Martinis Inc." On March 1, Second Bank conducted a proper search under the name of "James Bond Shaken Martinis Inc." and found no filings. Second Bank took a security interest in the equipment and after-acquired equipment of the debtor and properly filed. On April 1, First Bank properly filed an amendment under the name of "James Bond Shaken Martinis Inc." In August, the debtor declared bankruptcy. Who has priority as between First Bank and Second Bank?

A. First Bank has priority in all the equipment.
B. Second Bank has priority in all the equipment.
C. First Bank has priority in all equipment acquired by the debtor until March 1, and Second Bank has priority in all equipment acquired by the debtor after March 1.
D. First Bank has priority in all equipment acquired by the debtor until June 1, and Second Bank has priority in all equipment acquired by the debtor after June 1.

Question 12. Bitterroot Motors granted Creditor One a security interest in its inventory of cars, and Creditor One properly filed, listing the collateral as "inventory." Bitterroot Motors then sold a car, obtaining both cash and a trade-in car, and it used some of the cash from that sale to purchase a floor waxer. After 21 days, in which of the following property is Creditor One's security interest perfected?

A. The trade-in car.
B. The floor waxer.
C. Both A and B.
D. Neither A nor B.

Question 13. On January 2, a consumer debtor bought a home computer on credit from Sears and granted Sears a security interest in it. On January 5, the sheriff levied on the computer to satisfy a judgment creditor's judgment against the debtor. On January 25, Sears filed a financing statement. Who has priority in the computer as between Sears and the judgment creditor?

A. The judgment creditor, because judgment liens always have priority over security interests.
B. The judgment creditor, because Sears did not timely file its financing statement.
C. Sears, because it was perfected at the time the judgment creditor levied.
D. Sears, because it filed in time to obtain priority over the judgment creditor.

Question 14. On January 2, First Bank agreed to lend Debtor $50,000 on that day and another $50,000 on April 4. Debtor granted First Bank a security interest in Debtor's inventory, and First Bank properly perfected. The security agreement has a future advance clause. On February 2, the sheriff levied on Debtor's inventory to satisfy the judgment of a creditor. On April 4, with full knowledge of the levy, First Bank gave Debtor the second $50,000 pursuant to the agreement. Debtor used the money to buy inventory, and the sheriff levied on that inventory to satisfy the judgment. Who has priority as between First Bank and the judgment creditor in the second $50,000 worth of inventory?

A. First Bank, because it made the advance without knowledge of the levy.

B. First Bank, because it was committed to making the advance.

C. First Bank, because the advance was made within 45 days of the levy.

D. The judgment creditor, because a security interest is subordinate to the rights of a person that becomes a lien creditor before the security interest attaches.

Question 15. Mary resides in a state that has a statute that grants an auto repair shop a lien on an automobile that it has repaired as long as it retains possession of the automobile. The statute is silent on the priority of this lien. Mary bought a car from Nickel Cars on credit. Nickel took a security interest in the car and properly perfected. When the car broke down, Mary took it to Joe's Repair Shop. When Joe finished the repairs, he presented Mary with a bill for $400. Mary said she didn't have the money, so Joe said he would hold the car until she paid him. Meanwhile, Mary has defaulted on her obligation to Nickel. Who has priority in the car as between Joe and Nickel?

A. Joe, because Article 9 says a lien arising by operation of law has priority over a security interest.

B. Joe, because perfection by possession trumps other forms of perfection.

C. Nickel, because Article 9 says a security interest has priority over a lien arising by operation of law.

D. Nickel, because Joe did not give notice to Nickel of its claim.

Question 16. On February 1, Holland gave Bank a security interest in his tractor, and Bank properly perfected. The security agreement provided that Holland would keep the tractor in Florida. Nevertheless, on July 1, Holland took the tractor to Iowa and sold it to CB&O, a tractor dealer. On November 21, Jarrett bought the tractor from the inventory of CB&O. Who has priority as between Bank and Jarrett?

A. Jarrett, because Bank had four months from the time the tractor was taken to Iowa to refile in Iowa, and it did not refile.

B. Jarrett, because he bought from CB&O as a buyer in ordinary course of business.

C. Bank, because Holland breached the security agreement when he took the tractor to Iowa.

D. Bank, because Article 9 provides that a security interest is good against purchasers unless an exception applies, and no exception applies.

Question 17. Bank loaned Sam's Corporation $10,000, took a security interest in the inventory and equipment of Sam's Corporation, and properly filed. Later that year, when the corporation was having trouble paying its bills, Sam Jones, the President of Sam's Corporation, directed the corporate treasurer not to send withholding taxes to the IRS. The IRS assessed a tax lien against Sam Jones personally and properly filed. Sam's Corporation is in default under the security agreement with Bank. Both Bank and the IRS claim Sam Jones's personal property. Which party is entitled to it?

A. Bank, because it filed before the IRS did.

B. The IRS, because the Internal Revenue Code gives tax assessments priority over security interests.

C. The IRS, because Bank does not have a security interest in Sam Jones's personal property.

D. Neither party, because the IRS cannot assess Sam Jones personally for taxes owed by Sam's Corporation, and Bank does not have a security interest in Sam Jones's personal property.

Question 18. While the parties were negotiating the loan documents, First Bank asked Austin Furniture Company to grant the bank a security interest in its inventory. Before any security interest was granted, Austin, in an authenticated record, authorized First Bank to file a financing statement, which the bank filed on March 2. At this point, what does First Bank have?

A. An attached security interest.
B. A perfected security interest.
C. Both A and B.
D. Neither A nor B.

Question 19. In a communication that was not authenticated, First Bank proposed that, in return for a loan, Austin Furniture Company would grant it a security interest in certain property in which Austin had an interest. Austin then stated in an e-mail to First Bank that it agreed to all the terms proposed by First Bank. First Bank then loaned Austin the money. Later, Austin claimed that no enforceable security interest was created. Was a security interest created?

A. No, because Austin never authenticated the agreement.
B. No, because First Bank never authenticated the agreement.
C. Yes, because Austin authenticated the agreement.
D. Yes, because authentication is not required by either party.

Question 20. First Bank and Austin Furniture Company authenticated a security agreement on March 5. The agreement stated that, in consideration of the money First Bank loaned to Austin on February 1, Austin granted First Bank a security interest in its inventory. Is there an enforceable security agreement?

A. No, because there is no consideration.
B. No, because value was not given.
C. Yes, because there is consideration.
D. Yes, because value was given.

Question 21. With the debtor's authorization, First Bank properly filed a financing statement on March 2 and entered into a security agreement with the debtor on March 5. Second Bank entered into a security agreement with the same debtor on March 4 and properly filed on March 4. Which party has priority in collateral indicated in both security agreements?

A. First Bank, because it was first to attach.
B. First Bank, because it was first to file or perfect.
C. Second Bank, because it was first to attach.
D. Second Bank, because it was first to file or perfect.

Question 22. First Bank and a debtor entered into an effective security agreement on March 3, but the bank filed the financing statement in the wrong place on March 3. The debtor then showed Second Bank its security agreement with First Bank and explained that First Bank filed in the wrong place. The debtor and Second Bank then entered into an effective security agreement on March 5, and Second Bank filed the financing statement in the correct place on March 5. As between First Bank and Second Bank, which party has priority?

A. First Bank, because filing is irrelevant between the parties.
B. First Bank, if it can demonstrate that it made the incorrect filing in good faith.
C. First Bank, because Second Bank had actual knowledge of First Bank's security agreement and filing.
D. Second Bank, because it was first to file or perfect.

Question 23. First Bank has a properly filed security interest in equipment of Austin Furniture Company. Austin wants to use the equipment as collateral for a loan from Second Bank, but it is concerned about the existing security interest. Austin therefore presents to the filing office an amended financing statement terminating the filing of First Bank. What is the duty of the filing office in this situation?

A. It will file the termination and remove the financing statement of First Bank, leading Second Bank to conclude that it is first to file.
B. It will file the termination, requiring Second Bank to determine from the circumstances whether the termination is effective.
C. It will file the termination, requiring Second Bank to determine whether Austin's signature on it was authorized or not.
D. It will file the termination, requiring Second Bank to determine whether First Bank's signature on it was authorized or not.

Question 24. First Bank and Austin Furniture Company Inc. entered into a security agreement. Austin is a Delaware corporation with its principal place of business in Vermillion, South Dakota; First Bank is a Colorado corporation with its principal place of business in Denver, Colorado; and the collateral will be located in North Dakota. Where should First Bank file its financing statement?

A. Delaware.
B. South Dakota.
C. Colorado.
D. North Dakota.

Question 25. Homer Simpson bought a sofa on credit from Austin Furniture Co., signing a contract in which Homer promised to pay Austin $100 a month for 12 months and granted Austin a security interest in the sofa. Austin then borrowed money from First Bank and granted First Bank a security interest in Homer's obligation. How would you describe the collateral in the Austin–First Bank transaction?

A. An account.
B. Chattel paper.
C. A document.
D. Consumer goods.

Question 26. Assume Austin Furniture Co. granted First Bank a valid security interest in Austin's furniture to secure a loan, but First Bank did not properly file. Austin defaulted on its obligation. What remedies does First Bank have?

A. Get a judgment against Austin and execute on it.
B. Repossess the furniture.
C. Either A or B.
D. Neither A nor B.

Question 27. On April 1, Austin Furniture Co. granted First Bank a security interest in its inventory. First Bank properly filed a financing statement describing the collateral as inventory. On April 7, Austin took a chair out of inventory for an accountant to use in the sales office. What is the effect of that action on First Bank's security interest in the chair?

A. It is lost.
B. It becomes unperfected after 20 days unless First Bank amends the financing statement to describe the collateral as equipment.
C. It continues to be perfected until First Bank has knowledge of the changed use.
D. It continues to be perfected whether First Bank has knowledge of the changed use or not.

Question 28. First Bank has a security interest in Farmer's farm products in a state that has central filing for farm products. First Bank perfected by filing a financing statement in the proper place. Which of the following facts, if proven, would give a buyer of Farmer's farm products who registered with the Secretary of State its best claim that it takes free of First Bank's security interest?

A. The state's version of § 9-320(a) provides that a buyer of farm products takes free of a security interest.
B. First Bank did not send notice to the buyer.
C. First Bank's financing statement did not contain all information required by the Food Security Act.
D. The state has an agricultural lien statute that gives a superpriority to buyers.

Question 29. A creditor took a security interest in the debtor's checking account with its bank. To prevent another creditor other than the bank from getting priority in this collateral, what should the creditor do?

A. Properly file a financing statement.
B. Enter an agreement with the debtor and the bank in which the bank agrees to comply with instructions from the creditor without consulting the debtor.
C. Make it a joint account with the debtor.
D. Either B or C.

Question 30. Quarter Cars granted a security interest in its inventory to First Bank. Homer Simpson asked Quarter Cars to try to sell his personal car for him, and Quarter agreed. Quarter regularly sells used cars but rarely sells cars that belong to others. Does Article 9 apply to this transaction?

A. Yes, because the transaction was a consignment.
B. Yes, because Quarter took a security interest in Homer's car.
C. No, because the transaction was not a consignment for purposes of Article 9.
D. No, because First Bank only has a security interest in inventory, and the car is a consumer good.

Question 31. Alpha Co. regularly sells refrigerators to Beta Co. according to a sales agreement that states that Beta's payment is due 60 days after delivery. The agreement also states that "neither party may assign rights or delegate duties under this agreement." Alpha Co. borrowed money from Credit Co. and granted Credit a security interest in its accounts. When Alpha defaulted on its debt to Credit, Credit sent Beta a letter that was also signed by Alpha. The letter stated, "Pursuant to a security agreement between Alpha and Credit, your obligation to Alpha has been assigned to Credit. Please pay Credit." When Beta's payment to Alpha becomes due, should Beta pay Credit Co?

A. No, because under contract law, a clause restricting assignments is not enforceable.
B. No, because under Article 9, a clause restricting the assignment of a right to receive money is effective.
C. Yes, because under Article 9, a clause restricting the assignment of a right to receive money is not effective.
D. Yes, because under Article 9, the secured party always wins.

Question 32. A bank in Oklahoma is considering entering into a secured transaction with a business located on an Indian Reservation in the state. Which of the following should the bank assume?

A. As federal law, Article 9 applies on the Reservation.
B. The Oklahoma Article 9 applies to a Reservation in the state.
C. The Reservation may have adopted its own version of Article 9.
D. If the bank states in the contract that Oklahoma law applies, then Oklahoma Article 9 will apply.

Question 33. First Bank took a security interest in the winter wheat crop of a farmer. Which of the following would *not* be a sufficient description of this collateral in the financing statement?

A. Winter wheat crop.
B. Farm products.
C. Goods.
D. Agricultural lien.

Question 34. The senior partner of your law firm asks you to determine whether the property in which your client desires to take a security interest is a fixture. What is the best authority for your answer?

A. The definition of fixture in Article 9.
B. The definition of fixture in the state property law statutes.
C. Secondary sources like legal encyclopedias that explain what a fixture is.
D. The security agreement between the parties.

Question 35. Your senior partner asks you to draft language in a security agreement that will give your client a security interest in (1) the equipment the debtor presently has, (2) after acquired equipment, and (3) proceeds of equipment the debtor sells. After the words "Debtor hereby grants Creditor a security interest in Debtor's . . ." which of the following accomplishes this task in the fewest words?

A. Equipment.
B. Equipment and after acquired equipment.
C. Equipment and proceeds.
D. Equipment and after acquired equipment and proceeds.

Question 36. First Bank has a security interest in a debtor's fixtures that is subordinate to Second Bank's mortgage on the debtor's real property. When the debtor defaults, what advice would you give First Bank?

A. It cannot remove the fixtures under any circumstances.
B. If it has priority over all security interests in the personal property, it can remove the fixtures even if its interest is subordinate to the real property encumbrancer.
C. It can remove the fixtures if it pays for any damage to the real property encumbrancer.
D. It can remove the fixtures with the consent of the real property encumbrancer.

Question 37. Bank One loaned Debtor $20,000 in order to buy a van and took a security interest in the van. The van is used in Debtor's business to make deliveries. Bank One properly perfected. Debtor then filed for Bankruptcy under Chapter 11, owing $20,000 on the van. The trustee has determined that the value of the van is $15,000 and that in order to save money, Debtor dropped its collision insurance, which pays for damage to the van in the event of an accident. Failure to maintain collision insurance is an event of default under the security agreement. What should Bank One do?

A. Repossess the van because Debtor is in default.
B. Petition the Bankruptcy Court to lift the stay because of lack of adequate protection of Bank One's interest in the property.
C. Petition the Bankruptcy Court to lift the stay because the Debtor does not have an equity in the property and the property is not necessary to an effective rehabilitation.
D. Petition the Bankruptcy Court to have its $20,000 returned as a voidable preference.

Question 38. Assume in Question 37 the following facts: the loan and grant of security interest occurred on February 1, Bank One perfected on March 15, and Debtor filed its bankruptcy petition on April 1. Can the Bankruptcy Trustee avoid Bank One's security interest?

A. Yes, because the transfer is deemed made on March 15 and hence was made on account of an antecedent debt.

B. No, because the transfer is deemed made on February 1 and hence was not made on account of an antecedent debt.

C. No, because the security interest was a PMSI and Bank One had a grace period of 60 days to perfect.

D. No, because the security interest was an automatically perfected PMSI, so the date of any other perfection is irrelevant.

Question 39. A and B are partners in The A&B Shop. First Bank entered into a transaction in which it agreed to loan The A&B Shop $100,000 and The A&B Shop promised to repay the loan. As part of the transaction, A and B did not promise to repay the loan individually, but A granted First Bank a security interest in his baseball-card collection. Under Article 9, who is a debtor?

A. The A&B Shop only.

B. A only.

C. Both The A&B Shop and A.

D. Neither The A&B Shop nor A.

Question 40. A and B are officers of AB, Inc. First Bank entered into a transaction in which it agreed to loan AB, Inc. $100,000 and took a security interest in the equipment of AB, Inc. The agreement provided that First Bank had the right to modify the contract without notice. As part of the written transaction, A agreed to pay First Bank if AB, Inc. did not. AB, Inc. defaulted when a payment was due and First Bank immediately sued A. Is A liable to pay First Bank?

A. No, because First Bank must first make a claim against AB, Inc. before it can pursue its remedies against A.

B. No, because when a loan is secured, the creditor must first repossess the collateral before it can seek repayment of the debt.

C. Yes, because A is a secondary obligor.

D. Yes, because First Bank had the right to modify the contract.

Question 41. First Bank has a security interest in the inventory and after acquired inventory of Store that is properly perfected. Second Bank loaned Store the money to purchase an item of inventory, took a security interest in the item, and was properly perfected when Store received possession of the item. Does Second Bank have priority in that item over First Bank?

A. No, because Second Bank did not timely perfect.
B. No, because Second Bank did not give notice to First Bank.
C. Yes, because Second Bank complied with all the requirements for a superpriority.
D. Yes, because Second Bank had a PMSI.

Question 42. First Bank has a security interest in the farm products and after acquired farm products of Farmer that is properly perfected. Second Bank took a security interest in an item of Farmer's farm products that was not livestock and properly perfected within 20 days of Farmer's possession of the item. In order for Second Bank to have priority in that item, which of the following facts must be true?

A. Second Bank's security interest is a PMSI.
B. Second Bank perfected before Farmer got possession.
C. Second Bank gave notice to First Bank.
D. All of the above.

Question 43. In Nevada, the professional library of a judgment debtor used to carry on his business is exempt from execution up to a value of $10,000. On August 1, First Bank of Nevada (FB) loaned a Nevada lawyer $10,000 and took a security interest in the professional library the lawyer was using in his office. On September 1, a Judgment Creditor (JC) got a judgment against the lawyer for $10,000 and had the sheriff levy on the lawyer's professional library on September 1. FB filed on September 15. Who has the first claim to the library?

A. FB, because it has a PMSI and effectively filed.
B. JC, because the sheriff levied before FB effectively filed.
C. FB, because the property is exempt from execution but subject to a valid security interest.
D. The lawyer, because the property is exempt from execution.

Question 44. Compuco entered into an agreement described as a "lease" with Smith. Under the agreement, Smith was obligated to make payments of $180 per month for three years on a computer, and had an option to buy the computer at the end of that period for the market value at that time. The agreement also provided that on default, Compuco had the right to terminate the lease and take back the computer. Compuco immediately filed a financing statement. Six months later, Smith filed for bankruptcy. Which advice would you give the Bankruptcy Trustee?

A. Because the parties described the transaction as a lease, the transaction creates a lease.

B. Because under the facts the transaction creates a lease, the transaction creates a lease.

C. Because Compuco filed a financing statement, the transaction creates a security interest.

D. Because under the facts the transaction creates a sale, the transaction creates a security interest.

Question 45. In Question 44, what difference does it make whether the transaction created a lease or created a sale with reservation of a security interest?

A. If a lease, Compuco would get the property back subject to the leasehold interest; if a security interest, it would become an unsecured creditor in bankruptcy.

B. If a lease, Compuco would get the property back subject to the leasehold interest; if a security interest, it would be a secured creditor in bankruptcy.

C. If a lease, Compuco would become an unsecured creditor in bankruptcy; if a security interest, it would become an unsecured creditor in bankruptcy.

D. If a lease, Compuco would become an unsecured creditor in bankruptcy; if a security interest, it would be a secured creditor in bankruptcy.

Question 46. A security agreement between Debtor and Creditor is silent on both the expenses of sale and attorney's fees incurred in collecting the debt. In the course of a repossession, Creditor had to pay reasonable attorney's fees and incurred reasonable expenses. What can Creditor recover from the proceeds from the sale?

A. The attorney's fees.

B. The expenses.

C. Both the attorney's fees and the expenses.

D. Neither the attorney's fees nor the expenses.

Question 47. Before it distributed the proceeds from a sale, the creditor who conducted the sale received signed letters from two parties demanding a share of the proceeds of the sale. One of the parties is a secured creditor with a subordinate security interest, and the other has obtained a judgment against the debtor, but there has been no levy pursuant to the judgment. Which of these creditors, if any, should the creditor pay after it has paid itself?

A. The secured creditor only.

B. The judgment creditor only.

C. Both the secured creditor and the judgment creditor.

D. Neither the secured creditor nor the judgment creditor.

Question 48. Bank has a perfected security interest in Jeweler's inventory, which consists of a few items of high value. The security agreement conspicuously provides that Bank must consent to any sale by Jeweler, and Bank has never waived this right. A buyer wants to buy an item to wear as a ring. Jeweler tells the buyer that Bank "has a security interest" in the ring and, at the buyer's request, allows the buyer to read the security agreement. Jeweler then sells the ring to the buyer, who knows that Jeweler has not obtained the consent of Bank. Does the buyer take the ring free of the security interest?

A. No, because the buyer knew that the sale violated the rights of another person in the ring.

B. No, because the buyer knew of the existence of the security interest in the ring.

C. Yes, because the buyer was a buyer in ordinary course of business.

D. Yes, because the buyer bought the ring for personal, family, or household purposes.

Question 49. A bank agreed with a business that in connection with a substantial loan, the business would grant the bank a security interest in all of its personal property. The business authorized the filing of a financing statement. Both the security agreement and the financing statement described the collateral as "all personal property of debtor." Which of the documents contains a sufficient description of collateral?

A. The security agreement only.
B. The financing statement only.
C. Both the security agreement and the financing statement.
D. Neither the security agreement nor the financing statement.

Question 50. A debtor is in default and the secured creditor is trying to repossess the collateral. The debtor asks a friend if she would be willing to keep the collateral on her property to make it more difficult for the creditor to find it. The friend consults you for advice. What would you tell her?

A. The only consequence is that the creditor could attempt to repossess the property from her.
B. The creditor has no right to try to repossess the property from her, but the friend might be liable under state criminal statutes.
C. The creditor could attempt to repossess the property from her and she might be liable under state criminal statutes.
D. The creditor has no right to try to repossess the property from her and she is unlikely to be liable under state criminal statutes.

Question 51. Debtor is in default under its security agreement. Creditor hired Repo Man to repossess the collateral, a boat. Repo Man followed Debtor when he took the boat to a nearby lake. He waited until Debtor tied the boat up at a public dock and went into a restaurant. He then started the engine using locksmith's tools, untied the boat, and drove it to a boat dock, where he had a trailer waiting to take it away. Would a judge likely conclude there was a breach of the peace?

A. Yes, because Repo Man followed Debtor the same way a stalker would.
B. Yes, because Repo Man took the boat from a public place.
C. Yes, because Repo Man used locksmith's tools to start the engine.
D. No, because none of the above are breaches of the peace.

Question 52. First Bank of England took a security interest in property of a corporation named Safe Harbor Filings, Ltd. and filed its financing statement in the appropriate place under the debtor name "Safe Harbour Filings, Ltd." Second Bank, knowing of First Bank's security interest and filing, took a security interest in the same collateral and filed under the debtor name "Safe Harbor Filings, Ltd." In resolving the priority dispute between First Bank and Second Bank, which of the following facts is most significant?

A. The fact that Second Bank knew of the earlier security interest and filing.
B. The fact that First Bank did not use the debtor's exact full legal name on the filing.
C. Whether a reasonable searcher would have found First Bank's filing.
D. Whether the filing office's standard search logic would have found First Bank's filing.

Question 53. A disgruntled employee decided to interfere with his employer's credit by filing an unauthorized financing statement with the Secretary of State listing the employer as the debtor and various items of the employer's personal property as collateral. What is the employer's remedy?

A. Present an affidavit with the information required by statute to the Secretary of State so that the Secretary of State will remove the filing.
B. Demonstrate to the Secretary of State that the signature of the debtor on the financing statement is a forgery so that the Secretary of State will remove the filing.
C. File an information statement with the Secretary of State.
D. Because of the "open drawer" policy, there is nothing the employer can do that affects the filing.

Question 54. First Bank took a security interest in Debtor's accounts and filed on March 1. Second Bank took a security agreement in Debtor's accounts and filed on April 1. Third Bank took a security agreement in Debtor's accounts and filed on May 1. On June 1, First Bank and Second Bank entered into a subordination agreement in which they agreed that First Bank's security interest would be subordinate to Second Bank's security interest. Assuming all security interests were properly perfected, if Debtor declared bankruptcy on July 1, what would be the order of priority in the accounts?

A. First Bank, Second Bank, Third Bank.
B. Second Bank, First Bank, Third Bank.
C. Third Bank, Second Bank, First Bank.
D. First Bank, Third Bank, Second Bank.

Question 55. On January 1, First Bank took a security interest in the equipment and after acquired equipment of "Chip Production, Inc." and properly filed. At the time, the only equipment owned by the debtor was a red chip making machine. On February 1, the debtor changed its name to "Cheaper Chips, Inc." On March 1, Second Bank conducted a proper search under the name of "Cheaper Chips, Inc." and found no filings. Second Bank loaned money to debtor, took a security interest in the equipment and after acquired equipment of the debtor, and properly filed. On April 1, the debtor acquired a white chip making machine, and on August 1, the debtor acquired a blue chip making machine. On November 1, the debtor declared bankruptcy. In which chip making machines does First Bank have priority?

A. Red only.
B. Red and white.
C. Red, white, and blue.
D. None of them.

Question 56. Desert Motors, Inc., an Arizona corporation with its main office in Las Vegas, is in the business of selling new cars. Desert Motors granted Bank One a security interest in its inventory of cars. How should Bank One perfect? (Assume both Nevada and Arizona are title states.)

A. File with the Secretary of State of Arizona.
B. File with the Secretary of State of Nevada.
C. Have the security interest noted on the titles in Arizona.
D. Have the security interest noted on the titles in Nevada.

Question 57. Bank One loaned $5,000 to Burnham and took a security interest in Burnham's baseball-card collection. Bank One did not file. Burnham sold the baseball-card collection for $10,000 and used the money to buy an entry into the World Series of Poker. He finished second (he's not greedy) and won $5 million. He used part of the $5 million to purchase a Lamborghini for $175,000. Because he is in default, Bank One wants to foreclose on the Lamborghini. Can it do so?

A. No, because it never filed or perfected its security interest.
B. No, because the value of the Lamborghini is disproportionate to the amount of the debt.
C. No, because the Lamborghini is not proceeds.
D. Yes, because the Lamborghini is identifiable proceeds of the collateral.

Question 58. Compuco sold a computer on credit to Ace Motors, Inc. on May 1 and took a security interest in the computer. Ace Motors took delivery on that day. On May 4, to satisfy Judgment Creditor's judgment against Ace Motors, the sheriff levied on the computer. On May 15, Compuco filed. Who has priority as between Compuco and Judgment Creditor (JC)?

A. JC, because judicial liens have priority over security interests unless the lien statute provides otherwise.

B. JC, because Compuco had not filed or perfected at the time of the levy.

C. Compuco, because it was automatically perfected at the time of the levy.

D. Compuco, because it filed within 20 days after Ace Motors received the collateral.

Question 59. On January 2, First Bank agreed to lend Debtor $50,000 on that day and another $50,000 on April 4 of the same year. Debtor granted First Bank a security interest in Debtor's inventory and it was properly perfected. The security agreement has a future advance clause. On February 2 of the same year, the sheriff levied on Debtor's inventory to satisfy a judgment of Judgment Creditor (JC). On April 4, with full knowledge of the levy, First Bank gave Debtor the second $50,000 pursuant to the agreement. Debtor used the money to buy inventory and the sheriff levied on that inventory to satisfy the judgment. Who has priority as between First Bank and JC in the second $50,000 worth of inventory?

A. First Bank, because it made the advance without knowledge of the levy.

B. First Bank, because it was committed to making the advance.

C. JC, because the advance was made more than 45 days after the levy.

D. JC, because a security interest is subordinate to the rights of a person that becomes a lien creditor before the security interest attaches.

Question 60. Rachel bought a used car from CarCo on credit. CarCo took a security interest in the car and properly perfected. When the car broke down, Rachel took it to Joe's Repair Shop. Joe finished the repairs and presented Rachel with a bill for $400. Rachel said she didn't have the money, so Joe said he would hold the car until she paid. In this state, a statute provides that a mechanic has a possessory lien on a car, but the statute is silent on priority. Who has priority as between Joe and CarCo?

A. Joe, because the default rule is that a statutory lien has priority over a security interest.
B. Joe, because perfection by possession has priority over other methods of perfection.
C. CarCo, because the default rule is that a security interest has priority over a statutory lien.
D. CarCo, because Joe failed to give timely notice to CarCo of its lien.

Question 61. On January 8, ComputerCo sold Jim an Apple computer on credit and took a security interest in the computer. Jim planned to use the computer for personal purposes. On June 1, Jim took the computer to Joe's Computer Store and traded it in for a PC computer. On October 1, Mary bought the Apple from the inventory of Joe's Computer Store to use for personal purposes. Who has priority in the Apple as between ComputerCo and Mary?

A. Mary, because she bought it for personal purposes and ComputerCo had not filed.
B. Mary, because she bought it as a buyer in ordinary course of business.
C. ComputerCo, because Mary made no reasonable efforts to determine whether the computer was subject to a security interest.
D. ComputerCo, because Article 9 provides that a security interest is good against purchasers unless an exception applies, and no exception applies.

Question 62. Bank loaned Sam's Corporation $10,000, took a security interest in the existing equipment of Sam's Corporation, and properly filed. A few months later, Sam Jones, the President of Sam's Corporation, directed the corporate treasurer not to send withholding taxes to the IRS. The IRS assessed a tax lien against Sam's Corporation and Sam Jones personally and properly filed. Sam's Corporation is in default under the security agreement with Bank. Both the Bank and the IRS claim the equipment of Sam's Corporation. Which party is entitled to it?

A. The Bank, because it filed before the IRS did.
B. The IRS, because the Internal Revenue Code gives tax assessments priority over security interests.
C. The Bank, because the IRS must first pursue a remedy against Sam Jones personally.
D. The IRS, because the Bank does not have a PMSI.

Question 63. Assume that a jurisdiction has enacted § 9-503 Alternative A. A creditor loans money to a man who is known to all his creditors as Jon Smith, takes a security interest in property of Smith, and files in the name Jon Smith. However, Smith's birth certificate and driver's license use the name Jonathan Smith, which Smith has never used. The jurisdiction's search logic matches exact words, so a search for Jonathan Smith would not locate Jon Smith. Smith declares bankruptcy. Is the security interest perfected?

A. Yes, because the financing statement provided the individual name of the debtor.

B. Yes, because a reasonable searcher would have searched under both Jonathan Smith and Jon Smith and would have found the filing.

C. No, because the financing statement did not provide the legal name, which is the name on the birth certificate.

D. No, because the financing statement did not provide the name on the driver's license.

Question 64. Assume that FB loaned AA money on February 1. On March 5, FB and AA authenticated a security agreement that stated that in consideration of the money FB loaned to AA on February 1, AA granted FB a security interest in its inventory. Is there an enforceable security agreement?

A. No, because there is no consideration.

B. No, because FB did not file a financing statement.

C. Yes, because there is consideration.

D. Yes, because value was given.

 # Burnham's Picks

Question 1. Under the general rule of § 9-334(c), a security interest in fixtures is subordinate to the interest of an encumbrancer of the real property, such as the bank. That is the rule stated in response **D**. However, there is an exception under § 9-334(d) that arises when the security interest is a PMSI, the interest of the encumbrancer arose before the goods became fixtures, and the security interest is perfected by a fixture filing within 20 days after the goods become fixtures. Here, all of those requirements are satisfied, so the correct response is **C**. Responses **A** and **B** also represent exceptions to the general rule, but they are not relevant under these facts. To review this topic, see Chapter 18.B.

Question 2.   Article 9 makes a distinction between a *debtor*, who has an interest in the collateral, and an *obligor*, who owes payment of the obligation. See §§ 9-102(a)(28) and (59). Here, AB Inc. and A are obligors. According to § 9-102(a)(72), a *secondary obligor* is one whose obligation is secondary. That description fits A, who has agreed to pay if the principal obligor, AB Inc. does not. Therefore, the correct response is **A**. To review this topic, see Chapter 11.A.

Question 3.   Under § 9-609(b)(2), a lawful repossession must proceed "without breach of the peace." While breach of the peace issues are very fact-specific, it is probably fair to say that when no forced entry is made and there is no potential for violence, there is no breach of the peace. Here, the Repo Man found the car in the open, and it reasonably appeared that there was no potential for violence, so **D** is the best response. To review this topic, see Chapter 8.C.

Question 4.   Under § 9-615(a), the secured party must apply the cash proceeds to (1) lawful expenses, (2) the satisfaction of the obligations secured by the security interest under which the sale was made, and (3) the satisfaction of obligations secured by any subordinate security interest. Under subsection (d), if there is a surplus after those distributions are made, it must be paid to the debtor. Here, Creditor has paid expenses and is entitled to $60,000 to satisfy the obligation to itself. Auto Parts does not have a security interest, so it is not entitled to the proceeds of distribution. The balance must be paid to Debtor. Therefore, the correct response is **B**. To review this topic, see Chapter 10.A.

Question 5.   Under § 9-203, the security agreement must describe the collateral, and under § 9-108(c), a supergeneric description does not reasonably identify the collateral. Therefore, an enforceable security interest was not created. Furthermore, under the Federal Credit Practices Rules, 16 CFR § 444.1, it is a violation for a creditor to take "a nonpossessory security interest in household goods other than a purchase money security interest." Since it can be fairly assumed that "all personal property of debtor" includes household goods, the creditor has violated the Act. Therefore, the correct response is **C**. To review this topic, see Chapter 6.D and Chapter 7.E.

Question 6.   Under the general rule of § 9-201, a security agreement is effective against purchasers of the collateral. Exceptions include unperfected security interests under § 9-317(b), buyers in ordinary course of business (buyers from inventory) under § 9-320(a), and consumer buyers of consumer goods under § 9-320(b). The sale from Foster to Valdez does not fit any of the exceptions. Therefore, under the general rule, the secured creditor wins, and the correct response is **D**. Valdez has a claim against Foster for breach of the § 2-312 warranty of title. To review this topic, see Chapter 7.B, Chapter 15.B, and Chapter 15.C.

Question 7.   Under § 9-502(a), a financing statement must provide the name of the debtor as indicated in § 9-503(a). Under § 9-506(a), a financing statement that has minor errors is effective unless the errors make the financing statement "seriously misleading." Under subsection (c), if a search of the records of the filing office under the debtor's correct name using the filing office's standard search logic would disclose the financing statement, then the name provided does not make the financing statement seriously misleading. Therefore, the correct response is **C.** To review this topic, see Chapter 12.C.2.

Question 8.   Section 9-625 is captioned "Remedies for Secured Party's Failure to Comply With Article." It could be argued that the student is not a secured party and therefore the remedies do not apply. This argument would be bolstered by § 1-107, which provides that "[s]ection captions are part of [the Uniform Commercial Code]." Nevertheless, the text of § 9-625(b) provides that "any person is liable for damages in the amount of any loss caused by a failure to comply with this article," and the student, in filing a record without authorization, did not comply with § 9-509(a). The actual damages might include the increased cost of the alternative financing. Similarly, § 9-625(c) provides that a "person named as a debtor in a filed record" may recover $500 "from a person that . . . files a record that the person is not entitled to file under Section 9-509(a)." Therefore, the best answer is **C.** To review this topic, see Chapter 13.B.

Question 9.   This is a bit tricky. Recall that the § 9-322(a) rule for priority among conflicting security interests is "priority in time of filing or perfection," as long as there is no period after the initial filing or perfection when there is neither filing nor perfection. First Bank was initially perfected by filing. However, when First Bank filed a Termination Statement, perfection by filing was lost. Thus, it might appear that First Bank was unperfected when Second Bank became perfected. However, when it repossessed the collateral, First Bank became perfected by possession under § 9-313. Therefore, there was no period after the initial filing when there was neither filing nor perfection of First Bank's security interest. The correct response is **B.** To review this topic, see Chapter 13.B, Chapter 14.B, and Chapter 16.B.

Question 10.   These facts are based on the case of *In re Hilyard Drilling Co. Inc.* 840 F.2d 596 (8th Cir. 1988). Creditor 1 was the first to file or perfect under § 9-322, but was the perfection continuous? According to § 9-515(a), a filing is effective for five years, so Creditor 1's initial filing became ineffective on April 27, 2020. Although Creditor 1 filed a continuation statement, according to § 9-515(d), "a continuation statement may be filed only within six months before the expiration of the five year period." Here, that six-month period would begin on October 26, 2019. So Creditor 1 jumped the gun by filing on July 8, 2019, and since its continuation statement was not effective, its perfection lapsed. Under Bankruptcy Code § 544(a), the "strong arm clause," an unperfected security interest is not valid in bankruptcy. Under

§ 9-339, creditors are free to agree among themselves as to the order of priority of their security interests through a "subordination agreement." However, because Creditor 1 no longer had an effective security interest, the subordination agreement would be of no effect. Therefore, the correct response is **D.** To review this topic, see Chapter 13.C, Chapter 16.C, and Chapter 19.D.

Question 11.   Section 9-507(c)(2) covers the situation arising when a debtor changes its name:

(c) Change in debtor's name.

If the name that a filed financing statement provides for a debtor becomes insufficient as the name of the debtor under Section 9-503(a) so that the financing statement becomes seriously misleading under Section 9-506:

. . . .

(2) the financing statement is not effective to perfect a security interest in collateral acquired by the debtor more than four months after the filed financing statement becomes seriously misleading, unless an amendment to the financing statement which renders the financing statement not seriously misleading is filed within four months after the financing statement became seriously misleading.

Here, First Bank filed an amendment within four months from February 1, so it retains its priority in all equipment. The correct response is **A.** Note that if First Bank had not filed its amendment until after June 1, then the correct response would be **D.** To review this topic, see Chapter 13.D.2.

Question 12.   According to § 9-315(a), on disposition, a security interest continues in the identifiable proceeds of collateral. Both the trade-in car and the floor waxer are identifiable proceeds. But under § 9-315(d), the security interest becomes unperfected after 21 days unless:

(A) a filed financing statement covers the original collateral;
(B) the proceeds are collateral in which a security interest may be perfected by filing in the office in which the financing statement has been filed; and
(C) the proceeds are not acquired with cash proceeds.

Here, the trade-in car satisfies all three criteria, but the floor waxer does not satisfy (C), since it was acquired with cash proceeds. Therefore, the correct response is **A.** To review this topic, see Chapter 13.D.6.

Question 13.   Under § 9-317(a)(2), a security interest is subordinate to a person that becomes a judgment lien creditor before the security interest is perfected. Section 9-317(e) provides an exception for a purchase money secured party who files within 20 days after the debtor receives delivery of the collateral. Sears missed that deadline, but the exception for a purchase money secured party who files is not relevant here. Because Sears had a purchase money security interest in consumer goods, its security interest was automatically perfected under § 9-309(1). Under the general rule of § 9-317(a)(2), the creditor became a judgment creditor on January 5, which is after the security interest was perfected on January 2. Therefore, the correct response is **C**. To review this topic, see Chapter 14.E and Chapter 17.B.

Question 14. Section 9-323(b) provides:

> (b) **Lien creditor.** Except as otherwise provided in subsection (c), a security interest is subordinate to the rights of a person that becomes a lien creditor while the security interest is perfected only to the extent that it secures advances made more than 45 days after the person becomes a lien creditor unless the advance is made:
> > (1) without knowledge of the lien; or
> > (2) pursuant to a commitment entered into without knowledge of the lien.

Responses **A**, **B**, and **C** each enumerate a case in which the security interest is not subordinate to the rights of the lien creditor. However, response **A** is not true because First Bank had knowledge of the lien, and response **C** is not true because the advance was made more than 45 days after the levy. Only response **B** is factually applicable, so it is the correct response. To review this topic, see Chapter 17.B.2.

Question 15. Joe has a lien arising by operation of law. According to the default rule of § 9-333, the possessory lien has priority over the security interest unless a statute provides otherwise. Here you are told that the statute does not provide otherwise, so under the general rule, **A** is the correct response. To review this topic, see Chapter 17.C.

Question 16. This question is based on the facts of *Exchange Bank of Osceola v. Jarrett*, 588 P.2d 1006 (Mont. 1979). Under the general rule of § 9-201, a security agreement is effective against purchasers of the collateral. Exceptions include unperfected security interests under § 9-317(b) and buyers in ordinary course of business (buyers from inventory) under § 9-320(a). Here the Bank was perfected, as there was no requirement that it refile when the equipment was moved. Although it may initially appear that Jarrett is a § 9-320(a) buyer, because he bought from inventory, that section provides that the buyer from inventory takes free of a security interest "created by the buyer's seller." Here, the security interest was created by Holland, not by Jarrett's seller, CB&O. Since no exception applies, the security agreement is effective under the general rule, so **D** is the correct response. It is of course true that Holland breached the security agreement, giving Bank a claim against him, but that gives Jarrett no claim. To review this topic, see Chapter 15.C.

Question 17. Under § 6672 of the Internal Revenue Code, the IRS may impose the "100% penalty" against a "responsible person" who causes a business to fail to pay over withholding taxes. Therefore, the IRS claim against Sam personally is justified. As a general rule, § 6323(a) of the IRC provides that tax liens are subordinate to earlier filed security interests, but here there was no security interest that attached to the property of Sam individually. So the correct response is **C.** To review this topic, see Chapter 17.E.

Question 18. Under § 9-509(a), a person may file a financing statement if authorized by the debtor. There is no requirement that the debtor first grant a security interest. However, until a security interest is granted, there is no attachment under § 9-203, and § 9-308 provides that attachment is required for perfection. So under these facts, there is filing but there is neither attachment nor perfection. Therefore, the correct response is **D.** To review this topic, see Chapter 6.A and Chapter 12.B.

Question 19. Section 9-203 requires only the debtor to authenticate a security agreement. According to § 9-102(a)(7), "authenticate" means:

    (A) to sign; or
    (B) with present intent to adopt or accept a record, to attach to or
  logically associate with the record an electronic sound, symbol, or process.

The e-mail is probably an authenticated record. See Official Comment 9.b. to § 9-102. Therefore, the correct response is **C.** To review this topic, see Chapter 6.C.

Question 20. One of the § 9-203(b)(1) requirements for an enforceable security agreement is that "value has been given." Section 1-204 provides that "a person gives value for rights if the person acquires them . . . (2) as security for, or in total or partial satisfaction of, a preexisting claim." Under the common law, there would probably be no consideration for the debtor's grant of a security interest, for the debtor did not bargain for anything in return. However, it is not *consideration* but *value* that is required, and the scope of value is broader than that of consideration. Therefore, the best response is **D.** To review this topic, see Chapter 6.A.

Question 21. According to § 9-322(a)(1), "[c]onflicting perfected security interests . . . rank according to priority in time of filing or perfection." Here, First Bank filed on March 2 and Second Bank filed on March 4, so First Bank was the first to file or perfect. The correct response is **B.** To review this topic, see Chapter 16.B.

Question 22. According to § 9-322(a)(1), "[c]onflicting perfected security interests . . . rank according to priority in time of filing or perfection." Here,

First Bank is unperfected and Second Bank filed on March 5, so Second Bank was the first to file or perfect. The correct response is **D**. Note that to make the priority determination objective, knowledge is irrelevant. To review this topic, see Chapter 16.B.

Question 23. Austin was not authorized to file a termination statement. Nevertheless, the filing office is instructed by the Code to maintain an "open drawer" in which records are placed without any legal judgments being made. See §§ 9-519 and 9-520. The burden then falls on other creditors, such as Second Bank, to determine the validity of the filing. According to § 9-516, no signatures or "authentications" are required on a financing statement. Therefore, responses **C** and **D** are incorrect, and **B** is the correct response. To review this topic, see Chapter 13.B.

Question 24. According to § 9-301(1), the law of the jurisdiction in which a debtor is located governs perfection, and § 9-307(e) provides that a registered organization is located where it is organized. Since Austin is a Delaware corporation, First Bank should file in Delaware, so the correct response is **A**. To review this topic, see Chapter 12.D.

Question 25. In his agreement, Homer has promised to pay money to Austin, which evidences a monetary obligation, and he has also granted a security interest in the sofa to secure that monetary obligation. To classify collateral, we must look at it from the point of view of the debtor, and in the Austin–First Bank transaction the debtor is Austin. Austin has a record that evidences both a monetary obligation and a security interest, so it has *chattel paper* as defined in § 9-102(a)(11). Therefore, **B** is the correct response. To review this topic, see Chapter 4.B.

Question 26. According to § 9-601(a)(1), when the debtor defaults, the creditor has rights under Article 9, such as the right to repossess, but it also has the ordinary rights of a creditor, such as the right to proceed by judgment and execution. The correct response is **C**. Note that, as between the creditor and the debtor, perfection is irrelevant, so First Bank has the remedy of repossession even though it is not perfected. To review this topic, see Chapter 8.A.

Question 27. This item of collateral has now changed from inventory to equipment, making the financing statement misleading, because another creditor might not know that the security interest has attached to an item of equipment. However, according to § 9-507(b), "a financing statement is not rendered ineffective if, after the financing statement is filed, the information provided in the financing statement becomes seriously misleading under Section 9-506." Only a change in the debtor's name, as provided in § 9-507(c), affects the effectiveness of the financing statement. The correct response is **D**. To review this topic, see Chapter 13.D.

Question 28. The federal Food Security Act preempts the Article 9 rules on the disposition of farm products to a buyer. When the state has established central filing, in order to prevail over a buyer, the secured party must file an effective financing statement. See 7 U.S.C. § 1631(e)(2). That statute, and not Article 9, determines the contents of the financing statement. Therefore, the best response is **C**. To review this topic, see Chapter 15.C.

Question 29. Section 9-327 provides that a secured party with control of a deposit account has priority over a conflicting security interest, so the creditor should perfect by obtaining control. Under § 9-104(a), the creditor can obtain control by either method described in responses **B** and **C,** so the best answer to the question asked is **D**. Note, however, that § 9-327(4) provides that the creditor must use the method described in response **C** to obtain priority over the bank as well. To review this topic, see Chapter 14.C.

Question 30. According to § 9-109, Article 9 applies to a consignment. However, the definition of "consignment" in § 9-102(a)(20) provides that the transaction is a consignment if certain elements are satisfied, and one of the elements is that "the goods are not consumer goods immediately before delivery." Here, Homer's car was consumer goods immediately before delivery to Quarter, so this transaction is not a consignment under Article 9. The correct response is **C**. To review this topic, see Chapter 5.F.

Question 31. Under contract law, a nonassignment clause is generally enforceable according to its terms. However, to protect accounts receivable financing, § 9-406(d) provides that the term restricting assignment is not effective when it would impair the enforcement of a security interest. The correct response is **C**. To review this topic, see Chapter 9.E.

Question 32. Some Indian Tribes follow the state Article 9, but others may employ variations, including the Model Tribal Secured Transactions Act. Because the tribe is a sovereign with its own law on the reservation, the bank should make further inquiry. Therefore, the best response is **C**. To review this topic, see Chapter 2.A.

Question 33. Section 9-502(3) provides that the financing statement must indicate the collateral covered by the financing statement. Section 9-504(1) provides that the indication is sufficient if it provides a description of the collateral pursuant to § 9-108. Section 9-108(b)(3) provides that a specific listing is sufficient. "Winter wheat crop" would satisfy this requirement, so response **A** would be a sufficient description. Section 9-108((b)(3) provides that a type of collateral defined in the UCC is a sufficient description. "Goods" and "farm products," which are a subcategory of goods, satisfy this requirement, so responses **B** and **C** would be a sufficient description. An "agricultural lien" is defined in § 9-102(a)(5) as a statutory lien, so it is not a description of collateral. Therefore, the correct response is **D**. To review this topic, see Chapter 12.C.

Question 34.   While you want to start your research with Article 9, the definition of "fixture" in § 9-102(a)(41) refers you to real property law, which is state law. Therefore, response **A** is incorrect. A treatise might be helpful, but most treatises are not state-specific. Therefore, response **C** is incorrect. The best authority is the law of the jurisdiction, and the best place to start to find that law is the statutes, so **B** is the best response. That statute might include the intent of the parties as a factor, so the language of the security agreement may be helpful, but whether it is authoritative is dependent on the statute, so response **D** is incomplete. To review this topic, see Chapter 18.A.

Question 35.   According to § 9-203, the security agreement must contain a description of the collateral, so the description "equipment" is necessary. According to § 9-204(a), a security interest does not attach to after-acquired collateral unless so provided, so that language is necessary. According to § 9-315(a)(2), a security interest automatically attaches to proceeds, so that language is not necessary in the security agreement. Therefore, the correct response is **B**. To review this topic, see Chapter 7.C and D.

Question 36.   Under the general rule of § 9-334(c), the security interest in the fixtures is subordinate to the interest of the real estate encumbrancer. Therefore, the secured party cannot remove the fixtures, so responses **B** and **C** are incorrect. However, there is an exception under § 9-334 (f) if the real estate encumbrancer consents to priority, so response **D** is correct. To review this topic, see Chapter 18.B.

Question 37.   Because there is an automatic stay when a debtor files for bankruptcy, the bank may not repossess the van, so response **A** is incorrect. However, a creditor can obtain relief from the automatic stay under Bankruptcy Code § 362(d) if either of the situations described in responses B or C applies. Here, the debtor does not have an equity in the van since the amount of the debt is $20,000 and the value of the van is $15,000. However, the property is necessary for an effective rehabilitation since the debtor needs the van to operate its business. Therefore, response **C** is incorrect. However, there is a lack of adequate protection because the debtor dropped its collision insurance. Therefore, the bank probably qualifies for relief from the automatic stay, and response **B** is correct. To review this topic, see Chapter 19.B.

Question 38.   The security interest was granted on February 1, and it was perfected on March 15. Since perfection was more than 30 days after the grant, it is considered to have been made on March 15 under Bankruptcy Code § 547(e). Now if we apply the elements of a voidable preference under § 547(b), we see that the transfer was made on account of an antecedent debt and was made within 90 days of the filing of the petition. Therefore, the Bankruptcy Trustee can avoid the transfer as a voidable preference, so response **A** is correct. To review this topic, see Chapter 19.D.

Question 39.   Under § 9-102(a)(28), "'Debtor' means (A) a person having an interest, other than a security interest or other lien, in the collateral, whether or not the person is an obligor." Here, only A has an interest in the collateral, so **B** is the correct response. To review this topic, see Chapter 11.A.

Question 40.   A is a "secondary obligor" as defined in § 9-102(a)(72). Therefore, A is liable to pay the creditor when the obligor defaults and response **C** is correct. On default, a creditor does not have to first pursue its remedies against the collateral or against the obligor. To review this topic, see Chapter 11.A.

Question 41.   Second Bank will have a "superpriority" over First Bank if it complies with the rules of § 9-324(b), which are only for inventory. In addition to having a PMSI that is perfected when the debtor receives possession of the collateral, the creditor with the PMSI must send notice to the holders of perfected security interests in the collateral before the debtor receives possession. Here, Second Bank neglected to give notice to First Bank so it is not entitled to a superpriority and response **B** is correct. To review this topic, see Chapter 16.D.

Question 42.   Second Bank will have a "superpriority" over First Bank if it complies with the rules of § 9-324(a), which are for a PMSI in goods other than inventory and livestock. Farm products would qualify as goods that are not inventory or livestock. These rules require that the security interest be perfected within 20 days of the debtor's possession, but not necessarily prior to possession. The rules do not require notice to the secured party. Therefore, if Second Bank's security interest is a PMSI, it will have priority and response **A** is correct. To review this topic, see Chapter 16.D.

Question 43.   Exemption statutes bar judgment creditors from executing on the exempt property, but do not bar secured creditors from taking a security interest in it. Therefore, the bank's security interest in the books is valid and the judgment creditor's claim is not valid. The correct response is **C**. To review this topic, see Chapter 3.A.

Question 44.   Section 1-203 is used to determine whether a transaction creates a lease or a sale with reservation of a security interest. A court will look at the economic realities rather than the intention of the parties, so response **B** is incorrect. If a party files a precautionary financing statement under § 9-505, this fact should not be considered in the determination, so response **C** is incorrect. A right to recover the goods in the event of default is a right of both lessors and secured parties, so this is not a factor. Here, the lessee has the right to retain the goods on termination, but must pay the market value. This factor is likely to indicate that the transaction is a lease, so response **B** is correct. To review this topic, see Chapter 5.C.

Question 45. If a transaction creates a lease, then in bankruptcy, the debtor's interest in the goods is the leasehold interest, so the lessor gets the property back subject to that interest. If it is a sale with reservation of a security interest, then in bankruptcy the trustee can void unperfected security interests under Bankruptcy Code § 544(a). Here, the security interest was perfected, so if it was a sale, the seller would retain its security interest in bankruptcy. The correct response is **B**. To review this topic, see Chapter 19.D.

Question 46. Section 9-615(a) provides that after the sale, the secured party may apply the proceeds to the expenses of sale, but may apply the proceeds to attorney's fees only to the extent provided in the agreement. Here, the agreement is silent on attorney's fees, so response **B** is correct. To review this topic, see Chapter 10.A.

Question 47. Section 9-615(a) provides that after the sale, the secured party may distribute the proceeds to satisfy subordinate security interests or liens if the secured party has received an authenticated demand from the holder of the subordinate security interest or lien. Here, the judgment creditor has a lien, but it is not a lien on the collateral since there has not been a levy. Therefore, the secured creditor needs to pay only the secured creditor, so response **A** is correct. To review this topic, see Chapter 10.A.

Question 48. Under the general rule of § 9-320(a), a buyer in ordinary course of business takes free of a security interest even if it knows of the existence of the security interest. However, a buyer in ordinary course of business, according to § 1-201(b)(9), is one who buys "without knowledge that the sale violates the rights of another person in the goods." Here, the buyer knows that the sale violates the rights of the secured party, who has more than a security interest — the secured party also has the right to consent to each sale. The buyer is not a buyer in ordinary course of business and does not take free under § 9-320(a). The correct response is **A**. To review this topic, see Chapter 15.C.

Question 49. Section 9-108(c) provides that a supergeneric description such as "all the debtor's personal property" is not sufficient for the security agreement. However, § 9-504 provides that a financing statement sufficiently indicates the collateral if it indicates that the financing statement covers all assets or all personal property. Therefore, response **B** is correct. To review this topic, see Chapter 6.D.

Question 50. As long as it does not breach the peace, there is nothing to prevent a creditor from attempting to repossess the property in the hands of parties other than the debtor. While Article 9 does not address the topic, most states have statutes making it a crime to hinder enforcement of the security interest. Therefore, response **C** is correct. To review this topic, see Chapter 8.C.

Question 51. While the Code does not address what constitutes a breach of the peace, case law indicates that the described repossession would not breach the peace. Therefore, response **D** is correct. To review this topic, see Chapter 8.C.

Question 52. The filing was not in the name of the debtor. However, it might still be effective it the filing is not seriously misleading. The test under § 9-506(c) is whether the filing office's standard search logic would find the filing. Therefore, response **D** is correct. To review this topic, see Chapter 12.C.

Question 53. Under the "open drawer" policy, all filings should be available to searchers. Therefore, in most jurisdictions, the Secretary of State is not authorized to remove the filing. Instead, the employer can file an information statement pursuant to § 9-518, so that both the bogus filing and the information statement are available to a searcher. The correct response is **C**. To review this topic, see Chapter 13.B.

Question 54. Prior to the subordination, the priority is: First Bank, Second Bank, Third Bank. Under § 9-339, parties are free to agree to subordinate by agreement. Here, they agreed that First Bank would be subordinate to Second Bank. This agreement does not affect Third Bank's priority, so after the agreement, the priority is Second Bank, First Bank, Third Bank. Response **B** is correct. To review this topic, see Chapter 16.C.

Question 55. First Bank's security interest covered after-acquired equipment. However, when the debtor changed its name on February 1, First Bank had four months to file in order to perfect its security interest in equipment acquired by the debtor after that time. See § 9-506(c). The white chip making machine was acquired during that time, so the filing was effective to perfect the security interest in it. However, the blue chip making machine was acquired on August 1, which was beyond the four months. Therefore, as of November 1, First Bank is perfected and has priority in the red and white chip making machines, but not in the blue chip making machine. The correct response is **B**. To review this topic, see Chapter 13.D.

Question 56. The collateral should be characterized from the point of view of the debtor. Here, the cars are inventory in the hands of the debtor. Certificate of title statutes do not apply to collateral that is held as inventory by the debtor. See Chapter 14.D. Therefore, we follow the general rule that filing is made where the debtor is located and a corporation (a "registered organization") is located in the state under which it is organized. See § 9-307. Here, we are told that the debtor is an Arizona corporation, so filing is in that state and response **A** is correct. To review this topic, see Chapter 12.D.

Question 57. Perfection is irrelevant as between the debtor and the creditor (except in bankruptcy), so response **A** is incorrect. The value of the collateral is irrelevant, so response **B** is incorrect. A security interest attaches to the proceeds of the collateral, so this is a tracing problem to determine whether the Lamborghini is proceeds of the collateral. The facts indicate that the money used to purchase the Lamborghini is traceable to the baseball-card collection, so it is proceeds and response **D** is correct. Of course, as a practical matter it might be more difficult to trace the proceeds. To review this topic, see Chapter 7.C.

Question 58. While a judgment lien creditor has priority over an unperfected security interest under § 9-317(a), there is an exception for a PMSI. Under § 9-317(e), if the creditor with the PMSI files within 20 days after the debtor receives delivery of the collateral, then the security interest relates back to the date of attachment. Here, Compuco had a PMSI in the computer and filed on May 15, which is within 20 days of Ace's possession on May 1. Therefore, Compuco is considered perfected as of May 1 and has priority over the lien creditor who levied on May 4. Note that Compuco is not automatically perfected because automatic perfection applies only to a PMSI in consumer goods. Response **D** is correct. To review this topic, see Chapter 17.B.

Question 59. Section 9-323(b) provides that a perfected security interest in a future advance loses priority to a lien creditor if the advance is made more than 45 days after the person becomes a lien creditor. But there are exceptions if either the advance is made without knowledge of the lien or pursuant to a commitment entered into without knowledge of the lien. Here, the future advance was made on April 4, which is more than 45 days after the person became a lien creditor on February 2. The first exception does not apply because the advance was made with knowledge of the lien. However, the second exception applies because the creditor had committed to make the future advance on January 2, before it had knowledge of the lien. Therefore, the Bank has priority in the second $50,000 worth of inventory and response **A** is correct. To review this topic, see Chapter 17.B.

Question 60. Joe has a lien arising by operation of law. Under § 9-333, the default rule is that a possessory lien on goods has priority over a security interest. Here, the statute is silent on priority, so the default rule applies and response **A** is correct. To review this topic, see Chapter 17.C.

Question 61.   Since it took a PMSI in consumer goods, ComputerCo has a security interest that is automatically perfected. When the buyer sold it, the security interest remained attached under the rule in § 9-315(a)(1). Since Mary purchased from inventory, she initially appears to take free of the security interest under the "buyer in ordinary course of business" rule of § 9-320(a). However, that rule provides that a buyer takes free of a security interest "created by the buyer's seller," and here the security interest was created by Jim, not by Mary's seller, which was Joe's Computer Store. Therefore, the general rule applies and **D** is the correct response. Note that Mary's remedy is to make a claim against Joe's Computer Store for breach of the warranty of title in § 2-312. To review this topic, see Chapter 15.C.

Question 62.   This is a common situation. A debtor who has not paid its creditors often has not paid its taxes, so frequently there will be a tax lien filed against the debtor. Internal Revenue Code § 6323(a) treats the IRS like a secured creditor, so its lien is subordinate to a perfected security interest. Since the bank perfected first, it has priority and response **A** is correct. To review this topic, see Chapter 17.E.

Question 63.   Under Alternative A, known as the "only if" rule, the name on the driver's license is determinative. Because the secured party did not use the name on the driver's license, the financing statement is not an effective filing and response **D** is correct. Note that if the same facts took place in an Alternative B jurisdiction, the filing would have been effective because it provided the name of the debtor. To review this topic, see Chapter 12.C.

Question 64.   Response **B** is incorrect because it is not necessary to file a financing statement to make the security interest effective as between the creditor and the debtor. At common law, there would not be consideration if a person promises something (the grant of a security interest) in return for something the person already has (the loan of the money). However, for a security agreement to be effective, § 9-203 requires that "value" be given. "Value" as defined in § 1-204 includes not just consideration but also rights acquired "as security for . . . a preexisting claim." Here, the bank acquired the security interest as security for its loan. This is not consideration, but it is value, so response **D** is correct. To review this topic, see Chapter 6.A.

Table of Statutes

Index